Studies in Japanese Bilingualism

BILINGUAL EDUCATION AND BILINGUALISM

Series Editors: Professor Colin Baker, *University of Wales, Bangor, Wales, Great Britain* and **Professor Nancy H. Hornberger**, *University of Pennsylvania, Philadelphia, USA*

Other Books in the Series
Becoming Bilingual: Language Acquisition in a Bilingual Community
Jean Lyon
Bilingual Education and Social Change
Rebecca Freeman
Building Bridges: Multilingual Resources for Children
Multilingual Resources for Children Project
Child-Rearing in Ethnic Minorities
J.S. Dosanjh and Paul A.S. Ghuman
Curriculum Related Assessment, Cummins and Bilingual Children
Tony Cline and Norah Frederickson (eds)
English in Europe: The Acquisition of a Third Language
Jasone Cenoz and Ulrike Jessner (eds)
Foundations of Bilingual Education and Bilingualism
Colin Baker
Japanese Children Abroad: Cultural, Educational and Language Issues
Asako Yamada-Yamamoto and Brian Richards (eds)
Language Minority Students in the Mainstream Classroom
Angela L. Carrasquillo and Vivian Rodriguez
Languages in America: A Pluralist View
Susan J. Dicker
Learning English at School: Identity, Social Relations and Classroom Practice
Kelleen Toohey
The Languages of Israel: Policy, Ideology and Practice
Bernard Spolsky and Elana Shohamy
Multicultural Children in the Early Years
P. Woods, M. Boyle and N. Hubbard
Multicultural Child Care
P. Vedder, E. Bouwer and T. Pels
A Parents' and Teachers' Guide to Bilingualism
Colin Baker
Policy and Practice in Bilingual Education
O. García and C. Baker (eds)
The Sociopolitics of English Language Teaching
Joan Kelly Hall and William G. Eggington (eds)
Teaching and Learning in Multicultural Schools
Elizabeth Coelho
Teaching Science to Language Minority Students
Judith W. Rosenthal
Working with Bilingual Children
M.K. Verma, K.P. Corrigan and S. Firth (eds)
Young Bilingual Children in Nursery School
Linda Thompson

Other Books of Interest
Can Threatened Languages be Saved?
Joshua Fishman (ed.)
Encyclopedia of Bilingualism and Bilingual Education
Colin Baker and Sylvia Prys Jones

Please contact us for the latest book information:
Multilingual Matters, Frankfurt Lodge, Clevedon Hall,
Victoria Road, Clevedon, BS21 7HH, England
http://www.multilingual-matters.com

BILINGUAL EDUCATION AND BILINGUALISM 22
Series Editors: Colin Baker and Nancy Hornberger

Studies in Japanese Bilingualism

Edited by
**Mary Goebel Noguchi
and Sandra Fotos**

MULTILINGUAL MATTERS LTD
Clevedon • Buffalo • Toronto • Sydney

Library of Congress Cataloging in Publication Data

A catalog record for this book is available from the Library of Congress.

British Library Cataloguing in Publication Data

A catalogue entry for this book is available from the British Library.

ISBN 1-85359-490-3 (hbk)
ISBN 1-85359-489-X (pbk)

Multilingual Matters Ltd

UK: Frankfurt Lodge, Clevedon Hall, Victoria Road, Clevedon BS21 7HH.
USA: UTP, 2250 Military Road, Tonawanda, NY 14150, USA.
Canada: UTP, 5201 Dufferin Street, North York, Ontario M3H 5T8, Canada.
Australia: P.O. Box 586, Artarmon, NSW, Australia.

Typeset by Aarontype, Bristol.
Printed and bound in Great Britain by the Cromwell Press Ltd.

Contents

Preface

JOHN C. MAHER

A multilingual society is greater than the sum of its languages. A multi-cultural society has more interlocking layers and dimensions than the sum of its many cultures. The new paradigm required of postmodern Japan resides not in the celebration of micro-ethnicities, of mere 'difference', but in a growing awareness of social hybridity, life-style heterogeneity and cultural crossing. It is a creole aesthetic in which 'to be' means 'to freely choose'. The role of education in the making of a new model is crucial, since the purpose of much compulsory education has traditionally been to patrol the boundaries of social and linguistic conformity upon which the state depended for its continuity. Bilingualism is freedom.

All attempts to re-position Japan as a multilingual nation constitute a struggle with history. These attempts are not the work of minds happy enough with the reconstruction of the past offered by historians and folklorists. The efforts result rather from the need to critically inquire about basic concepts like 'tradition' and 'nation' and 'national language'. No concept can be protected from our critical eye, not even the term 'Japan' itself. Here we recall, for example, the term '*Japonesia*' (sic. '*Yaponesia*') coined by the novelist Shimao Toshio (1917–1986), incorporating the idea of the Japanese archipelago as a group of islands of varied cultures and languages.

The view of culture which has now become general consensus in the cultural critique of the late 20th century is that 'tradition' is less a seamless history stretching back into antiquity, but rather a product of the modern nation-state which seeks to explain its existence and legitimate and maintain its hegemony by the manipulation of heritage. It is the fate of history to be rigorously plundered for political expediency and to provide the raw material for a 'national tradition'. This has typically involved enshrining monolingualism (by means of a single 'national language') as the defining symbol of the nation.

The study of societal bilingualism is complex. No doubt the 'ethnic boom' helped change attitudes towards social diversity, but the newly welcome multiculturalism carries with it dangers also; students of bilingualism are therefore advised to be intellectually alert. Almost all narratives of marginalised peoples and languages are implicated in the reproduction of willful nostalgia. It is a familiar tale: the Scottish kilt (a clever invention by a London tailor), the rustic Breton in his fisherman's sweater, the winking Ainu bear with its raised paw beckoning to the *dai shizen* ('great nature') of frontier Hokkaido. The myths and metaphors of cultural identity may be harmless, but they can nevertheless radically distort the lives and wills of ordinary people who do not conform at all to what some others want them to be. To identify Scots Gaelic or Ainu with the pitiful or quaint or premodern is, once again, to seek to dominate the Other by means of spurious definitions. Indeed, as bilingual researchers in Australia are apt to stress, both state and media are quite happy to incorporate marginalised groups into the nation's multicultural image whilst at the same time diluting their claims to autonomy and language rights. They become ethnics with a good symbolic value but kept politically and socially peripheral. It is proper, therefore, that when language diversity is being discussed in Scotland or France or Japan that all people are given equal voice to describe who they are. Working with similar parameters of analysis, Japanese research on bilingualism can learn a great deal from the study of other situations and surely what I term here 'comparative bilingualism' is a rich intellectual quarry to explore.

It is well documented, in the states of Europe and Asia as well as in Japan, that the monolingual principle has been tied also to ideas of race and ethnocentrism. Nation-states as well as ethnic enclaves adopt familiar ideological strategies in order to maintain inner coherence and coercive allegiance. This may involve ideas about ethnic purity (even 'ethnic cleansing'), repressive language laws, and so on. Language has long served as an emblem of loyalty and identity for states and groups. The price of allegiance is usually high: the destruction of smaller or surrounding languages, coercion, the loss of freedom of choice.

The field of bi/multi-lingualism is a great teacher and sheds light on the process of history itself. When we begin to study how language variation ebbs and flows through the arteries of a particular society, quite suddenly hitherto disconnected events in human history boom across the world with many of the same stories. In 1788, a thousand Britons arrived in Australia in an armada of ships. It was a population of the impoverished, the landless and the criminal who were dispatched from a nation of huge wealth and poverty to build a colony. From that moment, the Dreamtime of Aboriginal Australians began to disintegrate and their language situation was to change forever. The following year saw also the great Kunashir-Menash Revolt in Hokkaido, the last battle of the Ainu to resist the Matsumae occupation. With the loss of this historic battle, the Ainu likewise came under the full sway of the emerging Japanese state, with its attendant policies of language removal and assimilation. In the same year, 1789, occurred the French Revolution, whose subsequent policies, elaborated in some detail, provided Europe's blueprint for the suppression of its hundreds of smaller languages and dialects.

In every country, in every age, multilingualism is a normal part of life. Numbers provide a clue to this: around 5000 languages co-exist in about 200 countries. Therefore, an enormous amount of contact is taking place, and Japan is no exception. A lagoon into which language rivers from all over the world have flowed, Japan is a rich melange, a mixture of diverse sounds and shapes. Should this be doubted, an observant eye and ear in the towns and countryside of Japan will tell the tale. The problem of the ideology of monolingualism is phenomenological: concerned with the structure of our seeing, rather than with what is or is not 'out there'. During the heady days of the rediscovery of multiculturalism in the 1970s in Canada, I made a visit to Toronto Metropolitan High School; I recall noticing a poster on a classroom wall which read: 'Monolingualism can be cured.' The problem presented by the monolingual view of society resides in a highly specific working ideology of language and society somatised into the body politic. It is the obligation of scholars to analyse this ideology and a starting point in the diagnosis of the psychosomatic nature of monolinguals has surely begun with this compilation of thoughtful and very welcome studies.

The scope and depth of the contributions, many of which derive from field work, raise this volume above the conventional level of review of the literature. This is pleasing. Now that the reality of Japan as a multilingual region is being rescued from the distortions of the 19th–20th century modernist paradigm, the ground can be cleared and a new garden planted. The work of renewal is also the formulation of new ways of speaking. By tracing the lines around what we now glimpse to be a bilingual Japan, we invoke the need for a different discourse – an *Ausseralltaglichkeit* – because the normal, everyday order – *Alltaglichkeit* – has been turned upside down. Books like *Studies in Japanese Bilingualism* are surely intended to create the new vocabulary of such a discourse.

This book has an applied orientation which relates to how bilingual education is implemented in a variety of situations. The educational emphasis is both fortuitous and necessary. It is important that the teaching of English or Japanese, Ainu or Korean, is not perceived, on the one hand, as an expression of the fetishism of a particular cultural minority in Japan, nor, on the other hand, as the legacy of so-called linguistic imperialism or cultural superiority. The learning and sustaining of any language is, I suggest, a matter of the quality of personal life. Language maintenance is, likewise, about justice and freedom in society for a particular language and people – adults and children – who happen to choose to love and learn a language. Language has no need of narcissistic or repressive endeavour on its behalf. Thus, the fate of English in Japan, the importance of regional dialects, the rich heritage of Korean, language maintenance for the children of Brazilian workers, Ryukyuan or Ainu language survival, are all interconnected.

It is the choice of bilingual-minded people either to build solidarities or struggle alone. This landmark collection of studies is pleasing, therefore, because scholars and educators in Japan are both enabled to organise and share their thoughts in common as well as open up a recognisable path ahead. In this endeavour, let us embrace the Ainu adage: *Naa somo kuokere* — 'the work is unfinished'.

Chapter 1

Introduction:
The Crumbling of a Myth

MARY GOEBEL NOGUCHI

This collection of papers addresses bilingualism in Japan. To many, the juxtaposition of the terms 'Japanese' and 'bilingualism' may seem like an oxymoron. Both inside and outside of the country, Japan has often been presented as a monolith and its people as highly homogeneous. In the seventies, the term 'Japan Inc' symbolised the Western perception of a government, business, educational system and workforce that operated as a single entity. With the curriculum and textbooks used in Japanese public education tightly controlled by the Ministry of Education, the ortho- graphy for writing the Japanese language prescribed by government regulations, and the accent used by television and radio announcers standardised by the public broadcasting network NHK (*Nippon hōsō kyōkai*), the language and culture of Japan appeared to be unequivocally uniform. In fact, so many books attempting to explain the unique nature of 'the Japanese' were published by Japanese and Western scholars that these works came to be considered a separate genre: *Nihonjinron*[1] (theories about the Japanese). So pervasive was this image of homogeneity that in 1986, the prime minister (Nakasone Yasuhiro) actually denied there were any minorities in Japan. What is more, the domestic press did not challenge him on this pronouncement.

The last decade, however, has seen a marked breakdown of this image. Minority groups have increasingly asserted their identity and demanded rights. A number of scholars have pointed out that language contact[2] has been common throughout Japanese history and that several linguistic minorities are firmly established in this country. Moreover, an economic boom has led to increasing movement across the nation's borders, with millions of Japanese travelling abroad for business, education and pleasure, and hundreds of thousands of people from other countries coming to Japan to work and study.

Meanwhile, the world has seen remarkable growth in research on bilingualism in the past two decades, with a wealth of studies on bilingual and immersion education programmes in Canada and the United States, as well as on societal bilingualism and codeswitching in multilingual communities around the world. Until recently, the bulk of this work focused on European languages and Western settings. However, scholars from other parts of the world have gradually begun adding to the research in this field, testing hypotheses and theories generated in North America and Europe on other language combinations to see if they can be applied universally or if other theories need to be developed.

It is hoped that *Studies in Japanese Bilingualism* will contribute to this growing body of research, adding greater depth to the understanding of some of the previously recognised minorities in this country, while also introducing new groups that have begun enriching the linguistic and cultural landscape of the nation in the eighties and nineties.

It must be emphasised that as this field of research has developed, the definition of the term 'bilingualism' has gradually been expanded and refined. Early researchers focused on fluency alone, following Bloomfield's (1933) lead in defining bilingualism to be the 'native-like control of two languages'. As research accumulated, however, linguists began to see that bilingualism is multi-faceted and complex. The *Encyclopedia of Bilingualism and Bilingual Education* specifies five issues that have been identified as creating difficulties in determining whether or not an individual is bilingual: (1) differences between measured language ability and actual language use (i.e. some people may be highly proficient in a language but rarely use it, while others may daily use a language that they are not highly proficient in), (2) variation in an individual's language proficiency in different skill areas, (3) dominance of one language, (4) separation of languages by function that may lead to competence lower than mono-lingual native speakers in both languages, and (5) variation in an individual's language proficiency over time (Baker and Jones, 1998). Such difficulties in determining the absolute minimum proficiency needed to label an individual 'bilingual' may have given rise to Haugen's mini-malist definition:

> 'Bilingualism ... begin[s] at the point where the speaker of one language can produce complete, meaningful utterances in the other language'. (Haugen, 1969, as exerpted in Grosjean, 1982: 232)

Subsequent researchers, while accepting Haugen's notion of a con-tinuum of fluency, have tended to take one of two tacts: (1) refining tests to measure skills in both languages and thereby isolate 'balanced bilinguals', or (2) stressing regular use of two languages as the defining feature of bilingualism (Grosjean, 1982). In *Studies in Japanese Bilingualism*, we have adopted the latter approach, embracing an extended view of bilingualism that encompasses a wide range of skill levels and focusing on language *use* rather than linguistic proficiency as we look at the way the presence of two languages in the environment affects the individual's identity and behaviour.

A Brief History of Language Contact in Japan

A great deal of the writing about Japan focuses on its geographical isolation and the fact that the Tokugawa Shogunate forcibly cut Japan off from the rest of the world for more than two centuries during the middle ages (approximately 1615 to 1854). However, recent scholarship (e.g. Katayama, 1996; Maher, 1996; Loveday, 1996) has shown that interaction between different languages and cultures played an important role in the formation of Japanese culture and that 'Japanese society has been involved in the processes of language contact since its earliest emergence' (Loveday, 1996: 26).

Some linguists surmise that the Japanese language evolved as a result of contact between the two main groups of in-migrants that inhabited the archipelago in prehistoric times. According to Maher (1996), the earliest inhabitants probably came from the south and spoke Austronesian (Malayo-Polynesian) languages. Later, Altaic-speaking groups migrated from the Korean peninsula and Sakhalin in the north. As the Austronesian- and Altaic-speaking peoples communicated with each other, their languages went through pidgin and creole stages in the process of being transformed into ancient Japanese (Maher, 1996; Loveday, 1996).

Ties with China, which appear to have begun in prehistoric times (Katayama, 1996), blossomed during the fourth and fifth centuries AD, when wholesale adoption of the more advanced Chinese systems of agriculture, technology and government led to rapid development of the Late Stone Age Japanese civilisation (Loveday, 1996: 26). The Chinese influence was further intensified by the official adoption of Chinese Buddhism in 594 AD (Loveday, 1996: 29). The medium for this transfer of technology and culture was the Chinese language (Loveday, 1996: 27). Since the Japanese had not yet developed a system of transcribing their own language, they also adopted the Chinese writing system, eventually adapting it for use in writing Japanese as well. Loveday (1996) categorises the language contact of the Nara Period (710–794) as a diglossic bilingual setting in which the high language, Chinese, was taught by native Chinese and Korean immigrants for use in documentation, religious writing and high literature, while Japanese served as the low language for everyday communication. The Chinese cultural influence lasted into the 12th Century and probably resulted in the greatest historical impact on the Japanese language.

Nonetheless, Loveday (1996) explains that language contact in Japan was not limited to this early period. Portuguese, Spanish and Latin words came into Japanese in the late 16th to early 17th Century with the arrival of Portuguese and Spanish missionaries and traders. The Dutch traders who were allowed access to Japan during its period of self-imposed isolation between the 17th and 19th Centuries introduced a wealth of scientific terms to Japan. Then after the country was opened up in the late 19th Century, English, German and French words, especially technological terms, were borrowed as Japan frantically tried to catch up with the West. And today Japan is undergoing another major period of language contact characterised by pervasive borrowing of English words, not all of which are adopted because Japanese equivalents are lacking (see Honna, 1995; Maher, 1991; Loveday, 1996). Loveday (1996: 77) points out that the largest European loan-word dictionary has 27,000 entries, and one study found that 82% of the new words in Japanese in 1975 were derived from European languages – mainly English.

In addition to the impact of foreign languages, Japan also has a history of internal language contact, for the nation itself was not culturally homogeneous. The Ainu people, who once occupied northern parts of the island of Honshu as well as Hokkaido (DeChicchis, 1995; Siddle, 1997), had their own culture and language which flourished until ethnic Japanese conquered all of the Ainu lands and established a policy of assimilation in the late 19th Century.

Similarly, the islands in what is now the southern prefecture of Okinawa were once united in a separate kingdom with its own culture and languages, which although they probably shared the same origins as the Japanese language, were different enough from it and from each other to be mutually unintelligible (Matsumori, 1995: 25). Even after the Ryukyu Kingdom was conquered by the Satsuma Clan of Kyushu (the southern-most main island of Japan) in 1609, the peoples of Okinawa remained ethnically distinct and continued to speak their own languages. It was not until the Meiji Period (1868–1912), when the Japanese government enforced an assimilation policy and insisted on the use of Japanese in educational institutions, that language shift took place (Matsumori, 1995: 33). Even today, many older Okinawans are bilingual, having a good command of both Japanese and one of the Ryukyuan languages.

Even excluding these indigenous minorities, the Japanese were not fully linguistically united until the early twentieth century. Pronunciations of certain sounds, overall intonation, syntax and grammar, a wide range of lexical items, and verb endings differed markedly around the country. In fact, regional dialects were so divergent that in some cases, com-munication was impossible. As late as 1960, a Japanese linguist noted that the dialects spoken in Kagoshima (in the southwest) and Sendai (in the northeast) were mutually unintelligible (reported in Twine, 1991: 208). Even today, Tokyoites and Osakans cannot always under-stand people from the Tohoku (northeast) region or from Kyushu (in the southwest).

The Origins of Japan's Monolithic Image

Given the diverse cultural and linguistic influences which have shaped contemporary Japanese society, one must ask why Japan is perceived to be a cultural and linguistic monolith.

A number of scholars trace the roots of this image to the nation-building policies of the Meiji government. (See, for example, Maher,

1995: 9, Weiner, 1997, and Twine, 1991.) In 1854, when America forced Japan to open its doors to trade after centuries of self-imposed isolation, many Japanese realised that their country was in a very weak position compared to the technologically advanced nations of the West. The feudal government was quickly overthrown and the nation's new leaders rushed to create a modern state strong enough to resist the type of subjugation that China and other Asian countries were experiencing. The goal of the government of the Meiji Period (1868–1912) was to create a unified, wealthy nation.

In *Language and the Modern State: The Reform of Written Japanese*, Nanette Twine (1991) explains how Japanese returning from study trips to Europe reported the benefits of Western systems of universal education and standardised written language. A national system of education was therefore established in 1872 and within a few years, enrollment was very near 100% (Benjamin 1997). The following year, the Ministry of Education published *kotobazukai* (language usage) glossaries and phrase sheets for use in teaching school children 'standard Japanese' so that they would not be inconvenienced by dialectal fragmentation (Twine, 1991: 213). According to Twine, the following decade saw a lively debate on whether Japanese should be standardised and its complex system of writing, which at that time was mastered only by the highly educated elite, should be simplified and written in a colloquial style. By 1886, however, a general consensus had been reached that to facilitate modern communication and universal education, the written language would have to be simplified, and before that could be done, the spoken language would have to be standardised (Twine: 216) so that people throughout the country could comprehend and produce texts based on a commonly understood lexicon, syntax and grammar.

Although there was initially some controversy about how to go about standardisation, it was soon generally accepted that the dialect of Tokyo would be the best choice as the standard language (Twine: 216). This dialect was already understood thoughout the country thanks to feudal systems that involved a great deal of travel between Edo (the city that was later renamed Tokyo) and the provinces. Moreover, as the language of the capital, the Tokyo dialect already had considerable prestige. Thus when the Ministry of Education published a reader in 1887, its introductory volume was written almost entirely in a colloquial style based on this dialect (Twine: 216). In this way, the government sought to familiarise young people all over the country with the syntax and grammar, terms and verb endings used in what was to become known as 'standard Japanese'.

Twine suggests that after the Japanese won the Sino-Japanese War in 1895, the concept of a national language took on significance as a unifying force and source of national pride. It was at this time that the Japanese language began to be referred to as '*kokugo*' – the national language

(p. 218). The tool that the government used to implement the adoption of a standard national language was the Ministry of Education, which set forth a detailed curriculum that was to be followed in all public schools throughout the country – a system that continues to this day. In 1900, the Ministry of Education instructed teachers to include lessons in 'standard Japanese' in their language classes; in 1901, the Ministry announced that the Japanese to be taught in schools was to be the language used by middle- and upper-class Tokyoites (Twine, 1991: 222). The next year, the National Language Research Council (*Kokugo chōsa iinkai*) was appointed, and one of the four areas it identified as a major problem in language reform was standardisation of both spoken and written Japanese (p. 220).

This standardisation of language and education created a sense of national unity at the expense of previously strong regional identities. Increasing emphasis was placed on the ideology of a single Japanese ethnic group (*minzoku*) which shared a common ancestry, history and culture (Weiner, 1997). Ancient myths which traced the Japanese imperial line back to gods who descended from heaven were used not only to create a feeling of consanguinity, but also to argue the superiority of the Japanese people and culture. This ideology was used as grounds for the assimilation of other ethnic groups – from the indigenous Ainu and Ryukyuans to the Koreans and Chinese who came under Japanese colonial control. Under the pretext that they were subjects of the god-Emperor, these peoples were deprived of their own languages and cultures (Nakano, 1995). Their very existence was often ignored as the myth of Japanese homogeneity was promulgated.

For example, in 1869 the Meiji government established the Colonisation Commission (*Kaitakushi*) to 'settle' the northern island of Hokkaido, which under the Land Regulation Ordinance (*Jisho kisoku*) of 1872 was declared to be unoccupied (Siddle, 1997: 23) despite the presence of well over 20,000 Ainu inhabitants (Otsuka, 1984a). With the establishment of Japanese control over the traditional Ainu lands came the implementation of the family registry law (*Koseki hō*), which required the adoption of Japanese family names by the Ainu (Otsuka, 1984b). The assimilationist policy of the Japanese government also led to the prohibition of traditional Ainu men's earrings and women's tattoos as well as the hunting and fishing upon which the Ainu way of life was based (Otsuka, 1984b). In place of the Ainu culture, agriculture was promoted and usage of the Japanese language was encouraged, especially in the special schools set up for the Ainu children (Otsuka, 1984b). Although attendance in these schools was at first low (less than 45% in 1901), by 1916 it had reached 94% (Otsuka, 1984b: 51), ensuring the acquisition of the Japanese language and culture by the young Ainu population. Thereafter, both the government and the Japanese public at large viewed the Ainu as a 'dying race' (Siddle, 1997: 24).

A similar programme to assimilate the Ryukyuan people followed. By 1939, the prefectural authorities in Okinawa had launched a campaign to 'homogenise Okinawa in line with the political and cultural dictates of the centre' (Steele, 1995: 43–44). This involved having Okinawans abandon traditional Ryukyuan funeral practices, dress and language 'in the interests of national unity' (Steele, 1995: 44).

Throughout the Japanese empire, education was standardised by fiat of the Ministry of Education and the use of 'standard Japanese' (*hyōjungo*) was enforced. Stories from Korea and Okinawa recount how children were punished for speaking their native tongues. (See, for example, Chapter 4 in this volume: 'Language and Identity in Okinawa Today,' by Osumi Midori.)

Of course, the drive for unification was not always unopposed, nor was the road to modern economic power always smooth. Steele (1995) describes how Yanagi Soetsu and other members of the *Mingei* (Folk Craft) Movement campaigned against assimilation in Korea and Okinawa. Maher and Yashiro (1995) mention increasing industrial strikes and other social unrest during the 1890s and early years of the twentieth century (p. 9). As Japanese society prepared for war, however, the surge in nationalistic sentiment, coupled with the workings of the secret police (*Tokkō keisatsu*), made it all but impossible for most Japanese subjects to resist nationalistic assimilation policies.

Defeat in World War II did not lead to the destruction of the ideological construct of a single Japanese culture and language. Although the US Occupation forces tried to encourage democracy and in 1947 disbanded the powerful Home Affairs Ministry (*Naimushō*), which had served as the driving force behind many of the nation's prewar social management campaigns, the Ministry of Education (*Monbushō*) was left in place (Garon, 1997) and continued its emphasis on a national curriculum taught in 'standard Japanese' (Twine, 1991). The Ryukyuan languages were lumped together under the term 'Okinawan dialect', and like other dialects and the Ainu language, were considered embarrassing symbols of provincialism which were inappropriate for use in education. Moreover, the large population of ethnic Koreans, many of whom had been brought to Japan forcibly before and during the war to work in mines and factories and on construction projects, were pressured to assimilate, often feeling forced to adopt Japanese-sounding names (*tsūshōmei*)[3] and use the Japanese language in most situations in order to avoid attracting negative attention.

Well into the 1990s, great emphasis was placed on standardisation in education.[4] Even now, teachers are limited in their choice of textbooks to a selection of four or five per grade for any one subject, and all of these texts have to pass a rigorous screening by the Ministry of Education. The textbook screening committee often dictates numerous changes.

Moreover, in the drive to maintain the perception of Japanese society as egalitarian, great effort is expended in making sure that educational experiences are the same for everyone. Cultural anthropologist Gail Benjamin (1997) notes that even the details of school life – for example, which plant is grown as a school project in which grade in elementary school (pp. 89–90) – are closely regulated to ensure that, as much as possible, all children get the same education in the same way (pp. 26–8). Benjamin also observes that the Japanese language texts used in public elementary schools often contain stories in which 'Differences between people based on social categories, such as occupations, region, income, gender, religion, age, disabilities, or even talents, are not presented as background or made the focus of situations in the stories' (p. 125). Because of the uniform nature of the Japanese education system, Benjamin argues, modern Japanese often experience their country as the very homogeneous nation it is commonly portrayed to be (p. 26).

It is perhaps for this reason that, despite the long history of language contact and cultural diversity outlined above, few Japanese seemed prepared to challenge Prime Minister Nakasone in 1986 when he declared that there were no minorities in Japan. The myth of national uniformity had, by the sheer force of the centrally controlled educational policy, been transformed into a reality experienced by a large portion of the Japanese populace.

Cracks in the Monolith

By the 1990s however, the myth of the Japanese monolith had slowly begun to crack as the older ethnic minorities found new voices and increasing numbers of Japanese widened their experiences by travelling and living abroad. Great influxes of newer groups of immigrants added a stronger international flavour to communities throughout the country, while new research focused on Japan's minorities.

The first of the older minority groups to begin reasserting its identity and thus exerting an influence on the national consciousness was probably the Ainu. Siddle (1997) recounts how national trends in student activism in the late 1960s and early 1970s were reflected in the Ainu community, first by groups of young Ainu who explored new ways of expressing their identity through the arts, then later by protest activities aimed at gaining more respectful treatment of their people and culture in the mass media. This led to greater discussion in the Ainu community about what the Ainu should expect from the government, and eventually, to a growing consciousness of 'being a separate people – indeed, a nation' (Siddle, 1997: 34). Subsequent efforts at language and culture revitalisation in one Hokkaido Ainu community are reported by Fred E. Anderson and Masami Iwasaki-Goodman in Chapter 3 of the present volume. The government response to this sense of a distinct identity on the part of the Ainu was a clear statement by the Welfare Minister in 1973 that the government did not view them as a separate people (*minzoku*).

The same year that the Welfare Minister made that statement, however, the Yay Yukar Ainu Ethnic Society was founded to revive the Ainu culture. This group went on to develop ties with organisations of indigenous peoples in other countries and took part in the World Aboriginal Conference in 1989 (*Japan Times*, Shibuya, 1997). Siddle (1997) reports that other Ainu groups also pressed for changes in laws and developed ties with other domestic minorities as well as with indigenous groups from other countries. By December 1992, the Ainu had gained international recognition and were invited to participate in the opening ceremonies for the United Nations International Year of the World's Indigenous People. In 1994, Kayano Shigeru was elected to serve as the first Ainu member of the Diet. Backed by the Ainu Association of Hokkaido (*Hokkaido utari kyōkai*), Kayano urged the government to abolish the discriminatory Hokkaido Former Aborigine Protection Law and enact a new law that would recognise the Ainu as indigenous people (*senjū minzoku*) and boost their economic welfare. This legislation was the first to admit the existence of an ethnic minority in Japan (*Japan Times* Kansai Edition, March 23, 1997).

Similarly, Okinawan identity and pride also underwent a strong resurgence and validation in the 1990s. Taira (1997) argues that one watershed was the August 1990 convention for overseas Okinawans (*Uchinanchu*) held to commemorate the 90th anniversary of the beginning of emigration from Okinawa to Hawaii and South America. Taira explains that the parades of overseas Okinawans wearing the national costumes of their adopted countries in Naha boosted the ethnic pride of the local residents, making them feel that they were 'not alone', but rather, were part of a worldwide community of Okinawans (Taira, 1997: 167). Two years later, the country celebrated the 20th anniversary of the return of Okinawa to Japanese control. Okinawan culture was the focus of numerous TV programmes, exhibits and concerts on the mainland, giving other Japanese a greater awareness of and respect for the distinct Ryukyuan culture. Around this time, several Okinawan pop music groups became very popular on the mainland – another boost to Okinawan pride. The most famous was the Rinken Band, which features songs written in a Ryukyuan language and using the Ryukyuan musical scale. One of their songs, 'Haru-dee-mun', was even included in a textbook for junior high school students (*Japan Times*, Naito, 1992).

Then in 1995 the rape of an Okinawan schoolgirl by three US servicemen ignited widespread protests over the large number of US bases in the prefecture. National media repeatedly reported the fact that Okinawa accounted for less than 1% of the nation's total land area and population but was forced to accommodate roughly three-quarters of the American troops stationed in the country and to provide approximately the same portion of the land used by the US military. As the prefectural governor continued to insist that the national government address this imbalance, both local residents and mainland Japanese became increasingly conscious of the distinct Okinawan identity. The interplay between these changing tides in ethnic identity and pride and attitudes towards Ryukyuan languages are explored by Osumi Midori in Chapter 4, 'Language and Identity in Okinawa Today.'

The developments in Ainu and Okinawan ethnic identity, as well as human rights movements around the world, inspired action on the part of a third ethnic minority – the nation's resident Koreans. As mentioned above, many Koreans were brought to Japan before and during the war to work in mines and factories and on construction projects, making up for a labour shortage caused by Japan's military campaigns (Maher and Kawanishi, 1995: 88). When Japan colonised Korea, it made Koreans Japanese citizens, but they were stripped of this citizenship in 1952 by the San Francisco Peace Treaty and subsequent enactment of the Alien Registration Law. Since that time, the Japanese government has allowed resident Koreans to become naturalised Japanese, but for years, one of the conditions of naturalisation was adoption of a 'Japanese-sounding' name. For this reason, as well as a desire to maintain their ethnic identity, a large number of Koreans refused to undergo naturalisation despite the permanence of their residence in this country. This situation continued through the third and fourth generations, so that even now, Koreans are still the largest group of foreign residents in Japan.[5] Moreover, many Koreans with ties to North Korea have continued to maintain their ethnic identity through Korean schools, as explained in Chapter 5 by Ann B. Cary.

Although they are not legally required to do so, most resident Koreans use a Japanese-sounding name, referred to as their *tsūshōmei* (normally used name), so that they do not have to constantly identify themselves as foreigners. (See Maher & Kawanishi, 1995, for an analysis of the reasons given for this custom.) Even so, they face various forms of discrimination in Japanese society. They are denied suffrage even though they are subject to the same taxes as Japanese citizens, and are also barred from holding jobs in the civil service, which includes many nursing positions and all teaching posts in public schools. Moreover, since Korean schools are not recognised as 'ordinary schools' by the Ministry of Education, their pupils were not allowed to participate in national sports competitions until recently,[6] and their graduates are still not allowed to take the entrance exams for public universities unless they take a high school equivalency test.

Many of these injustices have become the target of action by resident Koreans in the 1990s. The Foreign Residents' Voting Rights Party (*Zainichi-tō*) was formed and in February 1993, it filed a suit seeking voting rights for foreigners as well as the right of political parties organised by foreigners to run in elections in Japan. This suit was rejected by a court in December 1994 (*Japan Times* Kansai Edition, December 10, 1994), but the party has not disbanded. Changes made in the nation's election laws late that year made political parties eligible for state funding.

This gave greater momentum to the voting rights movement, which argued that this was a clear case of taxation without representation (*Japan Times*, Koseki, 1995). Another lawsuit over voting rights was therefore filed in April 1995 (*Japan Times*, Kansai Edition, April 9, 1995). Although this movement has not yet achieved success, it has drawn a great deal of attention to the discrimination suffered by foreigners in Japan.

Another campaign that has drawn media attention has been the drive to eliminate the nationality requirement for most civil service jobs. The government abolished this requirement for nurses, public health nurses and day-care centre workers at public facilities in 1986. Shortly thereafter (in 1988) Chong Hyang Gyun, a young resident Korean, became the first non-Japanese to get a job as a public health nurse. In 1994, when Chong had the seniority required to take an examination for a managerial post, she applied to do so. She was not allowed to take the examination (*Japan Times*, Sept. 14, 1994), so she sued, and eventually was awarded damages by the Tokyo High Court (*Japan Times* Kansai Edition, November 28, 1997).

In the field of education, too, resident Koreans have initiated campaigns to allow them to maintain their ethnic identity without suffering discrimination. In August 1996, a petition was presented to the Ministry of Education asking it to allow graduates from foreign high schools in Japan to take the entrance examinations for admission to the nearly 100 national universities in the country. Petitions regarding this policy were also filed by resident Korean students with the United Nations Sub-commission on Prevention of Discrimination and Protection of Minorities in 1995 and 1996 (*Japan Times* Kansai Edition, August 2, 1996).

A campaign was also launched to encourage resident Koreans to use their real (Korean) names. As a result, the Board of Education in Osaka Prefecture, which has the nation's largest concentration of resident Koreans, issued new guidelines in 1998 urging Korean school children to use their real names (*Japan Times* Kansai Edition, March 3, 1998).

One interesting aspect of these movements by Japan's older ethnic minorities is the networking that has gone on between the groups. Siddle (1997) mentions the ties the Ainu developed with other minorities. Another example of inter-group cooperation was seen in a series of concerts staged in 1994 featuring Korean and Okinawan musicians and trying to promote a positive image of minorities. Organizer Paggie Cho, a Korean resident of Japan, was quoted as saying 'Japanese can live richer lives by solving issues of discrimination and embracing the minorities in their midst' (*Japan Times*, Florence, 1994).

The Surge Towards Internationalisation

While the nation's minorities were reasserting their ethnic identities, many Japanese were taking on new identities of their own through cross-cultural experiences. From the 1970s onwards, Japanese companies made major inroads in foreign markets and began sending executives overseas to promote their exports and manage their investments. By the end of 1993, Japanese overseas investment stood at over $US 422 billion, and approximately 37,000 Japanese executives had been sent abroad to manage these companies, taking along 50,842 school-age children. This represented a 24% increase in the number of children of Japanese executives being educated abroad over 1987 (*Japan Times*, Tsuji, 1995).

The Ministry of Education estimates that approximately 12,000 to 13,000 of these school children return to Japan each year. Although the 1980s saw many reports of discrimination against these 'returnees' (*kikoku shijo*) because of their lack of Japanese language and social skills, the children's elite parents and the companies and organisations that sent them overseas soon began to pressure the government to faciliate their reentry so that the nation could benefit from their experiences (Goodman, 1990).

The Ministry of Education reports that 'returnees' now have a much easier time, as more schools have set special admission quotas that allow a limited number to enroll without passing the highly competitive standard entrance examination (*ippan nyūgaku shiken*) for the school. In 1996, entrance quotas for returnees were in effect at approximately 1700 senior high schools, 235 departments at 99 public universities, and 574 departments at 229 private universities around the country (*Japan Times* Kansai Edition, June 26, 1997). The image of returnees is now quite positive, and for many Japanese, the word 'bilingual' is associated with these children, as shown in Yamamoto Masayo's article 'Japanese Attitudes Towards Bilingualism: A Survey and Its Implications', Chapter 2 in this volume.

As overseas living and travel became more common, the popularity of foreign language lessons also increased. At first, the demand was mostly for English and other European languages, and large numbers of young Westerners were attracted to Japan by the promise of high-paying teaching jobs in companies and private language schools. To help meet some of this demand in the public school system, the Ministry of Education began bringing in young people from Western countries under the Japan Exchange and Teaching (JET) Program, which was launched in 1987. Participants in this programme work with Japanese teachers of their native language at the middle and high school level to provide an oral communication component for required foreign laguage classes in public schools. Ten years after its inception, the programme had a total of 5351 participants from 25 countries (*Japan Times* Kansai Edition, July 23, 1997).

The greater prestige of foreign languages and their increased importance on college entrance exams drove the nation's competitive schools to search for more effective ways of boosting their students' foreign language proficiency. It was not long before a Japanese school investigated the success of immersion programmes in Canada and the US and decided to try this system. In 1992, Katoh Gakuen, a private, family-run educational institution in Numazu, Shizuoka Prefecture, launched Japan's first English immersion programme in an elementary school. The program and its success are described in Chapter 10, 'Bilingual Education of Children in Japan: Year Four of a Partial Immersion Programme' by R. Michael Bostwick, the programme's director.

Accompanying this drive to improve foreign language education in Japan, there was also a recognition of the large gap between the number of students Japan sent abroad and the number of foreign nationals in Japanese schools. In 1983, the country was host to only 10,428 foreign students (*Japan Times*, Nagoya, July 3, 1996). That year the Ministry of Education launched the '100,000 Foreign Students Plan', which aimed to have that number of students from overseas studying in Japan by the year 2000. As a result of this drive to attract more foreign students with scholarships and special entrance examinations, the number of foreign nationals studying in Japan rose to 53,847 by May 1, 1995 (*Japan Times*, Nagoya, July 3, 1996). The vast majority of these students (49,212, or 91.5%) came from Asian countries, predominantly China and South Korea (*Japan Times*, Nagoya, July 3, 1996).

As Japan came to be recognised as an economic power, there was increasing insistence that it participate more in international aid activities. One area where demands were made was the acceptance of refugees. As a result of this international pressure, the Immigration and Refugee Recognition Law was introduced in 1982 (*Japan Times*, Fujimoto, 1993) and by 1994, Japan had accepted 9601 Indochinese as refugees (*Japan Times*, Nashima, 1994).

Another area where international pressure molded national policy concerned grievances that remained unresolved after World War II. Victims who may have felt they had nothing to gain from a nation reduced to ashes by defeat began to express resentment after Japan's robust economy brought it into the international limelight in the seventies and eighties. One group that had a direct impact on language contact in Japan was Japanese children who had been left behind in China during the hasty Japanese retreat near the end of the War. Known as Chinese 'War Orphans' (*zanryū koji*), many of these abandoned Japanese were raised by Chinese farmers. Repatriation of the War Orphans and their families began after the normalisation of Sino-Japanese relations in 1972, but only reached full swing after restrictions on their return were lifted and the responsibility of promoting their return was shifted onto the Japanese government by a bill passed by the Diet in 1994. By 1997, approximately 17,000 War Orphans and their families had been resettled at government expense. (See Chapter 6, 'Japan's Hidden Bilinguals: The Languages of "War Orphans" and Their Families After Repatriation From China', by Tomozawa Akie, for more on this group.)

The economic boom also spurred immigration by several other ethnic groups. In the mid-1980s, the country experienced a severe labour shortage, especially in the construction and manufacturing industries, where work was considered unattractive and was characterised in Japanese by three pejoratives starting with the letter 'k': *kitsui, kitanai, kiken* (difficult, dirty and dangerous). Many of these job openings were filled by illegal foreign workers coming from Pakistan, Iran, the Philippines and other Asian countries. The Labour Ministry reported that in November 1991, there were 210,000 illegal foreign workers in the country twice as many as the number in 1990 – and that most were from Asian countries (*Japan Times*, July 1, 1992).

Cultural friction and crimes involving these illegal workers led the government to look for new ways to alleviate the labour shortage. Apparently working under a theory that ethnic Japanese would deviate less from national norms and would therefore be better workers, the government amended the immigration control law in 1990 to make it easier for second- and third-generation Japanese from other countries to obtain work visas. As a result, the nation experienced a massive influx of South American *Nikkei* (people of Japanese ancestry) and their families, mostly from Brazil and Peru. By 1997, there were over 200,000 Brazilians of Japanese descent working in Japan (*Japan Times*, Maeda, 1997). Since employers who had good experiences with Nikkei often hired others, and the Nikkei themselves felt more comfortable living with people like themselves, these South Americans tended to become concentrated in certain areas. The most famous is the town of Oizumi in Gunma Prefecture, which has a large industrial complex that has experienced chronic labour shortages. In 1994, five percent of the town's population was reported to be South American (*Japan Times*, Nakamura, 1994). Chapter 7 explores the language environment of one group of Nikkei residents: Brazilians in Fujisawa City.

Despite the increase of legal immigration by Nikkei and Chinese War Orphans, many of whom took up jobs in the manufacturing industry, Japan continues to attract unskilled workers of other nationalities, most of whom do not have working visas. Although the number of foreigners who overstayed their visas has declined from a peak of approximately 299,000 in 1993, it has remained well over 270,000 since that time (*Japan Times*, Yamagiwa, June 13, 1996). As of January 1st, 1998, there were 276,000 foreigners in the country who had overstayed their visas and most of them were believed to be working illegally (*Japan Times*, June 17, 1998). By country, South Korea, Thailand, the Philippines and China were the sources of the largest numbers of illegal workers, with fewer coming from Peru, Iran, Malaysia, Taiwan, Bangladesh, Myanmar and Pakistan (Justice Ministry figures presented in *Japan Times*, Yamagiwa, June 13, 1996). In addition to these illegal workers who overstay valid visas, increasing numbers of Chinese job seekers have been smuggled into the country, mostly by Chinese brokers known as Snakeheads, who work in collusion with local crime syndicates (*Japan Times*, February 7, 1997).

Yet another factor in the rapid internationalisation of Japan is continuing urbanisation that has led to the depopulation of rural areas. As in many agricultural societies, the eldest son in Japanese farming families traditionally inherits the property and is expected to take care of his parents as they age. The growing independence of Japanese women, however, has meant that few are willing to endure the rigours of rural life or the demands of patriarchical families. To alleviate the dearth of brides for their young men, many rural communities have arranged meetings with young women in other Asian countries, especially the Philippines. In 1993, 20,092 Japanese men married non-Japanese women in Japan, and 32% of these marriages were to Filipinas (*Japan Times* Kansai Edition, September 10, 1994). Moreover, the Philippines reported that in the same year, 5418 women from the country married Japanese men, and more than 20,000 Filipino men and women had married Japanese in the past four years (*Japan Times*, Galvez, 1994). Meanwhile, the total number of international marriages in Japan rose from 5500 in 1970 to 27,000 in 1995 (*Japan Times*, May 25, 1997). While many of these international marriages have not succeeded because of unrealistic expectations on both sides, the Japanese press and other mass media have reported that some communities have taken measures to make the foreign wives feel more at home and welcomed the new customs they bring.

Taken together, this massive influx of people into Japan meant that the total number of registered foreign residents rose to 1.51 million as of the end of 1998. This is 1.2% of the nation's total population (*Japan Times* Kansai Edition, June 6, 1999). The growing foreign population has not only meant increasing cultural and linguistic contact in the community at large, it has also led to two other trends: a large jump in the number of children born to foreign parents in Japan, and a dramatic rise in the number of children in Japanese schools who lack Japanese language skills. The number of children born in Japan to at least one non-Japanese parent soared from 17,596 in 1987 to 32,434 in 1996 (*Japan Times*, Yoshida, 1998). Meanwhile, the number of foreign students in Japanese public schools surpassed 17,000 in 1998, a nearly 50% increase over 1995 (*Japan Times*, Parker, 1998). The problems faced by these children are described by Sharon Vaipae in Chapter 8, 'Language Minority Students in Japanese Public Schools', while factors that affect whether or not the children of mixed marriages become active bilinguals are explored by Mary Goebel Noguchi in Chapter 9.

The revitalising of the identity of Japan's older ethnic minorities, coupled with the emergence of several new ethnic groups, has spurred a number of changes in government policy at the local level. To give greater representation to its foreign population, the city of Kawasaki established a foreign residents' committee to advise the municipal government in late

1995, and Tokyo followed suit in 1997. Several local governments have opened up civil service employment opportunities to Koreans and other foreign nationals. Kochi was the first prefecture to abolish nationality requirements for government jobs in 1997. Kanagawa Prefecture and the cities of Yokohama and Osaka soon followed its lead. By August 1997, a survey revealed that roughly 80% of the nation's prefectural and municipal governments allowed foreign residents to apply for civil service jobs (*Japan Times* Kansai Edition, August 26, 1997).

Meanwhile, the Ministry of Education loosened restrictions on college entrance exams slightly, allowing the graduates of non-certified high schools (mostly ethnic Korean schools) in Japan who have passed a high school equivalency test to take entrance exams to public colleges for the first time in 1996 (*Japan Times* Kansai Edition, July 9, 1995). Moreover, starting in 1997, foreign students and foreign graduates of schools operated under the School Education Law were allowed to participate in national athletic meets.

Another area where Japan has recognised its increasing internationalisation is in providing access to information. Many government and non-governmental agencies now publish brochures in several languages, including Korean, English, Tagalog, and Chinese. Courts provide interpretation in as many as 25 languages. A number of these national groups have their own associations and news organs. In addition, multilingual radio stations have been established in a number of major cities, including Tokyo, Kobe, and Fukuoka.

If all this is not enough to explode the myth of Japanese cultural and linguistic homogeneity, a number of recent research collections have directly addressed the construct and forcefully presented counter-evidence. In 1991 a collection of papers in Japanese edited by John C. Maher and Yashiro Kyoko came out under the title *Nihon no Bairingarizumu* [Bilingualism in Japan]. Maher soon followed this with two collections of papers in English that he coedited: *Multilingual Japan* (1995) and *Diversity in Japanese Language and Culture* (also 1995). Soon after, Leo Loveday brought out *Language Contact in Japan: A Sociolinguistic History* (1996). Two other collections of papers on language and cultural contact in Japan also appeared: *Multicultural Japan: Palaeolithic to Post-modern* (edited by Denoon *et al.*, 1996), and *Japan's Minorities: The Illusion of Homogeneity* (edited by Michael Weiner, 1997).

Piecing Together the Whole Picture

Studies in Japanese Bilingualism strives to build on this foundation of research into language contact and cultural diversity in the nation in order to help bring into focus more pieces of the linguistic puzzle that is present-day Japan. The papers in this collection report field work on a number of the minorities in this country, both old and new. Many are based on surveys designed to give us a clearer, more up-to-date picture of how these minorities see themselves and their languages.

To frame our discussion of bilingualism in Japan, Chapter 2 reports on a survey by Yamamoto Masayo aimed at investigating whether there are common images of and attitudes towards bilinguals in this country. Yamamoto reports that in general, her respondents had positive images of bilinguals, but that their definitions of the term *bilingual* were rather strict and that they seemed to associate it with elite bilinguals — mainly Japanese who have acquired a high level of proficiency in English. Yamamoto then analyses the implications of these findings, stressing that the respondents' positive images may not extend to folk bilinguals such as the minority and immigrant groups discussed above. Indeed, Japan's powerful Ministry of Education has not yet considered bilingual education programmes or mother tongue maintenance for these groups.

The collection then moves on to chapters on Japan's oldest linguistic minorities — the Ainu, the Okinawans, and resident Koreans — looking at developments such as the Ainu revitalisation movement, the creative new mixtures of Okinawan vernacular expressions and standard Japanese used by Okinawan youth, and the evolving nature of ethnic Korean education in Japan. Next come chapters on two newer minorities, the Chinese 'War Orphans' and their families, and Nikkei Brazilians, followed by an overview of the situation of language minority children in Japan's public schools. We then examine some of the more elite groups of potential bilinguals: children born of marriages between Japanese and native speakers of English, and children in Japan's first English immersion programme in an elementary school. The final section of this book provides two studies on codeswitching, looking at a range of language proficiencies, from near balanced bilinguals at an international high school to limited-proficiency EFL (English as a Foreign Language) students. The volume closes with an overview of research on language attrition in Japanese contexts, with suggestions on applying research findings in this field to the development of effective language retention programmes for Japan's linguistic minorities.

One of the themes this collection of papers explores is identity. In Chapter 3 Fred E. Anderson and Masami Iwasaki-Goodman look at how those concerned with Ainu revitalisation in Nibutani, Hokkaido, are trying to balance the restoration of traditional values with modern realities, striving to develop new roles and new functions for the Ainu language that will reflect the identities of its speakers of the twenty-first century. In Chapter 4 Osumi Midori looks at how identity and language have interacted in Okinawa, exploring factors that have influenced the rate of language shift in various communities in the prefecture. Osumi also notes that young Okinawans are developing mixed modes of communication to assert a new ethnic identity for themselves. In Chapter 5 Ann B. Cary reports on Korean ethnic education in Japan. Although earlier research by Japanese and Japanologists tended to view this type of education as 'historically limited' or 'static', Cary argues that there is still vitality in Japan's Korean community and finds that it is committed to exercising its rights to its ethnic identity and language.

In addition to identity issues, *Studies in Bilingualism* explores the phenomena of language shift, maintenance and revitalisation. Three ethnic groups in Japan are found to be in the process of language shift: the Okinawans are nearing the end of this process, as shown by Osumi Midori in Chapter 4, while the Chinese War Orphans might be viewed as being in the midst of language shift, and the South American *Nikkei* may be seen to be at the beginning of the process.

The language environment of the Chinese War Orphans is covered in Chapter 6 by Tomozawa Akie, who conducted a survey of their language use. Her report examines when Japanese and Chinese are used, the subjects' attitudes towards maintaining their Chinese proficiency, and differences in language maintenance and attitudes according to the area in which these returnees are residing. Tomozawa suggests that the longer these families live in Japan, the greater the use of the Japanese language by the younger generation becomes. This rapid language shift has given rise to communication problems between the children and their parents and grandparents, for whom Chinese continues to be the dominant language.

In Chapter 7 Hirataka Fumiya, Koishi Atsuko and Kato Yosuke examine the language environment of Brazilian immigrants in the city of Fujisawa. The researchers use the results of a survey of 183 Brazilian residents to investigate the immigrants' Japanese language acquisition as well as their language use in their homes and workplaces. Japanese language education, mother tongue support programmes and other services available to the immigrants in the city are also outlined and analysed in terms of the immigrants' linguistic rights.

In contrast to the above three groups, the Ainu are often viewed as having already undergone language shift. However, the reassertion of their ethnic identity has led to a language revitalisation movement among the Ainu. In Chapter 3 Fred E. Anderson and Masami Iwasaki-Goodman examine the current state of this movement, with special emphasis on one children's language programme in the Hokkaido community of Nibutani. Their paper draws connections between the language situation in Nibutani and what is known about processes of language revival/revitalisation in other parts of the world, as per Fishman's (1992) Stages of Reversing Language Shift. Fishman's model suggests that bilingualism in revitalisation movements begins with a diglossic separation of languages according to function and situation. In the case of Ainu, the formal, ritualistic functions of the language (which are closely linked to the traditional culture) would appear to play a pivotal role in the development of stable bilingualism.

Children caught in between languages are the subject of Chapter 8. The school and classroom experiences of Japan's language minority students, as well as their linguistic and academic achievement, are reported in an extensive study by Sharon Vaipae which was based on surveys of teachers, parents and students, as well as interviews and classroom observation. Vaipae details the schools' assimilationist assumptions and practices, which minimise recognition of and response to students' limited achievement, and act to camouflage the resulting dysfunctional acculturation. She also explores administrative measures treating language minority students' educational needs, and reveals a hierarchy of institutionalised and systemic barriers to improving their accommodation and instruction in Japanese public schools.

Language acquisition is the focus of two other papers in this book, one on bicultural children, and the other on Japan's first English immersion programme. In Chapter 9 Mary Goebel Noguchi reports on a pilot survey of native English speakers in international marriages living in Japan. The survey was conducted to determine family and personal characteristics as well as family communication patterns which might promote or operate against the development of active use of two languages. Her findings suggest that it is more difficult for second and third children to become active bilinguals than it is for first children. Analysis of family communication patterns and the use of language strategies in relation to the development of children's binguality suggests that parents in mixed marriages do not need to limit their communication with their children to their native language (following a one person/one language approach) in order to ensure that their children become active bilinguals.

In Chapter 10 R. Michael Bostwick, the director of Japan's first English immersion programme in an elementary school, discusses the establishment and operation of the immersion programme and the students' progress in the first four years of the programme. He analyses both the children's acquisition of English and their development of Japanese literacy in comparison to their monolingual peers in Katoh Gakuen's regular programme and to Japanese national norms. Their test scores show that despite the great differences between the Japanese and English languages and the difficulty of written Japanese, these children, like so many in immersion programmes in other parts of the world, were able to acquire a high degree of proficiency in a second language without sacrificing academic achievement.

In Chapters 11 and 12, *Studies in Japanese Bilingualism* looks at a phenomenon that is inextricably bound up with language contact: code-switching. Both chapters present it as a positive phenomenon that allows bilinguals to achieve both social and linguistic goals. In Chapter 11 Yuriko Kite investigates the communication patterns of a group of near balanced bilinguals – high school students in an international school in Japan – using the concept of domain and the Markedness Model. She finds codeswitching to be the core of the students' in-group speech repertoire. Using markedness theory, Kite analyses survey results and the students' attitude toward their codeswitching as expressed in written passages. She concludes that codeswitching is the unmarked choice for informal communication with friends. She also finds that both students and faculty at the school hold relatively positive attitudes towards codeswitching, in contrast to negative views catalogued in previous studies conducted in other countries.

In Chapter 12 Sandra Fotos examines the use of codeswitching by college students studying English as a foreign language (EFL). This group is not normally considered bilingual, but Fotos argues that it constitutes Japan's largest pool of bilinguals. She suggests that classroom codeswitching by EFL students can enhance community membership and can also serve as a learning strategy to increase the salience of important input from the target language and foster student awareness of the limitations of their proficiency that serves to 'push' them to higher levels of output accuracy.

The volume concludes with an overview of language attrition — another phenomenon inextricably bound up with bilingualism. In Chapter 13 Lynne Hansen reviews the literature on language attrition in general and then hones in on research on language loss in Japanese contexts — a field to which the author herself has made substantial contributions. She then analyses possible applications of attrition studies in Japanese contexts, including their use in designing language retention strategies for language minority groups.

It is hoped that this wide range of studies on the language and identity of minority groups in Japan will provide new data that can be used to test and/or develop theories on language contact phenomenon, including language acquisition, maintenance, attrition, shift, revitalisation and codeswitching.

Notes

1. Japanese words and sounds in this book are transcribed using the Hepburn system of romanisation, with macrons (e.g. $\bar{o}$) used to symbolise the long vowels, except in personal and place names. Japanese names are presented in the traditional Japanese style, with the family name followed by the personal name.
2. Language contact is considered to be contact between peoples whose native languages differ and the resulting influences, both direct and indirect, on their languages.
3. See Maher and Kawanishi, 1995, for an explanation of the history of this practice and current reasons for its continuation.
4. In the late 1990s, international pressure as well as rising juvenile deliquency and increasing cases of 'school refusal' (in which children refuse to go to school) caused the Ministry of Education to reconsider its policy of standardisation. As a result, some changes are being planned to respect students' individuality and allow teacher innovation in lesson planning.

5. Estimates on the exact number of Korean residents of Japan vary. Yamagiwa Hiroshi reported in the *Japan Times* of November 19, 1996 that 600,000 of the 670,000 Koreans living in Japan had permanent residency status. Maher and Kawanishi (1995) estimate that when Koreans who have acquired Japanese citizenship are included, the total number of ethnic Koreans in Japan is approximately one million.

6. According to the *Japan Times* Kansai Edition of February 25, 1997, the 52nd National Athletic Meet held in Osaka in October 1997, was to allow Korean residents of Osaka Prefecture (home to approximately 180,000 Koreans, or one-fourth of the resident Koreans in Japan) to participate in the opening and closing ceremonies, and also allow foreign students and foreign graduates of schools operated under the School Education Law to compete in the meet itself for the first time. Students from schools affiliated with North Korean organisations, however, were still barred from participation.

References

Baker, C. and Jones, S.P. (1998) *Encyclopedia of Bilingualism and Bilingual Education.* Clevedon, UK: Multilingual Matters.

Benjamin, G.R. (1997) *Japanese Lessons: A Year in a Japanese School Through the Eyes of an American Anthropologist and Her Children.* New York and London: New York University Press.

Bloomfield, L. (1933) *Language.* New York: Holt, Rinehard and Winston.

DeChiccis, J. (1995) The Current State of the Ainu Language. In J.C. Maher and Yashiro K. (eds) *Multilingual Japan* (pp. 103–124). Clevedon, UK: Multilingual Matters.

Denoon, D., Hudson, M., McCormack, G. and Morris-Suzuki, T. (eds) (1996) *Multicultural Japan: Palaeolithic to Postmodern.* Cambridge, England: Cambridge University Press.

Garon, S. (1997) *Molding Japanese Minds: The State in Everyday Life.* Princeton, NJ: Princeton University Press.

Goodman, R. (1990) *Japan's 'International Youth': The Emergence of a New Class of Schoolchildren.* Oxford, England: Clarenden Press.

Grosjean, F. (1982) *Life With Two Languages: An Introduction to Bilingualism.* Cambridge, MA: Harvard University Press.

Honna N. (1995) English in Japanese society: Language within language. In J.C. Maher and Yashiro K. (eds) *Multilingual Japan* (pp. 45–62). Clevedon, UK: Multilingual Matters.

Japan Times
(articles without by-lines)

Ainu bill approved but void of legal rights. *Japan Times* Kansai Edition, March 23, 1997.

Applicant refused due to nationality. *Japan Times* Kansai Edition, September 14, 1994.

Businesses asked to avoid hiring of illegal workers. *Japan Times* Kansai Edition, June 17, 1998.

College entry open to German grads. *Japan Times* Kansai Edition, July 9, 1995.

Culture exchange going strong 10 years on. *Japan Times* Kansai Edition, July 23, 1997.

Foreign population totals 1.2%: Report. *Japan Times* Kansai Edition, June 6, 1999.

Foreign school grads want end to discrimination: Demand right to take college entry exams. *Japan Times* Kansai Edition, August 2, 1996.

International marriages on the rise. *Japan Times* Kansai Edition, May 25, 1997.

Korean kids urged to use real names. *Japan Times* Kansai Edition, March 3, 1998.

Korean residents file lawsuit demanding the right to vote. *Japan Times* Kansai Edition, April 9, 1995.

Koreans to participate in athletic ceremonies. *Japan Times*, Kansai Edition, February 25, 1997.

Labor shortage fuels illegal worker inflow. *Japan Times* Kansai Edition, July 1, 1992.

Local government jobs open to foreign residents. *Japan Times* Kansai Edition, August 26, 1997.

More mixed marriages reported last year. *Japan Times* Kansai Edition, September 10, 1994.

More schools open to returning students. *Japan Times* Kansai Edition, June 26, 1997.

Smuggling of Chinese into Japan proves to be a lucrative business. *Japan Times* Kansai Edition, February 7, 1997.

South Korean wins discrimination suit: Landmark civil service ruling. *Japan Times* Kansai Edition, November 28, 1997.

Voting rights denied to foreign residents. *Japan Times* Kansai Edition, December 10, 1994.

(*Japan Times* articles with by-lines)

Florence, M. (1994) Korean targets sour note of discord: Concerts push pluralism, rights, end to discrimination. *Japan Times* Kansai Edition, November 20.

Fujimoto M. (1993) Asian newcomers now viewed as integral elements of society. *Japan Times* Kansai Edition, January 7.

Galvez, V.C. (1994) More Filipinos marrying Japanese: Love cited as main reason. *Japan Times* Kansai Edition, September 23.

Koseki M. (1995) Debate over foreign suffrage gathers momentum. *Japan Times* Kansai Edition, February 21.

Maeda T. (1997) Do traditional Bon and samba mix? Gunma town struggles to embrace Japanese-Brazilian returnees. *Japan Times* Kansai Edition, August 19.

Nagoya S. (1996) Government promoting policies to attract overseas students. *Japan Times* Kansai Edition, July 3.

Naito Y. (1992) Roots vital to Rinken Band. *Japan Times* Kansai Edition, December 31.

Nakamura R. (1994) A Little Brazil springs to life in Gunma. *Japan Times* Kansai Edition, March 24.

Nashima M. (1994) Refugees adjusting to new home. *Japan Times* Kansai Edition, December 13.

Parker, G. (1998) Morality classes add lessons on foreigners. *Japan Times* Kansai Edition, May 22.

Shibuya T. (1997) Ainu revive traditional hunts: Group plans deer feast, rites. *Japan Times* Kansai Edition, March 6.

Tsuji M. (1995). Returnees find themselves at home: Living abroad is now less likely to mean alienation upon return. *Japan Times* Kansai Edition, September 14.

Yamagiwa H. (1996) Recourse eludes illegal aliens: Employers' attitude, lack of rights main complaints. *Japan Times* Kansai Edition, June 13.

Yamagiwa H. (1996) Voting rights cornering Koreans into identity row: North-South rivalry continues. *Japan Times* Kansai Edition, November 19.

Yoshida R. (1998) Mixed kids adding to meaning of 'Japanese'. *Japan Times* Kansai Edition, April 19.

Katayama K. (1996) The Japanese as an Asia-Pacific population. In D. Denoon, M. Hudson, G. McCormack and T. Morris-Suzuki (eds) *Multicultural Japan: Palaeolithic to Postmodern* (pp. 19–30). Cambridge, England: Cambridge University Press.

Loveday, L.J. (1996) *Language Contact in Japan: A Sociolinguistic History*. Oxford, England: Clarendon Press.

Maher, J.C. (1991) *Masumedia ni okeru eigo* [English in the mass media]. In J.C. Maher and Yashiro K. (eds) *Nihon no bairingarizumu* [Bilingualism in Japan] (pp. 17–33). Tokyo: Kenkyusha shuppan.

Maher, J.C. and Kawanishi Y. (1995) On being there: Koreans in Japan. In J.C. Maher and Yashiro K. (eds) *Multilingual Japan* (pp. 87–101). Clevedon, UK: Multilingual Matters.

Maher, J.C. and Yashiro K. (eds) (1991) *Nihon no Bairingarizumu* [Bilingualism in Japan]. Tokyo: Kenkyusha shuppan.

Maher, J.C. and Yashiro K. (1995) Multilingual Japan: An introduction. In J.C. Maher and Yashiro K. (eds) *Multilingual Japan* (pp. 1–18). Clevedon, UK: Multilingual Matters.

Maher, J.C. and Yashiro K. (eds) (1995) *Multilingual Japan*. Clevedon, UK: Multilingual Matters.

Maher, J.C. and Macdonald, G. (eds) (1995) *Diversity in Japanese Culture and Language.* London and New York: Kegan Paul International.

Maher, J.C. (1996). North Kyushu Creole: A language-contact model for the origins of Japanese. In D. Denoon, M. Hudson, G. McCormack and T. Morris-Suzuki (eds) *Multicultural Japan: Palaeolithic to Postmodern* (pp. 31–45). Cambridge, England: Cambridge University Press.

Matsumori A. (1995) Ryukyuan: Past, present, and future. In J.C. Maher and Yashiro K. (eds) *Multilingual Japan* (pp. 19–44). Clevedon, UK: Multilingual Matters.

Nakano H. (1995) The sociology of ethnocentricism in Japan. In J.C. Maher and G. Macdonald (eds) *Diversity in Japanese Culture and Language* (pp. 49–72). London and New York: Kegan Paul International.

Otsuka K. (1984a) *Ainu.* In *Nihon daihyakka zensho* [Encyclopedia Nipponica 2001] 1, 49. Tokyo: Shogakukan.

Otsuka K. (1984b) *Ainu minzoku no rekishi (Kaitaku ikō)* [The History of the Ainu People (After the Opening of Hokkaido). In *Nihon daihyakka zensho* [Encyclopedia Nipponica 2001] 1, 50–52. Tokyo: Shogakukan.

Siddle, R. (1997) Ainu: Japan's indigenous people. In M. Weiner (ed.) *Japan's Minorities: The Illusion of Homogeneity* (pp. 17–49). London and New York: Routledge.

Steele, M.W. (1995) Nationalism and cultural pluralism in modern Japan: Soetsu Yanagi and the mingei movement. In J.C. Maher and G. Macdonald (eds) *Diversity in Japanese Culture and Language* (pp. 27–48). London and New York: Kegan Paul International.

Taira, K. (1997) Troubled national identity: Okinawans. In M. Weiner (ed.) *Japan's Minorities: The Illusion of Homogeneity.* (pp. 140–177). London and New York: Routledge.

Twine, N. (1991) *Language and the Modern State: The Reform of Written Japanese.* London and New York: Routledge.

Weiner, M. (1997) The invention of identity: 'Self' and 'other' in pre-war Japan. In M. Weiner (ed.) *Japan's Minorities: The Illusion of Homogeneity* (pp. 1–16). London and New York: Routledge.

Chapter 2

Japanese Attitudes Towards Bilingualism: A Survey and Its Implications

YAMAMOTO MASAYO

Introduction

If a society holds certain attitudes toward bilingualism and associates these attitudes with a particular type of bilingual, then individual members of that group are likely to be affected. Members of a positively perceived category are more likely to be encouraged to maintain and advance their bilingualism. Conversely, members of a less positively perceived group will be less encouraged, if not, in fact, discouraged, to do so.

To investigate whether societal attitudes towards bilingualism can be detected in Japan, and if so, whether these attitudes are associated with specific types of bilinguals, a survey was conducted during the winter of 1993–1994. The subjects were asked to write down words they associate with the term *bilingual*, then to indicate whether they felt each term was 'positive', 'negative' or 'neutral'. The subjects' definitions of the word *bilingual* were also investigated, and the languages they associated with bilingualism examined. This paper presents the results of that study and discusses their implications for potential and actual bilinguals in Japan.

Historical Background

Japan has long been perceived and presented as a monolingual and ethnically homogeneous country by many mainstream Japanese. In 1986, Prime Minister Nakasone Yasuhiro even went so far as to claim that this characteristic was the determining factor in the educational superiority of Japanese over Americans, since, unlike America, Japan does not have to deal with 'minority groups of low intelligence, such as Mexicans and blacks' (*Asahi shimbun*, September 24, 1986 [translation by the present author]). Domestically as well as abroad, Mr. Nakasone's racist claim was rightfully criticised by many people. It seems, however, that his assertion of Japanese social homogeneity and monolingualism went unchallenged by mainstream Japanese.

Aside from this ethnocentric opinion of one politician, quite a few Japanese scholars in linguistics-related fields also share this monolithic view of their own society (e.g. Toyama, 1974; Suzuki, 1975; Higuchi & Nakamura, 1978; Iritani, 1988). In sharp contrast, their counterparts abroad are more cautious about defining a monolingual nation (Trudgill, 1974; Grosjean, 1982) or in designating Japan as one (Harding & Riley, 1986).

Yet despite its self-image, Japan has never actually been a genuinely monolingual country (Maher & Honna, 1994; Maher & Yashiro, 1995). As early as the Nara Period (710–794), the elite sector of Japanese society operated in a Japanese-Chinese diglossic bilingual environment (Loveday, 1996). Moreover, Japan has always had ethnic minority groups: indigenous Ainus and Ryukyuans, and especially in this century, resident Koreans, Chinese and other 'foreign' people as well.

In spite of the presence of these minorities, the view that Japan is a monoethnic and monolingual society has prevailed and has been reinforced through several crucial foreign and language policy measures taken by the governments of the times. One such measure was the policy of seclusion enforced by the Tokugawa government which drastically limited Japan's contact with the outside world for well over 200 years, from the 17th century to the 19th century. Another is a series of assimilation policies imposed upon minority groups such as the Ainu and the Ryukyuans. Among these was the Hokkaido Former Aborigines Protection Act, enacted by the Meiji government in 1899. The basic purpose of this policy was the 'Japanisation' of the Ainu, with the intention of forcing a language shift from the Ainu language to the Japanese language through education in school (Yamamoto, 1996a, 1996b). [See Chapters 1, 3 and 4 of this book for more on these assimilation policies and their effects.]

With such assimilative political pressures constantly imposed upon them, Japan's minority groups have become largely unseen and unheard by mainstream Japanese in modern times, and sociolinguistic issues such as the recognition and maintenance of their languages and ethnic identities have hardly been an issue among the Japanese majority.

Since around the middle of the 1980s, however, more people have been attracted to Japan from other areas of the world, especially from Asia and South America, due to Japan's economic prosperity and unfilled labour needs. Added to the 'older' groups of foreign residents named above, this influx of 'new' minorities during the last 15 years sharply increased the number of foreign residents of Japan. Figure 1 shows the total number of foreign residents registered to live in Japan under the Alien Registration Law and the breakdown for the two groups of minorities which increased the most since the middle of the 1980s: Asians and South Americans. In addition to legally recognised foreign residents, it has been estimated that approximately 300,000 more foreigners are living in the country illegally (Ministry of Labour, 1995).

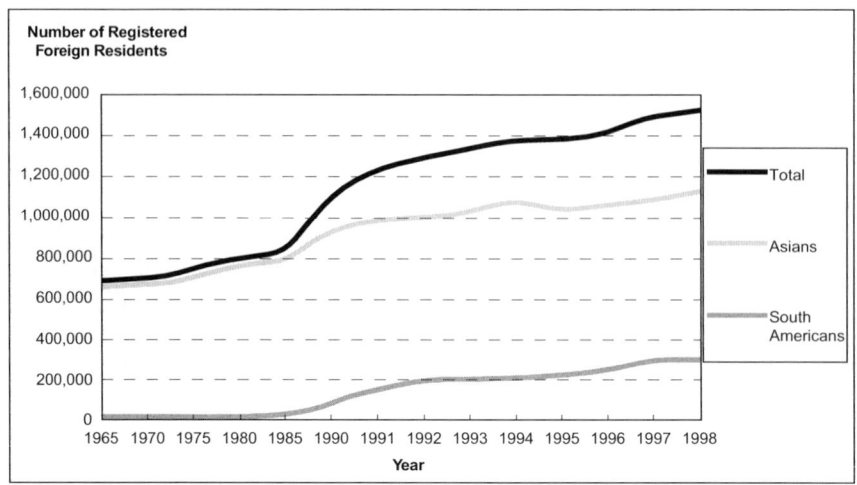

Figure 1 Registered foreign residents of Japan (1965–1997). (Source: Statistics Bureau, Management and Coordination Agency, 1998)

With this drastic demographic change, Japan is now in a gradual but certain process of social reorganisation, including its view of ethnic minorities. Issues of language are among the areas affected by this social reorganisation. Almost all activities in society, including business transactions, law enforcement, education, and mass media, have heretofore been conducted exclusively in the Japanese language. However, the recent increase of linguistically distinct segments of the population has required coping responses from the mainstream society, such as providing 'foreign children' with special Japanese language instruction (Ministry of Education, 1998) and staffing public employment agencies with interpreters (Ministry of Labour, 1995), to give but two examples.

Under such conditions, it may not be long before bilingualism/multilingualism will become one of the most significant issues faced by Japanese society. Prevailing attitudes towards bilingualism will strongly influence the societal response. If bilingualism in general is viewed positively, it may be encouraged in all groups. However, if it is viewed positively only under certain circumstances – in certain types of people or when it involves certain languages – then only some people will be encouraged to use two languages, while other groups may find it difficult to maintain one of their languages.

Types of Bilinguals and Language Maintenance

Two fundamental categories of bilinguals

Researchers have identified two fundamental categories of bilinguals. Those in the first group are termed *elite* (Skutnabb-Kangas, 1981) or *elective* bilinguals (Valdés & Figueroa, 1994). Bilinguals in this category are generally 'highly educated' (Skutnabb-Kangas, 1981: 97) and 'individuals who choose to become bilingual and who seek out either formal classes or contexts in which they can acquire a foreign language ... and who continue to spend the greater part of their time in a society in which their first language is the majority or societal language' (Valdés & Figueroa, 1994: 12).

The second category of bilinguals, called *folk* (Skutnabb-Kangas, 1981) or *circumstantial* bilinguals (Valdés & Figueroa, 1994), includes those who 'must learn another language in order to survive' (Valdés & Figueroa, 1994: 12) and 'have usually been forced to learn the other language' and 'often come from a linguistic minority' (Skutnabb-Kangas, 1981: 97). In this paper I will use Skutnabb-Kangas' terms, *elite* and *folk*, to refer to these categories of bilinguals.

Factors affecting the language maintenance/language shift of folk bilinguals

While elite bilinguals choose to learn another language and generally have the means to maintain their native tongue, folk bilinguals are migrants who are pressured to learn the language of their host country or minorities who have been forced to learn the majority language. Although some groups of folk bilinguals maintain their mother tongues in a mainstream society whose primary language is different from theirs, others undergo language shift, losing their original language after a generation or two.

Analysing the 1986 Australian national census, Clyne (1991) found that mother tongue maintenance rates were higher among groups from Southern Europe than among those from Northern Europe, and that immigrants from Eastern Europe tended to maintain their mother tongues more than those from Western Europe. Greek immigrants, for example, were found to have a strong tendency to maintain their mother tongue, with language shift towards majority language usage occurring in only 4.4% of the first generation. Even among the second generation (of endogamous marriages) only 8.7% used English as the sole means of communication at home. Data on Yugoslavian immigrants also revealed a low tendency to shift to English, with only 9.5% of the first generation and 18% of the second generation (of endogamous marriages) using English as their sole home language. On the other hand, Dutch immigrants were found to show a greater tendency to shift to English, with 48.4% of the first generation and as many as 85.4% of the second generation (of endogamous marriages) using English as the sole home language (Clyne, 1991).

In trying to explain these differences, Clyne suggested that cultural distance, including religion, is an important factor which affects the degree of first language retention. Groups who show a greater tendency to maintain their mother tongue 'are either racially different or have distinctive religious affiliation, world-views and practices ... that distinguish them markedly from mainstream ones ...' (Clyne, 1991: 66–68).

A variety of other social, demographic, and linguistic factors that may influence language maintenance have been suggested by other researchers (e.g. Conklin & Lourie, 1983; Giles, Bourhis & Taylor, 1977; Grosjean, 1982; Pauwels, 1991; Smolicz, 1981). Factors which are closely related to the present study are the attitudes of the minority group toward their own language, and the attitudes of the majority group toward the minority group (Grosjean, 1982). If the minority group has positive attitudes toward its own language, the group is more likely to try to maintain it. The minority group will also be encouraged to retain its language if the majority group regards the minority language positively.

In addition to attitudinal factors directly related to a specific minority and its language, attitudes toward the phenomenon of bilingualism itself may be critical in determining whether or not the mother tongue is maintained. Folk bilinguals are often said to be evaluated negatively. For example, according to Andersson & Boyer (1978), 'in California the label "bilingual" may connote "uneducated"' (p. 11). Likewise, Skutnabb-Kangas (1988) notes that '[b]eing bilingual has in several countries, especially the United States, been used almost as a synonym for being poor, stupid and uneducated' (p. 12). This connotation seems to contrast sharply with that of elite bilinguals. Skutnabb-Kangas (1981) cites Fishman about French/English bilingualism in the United States:

> If you have learnt French at university, preferably in France and even better at the Sorbonne, then bilingualism is something very positive. But if you have learnt French from your old grandmother in Maine, then bilingualism is something rather to be ashamed of. (p. 96)

Such negative attitudes toward folk bilingualism may have detrimental effects on mother tongue maintenance.

Types of bilinguals in Japan

Bilinguals in Japan, either actual or potential, may be categorised into four main groups:

(1) Mainstream Japanese studying a foreign/second language
(2) Japanese children repatriated after living abroad for an extended period (often called *kikoku shijo* or 'returnees')
(3) Offspring of parents who have different native languages
(4) Ethnic minorities (born and) residing in Japan

According to the definitions of elite and folk bilinguals presented above, it may be assumed that in the Japanese setting, mainstream bilingual

Japanese (Group 1) are elite bilinguals. Japanese returnees (Group 2) may also be considered elite if their native language (or one of their native languages) is Japanese. Members of both groups, as well as members of Group 3 (children whose parents have different mother tongues) may be evaluated more positively if the other language they use is English, which is highly esteemed in Japanese society (Yamamoto, 1995). On the other hand, members of Groups 2, 3 and 4 who do not speak Japanese as (one of) their native language(s) would be categorized as folk bilinguals.

Survey

To investigate whether there are prevailing attitudes towards bilingualism in Japan and whether specific attitudes are associated with particular types of bilinguals or potential bilinguals in Japan, the author conducted a survey between the winter of 1993 and the spring of 1994.

Questionnaire design and administration procedure

The subjects were provided with a short questionnaire (Appendix) and were requested to answer each question according to oral instructions given by the author. The survey instrument was written in Japanese and all instructions were given in Japanese. The questionnaire consists of two main sections: one to investigate the subjects' attitudes towards bilinguals and the other aimed at examining their definitions of the term *bilingual.*

A variety of methods to measure attitudes in relation to language have been proposed (e.g. see Edwards, 1985; Baker, 1992). One of them is to measure, often with a Likert scale, the subjects' responses to a list of statements regarding languages or their speakers (e.g. Baker, 1993; Garrett *et al.*, 1994). Another is to directly interview subjects (e.g. Oyetade, 1996). Among other well-known methods are the Semantic Differential technique and the Matched-Guise technique.

None of these techniques suited the purpose of the study precisely, since the author wanted to investigate the images evoked in Japanese subjects by the term *bilingual* and try to examine whether these images were positive, negative or neutral. This study therefore employed a free association technique to elicit spontaneous responses. In the blanks below the heading 'Images' on the questionnaire (see Appendix for English translation), the subjects were orally instructed to write up to five words which are evoked in their minds by the term *bilingual.* The resulting lists make it possible to investigate whether or not the subjects have common associations with the term *bilingual.*

However, the image words elicited in this way do not necessarily provide attitudinal information. If an attitude is 'a disposition to react favourably or unfavourably to a class of objects' (Edwards, 1994: 97) or 'a tendency to respond in a certain manner when confronted with certain stimuli' (Oppenheim, 1992: 174), then it is necessary to find out how favourably or unfavourably the subjects perceive those images. Thus, after completing their list of words associated with the term *bilingual*, the subjects were orally instructed to classify each of their own responses as positive, neutral or negative by checking boxes marked '+' for 'positive', '±' for 'neutral' and '−' for 'negative'.

Then, in the third step, the subjects were presented with five definitions of the term *bilingual* prepared by the author and were orally instructed to circle as many as they thought appropriate. These definitions covered a range of possibilities, from the ideal image of a bilingual as someone with native-like control of all aspects of two languages (e.g. Bloomfield, 1933), to a minimalist definition of a receptive bilingual. English translations of the definitions provided on the questionnaire are:

(1)   A person who possesses abilities in all four skills (speaking, listening, writing and reading) in two languages equivalent to the skills of native speakers of each language.
(2)   A person who is not as proficient as the person described in '1', but who can communicate well enough in daily life in both languages.
(3)   A person who is competent in all four skills (speaking, listening, writing and reading) in one language but whose proficiency in the other language is on the level of giving greetings.
(4)   A person who can neither write nor read in either language but who can speak and understand both.
(5)   A person who can neither write nor read in either language, nor speak in one of the languages, but who can comprehend both languages when spoken.

After marking the definitions they thought fit the term *bilingual*, the subjects were asked whether, by those criteria, they would rate themselves bilingual or not.

Finally, the subjects were given an unexpected question: they were asked to specify what language(s) they had had in mind when they were answering all the previous questions. The purpose of this question was to find out whether the subjects' attitudinal traits toward bilinguals were associated with particular bilingual groups or not. In order to avoid contaminating the responses, the author had been very careful not to mention any particular language in either the questionnaire or the oral instructions.

Subjects

Due to time and financial constraints, the subjects of the study were not randomly selected. They were a convenience sample of intact classes, one the College of Letters at a university in the Kansai area, and the other in the College of Engineering at a university in the Chubu area. Of the total 144 students in the surveyed classes, 100 (female = 65, male = 35) were in the College of Letters at the former university and 44 (female = 2, male = 42) were in the College of Engineering at the latter university.

Results and Discussion

Words associated with bilinguals

The 144 subjects wrote a total of 607 responses, or an average of 4.2 words or phrases, that were evoked in their minds by the term *bilingual*. In compiling these responses, the author grouped those that incorporated the same word stem, concept or core word in a phrase. For example, *kokusaiteki* (international), *kokusai-ha* (international-minded person), and *kokusaijin* (an international or cosmopolitan person) were all grouped together under the core concept *kokusai* (international). In some cases, the same subject wrote more than one word or phrase belonging to a single image or concept group: e.g. both *kashikoi* (intelligent) and *chiteki* (intellectual) were among the responses on one questionnaire. The most frequent responses (in terms of these image groups) are presented in Table 1.

Of the large number of different responses, words or phrases incorporating *kokusai* (international) appeared most often ($n = 78$, 12.9%). Other frequent core words or concepts included *kakkoii* (cool, $n = 31$, 5.1%), *kashikoi* (intelligent, $n = 30$, 4.9%), *eigo* (English, $n = 24$, 4.0%), *urayamashii* (enviable, $n = 16$, 2.6%), *sugoi* (awesome, $n = 10$, 1.6%), *gaikoku-no* (foreign, $n = 10$, 1.6%) and *tsūyaku* (interpreter, $n = 10$, 1.6%).

Table 1 Words most frequently associated with bilinguals

Images (English Equivalent)	n	% of Responses
kokusai (international)	78	12.9%
kakkoii (cool)	31	5.1%
kashikoi (intelligent)	30	4.9%
eigo (English)	24	4.0%
urayamashii (enviable)	16	2.6%
sugoi (awesome)	10	1.6%
gaikoku-no (foreign)	10	1.6%
tsūyaku (interpreter)	10	1.6%

*Italicised words are romanised Japanese. Synonymous variations are combined.

Subjects' evaluations of their images of bilinguals

Table 2 shows the image words on the subjects' lists, sorted by the subjects' own evaluations: positive, neutral or negative. Due to space limitations, only a few of the most frequent core words and concepts under each evaluation category are included.

Of the total 607 responses recorded, 362 (59.6%) were rated as positive, 179 (29.5%) as neutral, and only 66 (10.9%) as negative. Among the positive concepts, those most often given were 'international', 'cool', and 'intelligent'. Interestingly, 'international' was also the most common neutral image cited, followed by 'foreign'. Like 'international', 'English' was seen as positive by some of the respondents and as neutral by others. Among the concepts rated as negative, 'self-important', 'cold', 'not proficient in Japanese', and 'not proficient in either language' were the most frequent. (See Figure 2.)

The subjects' responses were sorted by sex and by the course the students were enrolled in (see Figures 3 and 4). Chi-square analysis showed

Table 2 Images associated with bilinguals, sorted according to subjects' evaluations

Evaluation	Images (English Equivalent)	n	% of Words Evaluated This Way
Positive Images n = 362	*kokusai* (international)	49	13.5%
	kakkoii (cool)	31	8.6%
	kashikoi (intelligent)	30	8.3%
	eigo (English)	18	5.0%
	urayamashii (enviable)	16	4.4%
	sugoi (awesome)	10	2.8%
	tsūyaku (interpreter)	10	2.8%
	Other words	198	54.7%
Neutral Images n = 179	*kokusai* (international)	29	16.2%
	gaikoku-no (foreign)	10	5.6%
	josei (female)	7	3.9%
	eigo (English)	6	3.4%
	Other words	127	70.9%
Negative Images n = 66	*erasō* (self-important)	5	7.6%
	tsumetai (cold)	3	4.5%
	nihongo ga tadotadoshii (not proficient in Japanese)	3	4.5%
	ryōhō no gengo ga hanpa ni narisō (not proficient in either language)	3	4.5%
	docchi tsukazu (ambivalent)	2	3.0%
	Other words	50	75.8%

* Italicised words are romanised Japanese. Synonymous variations are combined.

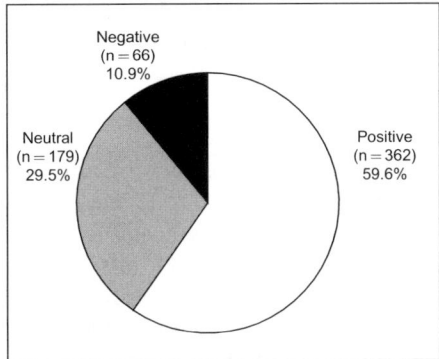

Figure 2 Self-evaluations of images of bilinguals (all subjects, $N = 607$)

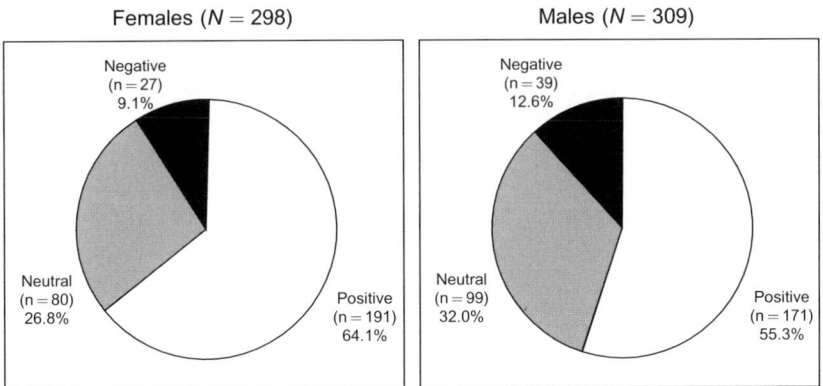

Figure 3 Self-evaluations of images of bilinguals, subjects sorted by sex

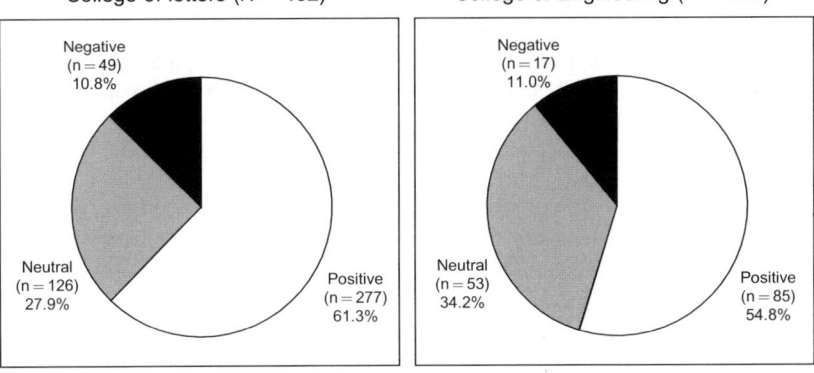

Figure 4 Self-evaluations of images of bilinguals, subjects sorted by course of study

no significant differences in images either by sex ($\chi^2 = 5.106$, df $= 2$) or by the course the students were enrolled in ($\chi^2 = 2.366$, df $= 2$).

Definitions of 'bilingual'

Figure 5 is a graphic depiction of the definitions of a bilingual that were provided on the questionnaire. Proficiency levels in each of the four skills and in each language are shown symbolically on a matrix. Among the five definitions presented to the subjects (also included in Figure 5), number 1 defines *bilingual* the most stringently, stipulating native proficiency in all four skills in both languages. Definition 2 is less strict, allowing a person less proficient but nevertheless competent in all four skills in both languages to be included. Those covered by Definition 3 are more likely to be essentially monolingual but with an incipient command of another language. Literacy is not required according to Definitions 4

Skill	*Speaking*		*Listening*		*Writing*		*Reading*	
Definition number	*L1*	*L2*	*L1*	*L2*	*L1*	*L2*	*L1*	*L2*
1	$\odot^n$	$\odot^n$	$\odot^n$	$\odot^n$	$\odot^n$	$\odot^n$	$\odot^n$	$\odot^n$
2	$\odot$	$\odot$	$\odot$	$\odot$	$\odot$	$\odot$	$\odot$	$\odot$
3	○	□	○		○		○	
4	○	○	○	○				
5	○		○	○				

Definitions presented on the questionnaire (English translation)
1. a person who possesses abilities in all four skills (speaking, listening, writing and reading) in two languages equivalent to the skills of native speakers of each language
2. a person who is not as proficient as the person described in '1', but who can communicate well enough in daily life in both languages
3. a person who is competent in all four skills (speaking, listening, writing and reading) in one language but whose proficiency in the other language is on the level of giving greetings
4. a person who can neither write nor read in either language but who can speak and understand both
5. a person who can neither write nor read in either language, nor speak in one of the languages, but who can comprehend both languages when spoken

$\odot^n$ = as proficient as native speakers
$\odot$ = proficient but less than $\odot^n$
○ = proficient (proficiency level not mentioned)
□ = incipient
blank = incapable

Figure 5 Graphic depiction of survey definitions

Table 3 Definitions of 'bilingual' chosen by subjects (multiple choices allowed)

Definition (s) Chosen	All Subjects N = 144	Sex		College	
		Female n = 67	Male n = 77	Letters n = 100	Engineering n = 44
1 only	33 (22.9%)	21 (31.3%)	12 (15.6%)	32 (32.0%)	1 (2.3%)
1 & 2	53 (36.8%)	24 (35.8%)	29 (37.7%)	34 (34.0%)	19 (43.2%)
1, 2 & 4	31 (21.5%)	7 (10.4%)	24 (31.2%)	9 (9.0%)	22 (50.0%)
1 & 4	3 (2.1%)	2 (3.0%)	1 (1.3%)	3 (3.0%)	0 (0.0%)
1, 4 & 5	2 (1.4%)	1 (1.5%)	1 (1.3%)	2 (2.0%)	0 (0.0%)
2 only	12 (8.3%)	8 (11.9%)	4 (5.2%)	12 (12.0%)	0 (0.0%)
2 & 3	1 (0.7%)	1 (1.5%)	0 (0.0%)	1 (1.0%)	0 (0.0%)
2 & 4	7 (4.9%)	3 (4.5%)	4 (5.2%)	5 (5.0%)	2 (4.5%)
3 only	1 (0.7%)	0 (0.0%)	1 (1.3%)	1 (1.0%)	0 (0.0%)
4 only	1 (0.7%)	0 (0.0%)	1 (1.3%)	1 (1.0%)	0 (0.0%)

and 5: Definition 4 requires oral productive abilities in both languages, but Definition 5 allows a person who can only speak one language to be considered bilingual as long as s/he is capable of comprehension in both languages.

As explained above, the subjects were instructed to circle as many of the definitions of 'bilingual' on the survey instrument as they thought appropriate. The results are presented in Table 3.

Very few of the subjects (1.4%, $n = 2$) included Definition 3 (someone whose proficiency in her or his second language is on the level of giving greetings) among their choices. Likewise, only two subjects (1.4%) included Definition 5 (a non-literate receptive bilingual) among their choices, and none of the respondents chose Definition 5 only. Thus, most subjects appeared to feel that listening comprehension in a second language was not enough to qualify a person as a bilingual: a certain level of speaking ability in both languages is also required. In fact, a good portion of all the subjects (68.1%, $n = 98$) selected Definition 1 or 2, or both, indicating that they consider a certain command of all four skills in both languages necessary. A third of these ($n = 33$) indicated that only those meeting the most stringent definition (Definition 1) are entitled to be called bilingual. On the other hand, nearly a third of all the subjects (30.6%, $n = 44$) included non-literates (Definition 4) in their definition of bilingual, as long as they are capable of speaking and understanding both languages. These results are depicted in Figure 6.

The responses were analysed to see if there was a difference in the way the female and male subjects defined *bilingual*. The results are presented in

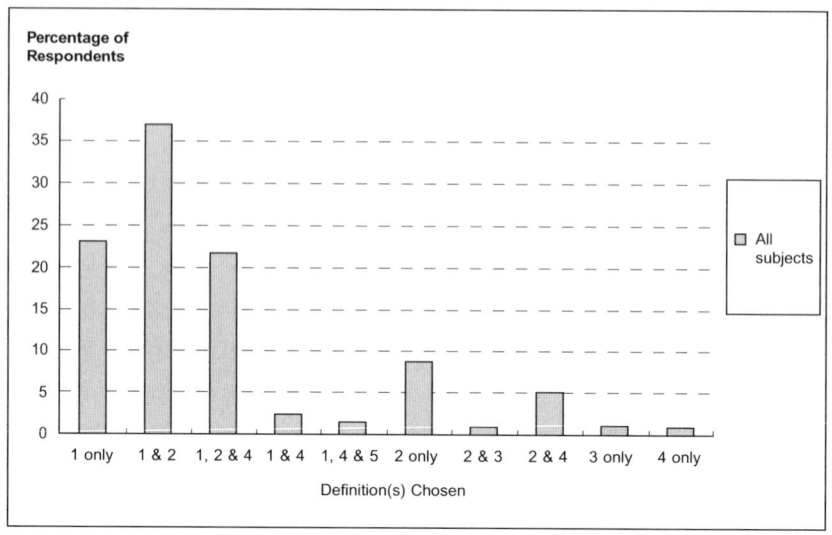

Figure 6 Definitions of 'bilingual' chosen (all subjects)

graph form in Figure 7. From the graph, it would appear that the female subjects had a tendency to define *bilingual* more strictly than the male subjects, and that fewer female subjects accepted non-literates, even ones with oral capabilities in both languages. However, the difference in response between the female subjects and the male subjects was not statistically significant ($\chi^2 = 16.443$, df $= 9$).

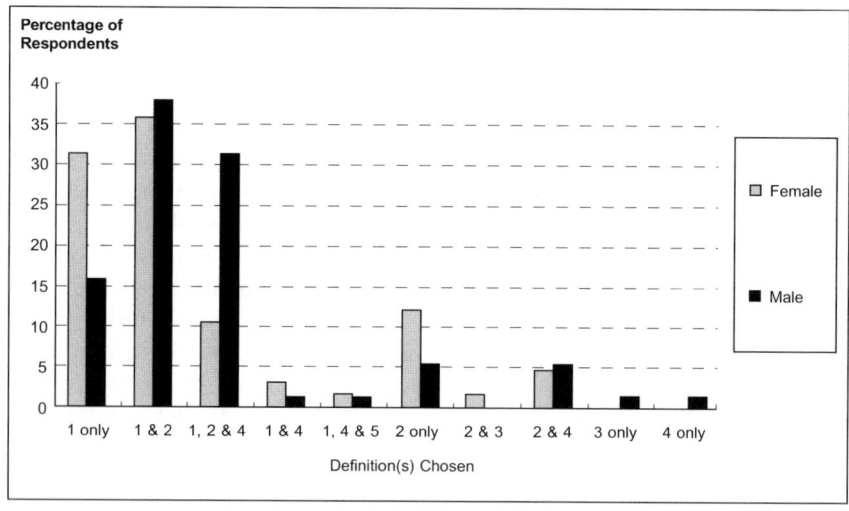

Figure 7 Definitions of 'bilingual' chosen, subjects sorted by sex

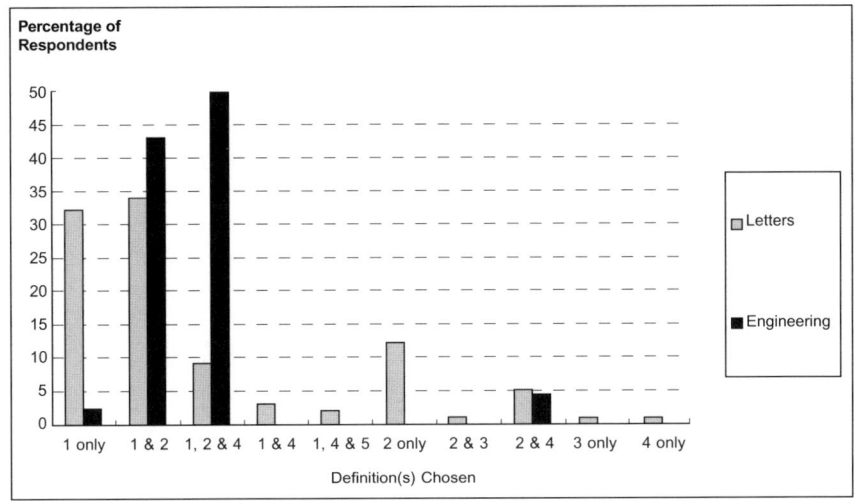

Figure 8 Definitions of 'bilingual' chosen, subjects sorted by course of study (college)

The responses were also sorted according to the students' course of study, and a significant difference was found between the subjects in the two colleges ($\chi^2 = 45.155$, df $= 9$, $p < 0.001$). While the proportion of subjects who accepted both Definition 1 and Definition 2 is roughly comparable for students in both colleges (Letters: 34.0%, $n = 34$; Engineering: 43.2%, $n = 19$), the number who accept only individuals with native-speaker proficiency in all four skills in both languages, as stipulated in Definition 1, is far greater among the subjects in the College of Letters (Letters: 32.0%, $n = 32$; Engineering: 2.3%, $n = 1$). These results are presented in graph form in Figure 8.

Self-evaluation of bilingual ability

Based on the definition(s) of *bilingual* they chose, the subjects were requested to judge if they consider themselves bilingual or not. Only 6.3% ($n = 9$) of the subjects felt that they were bilingual, as shown in Figure 9. The respondents' evaluations of their own bilingual ability were statistically independent of sex ($\chi^2 = 2.213$, df $= 1$) and course of study ($\chi^2 = 2.770$, df $= 1$).

Examination of the definitions chosen by the nine subjects who evaluated themselves as bilingual revealed an interesting point. All nine included the strictest definitions of *bilingual* – Definition 1 or 2 (or both) – among their choices, but acceptance of non-literate bilinguals (Definitions 4 and 5) diverged substantially according to the subject's course of study. Four out of the five engineering students included Definition 4

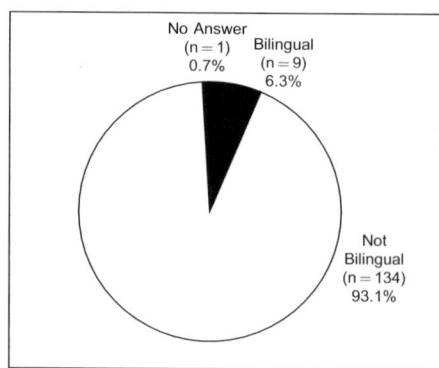

Figure 9 Self-evaluation of bilingual ability ($N = 144$)

(a non-literate person with the ability to speak two languages) among their choices, but only one of the four subjects in the College of Letters accepted either Definition 4 or Definition 5. The remaining three accepted only Definitions 1 and/or 2, which require proficiency in all four skills in both languages.

Since the sample size is small and it is impossible to know specifically which one of the selected definitions was the basis for their self-judgments, the following is mere speculation, but it appears that the bilingual humanities majors evaluated their linguisitic abilities more strictly than the engineering majors did. It stands to reason that students majoring in humanities are more likely to be sensitive to language and how it is used – accuracy, appropriateness, articulation, fluency, and so forth – and more likely to set a high standard for bilingual proficiency.

Languages associated with bilingualism

Table 4 shows the responses to the unexpected question regarding what languages the subjects had had in mind while answering the preceding questions. Among the wide variety of language combinations given, the two-language combination of 'Japanese and English' was most frequently cited (73.6%, $n = 106$). If multiple-language combinations including both Japanese and English are also counted, then the proportion rises to 79.2% ($n = 114$).

In contrast, only 1.4% ($n = 2$) of all the subjects mentioned 'Korean and Japanese', and only 2.8% ($n = 4$) included Chinese as one of the languages, even though ethnic Koreans and Chinese are two of the largest potentially bilingual groups in Japan. The subjects in general did not associate the term bilingual with the languages that these groups may speak. Instead, the majority of them identified the term with 'Japanese and English ($+ \alpha$)'.

Table 4 Language combinations associated with bilinguals

Language Combinations	n	% of Responses
Japanese and English	106	(73.6%)
Japanese, English and Chinese	2	(1.4%)
Japanese, English and German	1	(0.7%)
Japanese, English and French	1	(0.7%)
Japanese, English and Italian	1	(0.7%)
Japanese, English and Indonesian	1	(0.7%)
Japanese, English and some Asian language	1	(0.7%)
Japanese, English, French and German	1	(0.7%)
Japanese and German	1	(0.7%)
Japanese and another language	2	(1.4%)
Japanese and some foreign language	1	(0.7%)
Japanese and mother tongue	1	(0.7%)
Japanese and no specific language	2	(1.4%)
Korean and Japanese	2	(1.4%)
Mother tongue and English	1	(0.7%)
Mother tongue (Cantonese) and English	1	(0.7%)
Mother tongue, English and some foreign language	1	(0.7%)
English and French	1	(0.7%)
English, French and Chinese	1	(0.7%)
English and some other language	2	(1.4%)
No specific languages	3	(2.1%)
No response	11	(7.6%)
Total	144	(100.0%)

Conclusion

Despite some limitations, the present survey revealed specific attitudinal traits toward bilingualism in Japan. While it is necessary to pursue this issue further with more broadly distributed surveys, three main points became clear from the survey results presented above.

(1) Bilinguals were generally associated with relatively positive images.
(2) The definitions of *bilingual* selected by the subjects were relatively strict: bilinguals were expected to have a rather good command of at least the speaking and listening skills in both languages, and preferably all four skills.

(3) To most subjects, the term *bilingual* refers to a speaker of Japanese and English, but not to speakers of other languages.

These results suggest that to the subjects of this study, the term *bilingual* refers to elite bilinguals. Bilinguals are perceived to be people such as the EFL learners in Group 1 above (and a certain segment of the returnees in Group 2) who speak Japanese as a native language and have managed to achieve a high level of proficiency in English, which is considered important for success in education and professions in Japan. Most of the survey subjects did not think that they had reached levels of foreign language proficiency high enough to claim to be bilinguals themselves, and many felt envious of those who have. Positive images related to bilinguals may have been derived from these feelings of envy.

The tendency for the subjects to associate the term *bilingual* only with elite bilinguals implies that their positive images of bilinguals may not apply to folk bilinguals such as the offspring of parents who have different languages (Group 3) and Japan's ethnic minorities (Group 4), as well as returnees whose mother tongue is not Japanese. In fact, bilinguals who are not considered elite may be evaluated quite differently, in much the same way as folk bilinguals are considered in many other societies.

The implications of this study's findings should cause concern. We see a hint of the positive image of elite bilinguals in recent deliberations in the Ministry of Education. Under the present national curriculum, foreign language education (usually in the form of English classes) begins in junior high school, but the Ministry is currently considering starting English education at the elementary school level instead. The purpose would obviously be to promote elite bilingualism for children whose mother tongue is Japanese. Some native Japanese-speaking children may benefit from this scheme (and some English-speaking children may benefit as well).

However, what about children whose mother tongue is neither Japanese nor English? As of September 1997, there were 17,296 students who were considered to need JSL (Japanese as a second language) instruction in public schools (elementary through high school level) throughout Japan (Ministry of Education, 1998). The mother tongue of 97.4% of these children is a language other than English. It does not seem that the scheme under consideration by the Ministry of Education is intended to include the maintenance and development of their mother tongues.

I have argued elsewhere (Yamamoto, 1994, 1996b) that their bilingualism should be considered to be as valuable as the elite bilingualism of Japanese children. Programs designed to promote these children's bilingualism should be offered as well. Needless to say, the primary goal of such programmes should be to develop the children's proficiency in their mother tongue as well as in Japanese.

One way to implement such a programme would be by offering alternatives to English language study. In an area where many Korean people are living, for example, Korean language classes could be offered in addition to English classes. In this way children would have a choice. Likewise, Chinese could also be offered as an alternative in a school district where many Chinese families reside. So could Spanish and Tagalog.

Another possibility (suggested in Yamamoto, 1994) would be employing distance-learning through computer networks. A programme of this type would be most efficient where children of the same language background are scattered, as is often the case in Japan (Ministry of Education, 1998). It would allow one language teacher to serve many students. Such a plan would also permit students to move from one geographic area to another without a loss of access to language learning support. This type of programme has already been implemented in Japan on an experimental basis in a joint project between St. Andrew's University and Nippon Telegraph and Telephone Corporation (Yamamoto, 1998 and forthcoming; NTT Corporation & St. Andrew's University, 1999).

However, even if children whose mother tongue is neither English nor Japanese do manage to acquire bilingual proficiency through such programmes, they will still not be the kind of bilinguals that the subjects of the present survey had in mind. So we need to ask: how would they be perceived? What kind of image would their bilingualism have?

These questions speak to the problem of Japanese perceptions of bilinguals, and with the population of foreign residents rising rapidly, the answers to these questions will take on increasing significance.

Acknowledgements

This paper is a revised and expanded version of a paper published in the inaugural issue of *The Japanese Journal of Language in Society* (1998) (1 (1), pp. 11–18), and portions are reprinted by permission of the editor. I wish to express my gratitude to Professor John Maher of International Christian University and Professor James Swan of Nara University for their many valuable comments on this paper.

References

Andersson, T. and Boyer, M. (1978) *Bilingual Schooling in the United States.* Austin, Texas: National Educational Laboratory Publishers.

Asahi shimbun (1986) *Chiteki suijun hikui bei: Shushō hatsugen ni bei de hampatsu* [US Intelligence Low: American Hackles Raised by PM's Remark], *Asahi shimbun* Morning Edition, September 24: 1.

Baker, C. (1992) *Attitudes and Language.* Clevedon, UK: Multilingual Matters.

Baker, C. (1993) *Foundations of Bilingual Education and Bilingualism.* Clevedon, UK: Multilingual Matters.

Bloomfield, L. (1933) *Language.* New York: Holt, Rinehart and Winston.

Clyne, M. (1991). *Community Languages: The Australian Experience.* Cambridge, UK: Cambridge University Press.

Conklin, N.F. and Lourie, M.A. (1983) *A Host of Tongues: Language Communities in the United States.* New York: The Free Press.

Edwards, J. (1985) *Language, Society and Identity.* Oxford, UK: Basil Blackwell.

Edwards, J. (1994) *Multilingualism.* London: Penguin Books.

Garrett, P., Griffiths, Y., James, C. and Scholfield, P. (1994) Use of the mother-tongue in second language classrooms. *Journal of Multilingual and Multicultural Development,* 15 (5), 371–83.

Giles, H., Bourhis, R. and Taylor, D. (1977) Towards a theory of language in ethnic group relations. In H. Giles (ed.) *Language, Ethnicity and Intergroup Relations* (pp. 307–49). London: Academic Press.

Grosjean, F. (1982) *Life with Two Languages: An Introduction to Bilingualism.* Cambridge, MA: Harvard University Press.

Harding, E. and Riley, P. (1986) *The Bilingual Family: A Handbook for Parents.* Cambridge, UK: Cambridge University Press.

Higuchi T. and Nakamura T. (1978) *Gengo to bunka* [Language and culture]. In Tanaka H. (compiled) *Gengogaku no susume* [Introduction to Linguistics]. Tokyo: Taishukan shoten.

Iritani T. (1988) *Gengo-shinrigaku no susume* [Introduction to Psycholinguistics]. Tokyo: Taishukan shoten.

Loveday, L.J. (1996) *Language Contact in Japan: A Sociolinguistic History.* Oxford, UK: Clarendon Press.

Maher, J.C. and Honna N. (eds) (1994) *Atarashii nihon-kan sekai-kan ni mukatte: Nihon ni okeru gengo to bunka no tayōsei* (Towards a New Order: Language and Cultural Diversity in Japan). Tokyo: Kokusai shoin.

Maher, J.C. and Yashiro K. (ed.) (1995) *Multilingual Japan.* Clevedon, UK: Multilingual Matters.

Ministry of Education (1998) *Heisei 9 nendo nihongo kyōiku ga hitsuyōna gaikokujin jidō seito no ukeire jōkyō to ni kansuru chōsa no kekka* [Results of the 1997 Survey on Acceptance and Instruction of Foreign Children and Students Needing Japanese Language Education]. Tokyo: Ministry of Education.

Ministry of Labour (ed.) (1995) *Labour White Paper: 1995.* Tokyo: Nihon rodo kenkyu kiko.

NTT Corporation and St. Andrew's University (1999) *Shōsū-gengo wo bogo tosuru jidō/seito no bogo-hoji/shinchō kyōiku hōkokusho.* [Project Report on Mother Tongue Maintenance and Development Education for Minority Language Students]. Osaka: St. Andrew's University.

Oppenheim, A.N. (1992). *Questionnaire Design, Interviewing and Attitude Measurement.* London: Pinter.

Oyetade, S.O. (1996) Bilingualism and ethnic identity in a Nupe-Yoruba border town in Nigeria. *Journal of Multilingual and Multicultural Development* 17 (5), 373–84.

Pauwels, A. (1991) Managing multilingualism in Australia: Issues in language maintenance and intercultural communication affecting ethnolinguistic minorities. Paper presented at the Language Management for Multi-cultural Communities symposium, chaired by J.V. Neustupny, conducted at a meeting of the National Language Research Institute, Tokyo.

Skutnabb-Kangas, T. (1981) *Bilingualism or Not: The Education of Minorities.* Clevedon, UK: Multilingual Matters.

Skutnabb-Kangas, T. (1988) Multilingualism and the education of minority children. In T. Skutnabb-Kangas and J. Cummins (eds) *Minority Education: From Shame to Struggle* (pp. 9–44). Clevedon, UK: Multilingual Matters.

Smolicz, G. (1981) Core values and ethnic identity. *Ethnic and Racial Studies* 4, 75–90.

Statistics Bureau, Management and Coordination Agency (ed.) (1998) *Japan Statistical Yearbook: The 48th Edition (1999).* Tokyo: Japan Statistical Association.

Suzuki T. (1975) *Tozasareta gengo: Nihongo no sekai* [Closed Language: The World of Japanese]. Tokyo: Shinchosha.

Toyama S. (1974) *Josei no ronri* [Women's Logic]. Tokyo: Chuo koronsha.

Trudgill, P. (1974) *Sociolinguistics: An Introduction.* Middlesex, UK: Penguin Books.

Valdés, G. and Figueroa, R.A. (1994) *Bilingualism and Testing: A Special Case of Bias.* Norwood, NJ: Ablex.

Yamamoto M. (1994) *Bogo kyōiku: Shōsū-gengo bogowasha no bogo hoji, shinchō kyōiku.* [Mother Tongue Education: Education for the Maintenance and Development of Minority Language Mother Tongues]. *The Language Teacher* 18 (4),10–12, 25.

Yamamoto M. (1995) Bilingualism in international families. In J. C. Maher and Yashiro K. (eds) *Multilingual Japan* (pp. 63–85). Clevedon, UK: Multilingual Matters.

Yamamoto M. (1996a) A brief history of Japanese official policies of Ainu segregation and assimilation, with a focus on language policy. *St. Andrew's University Bulletin of Research Institute* 22 (1), 83–92.

Yamamoto M. (1996b) *Bairingaru wa donoyōnishite gengo wo shūtokusuru no ka* [How Bilinguals Acquire Their Languages]. Tokyo: Akashi shoten.

Yamamoto M. (1998) *Nihon no genjō wo fumaeta bairingaru-kyōiku: Kaihatsu, jisshi e no mosaku* [Bilingual education in the Japanese context: A trial of its development and implementation.] Paper presented at the Bilingual Education Roundtable of the Intercultural Education Society, Japan, Tokyo.

Yamamoto M. (Forthcoming) '*Bogo kyōiku*' *jisshi e no mosaku: Kompyūta riyō no enkaku kyōiku* [An attempt to implement 'mother tongue education': Distance-learning through computer networks]. In Yamamoto M. (ed.) *Nihon no bairingaru kyōiku: Kodomotachi ga motsu senzai bairingaru nōryoku no kenzaika wo hakaru kyōiku* [Bilingual Education in Japan: Education to Realize Children's Potential Bilingual Abilities]. Tokyo: Akashi shoten.

Appendix

Questionnaire (translated into English)

Sex: ☐ F ☐ M **Age:** _____ years old

* Images

_____ : ☐ + ☐ ± ☐ –

_____ : ☐ + ☐ ± ☐ –

_____ : ☐ + ☐ ± ☐ –

_____ : ☐ + ☐ ± ☐ –

_____ : ☐ + ☐ ± ☐ –

* Definitions

1. a person who possesses abilities in all four skills (speaking, listening, writing and reading) in two languages equivalent to the skills of native speakers of each language
2. a person who is not as proficient as the person described in '1', but who can communicate well enough in daily life in both languages
3. a person who is competent in all four skills (speaking, listening, writing and reading) in one language but whose proficiency in the other language is on the level of giving greetings

4. a person who can neither write nor read in either language but who can speak and understand both

5. a person who can neither write nor read in either language, nor speak in one of the languages, but who can comprehend both languages when spoken

According to the definitions that I chose, I am

☐ bilingual   ☐ not bilingual

Chapter 3

Language and Culture Revitalisation in a Hokkaido Ainu Community

FRED E. ANDERSON AND MASAMI IWASAKI-GOODMAN

Introduction

Although recent immigration and internationalisation may be said to have made Japan increasingly multilingual and multicultural, the Ainu[1] people native to Hokkaido, Sakhalin and the Kurile Islands are testimony to the fact that the country — at least conceived in terms of its present-day political boundaries — has never been monolingual or monocultural. It is a matter of debate how long the Ainu have occupied what is called Ainu Mosir[2] — the Ainu homeland, primarily Hokkaido, the northernmost major island of Japan — but it is the view of the Ainu community (and the view that will be adopted in this paper) that they are the indigenous people of this region.[3] Similarly, the origins of the Ainu language, at least from the point of view of Western-trained linguists, remain unconfirmed. While a relationship with Japanese or other languages is a distinct possibility, it is generally agreed that any such relationship is a remote one. Because of this, the Ainu language is widely characterised in linguistic survey texts as a *language isolate*; that is, a language which has no proven genetic affiliation with any other extant language (see, e.g. O'Grady, Dobrovolsky, and Aronoff, 1991; Shibatani, 1990).[4]

Following several centuries of increasing economic control over Hokkaido by the Japanese, assimilation of the Ainu into Japanese society in the later nineteenth century gave rise to a century of suppression of Ainu ethnicity. As a result, the language and cultural practices of the Ainu gradually faded from public view during the twentieth century. Over the last few decades, however, as one facet of a growing movement of ethnic and cultural renewal, Ainu language and culture programmes have sprung up within communities throughout Hokkaido.

This paper describes the efforts of the Ainu community of Nibutani in the Hidaka region of Hokkaido to reverse the decline in the use of its indigenous language and promote Ainu cultural awareness. The combined effort of a sociolinguist (Anderson) and a cultural anthropologist (Iwasaki-Goodman), this investigation is a case study which has as its goal the investigation of processes that characterise the Ainu movement at the community level. By qualitatively focusing on what is happening in one community, it is believed that insights of a type not available through broad-based surveys or quantitative studies can be obtained. The data used in the paper are the result of fieldwork within the Nibutani community, consisting of observations of language classes and community activities, and interaction with key informants, combined with the study of documents and papers produced by persons most concerned with the movement.

Although attempts will be made to relate the Nibutani programme to more general issues and theory in language revival and revitalisation, it is not the authors' intention to replicate more comprehensive reviews of the current state of Ainu language and culture that have appeared in English in recent years (e.g. Sjöberg, 1993; DeChicchis, 1995), but rather to focus on the language programme of a single community by looking at the people, events and attitudes that have shaped the programme.

Historical Background[5]

Traditionally, the Ainu people harvested local wildlife such as deer, bear and salmon for food, and utilised various wild plants for food, medicine, clothes and other household goods. Ainu culture was thus distinct from Japanese agricultural society not only in its language, but by virtue of the fundamental livelihood of the Ainu people.[6]

Japan began to extend economic control over *Ezo* (the name by which Hokkaido was then known) in the fifteenth century, particularly at seaports. Over the next few hundred years this control gradually increased, so that by the seventeenth century Ainu people were subjected to forced labour at Japanese fishing stations. By the end of the eighteenth century, Japan's economic control over *Ainu Mosir* was more or less complete; nevertheless, Japanese dominance had not yet been extended to the realm of the culture; the Ainu people were still able to maintain their language and traditional practices and values. However, this began to change in the early nineteenth century after the Japanese Shogunate took direct control of Ezo, and Ainu people were forced to adopt agriculture.

A major turning point toward cultural assimilation came in 1867 with the Meiji Restoration, when Ezo was officially incorporated as a part of Japan, and renamed Hokkaido. The Ainu community deteriorated seriously when the Meiji government implemented its assimilation policy, imposing various laws that in effect prohibited the Ainu from practicing their traditional hunting and fishing. In 1883, for example, a law was enacted to control salmon fishing, resulting in the banning of salmon fishing in the rivers where the Ainu people traditionally harvested salmon.

The final blow, as described by Ogawa (1993) and Sjöberg (1993: 123–4) came in 1899 in the form of the 'Hokkaido Former Aborigines Protection Act' (*Hokkaidō kyūdojin hogohō* in Japanese), by which Ainu people were to be assimilated into the Japanese agricultural society and given rights as Japanese citizens. The result, however, which was hastened by the 'Regulations for the Education of Former Aboriginal Children' of 1901 (also discussed in Ogawa, 1993), was the loss of traditional Ainu hunting and gathering grounds and their traditional system of education,[7] and hence, their livelihood and the foundation for their ethnicity. According to Ogawa (1993: 240):

> The Protection Act centred around agriculture and education. The first four clauses covered land grants. Five hectares was allotted only to those who agreed to take up farming; no assistance was provided for those making a living by other means. The land grants themselves were in essence an extension of the previous 'reservations' and were not intended to enable the Ainu to maintain their traditional lifestyle. Clause Seven stipulated that 'a child from a poor Former Aboriginal family may be provided with expenses for lessons on entering school', while Clause Nine provided for 'elementary schools to be constructed at national expense in Former Aborigine villages.'

Ogawa (1993: 241) describes the educational system developed for the Ainu as 'a system based on discrimination.' Special lessons were enacted for the explicit purpose of reforming Ainu customs, and use of the Japanese language was enforced. Thus, with their traditional way of life disturbed, and with Japanese now the language of education, the Ainu people began to use their native language less and less, and it entered a state of endangerment. Fortunately, efforts were made by the Ainu community and scholars during the twentieth century to preserve the spoken language through recordings and transcriptions (e.g. Kindaichi and Kannari 1959–1968). Without the resources that arose from these efforts, along with various grammatical and descriptive studies of Ainu – particularly those of eminent Japanese linguist Kindaichi Kyosuke[8] (Kindaichi, 1960) – the current efforts at teaching the language would be considerably more difficult.

Perspectives on Language Shift

Outsider and insider views: Decline vs. revitalisation

No one doubts that over the past century, the Ainu language has undergone an enormous decline in usage, what sociolinguists refer to as 'language shift' (Fishman, 1991; Romaine, 1995). Yet the current status of the language is subject to interpretation. On the one hand, it is popular for linguists, anthropologists, and scholars of Ainu studies to talk about the decline and imminent death of Ainu. The following statement by linguist Michael Krauss (1992: 4), made during general discussion of endangered languages, is representative of this point of view:[9]

On and on this sad litany goes, and by no means only for Native
North America. Sirenikski Eskimo has two speakers, *Ainu is perhaps
extinct*, Ubykh, the Northwest Caucasian language with the most consonants, 80-some, is nearly extinct, with perhaps only one remaining
speaker [italics are the present authors'].

Within Ainu communities, however, the language-death perspective is
often seen as the outsiders' point of view. Moreover it is a perspective
that is resented as both inaccurate and as harmful to the Ainu cause.
Nibutani Ainu elder Kayano Shigeru, the key figure in the Nibutani Ainu
language revitalisation, a scholar of Ainu language and culture and a
former politician, has noted that,

> With only a few exceptions, most scholars since the early decades of
> this century have continued to state in papers and lectures that Ainu
> language and culture are dead, and that we are a 'dying race'. How
> many of them have tried to help us in preserving and transmitting our
> culture? Almost none. (1993: 365–366)

Similarly, when discussing the practice of usurpation of Ainu cultural
property in the name of scholarship which was common in the past, Siddle
(1993: 41) notes that, 'The Ainu were seen as a "dying race"'. He continues: 'For anthropologists, the Ainu, living or dead, became mere items
of data.'[10] However, as ethnographers, the present researchers are striving
to address the insiders' point of view. Within the Ainu community, at least
since the early 1980s, Ainu have regarded their language and culture as
being in a state of renewal. Therefore, we suggest that 'revitalisation'
serves as a better metaphor than 'decline.'

Among academic scholars, the work of sociologist of language Joshua
Fishman (1991) on reversing language shift supports this metaphor.
Though Fishman's work makes no specific mention of Ainu, it does attempt
to address the needs and desires of *speakers* of endangered languages – not
simply of linguists and anthropologists – by making prescriptions for
language and culture renewal based on analysis of the successes and
shortcomings of language movements in various parts of the world.
Indeed, the discrepancy between outsider and insider perspectives in the
case of Ainu is not surprising considering the more general tendency, as
described by Fishman (1991: 381), for linguists and sociolinguists to
concentrate their efforts on the ' "minus" side of the ledger' of language
change and culture change (e.g. language attrition–shift–endangerment–
loss–death), 'while studies of revival, restoration, revitalisation and resta-
bilisation remain proportionately few and far between.'

Revitalisation vs. revival

At this point it will be useful to clarify why the term *revitalisation* is
used to describe the phenomenon of ethnolinguistic renewal in preference

to the similar label, *revival*, or to what Fishman (1991) refers to more generally as *Reversing Language Shift* (RLS).[11] While the initial impression might be that the Ainu case is one of revival rather than revitalisation, since the spoken language has been replaced by Japanese in the daily life of the community, a closer look suggests that revitalisation is equally pertinent as a metaphor and is more in line with the insider point of view.

In Nibutani and other Ainu communities which the researchers have examined, Japanese-Ainu code-mixing and codeswitching are practiced to some extent to this day. According to an Ainu informant in Nibutani, older community members and shopkeepers are sometimes overheard switching between Ainu and Japanese in everyday conversation. Even among community members who are monolingual speakers of Japanese, including non-Ainu residents of predominantly Ainu communities, certain Ainu words and expressions are reported to be a part of the local lexicon. As an illustration of this, a young woman of mixed Ainu-Japanese parentage who had grown up in Nibutani as a monolingual Japanese speaker, related an experience that she had had while living outside of Nibutani.

> While out with some friends, I used the word *kankan* – a common expression in Nibutani – to refer to *horumon* [the standard Japanese term for 'grilled tripe']. It was only when I saw how puzzled my companions were, since they did not understand what I meant by *kankan*, that I came to realize that this was an Ainu word, and not Japanese at all. (Field note, 1997)

Indeed, the popular assumption implicit in much of academic linguistics – that 'languages' are discrete and translatable entities – can blind one to the reality of how language is actually used. In communities where linguistic contact is a fact of life, the switching and mixing of languages and the borrowing of items from one language for use in another are the rule rather than the exception.

Codeswitching and code-mixing aside, however, there is anecdotal evidence that the number of actual Ainu speakers may be considerably greater than is commonly believed, particularly if one includes receptive competence (the ability to comprehend the spoken language). Kayano (1993: 365) writes:

> According to academics, there are perhaps twenty native speakers of Ainu left. I believe this is wrong. Although one can argue about the degree to which they are fluent in Ainu, there are in fact many more Ainu speakers. When I go to a village for recording and tell a 'wepeker' [= *uepeker*, a traditional folktale] to people of about my age [late 60s], they listen intently. Many say afterwards that although they cannot repeat it they can more or less understand the story. In short, they can comprehend Ainu although they cannot speak it. Those who have this comprehension can soon come to be able to speak the language.

Kayano goes on to describe the case of an elderly woman in his town who possessed just such a receptive knowledge of Ainu, and was able to build on it to acquire speaking ability in Ainu within a very short time. Judging from the percentage of Ainu in his village with a similar receptive competence, Kayano estimated that around 10% of the reported Hokkaido Ainu population of 25,000,[12] or about 2500 people, can understand Ainu when they hear it. This is far more than the usual estimates.

Similarly, an anecdote reported in Honda (1997b: 95–96) also suggests that there may be many more Ainu speakers than is commonly reported if one broadens one's definition of what a speaker is. Honda describes an incident that she observed while listening to a recitation of a *yukar* (epic tale) with a group of elderly Ainu women on a bus on the way to an Ainu culture festival. As the tape of the *yukar* began, a hush fell over the bus. Looking around, Honda noticed that everyone was moving their body and tapping on their knees to the rhythm of the *yukar*, and eventually the bus was filled with the sound of stomping feet. When the tape finally finished, there was a round of applause, together with sighs and cheers, and women could be overheard commenting on how good the recitation had been and the kind of nostalgia it evoked. One women commented, 'it would have been even better if I could have understood the meaning of the words,' to which everyone laughed. Honda notes:

> The question is often raised of how many people there are in the present day who understand the Ainu language. In this situation, one cannot really count these older ladies as among 'those who understand.' However, I have long felt that it is absurd to include such people – those who are totally absorbed in the long *yukar* and move their bodies and souls to it – as among 'those who do not understand.' (pp. 95–96; translation by the present authors)

Like Kayano's story, this anecdote suggests that the distinction between a speaker and a non-speaker of Ainu is anything but clear, and that there remains considerably greater implicit knowledge of Ainu than is commonly acknowledged.

The role of bilingualism in language revitalisation

Another point in need of clarification is the relationship between language revitalisation and bilingualism. Although to sociolinguists there are many obvious connections, this is not necessarily true for members of the community whose language is the target of revitalisation. To members of a minority culture trying to restore the culture that has been lost, becoming bilingual may not be an important goal. Nevertheless, work that has been done on language revival and revitalisation in various contexts suggests that bilingualism is more than a bi-product of a language revitalisation movement; rather, if the movement is to be successful, bilingualism should play a central role.

> What hope or purpose is there for a community's sociocultural, econo-technical and political self-regulation if the upper societal spheres are dominated by another language? Well, there is still the opportunity to function in these latter spheres via societal bilingualism, i.e. via the co-mastery of the generally employed language of those spheres, by means of exposure to institutions of education and work and to other life experiences that go beyond intimacy, family and local community. (Fishman, 1991: 5)

What Fishman advocates is the attainment of language revitalisation through a kind of diglossic bilingualism – that is, through the conscious use of different languages or language varieties within different domains of the society.[13]

In the Ainu situation, Japanese would remain the language of choice in what Fishman calls the 'upper societal spheres', whereas Ainu would, ideally, serve as the language of 'intimacy, family and local community.' Fishman's prescription calls for the establishment of priorities whereby communities should first concentrate on promoting the language at the community/family level and not expend energy on the higher order spheres over which they likely have little control (i.e. the schools, media and governmental institutions of the dominant society) until the language is firmly re-established at the local level. In many cases, according to Fishman, such diglossic bilingualism may represent the most desirable level of language revitalisation for the community in question, and there may be little need to tamper with the higher order.

Language and culture

The relation between a language and its culture is one that is widely recognised and brought to the fore both by Ainu elders and scholars of endangered languages. Kayano (1994a, 1994b) illustrates this by describing a conversation that took place among the three most fluent Ainu speakers in his village, his father and two of his father's friends, in the early 1950s. The three agreed that, 'The first among us to die is the luckiest', because the other two would be alive to perform the traditional ritual that guides passage to the other world. As it turned out, his father died first and was therefore the 'luckiest.' Kayano (1994b: 106–107) concludes that, 'The desire to die early simply for the sake of a meaningful funeral shows the extent to which culture and language are important to us Ainu.'

Elsewhere, Kayano (1993: 361) describes the high value placed on language itself in the traditional Ainu community, explaining how the use of language to settle quarrels 'was one of the basic principles of daily life. We teach our children that human language is mightier than the sharpest sword or poison arrow.'[14]

In relation to endangered languages more generally, linguist Ken Hale (1992: 36) has discussed how language, culture and 'intellectual wealth' are invariably linked:

> Of supreme significance in relation to linguistic diversity, and to local languages in particular, is the simple truth that language – in the general, multi-faceted sense – embodies the intellectual wealth of the people who use it .... Some forms of verbal art – verse, song, or chant – depend crucially on morphological and phonological, even syntactic properties of the language in which it is formed. In such cases the art could not exist without the language, quite literally.

The rich repertory of traditional verbal art was always a significant part of Ainu cultural life, and more recently it has played an important role in the preservation and revitalisation of the language. When Ainu elders who were fluent in the language began passing away, an effort to preserve the language began by recording the speech of those who were still alive, especially their recitations of *yukar* (epic poetic tales of history and ancient heroism) and *uepeker* (folk tales in prose). These recordings account for most of the spoken models of Ainu currently available to Ainu language learners, and their written transcriptions are also used in language teaching.[15] The spoken and written materials serve as input in vocabulary, grammar and pronunciation, and also as important cultural input. Traditionally, *yukar* and *uepeker* were not only for entertainment, but also served important functions in the socialisation and education of children. The stories contain lessons on how to behave in various social situations (Honda, 1997b), and this cultural knowledge, as well as linguistic information, is preserved in them. Along with other aspects of Ainu intellectual wealth – songs, dances, and knowledge about native plants, geography and wildlife – *yukar* and *uepeker* are an important part of the language teaching effort in Nibutani.

Language and Culture Revitalisation in Nibutani

The Ainu language movement in Hokkaido

The Nibutani Ainu language programme is part of a more general cultural revitalisation movement that has spread across Hokkaido. According to a list compiled by the Hokkaido *utari kyōkai* (Hokkaido Ainu Association), as of April 30, 1998 there were 14 Ainu language programmes in Hokkaido offering classes for adults. In addition to the Nibutani programme, which was the first, there are classes in Asahikawa, Urakawa, Kushiro, Sapporo, Shiraoi, Akan, Chitose, Shizunai, Mukawa, Obihiro,

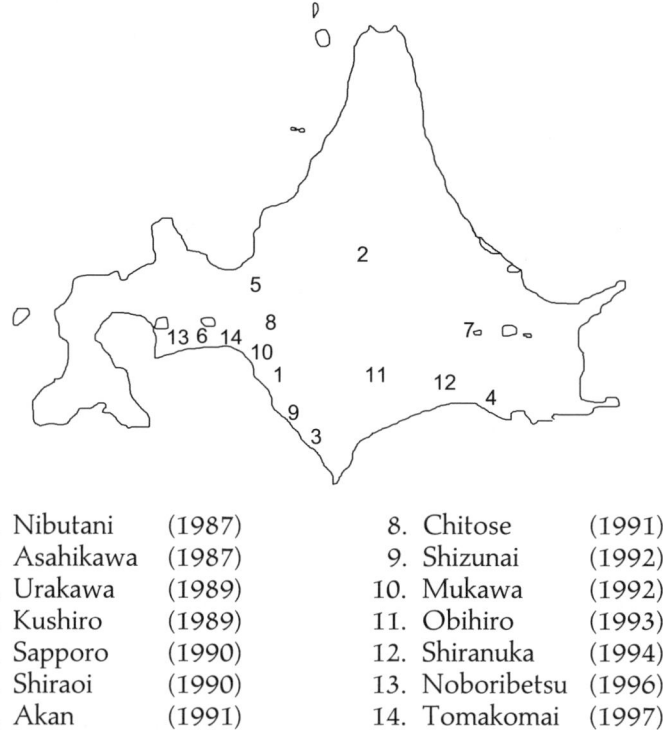

1. Nibutani	(1987)	8. Chitose	(1991)
2. Asahikawa	(1987)	9. Shizunai	(1992)
3. Urakawa	(1989)	10. Mukawa	(1992)
4. Kushiro	(1989)	11. Obihiro	(1993)
5. Sapporo	(1990)	12. Shiranuka	(1994)
6. Shiraoi	(1990)	13. Noboribetsu	(1996)
7. Akan	(1991)	14. Tomakomai	(1997)

Map 1 Locations of Ainu language programs in Hokkaido
(date of official recognition by Utari Kyokai in parentheses)

Shiraoi, Noboribetsu, and Tomakomai. The locations are shown on Map 1, accompanied by the dates when each programme was recognised as an official component of the Utari Kyokai. In some cases, however, the programme began prior to its official recognition by the association. This is true of the Nibutani program, which was actually founded in 1983.

As the dates on the map indicate, these programmes began to be officially established in the 1980s. However, the seeds of the linguistic revitalisation movement were actually sown much earlier. Honda (1997a) points out that throughout the 1970s Ainu language/culture study groups arose in Sapporo, Nibutani, Akan, and Asahikawa, so that in 1979 the Utari Kyokai, responding to the growing interest in Ainu language and culture studies, established an outdoor classroom for the transmission of traditional knowledge, as well as an Ainu language course.

Ainu language programmes developed in the various regions of Hokkaido in response to the needs of the local people. Therefore, the histories of their development differ, as do their present curricula. The number of students who have registered for the classes also varies, ranging between 13 and 55 as of 1996. Most classes meet weekly or semi-weekly throughout the year, while a few classes meet intensively during certain periods of time, especially winter or summer. Textbooks are used in all programmes, though the methods used in teaching the Ainu language vary. Some programmes emphasise conversational skills alone, whereas others teach conversation in the context of cultural activities such as dances, songs and cooking. The Nibutani programme is one which emphasises the relationship between language and culture.

While it is beyond the scope of this paper to describe each of these programmes, it should be noted that they have been characterised by steady growth. No programme has folded since its inception.

The Nibutani community

Nibutani is one of the 15 administrative sub-districts within the township of Biratori (*Biratori-chō*), approximately two hours drive southeast of Sapporo. (See Map 1.) According to the 1996 Biratori Town Informational Manual (Biratori-cho, 1996), the population of Biratori as of the end of December 1995 was 6932. Nibutani has a population of 478 people, about 70% of whom are Ainu (Biratori-cho, 1974).

While agriculture and dairy farming are the main industries in Biratori, the people of Nibutani depend heavily on tourism. The Nibutani Ainu Museum, which is operated by the city, is located in the centre of Nibutani and serves as a major tourist attraction. The Shishirimuka Nibutani Ainu Museum is owned by Kayano Shigeru, the founder of the Nibutani Ainu language programme, and lies within walking distance of the city-operated museum. There are shops which sell Ainu crafts and souvenirs between these two museums. The Nibutani Children's Library, where Ainu language classes are held, is near the Shishirimuka Museum. (See Map 2.)

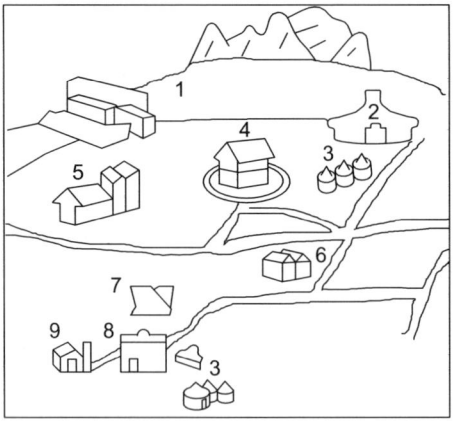

1. Saru River and Nibutani Dam
2. Nibutani Ainu Museum
3. Traditional Ainu dwellings (part of Nibutani Ainu Museum)
4. Munroe Memorial House
5. Nibutani Elementary School
6. Post Office
7. Kindaichi Kyosuke Memorial
8. Shishirimuka Nibutani Ainu Museum
9. Nibutani Children's Library (site of Ainu language classes)

Map 2 Significant locations in Nibutani

According to the Biratori Town History (Biratori-cho, 1974), Nibutani is presently known as the community with the highest concentration of Ainu in Hokkaido. The record of Ainu settlement in this area can be traced as far back as the fourteenth century. In the late nineteenth century, expansion of Japanese territory from the southern part of Hokkaido affected the Ainu of Nibutani, and the town history (Biratori-cho, 1974) describes the beginning of the hardship for the Ainu residents. At this time, approximately one-third were taken away from the village and forced to work in the fishing ports for minimal pay.

Nibutani linguistic 'hero'

As noted by Craig (1992), all successful language rescues have linguistic 'heroes' who lead the way, and this is certainly true of the programme at Nibutani. One could not begin to do justice to the Ainu language revitalisation movement there without a discussion of its leading figure, Kayano Shigeru.

Kayano is an Ainu elder who served on the Biratori Town Council for several terms and then, from August, 1994 to July, 1998, served as the first Ainu parliamentarian in the Japanese House of Counselors. He is a self-taught ethnologist and linguist who has authored over 40 books in Japanese on traditional Ainu crafts and language. Some of these, such as *Our Land Was a Forest* (1994b), an autobiographical work, and *Romance of the Bear God* (1985), a collection of folktales, have been translated into English. However, his most significant contribution may be his recent (1996) Ainu-Japanese dictionary, which represents a lifetime of research.

As a child growing up in the 1920s and 30s, Kayano became bilingual by using Japanese at school and Ainu at home. As he described it in a keynote lecture for the 1993 Nibutani Forum, an international gathering for indigenous peoples, his grandmother served as his major source of input for Ainu.

> As of today, 1993, I am the youngest of the few Ainu who can still understand and speak the Ainu language. My grandmother was my teacher and she spoke no Japanese at all. The conversation she had with me, her grandchild, was carried out only in the Ainu language, and I spoke Japanese with my parents and brothers. So, somehow I learned to speak both the Ainu and Japanese languages equally well. However, when I think or try to say something, first I think in the Ainu language, and then translate it into the Japanese language. That's my thought process. My basic thought process is pretty much Ainu, using the Ainu language. (Kayano, 1994a: 17)

Kayano began teaching the Ainu language to Ainu children in Nibutani in May of 1983. He began with nine students, many of whom were his own nephews and nieces. His original idea had been to establish a daycare facility for Ainu children where the Ainu language would be taught as part of the curriculum. However, since the Japanese government did not approve of his plan, Kayano set up an Ainu language programme for children instead (Kayano, 1994b).

However, linguistic revitalisation is not something that can be achieved by only one person. Kayano's efforts have been supported by many others throughout the course of the Nibutani movement. Many of the assistants are ethnically Ainu but not native speakers of the Ainu language. Others are actually Japanese both ethnically and linguistically.[16]

One example of the latter, a long-time assistant of Kayano, was cast into the role of Ainu language instructor in a rather roundabout way.[17] She was born and grew up in Kanazawa, Ishikawa Prefecture, in central Japan, and it was only when she entered Hokkaido University that she learned about Ainu people. As her interest in the Ainu grew, she studied Ainu history, but did not study the language while a university student. After graduating, she moved to Nibutani to work under Kayano, who was just starting the Ainu language programme for children. After several classes, Kayano became ill and was hospitalised, a situation that forced her to fill in for him in his classes. Since she herself was still a beginning learner of the language, she spent time at Kayano's bedside before each class and learned enough to be able to teach the children. After Kayano recovered, she continued studying the Ainu language and culture under his tutelage while teaching in the children's language programme.

In the years after its inception, the Nibutani programme branched out into separate components for children and adults. The children's programme was divided into two separate courses, one for young children (elementary and junior high school age) and one for high school students. Kayano continued to teach the language classes for adults even during his tenure as a National Diet member, returning to Nibutani on weekends. However, he eventually delegated responsibility for the children's programme to assistants. As interest in the programme grows and more people become qualified to teach the language, it is likely that the responsibilities for the programme will be diffused to a greater degree in the future.

In describing the curriculum in the following section, the focus will be on the children's programme, as this is the most unique aspect of the Nibutani programme and the one that is likely to have the greatest positive effect on the revitalisation of the language.

Children's programme curriculum[18]

The Nibutani programme is unique among the Hokkaido Ainu programmes in that it started as a language course for children and later developed to include classes for adults. To our knowledge, it remains the only programme to have separate children's classes. This is important

Table 1 Schedule of 1996 children's Ainu language/culture class

Date/Time	Content	Location
April 13 (Sat.) 14:00~	Opening of class; Words (1)	Nibutani Children's Library
April 27 (Sat.) 14:00~	Words (2); Plants in spring	Nibutani Children's Library
May 4 (Sat.) 10:00~	Spring outing in mountains	Mountains around Nibutani
May 25 (Sat.) 14:00~	Words (3)	Nibutani Children's Library
June 2 (Sun.)	Bus Excursion	Otaru Transportation Museum, etc.
June 22 (Sat.) 13:00~	Digging toreputa (wild lily) roots	Mountains around Nibutani
July 13 (Sat.)	Drawing of trees	Nibutani Ainu Culture Museum
July 27 (Sat.) 14:00~	Ainu Conversation (1)	Nibutani Children's Library
Late July or early August	Summer camp	
Sept. 14 (Sat.) 14:00~	Ainu stories (1)	Nibutani Children's Library
Sept. 28 (Sat.)	Trees (names and nature)	Nibutani Ainu Culture Museum
Oct. 12 (Sat.) 14:00~	Conversation (2)	Nibutani Children's Library
Oct. 26 (Sat.) 14:00~	Ainu stories (2)	Nibutani Children's Library
Nov. (Sun., date undecided)	Ainu traditional cuisine	Nibutani Children's Library
Nov. 9 (Sat.)	*Shitokara* (making *shito*)	Nibutani Children's Library
Nov. 23 (Sat.) 14:00~	Conversation (3)	Nibutani Children's Library

Date/Time	Content	Location
Dec. 8 (Sun.) 13:00~	2nd Ainu Culture Class	Nibutani Ainu Culture Museum
Dec. 21 (Sat.) 14:00~	Preparation for *Shishirimuka* Culture Festival	Nibutani Children's Library
Jan. 11 (Sat.) 14:00~	New Year's Party	Nibutani Children's Library
Jan. 25 (Sat.) 14:00~	Preparation for *Shishirimuka* Culture Festival	Nibutani Children's Library
Feb. 8 (Sat.) 14:00~	Preparation for *Shishirimuka* Culture Festival	Nibutani Children's Library
Feb. 15 (Sat.) 14:00~	Preparation for *Shishirimuka* Culture Festival	Nibutani Children's Library
Feb. 22 (Sat.) 13:30~	*Shishirimuka* Ainu Culture Festival	Nibutani Children's Library
March 8 (Sat.) 14:00~	Review (1)	Nibutani Children's Library
March 22 (Sat.)14:00~	Review (2); Closing Ceremony	Nibutani Children's Library

from the perspective of language preservation, since children are the key to maintaining a language, as stressed by Krauss (1992: 4) in his article on endangered languages:

> The question for us here is this: how many languages still spoken today are no longer being learned by children? This is a key question, as such languages are no longer viable, and can be defined as moribund, thus to become extinct during the century nearly upon us.

In Nibutani, the language programmes for both children and adults focus on language within the context of broader cultural activities. From the beginnings of the programme, Kayano has been adamant that language teaching cannot be separated from culture. In fact, his earliest lessons for children were taught through outdoor field trips where students learned the Ainu names and traditional functions of native plants, while exploring the plants through the five senses. Children's classes for elementary and junior high school students were scheduled twice each month on Saturday afternoons – not often enough for the children to develop fluency in the language, but sufficient to give them a feeling for the language and the culture. Continuity is encouraged in the children's programme by awarding long-term serious students with subsidised trips to Canada to visit first-nation communities.[19]

The schedule of the children's language programme for elementary and junior high school is decided at the beginning of the school year. (See Table 1 for an example.) The instructor follows this schedule, making adjustments to meet circumstances that arise throughout the year.

There are four major components of the curriculum, the first three of which have been a part of the programme for some time, and the fourth, a later addition (Honda, 1997b): (1) study of the words and sentence structures of Ainu, through handouts and games; (2) practice of traditional Ainu songs and dances; (3) acquisition of traditional knowledge of Ainu ancestors through outdoor field trips; and (4) study of Ainu folk tales to enhance understanding of traditional customs and values. Each of these components will be discussed below.

The class often begins with an explanation of the words and sentences given on a blackboard or handouts. Since Ainu idioms tend to be segmentable into separate meaningful morphemes,[20] the idioms are often explained according to the meaning of these segments. For example, the expression, *yainikoroshima* is composed of three morphemes: *yai* meaning 'myself', *nikor* meaning 'fold,' and *oshima* meaning 'go into.' The meaning of the idiom is explained after the children learn the meanings of the parts. In this case, *yainikoroshima* means to fold oneself into one's own skin, hence 'feeling embarrassed.'[21] Following the introduction of the words and expressions, cards and physical movements are used to encourage the students to experience them on a deeper level. Games are also used extensively.

Traditional dances and songs also play a significant role in the children's programme. The children are introduced to these in class and practice them intensively for special events such as the *Shishirimuka* Culture Festival in February. Although they learn to both sing and dance, the children are sometimes accompanied by elderly people who sing for their dances. In addition to performing the common dances already known to most of the local people, there have been recent attempts to teach the children less familiar dances, reconstructing them from recordings made about 40 years ago.

A walk in the woods behind the Children's Library provides the children with an important field opportunity to learn the words for trees and plants, and to acquire traditional knowledge. Since many of the wild plants were used as folk remedies, children learn their remedial functions along with the names. Games using plants, branches and vines are an important part of the Ainu language curriculum.

Reading of Ainu folk tales has recently become an important part of the curriculum. Although this is done largely in Japanese (the children's comprehension is not at a level where they would be able to understand the stories solely in Ainu), the folktales have been found to be an effective way to introduce intangible elements of traditional Ainu life. While enjoying the stories, the children learn about everyday customs, social norms and values associated with various persons, gods, and situations. As they listen to more and more stories, they come to recognise how particular aspects of traditional Ainu behaviour and lifestyle differ from those of contemporary Japan.

As of June 1998, there were 18 students registered in the children's class, with an average of about 12–13 attending at any one time. While this number was down somewhat from previous years, the decrease does not point to failure. Rather, the reason for the lower enrollment was that Ainu culture had recently been adopted as a part of the regular curriculum at Nibutani Elementary School, so some children now felt less of a need to attend the Saturday classes. The decreased enrollment can therefore be seen as a sign that the programme had been successful enough to influence the local school system. With the Ainu 'culture' aspect now being covered to some extent in public school, the focus of the Saturday classes had begun to change, moving toward a stronger focus on the language *per se*.

Tradition and Transition

As seen above, teaching the traditional culture plays a prominent role in the Ainu language programme of Nibutani. Yet community members recognize the need to focus not only on past traditions, but also to adapt the Ainu language to the culture and lifestyles of the Ainu of the late twentieth century. One such adaptation is the publication in Nibutani since March of 1997 of an Ainu-language newsletter, *Ainu Taimuzu* (Ainu Times). Articles in the newsletter are presented in the Ainu language – written in both Japanese katakana script and romanized alphabet – with only brief commentaries in Japanese.

The issue of tradition vs. transition is an issue not only with the Ainu, but is inherent in language and culture revitalisations worldwide. It is not a problem that is easily resolved. It has been argued on the one hand that too much purism in a language revival or revitalisation may reduce the language's chances for survival, whereas structural compromise and healthy innovation can enhance the chances (Dorian, 1994). On the other hand, it can equally be argued that even where the *explicit* goal of a programme is restoration of the traditional culture, this does not have to hinder the movement if it serves as a catalyst for a necessary transformation (Bentahila and Davies, 1993). However, as Bentahila and Davies (1993) contend, the complete restoration of a culture in its traditional form may be impossible.

アイヌタイムズ　１９９７年（平成９年）３月２０日　木曜日　創刊号

アイヌタイムズ

＜創刊の言葉＞

タント　アイヌタイムズ　ア・カラ　ワ、
エアラキンネ　ア・エヤイコプンテク。
タン　新聞　ヌカラ　ワ　ウエピリカレ　ヤン。
アウタリ　オピッタ　ウトゥラ・アン　ワ　アリキキ・アン　ロ！

tanto Aynu-*taimuzu* a=kar wa,
earkinne a=eyaykopuntek.
tan *Sinbun* nukar wa uepirkare yan.
a=útari opitta utura=an wa arikiki=an ro!

[萱野　志朗]

★アイヌ　オッカイポ　ヤイエイソイタク
★aynu okkaypo yayeysoytak

カニ　アナクネ　アイヌ
モシリ　シシリムカ　テエ
タ　レヘ　ピパウシ　コタ
ン　タネアン　レヘ　ニプ
タイ　コタン　コアパマカ
　アイヌ　オッカイポ　萱
野志朗　ク・ネ　ルウェ
ネ。
　アイヌ　ク・ネ　コロカ
　ク・スクプ　ラポク
ク・イェ　イタク　アナク
ネ　シサム　イタク　トゥ
ラノ　シサム　プリ　パテ

ク　ネ　ア　クスク　ク・ヤ
イヌ　ヒ　カ　シサム　ヤ
イヌ　シサム　プリ　パテ
ク　ネ　ア　ペコロ　ク・
ヤイヌ　ヒ　カ　アナクネ
　ケシカシケ　ソモ　ルウ
エ　ネ。
　シネ　オッカイポク・
ネ　コロカ　スクプ　トゥ
ラシ　ネプ　ネプ　イヌ
ネ　ヤ　オヤ　オヤ　プ
ク・ヌ　ルウェ　ネ　ネヒ
オロタ　コナハ　萱野茂

イェ　イタク　ク・ヌ　ヒ
シネプ　ク・イェ　ナ、
ヌ　ワ　エン・コレ　ヤン
アニ。
　コナハ　ナ　ナ　ペウレ
ヒ　タ　トオプ　シシリ
ムカ　エトコホ　ワノ　流
送　セコロ　ア・イェ　ネ
プキ　キ　ヒ　タ　アイヌ
ウタラ　カ　インネ　ワ
オカ。　ネ　トゥムフ
タ　アイヌ　アッカリ　イ
ンネ　シサム　オカ　ルウ

Figure 1 Front page of the inaugural issue of the *Ainu Times* (March 20, 1997). Reproduced by permission of the editor of the *Ainu Times* (Kayano Shiro).

The question of how to bridge the Ainu past with the present may appear to be complicated by a lack of continuity in the culture. That is, with the Ainu culture repressed for so long, an historical link between the late nineteenth century and the end of the twentieth is missing. It is thus difficult to establish an Ainu identity other than that which has been perpetuated by museums. Indeed, many Japanese have an image of 'Ainu culture' based almost entirely on the traditional hunting-gathering lifestyle, rather than on the present Ainu reality (Yoneda, 1996).

Within Ainu communities, however, there is not a lack of continuity in the culture, even if this culture was in the past largely hidden from the view of outsiders for fear of discrimination or sometimes even legal sanctions. Ainu culture and language have been kept alive in various, if subtle and often subconscious, forms, from codeswitching and code-mixing on the level of interpersonal interaction to the recording and translation of traditional verbal art among scholars, and through the enactment of traditional rituals (using prescribed linguistic routines) within specific communities. Encouraged by the recent movement toward revitalising traditional Ainu culture, numerous Ainu are now consciously trying to learn from their elders in order to reassemble the pieces of their culture, and re-establish their identity in the present. In so doing, the rituals and verbal art forms from the past are as much a means to an end as they are an end in themselves: These are where the language, and its associated values, have best been preserved. It is not, therefore, so much a matter of returning to the past as it is of making the fullest use of the resources that the past has to offer the present. Sjöberg (1993: 184) discusses this synthesis between the past and the present in terms of Ainu cultural mobilisation on a broader level than that of the language alone:

> A defining feature of Ainu cultural change is the emphasis placed on ideologies rooted in their cultural mobilisation. This includes the intro-duction of Ainu crops and vegetables, the establishment of national parks in areas of historic importance and the establishment of Ainu knowledge centres, where lectures in their oral language, history and culture as well as in Ainu weaving and wood-carving techniques, are undertaken. This does not necessarily mean that they seek to exit from the nation of which they are part, nor that they strive to exist between two sectors, a 'traditional' and a modern. It would be wrong to conclude that their strategies contrast with the life of the present. Such views derive from the assumption that 'tradition' and change stand in a dualistic relationship to one another, while in practice there exists a synthesis between the two.

In the course of Nibutani Ainu language revitalisation, a number of other issues have arisen, some involving the individual identities of the language learners. In the early stages of the Nibutani programme, many children were said to be hesitant about attending Ainu language classes lest they be identified as Ainu and therefore subject to discrimination. (See Sjöberg, 1993: 171–174, or Kayano, 1994a, for a more detailed discussion of discrimination against the Ainu.) While discrimination is reportedly much less of a problem now than it use to be, self-consciousness about Ainu ethnicity in the face of possible prejudice continues to be a concern for some of the children, particularly when moving up from Nibutani Elementary School, which is predominantly Ainu, to Biratori Junior High, which is primarily Japanese (Yoneda, 1995).

A related issue discussed in Yoneda concerns the role of the Japanese participants in the Ainu language programme. Ainu ethnicity is not a requirement for becoming an Ainu language learner; in fact, a number of the children in the Nibutani programme are Japanese. Yet they sometimes express confusion over their role in the programme. If they are not Ainu, do they actually have the right to be representing Ainu culture? Indeed, with many Ainu today having Japanese blood, and with ethnic Japanese and Ainu living in close proximity of one another, questions of ethnicity and identity – and of who is or is not qualified to carry on the movement – are likely to become even more significant in the future. As Bentahila and Davies (1993: 371) have argued:

> The results [of a language revival or revitalisation movement] may include the establishment of what is in effect a new variety of the language, used in new contexts and adopted by a new type of speaker. It may no longer serve as a widely used medium of communication among the type of people with whom it was originally associated, but instead acquire new functions for another group, and be assigned roles it could never have assumed in its heyday.

Those concerned with the Ainu revitalisation in Nibutani are aware of the need to balance the restoration of traditional values with modern realities. Yet the way in which the balancing will be done, and the kinds of linguistic and cultural transformations that will result as we enter the twentieth century, remain unclear.

Acknowledgements

We are grateful to Kayano Shigeru and the people of Nibutani for allowing us to observe Ainu language classes and gather information in their community. We would also like to thank the Hokkaido *utari kyōkai* (Hokkaido Ainu Association) for providing information on Ainu language programmes throughout Hokkaido, and Kayano Shiro for granting permission to reprint a section from the *Ainu Times*. Additional thanks go to Honda Yuko for her valuable comments on earlier versions of this manuscript.

Notes

1. The romanisation *Ainu* is used throughout this paper to describe this group of people and their language, since it is the most common romanisation found in works written in English. An alternate spelling, *Aynu*, is also found in certain contexts, including Kayano Shigeru's Ainu-Japanese dictionary (Kayano, 1996), which the present paper follows for all other Ainu words.

2. *Mosir* is itself a compound, being derived, according to Kayano (1996), from components meaning 'quiet earth' (*shizuka + daichi* in Japanese). For a more complete interpretation of *Ainu Mosir* (also romanised as *Ainu Moshir* or *Ainumoshir*), see DeChicchis (1995).

3. Legislation passed by the Japanese Diet in 1997 recognises the Ainu as an ethnic minority with a distinct culture worthy of preservation. While this is the first legislation of its type, and while at one level it reverses the legislation passed in 1899 that assimilated Ainu into Japanese society, it is criticised by many for falling short of recognising the Ainu as the indigenous people of Hokkaido. It does, however, provide official recognition of the fact that Japan is not a monolingual, monocultural nation, and calls for preservation of Ainu culture.

4. This is despite much speculation over the past century about possible relations not only with Japanese, but with numerous languages of the Pacific, the Asian mainland, and even Europe. One recent and ambitious attempt to uncover genetic relations between Ainu and other languages is that of Patrie (1982), who proposed, based on examination of lexical data, that Ainu, Japanese and Korean formed a subgroup of the Altaic language family that stretches across much of the Asian continent. However, like other, less rigorous attempts that have preceded it, Patrie's classification remains highly controversial. (See Shibatani, 1990, for an overview of the debate over historical relations, as well as a discussion of structural characteristics that make Ainu distinct from Japanese.)

5. What is presented here is a very rough sketch. Readers looking for more detailed historical information in English are referred to Sjöberg (1993).

6. Some recent research, however, suggests that the Ainu, even in the traditional society, may have been involved in limited agriculture in addition to their major activities of hunting and gathering (Kikuchi and Fukuda, 1989; Kikuchi, 1994; Osumi and Murai, 1997; Irumada, Kobayashi, and Saito, 1999).

7. 'Education within Ainu society was informal in the sense that it was an inseparable aspect of daily life and religious belief, functioning through children's games, rites of passage and other ceremonial occasions.' (Ogawa, 1993: 237).

8. Where Japanese names appear in this article, the Japanese practice of placing the surname before the given name will be followed.

9. Krauss's essay appeared in the prestigious linguistics journal *Language* as one of a series of essays by various scholars on the topic of endangered languages. Although the passage from the essay quoted here is criticised, this is not intended as a commentary on the entire paper, which, like the other essays in the series, was written to draw readers' attention to the plight of endangered languages. Papers by Craig (1992) and Hale (1992) cited elsewhere in the present article are part of the same series.

10. The suspicion toward academic scholars is a result of more than simply the resentment of their 'language death' perspective. In another paper, Kayano (1994a: 33) discusses how large numbers of Ainu artifacts and antiques were removed from Nibutani over the years in the name of scholarship, some as recently as the mid-1980s, and some of which were later sold for profit.

11. Although *revitalisation* and *revival* are sometimes used interchangeably, they have rather different connotations (Dorian, 1994; Hornberger and King, 1996). 'Revival' suggests the reintroduction of a language that is no longer in use, whereas revitalisation implies efforts to 'impart new vigour in a language already in use through increasing the language's domains' (Hornberger and King, 1996: 428; citing Paulston, 1994).

12. An accurate count of the Ainu population is not available. According to Kayano (1994), the number is estimated at 25,000 based on records of membership in the Hokkaido *utari kyōkai* (Hokkaido Ainu Association), the prefecture-wide Ainu association. However, since membership in the association is by application by those who identify themselves as Ainu (the official definition of which, according to Sjöberg [1993: 152] 'is consanguinity, or by marriage, including adopted children), the actual number may be much larger. Kayano (ibid.) has estimated it as 50,000. Sjöberg writes that the figure should, according to the Ainu, be around 300,000, and that 'the Ainu say that their unwillingness to register as Ainu reflects their disapproval of the ways in which their situation is officially handled' (p. 152). Fear of possible discrimination (see Kayano, 1994) is another reason why many may be hesitant to declare themselves as Ainu. Although in the past Ainu could often be distinguished from Japanese by physical features alone (e.g. fairer skin, rounder eyes, and more hirsute bodies) intermarriage with Japanese has made this difficult if not impossible in most cases, so that it is easier for many Ainu to deny their ethnicity if they so choose.

13. The term *diglossia* was first employed by Ferguson (1959) to describe how speakers of certain languages switch between standard and local dialects according to the speech situation. The term has come to be used to describe situationally patterned use of language in a wide variety of contexts, between distinct languages as well as between dialects of a single language.

14. It is interesting to contrast this view with the mistrust of verbal communication that is often ascribed to Japanese culture, e.g. Lebra (1976: 252): 'Among the behaviour patterns that have appeared again and again [in the literature on Japanese culture] is the stress upon nonverbal communication, or mistrust of words.'

15. Ainu was an unwritten language prior to its study and transcription by Western and Japanese scholars. Currently there are two major systems of writing that are used to represent Ainu: romanised script (primarily in linguistic studies and in studies written in Western languages), and a modification of the Japanese katakana syllabary (for Ainu language teaching materials and Ainu publications within Japan), though there is not complete standardisation within either writing system. Katakana, the Japanese writing system used mainly to represent foreign loanwords, has been adapted to Ainu to reflect its different phonology, which includes word-final consonants that are not found in Japanese.

16. The fact that non-native speakers should be among the linguistic rescuers is actually quite common among revitalisation movements (Craig, 1992; Bentahila and Davies, 1993), but normally these are educated and urbanized members of the ethnic group who later choose to return to their ethnic community. It is of course also common for professional linguists and anthropologists who have no ethnic connections to a community to be involved in efforts at linguistic and cultural reconstruction and preservation, but normally they would operate at a somewhat more detached level.

17. This is described in more detail in Japanese by Honda (1997b).

18. This section describes the Nibutani programme primarily up until early 1997, and to a limited extent through mid-1998. Since that time, the authors have learned, numerous changes have been taking place in the structure of the programme. A full explanation of these, however, is beyond the scope of the present paper. The information given here is thus best seen in historical perspective, as an example of how the programme was structured at a given period in time rather than as a definitive description.

19. 'First-nation' is a term commonly used to refer to Canadian native communities.

20. Ainu is generally classified by linguists as a polysynthetic language, in which various morphemes can be incorporated into the verb (see Shibatani, 1990, for a discussion of the grammatical structure).

21. This example is also explained in Kayano (1993:361) as *ku-yai-nikor-oshima*, 'I am so ashamed that I want to hide by folding myself into my own skin' [where *ku* = 'I'].

References

Bentahila, A. and Davies, E.E. (1993) Language revival: restoration or transformation? *Journal of Multilingual and Multicultural Development* 14 (5), 355–74.

Biratori-cho (1996) *Biratori chōsei yōran* [Biratori Town Informational Manual]. Biratori-cho, Hokkaido.

Biratori-chōshi hensan iinkai [Biratori Town History Editing Committee] (1974) *Biratori chōshi* [Biratori Town History]. Biratori-cho, Hokkaido: *Biratori-chōshi hensan iinkai* [Biratori Town History Editing Committee].

Craig, C. (1992) A constitutional response to language endangerment: The case of Nicaragua. *Language* 69 (3), 17–24.

DeChicchis, J. (1995) The current state of the Ainu language. *Journal of Multilingual and Multicultural Development* 16 (1/2), 103–24.

Dorian, N.C. (1994) Purism vs. compromise in language revitalisation and language revival. *Language in Society* 23, 479–94.

Ferguson, C.A. (1959) Diglossia. *Word* 15, 325–40.

Fishman, J.A. (1991) *Reversing Language Shift: Theoretical and Empirical Foundations of Assistance to Threatened Languages*. Clevedon, UK: Multilingual Matters.

Hale, K. (1992) On endangered languages and the safeguarding of diversity. *Language* 69 (3), 1–3.

Honda Y. (1997a) *Ainugo kyōshitsu* – Biratori [Ainu language classroom – Biratori]. In Kubota J., Kuritsubo Y., Noyama K., Hino T., and Fujii S. (eds) *Kōshō bungaku 2: Ainu bungaku* [Oral Literature 2: Ainu Literature] (pp. 353–67). Tokyo: Iwanami shoten.

Honda Y. (1997b) *Futatsu no kaze no tani: Ainu kotan de no hibi* [The Valley of Two Winds: Life in an Ainu 'Kotan']. Tokyo: Sanshodo.

Hornberger, N.H. and King, K.A. (1996) Language revitalisation in the Andes: Can the schools reverse language shift? *Journal of Multilingual and Multicultural Development* 17 (6), 427–41.

Irumada N., Kobayashi M., and Saito T. (eds) (1999) *Kita no naikai sekai* [The World of the Northern Inland Sea]. Tokyo: Yamakawa shuppansha.

Kayano S. (1985) *The Romance of the Bear God: Ainu Folktales*. Tokyo: Taishukan Publishing Co.

Kayano S. (1993) Ainu ethnic and linguistic revival. In N. Loos and T. Osanai (eds) *Indigenous Minorities and Education: Australian and Japanese Perspectives of Their Indigenous Peoples, the Ainu, Aborigines and Torres Strait Islanders* (pp. 360–367). Tokyo: Sanyusha Publishing Co.

Kayano S. (1994a) The current situation of the Ainu in Japan. In Nibutani Forum Organizing Committee (ed.) *Gathering in Ainumoshir, the Land of the Ainu: Messages from the Indigenous Peoples of the World* (pp. 16–35). Tokyo: Yushisha.

Kayano S. (1994b) *Our Land Was a Forest: An Ainu Memoir*. Boulder, CO: Westview Press.

Kayano S. (1996) *Kayano shigeru no ainugo jiten* [Kayano Shigeru's Ainu Dictionary]. Tokyo: Sanseido.

Kikuchi I. (1994) *Ainu minzoku to nihonjin* – *Higashi ajia no naka no ezochi* [The Ainu people and the Japanese – The Land of Ezo Within East Asia]. Tokyo: Asahi shimbunsha.

Kikuchi T. and Fukuda T. (eds) (1989) *Kita no chūsei tsugaru, hokkaidō yomigaeru chūsei 4* [The Middle Ages in the North, Tsugaru and Hokkaido: Recalling the Middle Ages, Volume 4]. Tokyo: Heibonsha.

Kindaichi K. (1960) *Ainugo kenkyū. Kindaichi kyōsuke senshū* [Research on the Ainu Language. Selected Works of Kindaichi Kyosuke.] Tokyo: Sanseido.

Kindaichi K. and Kannari M. (1959-68) *Ainugo jojishi yukarashū* [Ainu Epic Yukar Collection]. Tokyo: Sanseido.

Krauss, M. (1992) The world's languages in crisis. *Language* 68 (1), 4–10.

Lebra, T.S. (1976) *Japanese Patterns of Behavior*. Honolulu: University of Hawaii Press.

Loos, N., and Osanai T. (eds) (1993) *Indigenous Minorities and Education: Australian and Japanese Perspectives of Their Indigenous Peoples, the Ainu, Aborigines and Torres Strait Islanders*. Tokyo: Sanyusha Publishing Co.

Ogawa M. (1993) The Hokkaido Former Aborigines Protection Act and assimilatory education. In N. Loos and Osanai T. (eds) *Indigenous Minorities and Education: Australian and Japanese Perspectives of Their Indigenous Peoples, the Ainu, Aborigines and Torres Strait Islanders* (pp. 237–249). Tokyo: Sanyusha Publishing Co.

O'Grady, W., Dobrovolsky, M., and Aronoff, M. (1991) *Contemporary Linguistics: An Introduction* (2nd edn). New York: St. Martin's Press.

Osumi K. and Murai S. (eds) (1997) *Chūsei kōki ni okeru higashi ajia no kokusai kankei* [International Relations in East Asia in the Latter Middle Ages]. Tokyo: Yamakawa shuppansha.

Patrie, J. (1982) *The Genetic Relationship of the Ainu Language.* Honolulu: University of Hawaii Press.

Paulston, C.B. (1994) *Linguistic Minorities in Multilingual Settings: Implications for Language Policies.* Amsterdam: John Benjamin Publishing Company.

Romaine, S. (1995) *Bilingualism.* Oxford: Blackwell.

Shibatani M. (1990) *The Languages of Japan.* Cambridge: Cambridge University Press.

Siddle, R.M. (1993) Academic exploitation and indigenous resistance: The case of the Ainu. In N. Loos and Osanai T. (eds) *Indigenous Minorities and Education: Australian and Japanese Perspectives of Their Indigenous Peoples, the Ainu, Aborigines and Torres Strait Islanders* (pp. 40–51). Tokyo: Sanyusha Publishing Co.

Sjöberg, K.V. (1993) *The Return of the Ainu: Cultural Mobilization and the Practice of Ethnicity in Japan.* Chur, Switzerland: Harwood.

Yoneda (Honda) Y. (1995) *Nibutani ainugo kyōshitsu no kodomotachi* [The children of the Nibutani Ainu classroom]. Paper presented at the *Kokusai rikai suishin jigyō: Ainu minzoku no ima* [Project for the Advancement of International Understanding: The Ainu People Today], Tokyo.

Yoneda Y. (1996) *Ainugo kyōshitsu ni okeru 'ainu bunka' no kyōzai no mondaiten ni tsuite* [Problems with Teaching Materials for 'Ainu Culture' in the Ainu Language Classroom]. *Hokkaidō-ritsu ainu minzoku bunka kenkyū sentā kenkyū kiyō* [Bulletin of the Hokkaido Prefectural Center for Research on Ainu Culture] 2, 123–148.

Chapter 4

Language and Identity in Okinawa Today

OSUMI MIDORI

Introduction

Identity and language are inextricably intertwined. Language is so essential to human life that almost everything around us is expressed by and conceptualised through it. Yet the world is viewed and analysed in a very different manner according to the language one speaks. Plurality is expressed in some languages but not in others. Some tongues have a complex gender or noun class system, while others have none. The degree of abstraction or the semantic domain of a word is only rarely the same as the 'corresponding' term in another language. Using a non-native language therefore results in a great handicap for the speaker. In this respect, ruling through language may be the most powerful though invisible form of colonialism.

In many countries, however, the use of only one or a few predominant languages is encouraged as a result of national, economical, or political priorities. National interests often put people who speak minority languages at a major disadvantage. Today, the rate at which languages disappear seems to be far greater than ever before in human history, and the future viability of minority languages has recently become a serious concern among linguists. Some linguists suggest that many languages will not survive beyond the next generation (Dixon, 1991).

The loss of a language means that the most essential part of a human community is lost, since the language is the patrimony of the people, the reflection and the means of their recognition of the world. Indeed, a language and the identity of its speakers are so inextricably intertwined that the 'destruction of a language is the destruction of a rooted identity' (Fishman, 1991: 4). While many languages have been pushed to the verge of extinction and it may well be too late to save them, people do struggle to protect their linguistic heritage.

With language being such an essential part of a human community and its individual members, one must ask: Is it possible for a community to reassert its identity through the creative use of its language? And is this possible even after a community has experienced language shift? These are the questions this paper will strive to answer as it looks at the linguistic situation in Okinawa today.

Okinawans currently constitute Japan's largest ethnic minority, with approximately 1.3 million living in Okinawa Prefecture and the Amami Islands. Another 300,000 Okinawans live in other areas of Japan, while a similar number are dispersed outside of Japan, mostly in Hawaii and the Americas (Taira, 1997: 142). In this paper, I will examine the linguistic history of this group, shifts in its identity, and the interaction between the two.

In making this exploration, I will begin by giving a brief history of Okinawa and its languages. After describing the general trend towards language shift from the vernacular Okinawan languages to standard Japanese in the twentieth century, I will analyse variations in this pattern, looking at differences in language use according to local and regional attitudes, as well as lifestyles and activities people are engaged in. I will then examine the current usage of language in Okinawa, explaining how and when Okinawan vernaculars (*Uchinaaguchi*) are used. In particular, I will focus on the language use of Okinawan youth, as revealed by a survey of university students I conducted in late 1996 to explore attitudes toward and use of the vernacular languages in Okinawa. I will also examine how Okinawan languages have influenced the variety of Japanese used in Okinawa, which is known as *Uchinaa-Yamatoguchi*, and explain how it differs from standard Japanese. I will then investigate new developments in *Uchinaa-Yamatoguchi*, including creative mixtures of Okinawan and standard Japanese by Okinawan youth. I will also report on factors that have contributed to an overall increase in self esteem on the part of Okinawans in the past decade, and suggest that this reevaluation of Okinawan culture has been a factor in the development of new forms of expression by Okinawan youth. In this way, I will try to show how language and identity are more fluid and capable of transformation than often imagined.

Historical Background

The Ryukyu archipelago is a chain of islands that extends southwest from Kyushu, the southernmost of Japan's main four islands, almost all the way to Taiwan. Most of these islands are now grouped into a single political unit, the Japanese prefecture of Okinawa; however, the islands of the Amami-Oshima group, which were once part of the Ryukyu Kingdom, are assigned to Kagoshima Prefecture.

The Ryukyus were already inhabited during the paleolithic period, as we know from human fossils dating back approximately 18,000 years that were found at Minatogawa near Naha (Hanihara, 1994). These prehistoric fossils are considered to be very significant in exploring the prototype of the modern Japanese.[1] The Ryukyus (except for the Miyako and Yaeyama island groups) and mainland Japan are believed to have shared the neolithic Jomon culture, which is characterised by rope patterned pottery (Takara & Dana, 1993: 7). The genealogical relation between the Okinawan languages and standard Japanese is also well known, having been established by the end of the last century (Chamberlain, 1895).

After about 300 BC, however, the Okinawan culture started to diverge from that of mainland Japan. Where the Ryukyuans interred their dead in funerary urns, the Japanese cremated the deceased. While pork was a mainstay of the Ryukyuan diet, Japanese traditionally ate little meat (Taira, 1997: 43). The architecture and clothing of the two ethnic groups were also quite distinct.

The languages of these two groups also diverged in many aspects of phonology, grammar and lexicon, and it is believed that the two separated some time between the 5th and 8th century AD (Matsumori, 1995: 23). Nonetheless, a number of features of archaic Japanese appear to have been preserved in different places and islands in the Ryukyu archipelago, albeit with various stages of phonological transformation (such as /p/ changing to /f/ or /h/).[2] Okinawans also use a number of words that were used in mainland Japan in the 8th to 9th century, including *warabi* (meaning 'child'), and *shitimiti* ('early morning'). Many Okinawan words also share features with those of the Kyushu dialect. Yet despite these similarities and the fact that the languages spoken in Okinawa are often referred to as the 'Okinawan dialect of Japanese', it should be emphasised that they are mutually unintelligible.[3]

I should also stress that there is not just one language indigenous to Okinawa. Nakamoto (1988: 191–192) classifies the Okinawan vernaculars into two main groups: the North Ryukyu and the South Ryukyu. The North group is broken down into the Amami dialects and the Okinawa dialects, and the South group into the Miyako, the Yaeyama, and the Yonaguni dialects. Here, again, the word 'dialects' is used, but many of varieties of Okinawan are mutually unintelligible.

Matsumori summarises the situation as follows:

> ... the various dialects that are now categorised as Ryukyuan are by no means a single language, but a conglomeration of different dialects, many of which are mutually unintelligible. Furthermore, the speakers of Ryukyuan claim that even within one particular dialectal region, vernaculars differ so much that they cannot communicate with the speakers of other islands in the region (p. 25).

Matsumori explains that Okinawans can understand speakers of other dialects if they come from nearby areas, but not if they come from further away. Thus, she posits that these vernaculars are 'points in a continuum rather than ... mutually discrete entities' (p. 25). Given this fact, she explains that 'the exact number of vernaculars is not known; it depends on how dialects are defined.' Indeed, Okinawa is an area of great linguistic diversity, and is significant both for diachronic and dialectal studies.

One of the reasons for this great variation in regional language may be that the peoples of the Ryukyus apparently lived in small and separate communities until the 12th century, when they began to form regional groups. Then in the mid 14th century, clan chiefs divided the islands into three regions. Each rushed to establish a tributary relationship with China. After several power struggles among them, the first dynasty of the Okinawan nation state was established in 1429 (Takara and Dana, 1993: 10–14).

The kingdom flourished with the growing and lucrative trade with China.[4] During the reign of the third king of the second dynasty (1477–1527), the Ryukyuan people adopted the dialect of the capital, Shuri, as the lingua franca of the kingdom. Shuri continued to fulfill this role until the late 19th century (Matsumori, 1995).

Trading by the Ryukyuans continued to expand, extending as far as Malacca and Siam (Takara & Dana, 1993: 30–33). This prosperity, however, served as a magnet to draw in the Japanese from the north. In 1609, the Shimazu clan of the Satsuma area of Kyushu moved into the Ryukyu Kingdom in order to profit from this external trade, colonising the area between Amami-Oshima and the Yoron-to islands. Despite this outside rule, however, the Ryukyu Kingdom officially remained intact and the vernacular languages continued to be used for another 270 years (Matsumori, 1995: 21).

Then in 1879 the Meiji government disbanded the clan system that had been maintained by the deposed Edo Shogunate and established Okinawa as a prefecture. Thereafter, the area was ruled directly from Tokyo. Around the same time, in an effort to break down the old feudal turfs and build a unified nation state, the Japanese government adopted a policy of linguistic standardisation for the entire country under the slogan *futsūgo* (common language) and later, *hyōjungo* (standard language). [See Chapter 1 for a more detailed explanation of this policy.] Interestingly, the Okinawan government took a very positive attitude toward the 'standardisation' of the language, linking it to modernisation, and was the first prefectural government to adopt these slogans after the national government promulgated them (Matsumori, 1995: 32).

To promote the acquisition of 'standard Japanese', a conversation school was set up in Okinawa in 1880 (Takaesu, 1994: 1). Mass media and communication with people from the mainland soon brought the Japanese language into the lives of common people in Okinawa.

The trend to accept standard Japanese was spurred in part by the increased mobility of the Okinawan population. Many young people began leaving Okinawa for jobs in the cities of mainland Japan, where they were forced to learn Japanese. Recognition of the linguistic handicap they faced accelerated the push for acquisition of standard Japanese back home, leading to a massive shift from predominantly monolingual communities to societal bilingualism. In fact, during the first half of this century, the desire for modernisation was so great in the prefecture that there was apparently very little concern over the decline of the local languages (Matsumori, 1995: 32).[5]

Another factor in the rapid shift towards bilingualism was the increased need for a lingua franca within Okinawa. As mentioned above, many of the Okinawan 'dialects' are mutually unintelligible. While Shuri had served as the official lingua franca of the Ryukyu Kingdom, it was not widely known. As modernisation led to greater mobility, Okinawans felt an increased need to be able to communicate with people from other areas of Okinawa as well as with mainland Japanese. Widespread acquisition of standard Japanese allowed them to do both.

However, by far the biggest factor in the shift away from Okinawan languages towards standard Japanese was undoubtedly the switch to Japanese as the language of instruction in educational institutions. In the years immediately preceding World War II, school children in Okinawa were forbidden to use their native language, even on the playground. Pupils caught using Okinawan expressions at school were forced to wear a tag called a *hōgen-fuda* (literally, 'a dialect tag') on a string hung around their necks as a punishment (personal communications from Miyagi Shizu, Hokama Shuzen and other Okinawans). A pupil wearing the *hōgen-fuda* would have to keep it on until somebody else used an Okinawan expression; the tag would then be passed on to the new offender. Since the last pupil wearing the tag at the end of the day was scolded by the teacher, children devised ways of getting rid of it. They found that a good way was to hit another pupil; the struck child would invariably cry out '*Agaa*' (ouch) and be forced to don the tag himself. This system was said to have been voluntarily adopted by junior high school students in 1907, but was later enforced by all Okinawan schools as the standardisation policy was intensified starting in 1917 (Matsumori, 1995: 32).

The negative image of the vernacular languages was further exacerbated during World War II, when it was rumored that people who used Okinawan languages could be shot by Japanese soldiers, who might take them for spies speaking an unintelligible language.

A recent survey by Ono and Hokama (reported in Ono, 1995) concerning people's ability in and consciousness of Okinawan languages confirmed how successful the 'standardisation' of language was in Okinawa. Interestingly, this study showed that older Okinawans are not only better than younger ones at speaking Okinawan languages, but they are also more confident in speaking standard Japanese. In fact, older people reported that they could choose either standard Japanese or Okinawan language according to the occasion. In contrast, younger people expressed little confidence in their ability to speak either. People over the age of 65 generally were found to be able to speak standard

Japanese (with an Okinawan accent) as well as one of the Okinawan languages. Those around the age of 50, depending upon the area they were brought up in and who they socialised with, could usually speak one of the Okinawan languages fairly well, but only with the right people and on the right occasion. Okinawans between 35 and 50 generally understood a spoken Okinawan language, but could not speak it well. Younger people, however, were often found to be unable to even understand the language of their area.

Thus, during the last century, most Okinawan communities have gone from a predominantly monolingual Okinawan language speaking society to a state of bilingualism without diglossia, a stage along the way to becoming monolingual in standard Japanese (Matsumori, 1995: 19). Though there are still hundreds of thousands of speakers, Okinawan vernaculars are no longer passed on to the younger generation the way they used to be.

At present, we do not hear much Okinawan in the cities of the archipelago. I personally heard Okinawan spoken in all its vividness for the first time several years ago, when I was hospitalised in Nago (in North Okinawa, where I lived) and shared a room with three elderly women. I could not understand a word they spoke with their visitors. Since then, after observing different situations and talking to students and area residents, I have realised that Okinawan languages are still actively spoken in some areas, among some people, and in some situations – even among students. That is, Okinawan is used less, but is still alive in different forms. In this paper, I will try to describe what these forms are.

Use of Okinawan Languages Today

Locale, attitude and language maintenance

In the previous section, I described how standard Japanese infiltrated Okinawan people's lives, leading to the dwindling use of the vernacular languages. People's generally cooperative attitudes toward 'standardisation' partly helped this shift. It is interesting to note, however, that there is substantial variation in the amount of Okinawan language used in different regions in Okinawa, and even among different villages in the same area. I would like to begin my exploration of language and identity by noting some of the differences I personally observed when I lived in Okinawa for three years between 1994 and 1997.

Serafim (1991) generalises that in language shift, the new language usually is first adopted by the cultural elite in the cities and 'gains a foothold as the language of public discourse'. It then supplants the indigenous tongue in more and more situations, until the original language is reserved for use at home and possibly in the market, and is eventually pushed out there too (p. 4). If this is true, people in rural areas would be more likely to retain command of their native language than those in cities.

I was surprised to find that this is not the case in Okinawa. I noticed that people from the capital area of Naha and the large city of Shuri retained their proficiency in an Okinawan language better than people in other areas. Another place where I found many who could speak an Okinawan language was Itoman, a fishing port in the southern part of Okinawa island where tradition has been well preserved.

Compared to the people in these cities, who have a great deal of contact with mainland Japanese, people living on remote islands such as Miyakojima are cut off from outside contacts and should find it easier to maintain their local language. In reality, however, I found that the people in such rural areas were the first to convert themselves to speakers of standard Japanese. I suspect the reason for this difference is that people from the countryside tend to be insecure about their identity and feel inferior to residents of Naha or mainland Japan. They therefore adopt the language of the seemingly 'superior' group in an attempt to improve themselves. In contrast, people with more self-confidence or a greater pride in tradition appear to be less willing to let go of a part of their identity or tradition.

This hypothesis on the link between self esteem and language maintenance could also explain why Okinawans in general accepted the shift to standard Japanese more readily than people in any other area of Japan. As an oppressed people, they had a harder time maintaining their pride than residents of prosperous fiefdoms such as Satsuma (in Kagoshima Prefecture) or those who lived in the ancient capital of Kyoto – areas where people proudly eschew standard Japanese and adhere to the local dialect to this day.

Further support for this hypothesis comes from a comparison of the language use in two villages I visited in northern Okinawa. The first was Nakijin, a village adjacent to the city I resided in during my stay in Okinawa. Nakijin is an ancient castle town, built by a clan chief who ruled North Okinawa in the 14th century. It is made up of a number of distinct communities, each with its own dialect that differs slightly from the others. The town has a quarter that used to serve as the residential area for the warrior class, who lived apart from the town's merchants and other lower classes. The residents of this quarter still speak with a different accent than the other people of the village, and also have a more developed range of honorific expressions.[6]

The local Okinawan language is still strongly retained in Nakijin. One of my students from this village was among the most fluent speakers of an Okinawan language in his age group. The people of this village appear to be quite proud of their historical heritage. Although on the surface they belittle their language, saying that it is a rural accent and inferior to the language spoken in Shuri or Naha in the south of Okinawa, they do not hesitate to use it. The fact that most of the villagers are engaged in farming, raising cattle or agricultural crops and following a traditional lifestyle, and that few new settlers have moved into the village, may be other reasons why their Okinawan language has been maintained.

The situation I found in Ogimi, another village in northern Okinawa that I visited for research purposes, was quite different. Inhabitants there, mostly elderly people, chose to converse in standard Japanese. A 91-year-old lady of this village, who served as an informant for my research on Okinawan language use, spoke beautiful standard Japanese. She told me how a *hōgen-fuda* (explained above) had been used at the elementary school she attended. She also explained that parents and other villagers had worked very closely with the school in encouraging children to learn standard Japanese. Her parents had spoken to her in standard Japanese even though they used the local vernacular tongue with each other.

In her recollection, everybody in Ogimi tried hard to speak standard Japanese, including a fish vender. She actually remembered when the vender changed her call from '*Io konsoore*', Okinawan for 'Would you like to buy some fish?' to its standard Japanese equivalent, '*Sakana kaimasen ka.*' According to my informant, the people of Ogimi had always had an inferiority complex about their language vis-à-vis the one spoken in the capital of Okinawa; therefore, they willingly abandoned it when the opportunity arose to adopt standard Japanese. They would still speak their local language among themselves because it was their mother tongue, but they also made sure that their children would be good at standard Japanese.

The two villages mentioned above show an interesting contrast: a young person from the former can speak an Okinawan language fairly well, while those from the latter village cannot. A lady of around 55 years of age from Nakijin told me that she remembered people of her village complaining to a child speaking in standard Japanese, 'Why can't you speak your own language?' The exact opposite reaction was heard in Ogimi: There, my 91-year-old informant told me, adults used to say, 'Oh, don't use *Uchinaaguchi* (Okinawan). Speak proper Japanese.' This difference in attitude resulted in major differences in the next generation's ability to use Okinawan languages.

Language and traditional activities

In addition to the above-mentioned effect of attitude on language maintenance or shift, I also found that the destiny of some words and expressions was directly tied to the fate of the activities they were related to. A number of words that older people remembered had gone out of use with the customs they named. *Habusarii*[7] is the word for a wreath of straw used as a buffer between the head and a load of things carried on it. As Okinawans stopped carrying things on their heads, this term disappeared. Similarly, the term *uriyasumii*, which refers to the wet period during which children skip school to help their parents plant potatoes, has gone out of use with the passing of the rural lifestyle. Other outdated expressions include *tamunuu*, which means firewood, *pagama*, an iron pot used for cooking rice, *bindaree*, a washbasin, *gujinmii*, a trench filled with straw beside an animal pen, in which rain water mixes with animal excrement to make compost, and *huuru*, the name for a pig pen attached to a toilet, where the excrement could be used to feed the pigs. Examples of such words that have disappeared with social and cultural changes appear in Table 1 below.

On the other hand, Okinawan languages are kept alive in theaters featuring a local drama form called *uchinaa shibai* because the plays depict Okinawan customs and manners. I happened to see some of these plays broadcast on TV with Japanese subtitles, but was told that the subtitles never conveyed the nuances of the Okinawan language. The language is essential in these plays. The expressions used in them are often very imaginative and vivid. One example is the threat *namanee, kubinujaani, bin'nu hutana shiwadunaisa*, which means, 'I will rip your neck off and make it into a bottle top' (Kyan, 1996: 30—31). Another *is iibii nagete miinu gyun'do*, which is translated as 'I'll throw my finger and pull your eyes out' (Kyan, 1996). Another imaginative expression from a drama is *On'na dakeagata satuga umarijima morin'ushinukete kogatanasana*: 'Over Mount On'na my lover lives. I want to make him come this way by pushing the mountain aside' (Kyan, 1996; Hokama, 1995: 135—136). These lively expressions surely help attract an audience and keep this type of theater — and its language — alive.

Table 1 Okinawan expressions which have died out due to social or cultural changes

Okinawan Term	English Equivalent	Okinawan Term	English Equivalent
bindaree	a washbasin	*pachimaa*	hand towel
pagama	an iron rice pot	*sanagee*	ladle
michigee	wooden spoon	*baaki*	basket
sagijooki	hanging basket	*hichubibanki*	wild strawberry
hichina	tiny stool for sitting on	*tamunuu*	firewood
gujinmii	a compost trench	*huuru*	pig pen attached to a toilet
ishinagu	stone marbles	*unjooni*	a swing
habusarii	wreath-shaped head cushion	*uriyasumii*	seasonal absence from school

Another art form that seemed to promote the maintenance of Okinawan languages is poetry. Like Japanese poems, *ryūka* and *kyōka* are composed of lines with a specific syllable count. However, where Japanese poetry incorporates lines of seven and five syllables (with a total of 17 or 31 syllables), these Okinawan poetic forms consist of three eight-syllable lines followed by one six-syllable line (for a total of 30 syllables). Because their rhythm, as well as the themes taken up, are directly related to the language used, these poetic forms help maintain Okinawan languages. On a number of occasions during the three years I lived in Okinawa, I heard people recite old poems or their own compositions using authentic Okinawan words and expressions (which were virtually unintelligible to me).

Language and Attitudes of Okinawan Youth: Student Survey

As we have seen, Okinawa appears to be undergoing a process of language shift from Okinawan vernaculars to standard Japanese, although Okinawan languages are still used in some areas and for some activities. To get a better idea of the current linguistic situation and possible future trends, I conducted a brief, exploratory survey on language use and attitudes in November, 1996. My purpose was to investigate: (1) knowledge and frequency of use of Okinawan languages, (2) attitude towards Okinawan languages, Japanese, and mixtures of these languages, and (3) Okinawan words and expressions used in daily life.

The questionnaire was distributed at a university festival. Two-hundred and thirty people filled it out on a voluntary basis. Ninety percent of the respondents were students between 18 to 21 years of age. Ninety-six percent were Okinawans. No assessment of the reliability or validity of the questionnaire was made, as this survey was intended only to generate hypotheses and suggest areas for future research. A translation of the survey instrument is provided in the Appendix. The responses are summarised below.

Knowledge of Okinawan languages

The subjects were first asked to assess their own productive and receptive proficiencies in Okinawan languages (*Uchinaaguchi*), marking one of five or six levels to indicate how well they speak and understand the local vernacular. None of the 230 respondents marked either of the two highest levels of productive ability indicating that they could speak an Okinawan language 'very well' or 'fairly well'. About half marked the fourth highest level, indicating that they could speak 'only very little'. Most of these respondents also answered that they could understand it 'partly' when spoken to. All the rest except a dozen answered that they 'hardly' understood any Okinawan. Out of the 12 who indicated that they could speak 'a little' (the third highest choice on the questionnaire), eight were over 40 years old and two were over 35.

The next two questions asked what language the respondents used at home and what language they used with friends. All responded that they generally use *Uchinaa-Yamatoguchi* – the Okinawanised version of standard Japanese – in both cases.

Respondents were next asked to write at what times or in what situations they hear Okinawan vernaculars spoken. Most answered that they hear such language when conversing with their grandparents, or, rarely, with their parents.

Although most of the young people surveyed indicated that they could not speak an Okinawan vernacular, when asked, they could write down many Okinawan expressions they used on particular occasions (though they were generally mixed with standard Japanese). Most of the respondents indicated that they used these expressions when they 'fight' or 'joke' with each other. In other words, their Okinawan is limited to certain kinds of intimate, personal or emotional contexts.

Attitudes towards language

The Okinawan language used among the prefecture's youth is some-times perceived as 'not acceptable' or even 'vulgar' by elderly people. The survey therefore explored how young people themselves felt about Okinawan languages and the Okinawanised form of standard Japanese known as *Uchinaa-Yamatoguchi*. First the questionnaire asked, 'What do you feel about Okinawan?' Respondents were given five different state-ments designed to express a range of positive and negative feelings toward the local languages; multiple responses were allowed. The most positive choice was: 'Okinawan should be spoken more often'; next was: 'I am interested in Okinawan, and would like to learn and use it if I could.' The other three choices were more negative: 'Okinawan is the language of elderly people', 'We had better learn standard Japanese rather than Okinawan', and 'It is not useful any more in modern society.'

The majority of the respondents answered that they were 'interested in Okinawan and want to learn and use it if [they] could'. However, at the same time, almost all also marked 'Okinawan is the language of elderly people', and 'It is not useful anymore in modern society,' suggesting that they felt there is no way to go back to using the traditional language, since society has changed.

Next the questionnaire asked, 'When you use Okinawan expressions or *Uchinaa-Yamatoguchi*, what is the reason?' The subjects were asked to select one of four responses: (1) 'Okinawan is our traditional language that should be maintained', (2) 'We can express ourselves better using them',

(3) 'I feel I am an Okinawan', and (4) 'It keeps people together; we feel we are comrades'. The most common responses were the third and first, suggesting that Okinawan expressions are tied to the respondents' identity as Okinawans, and that they also do not want to let tradition die out. Many respondents also marked the fourth answer, indicating the role of language as a unifying factor. In my own observation, too, I found that students from other parts of Japan who picked up Okinawan expressions seemed to be more easily accepted by their Okinawan peers.

Next the subjects were asked to write their own answers to the question, 'What do you feel about recent *Uchinaa-Yamatoguchi* expressions used by young people?' Approximately 15% of the respondents expressed concerns such as, 'It hinders the proper acquisition of Okinawan,' and 'Creating expressions with no discipline leads to degradation in the current Japanese language'. Respondents over 40 expressed some strong opinions. For example, one wrote, 'The Okinawan language used by the youth is not right. They should not try to use it at all if their knowledge of it is imperfect.' Another answered, 'I can't stand their language. It's neither Okinawan nor Japanese. They had better learn proper Japanese rather than trying to learn Okinawan.'

Okinawan words and expressions in use today

After checking on knowledge of and attitudes towards Okinawan vernaculars and recent developments in *Uchinaa-Yamatoguchi*, the questionnaire asked the subjects to write down 'words or expressions in Okinawan which you use or hear sometimes' and to explain their meanings if possible. In this section, I will present the words given by the respondents as well as those I collected during my stay, mainly from people in North Okinawa. In reporting this data, I will try to examine what kinds of words are better preserved, and in which direction the language is changing today.

Okinawan expressions still in use today (though some are slightly modified) are listed below. The list is not exhaustive. The items have been grouped for easier analysis. In general, they tend to be terms referring to different types of people, body parts, feelings, culturally specific customs, rituals, and foods, and emphatic expressions.

Types of people

Many of the Okinawan expressions still in use contain the suffixes [-aa], [-mun], or [-chu] , all of which mean 'a person who . . .'. A number of these terms are listed below with their English equivalents in parentheses. Similar Japanese expressions, when available, are provided in brackets.

-aa
teefaa (joker)
turubayaa [manuke] (blockhead)
gachimayaa [kuishinbō] (glutton)
yukacchaa [kizoku] (nobles)
ashibaa [asobinin] (play boy)
yoogaraa [yaseppochi] (skinny person)
nachibusaa [nakimushi] (cry baby)
rikiyaa [dekiru hito] (clever person)
tanchaa [tankimono]
    (short-tempered person)

afaa [ahō] (fool)
niibuyaa (sleepyhead)
yukusaa [usotsuki] (lier)
danpachaa [tokoya] (barber)
hingaa (dirty person)
wajiyaa (angry person)
huraa [baka] (stupid person)
haru achaa [hyakushō] (farmer)
umuyaa [koibito] (lover)

-mun
shikamun [okubyō] (coward)

waayanamun [warui hito]
    (bad person)

-chu
uekinchu [kanemochi] (rich person)

shimanchu [shimano hito]
    (islander)

-guwaashii (suffix meaning 'a person pretending to be ...')
shiijaaguwaashii (a person pretending to be old)

Personal pronouns, kinship terms

munchuu (relatives)
waa (I)
anmaa (Mom)

uchinaamuukuu (son-in-law from outside)
yaa (you)
shiijaa (elders)

Body parts and physical appearance

chiburu [atama] (head)
chiimagaa (big breasts)
churakaagii [bijin]
    (pretty woman)

meegoosaa [genkotsu] (fist)
shimajiraa [shimagao] (island face)
miibuu (absess in the corner of
    the eye)

Animal and plant names

piituu [iruka] (dolphin)
waa [buta] (pig)
gooyaa [nigauri] (gourd)
jiimaami [piinattsu]
    (peanuts)

hiijaa [yagi] (goat)
mayaa [neko] (cat)
naabeeraa [hechima] (sponge cucumber)
sunui [mozuku]
    (*Spermatochnaceae* seaweed)

Cooking terms

maasu [shio] (salt)
irichaa [itame] (stir fry)

anda [abura] (oil)
ajikuutaa (strong taste)

Feelings

Many of the Okinawan expressions concerning feelings of compassion shared and cherished in Okinawan society are compounds containing the term *chimu*, which means liver. *Chimu* is a cognate of the word *kimo* in standard Japanese, which is used in expressions concerning courage or spirit, as in *kimo ni meijiru* (engraved on the heart [literally liver]) and *kimo wo tsubusu* (be terrified out of one's senses [literally, to destroy one's liver]). Some of the Okinawan expressions incorporating *chimu* are listed here.

chimugukuru (affection)   *chimu gurisan* (feel sorry for, sympathize)
chimuiri (heartfelt)   *chimuyamii* (heartache)
chimudondon (heartbeat)   *chimunjasun* (compassion)

Okinawan customs, traditions and religious terms

yuimaaru (harmony)   *kajimayaa* (the 97th anniversary of
yuta (psychic)   one's birth)
tootoome (memorial tablet)   *ugan* [*ogami*] (prayer)
utaki (sacred place)   *unjami* (god of the sea)
mooashibi (kind of a   *hinpun* (screen wall to keep out
    beach party)   evil spirits)
suuji (celebration)

Diminutives

The suffix *-gwaa* is a diminutive that can be attached to many nouns, as in the following examples. The Japanese terms shown in brackets here are the stem words without the diminutive.

shimagwaa [*shima*] (islet)   *tanagwaa* [*tana*] (small shelf)
shiruugwaa [*shiro*] (little white one)

Verbs, adjectives, other inflected terms

kamii [*tabero*] (eat!)   *butturuu* [*deppatteiru*] (sticking out)
kwaasattan (be cheated)   *nadaguruguruu* (weep)
abiree (speak up)   *geren* (stupid)
magii (big)   *hagoo* (dirty)
chura [*kirei*] (beautiful)

Emphatics, interjections, etc.

akisamiyoo (oh, no!)   *chaa* (always)
miikusuppi (a tiny bit)   *chibariyoo* [*ganbare*] (cheer up)
hasshi (when surprised)   *shittaihyaa* [*yatta*]
yami (suffix for a question)   (yeah! well done!)

> *kurusarindoo* (you'll be
>   beaten up)
> *shini* (very)
> *jiraa* [*mitaina*] (... like)
> *too* (now, then; oh!)

> *haisai* (hello)
> *kusuu* (very bad)
> *saaranai* (at once)
> *annii* (isn't it?)

Apparent cognates with different meanings

There are many Okinawan words in common use which have Japanese cognates with slightly different meanings. Often Okinawans use them when speaking Japanese without really recognising the differences. A few are shown in Table 2 with the apparent cognate and its English equivalent.

It should also be mentioned that there are differences between Okinawan usage and standard Japanese in terms of pragmatics. Okinawan languages traditionally have no formulaic expressions of greetings such as *Ohayō* (Good morning) and *Kon'nichiwa* (Good day; Hello). Instead, in Okinawan languages the other's actions are mentioned, as in the morning greeting *ukimisoochi* [literally, 'You got up'] (Nakamoto, 1982). These habits are changing now, though Japanese from the mainland still sometimes misunderstand Okinawans, claiming that 'they do not greet properly' because of this difference in pragmatic language use.

Okinawanised Japanese: *Uchinaa-Yamatoguchi*

Although great efforts have been made by the school system and many Okinawans themselves to instil use of the language officially recognised as '*hyōjungo*' (standard Japanese), in fact, the 'standard Japanese' used in

Table 2 Apparent Okinawan/Japanese cognates with different modern meanings

Okinawan Term (English Equivalent)	Apparent Japanese Cognate (English Equivalent)	Actual Japanese Equivalent
ganjuu (strong, healthy)	*ganjō* (strongly built)	*kenkō*
wata (belly)	*wata* (guts)	*hara*
jootoo (good)	*jōtō* (excellent quality)	*ii*
ippee (really)	*ippai* (full, lots)	*hontō*
deeji (very)	*daiji* (important)	*totemo*
chiri (rubbish)	*chiri* (dust)	*gomi*
nakami (guts)	*nakami* (contents)	*motsu*
nishi (north)	*nishi* (west)	*kita*
teegee (easygoing)	*taigai* (mostly)	*iikagen*

Okinawa is heavily influenced by Okinawan languages. It is partly the result of efforts by the older generation to imitate standard Japanese without much formal training. The Japanese spoken by the majority of Okinawans at present is called *Uchinaa-Yamatoguchi*: 'Okinawan Japanese'.

Pronunciation

Uchinaa-Yamatoguchi has distinctive pronunciation characteristics that derive from the difference in the phonemic systems of Okinawan languages and standard Japanese. While standard Japanese has five vowels (/a/, /i/, /u/, /e/, /o/) Okinawan languages generally have three vowels (e.g. /a/, /i/, /u/ in Naha), although there are four in some areas. Thus, in Okinawan languages, one vowel sound is used to represent two different vowels in standard Japanese, as shown in Figure 1.

Because of this difference between Japanese and Okinawan languages, mixtures of the vowels from the Japanese and Okinawan systems is sometimes observed in *Uchinaa-Yamatoguchi*. The /u/ sound in Okinawan languages corresponds to both the /o/ and /u/ sounds in standard Japanese, so hyper correction is occasionally seen in the 'standard Japanese' spoken in Okinawa. For example, the word *udewa* (bracelet) in standard Japanese is pronounced *odewa*, while *suwaru* (sit) in standard Japanese becomes *sowaru* in *Uchinaa-Yamatoguchi*. Moreover, the /e/ sound in standard Japanese is often pronounced with an on-glide [j], so that *eigo* (English) in standard Japanese becomes [*jeigo*] in *Uchinaa-Yamatoguchi*.

Uchinaa-Yamatoguchi also shows the influence of Okinawan consonant systems. For example, since [d] and [r] are allophones in some of the Okinawan dialects, they are often interchanged in *Uchinaa-Yamatoguchi*. Thus, *rippa* (excellent) in standard Japanese is often pronounced *dippa*, *rōsoku* (candle) becomes *doosoku*, and *karada* (body) may be pronounced *karara*. Similarly, the [k] and [g] sounds are sometimes interchanged by Okinawans, so that *kani* (crab) in standard Japanese is pronounced *gani* and *kujira* (whale) becomes *gujira* in *Uchinaa-Yamatoguchi*. In some areas, the [k] and [g] sounds can be pronounced [kwa] and [gwa] in *Uchinaa-Yamatoguchi*, so that the standard Japanese word for company — *kaisha* becomes *kwaisa* and *gaikoku* (foreign country) is pronounced *gwaikoku*. Moreover, although standard Japanese does not combine the [t] sound with [i] or [u], (having the

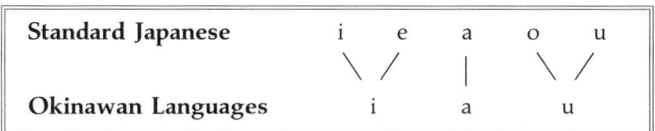

Figure 1 Vowel correspondences between standard Japanese and Okinawan languages

Table 3 Lexical differences between standard Japanese and *Uchinaa-Yamatoguchi*[8]

Uchinaa-Yamatoguchi	Standard Japanese	(English Equivalent)
hajii	*kaze*	(wind)
tui	*tori*	(bird)
pushi	*hoshi*	(star)
chichi	*tsuki*	(month)
mii	*me*	(eye)
chu	*hito*	(person)
nuu	*nani*	(what)
chuu	*kyō*	(today)

sounds ['chi'] and ['tsu'] instead), in *Uchinaa-Yamatoguchi*, as in Okinawan languages, [t] may occur in front of [i] or [u], as it does in the word *piituu* (dolphin). Similarly, [f], which does not occur in standard Japanese, is also heard in *Uchinaa-Yamatoguchi*: e.g. *afaa* (a fool).

Lexicon

A number of common words used in Okinawa differ from those used on the mainland, though in many cases, these terms are cognates whose Okinawan pronunciation differs from that of standard Japanese. Examples of lexical differences between standard Japanese and *Uchinaa-Yamatoguchi* are shown in Table 3.

Usage

As mentioned above, Okinawans are often not aware of the distinction between their version of 'Japanese', which they call *Uchinaa-Yamatoguchi*, and the mainland variety. There are many words and expressions used in *Uchinaa-Yamatoguchi* which, much like the apparent cognates in Okinawan languages discussed above, have the same form as standard Japanese terms but have a different meaning or use than the *Yamato* (mainland) equivalent. Some examples are explained below.

Words indicating aspects or moods

A number of verb inflections and words indicating aspect and mood have different uses in standard Japanese and *Uchinaa-Yamatoguchi*. *Hazu*, for example, is used on the mainland when something is 'due, scheduled, or supposed to occur', indicating a high degree of probability. However, in *Uchinaa-Yamatoguchi*, it is used to indicate a much lower degree of certainty – closer to 'probably' or 'may ...'. The phrase *kuru hazu*, for example, is used in *Uchinaa-Yamatoguchi* in much the same way as a similar Okinawan phrase, *chuuruhaji*, which means 'may come', while on the mainland, *kuru hazu* means 'supposed to come' or 'due to come'.

On the mainland, the auxiliaries *mashō*, *yō* and *ō* are often combined with the particle *ne* after a verb at the end of a sentence and used to make a suggestion like *ikimashō ne* ('Let's go'). However, the meaning of this combination is different in Okinawa, where it is used to indicate the speaker's will or volution, so that *ikimashō ne* means 'I will go' in *Uchinaa-Yamatoguchi*. This same construction is also used to make an informal request in *Uchinaa-Yamatoguchi*. Thus, depending upon the context, *ikimashō ne* may mean 'Please go.' Likewise, *kariyō ne* can be used to make an informal request to borrow something ('Lend this to me, will you?') in *Uchinaa-Yamatoguchi*, whereas to make this type of request on the mainland, one would use the phrase *kashite ne*.

Moreover, in standard Japanese, the noun *wake* means 'reason, cause or circumstance' and is used at the end of a sentence that explains why something happened or what a situation is. However, in Okinawa, *wake* is often used at the end of a sentence even when the speaker is not explaining causes or circumstances; instead it adds emphasis or finality, as in the statement *ii da wake* ('It is all right'). In standard Japanese, one might say, *ii no da* or *ii desu* under similar circumstances.

The auxiliary verb *iru* (be) is also used with a slight difference in *Uchinaa-Yamatoguchi*. When combined with another verb, *iru* generally makes a present or progressive in standard Japanese, but in Okinawa it is combined with verbs in cases where the perfect tense indicator *ta* would be used in standard Japanese. For example, an Okinawan might say *Jūgo-nin mo kite-ita* where someone from the mainland would say *Jūgo-nin mo kita* (Fifteen people came). Similarly, *Koko ni kite kara kenkō ni natte iruyo* would be used to say 'I have become healthy since I came here' in *Uchinaa-Yamatoguchi*. The Okinawan phrase sounds strange in standard Japanese, as it would be taken to mean 'I am getting healthy since I came here.' Instead, *Koko ni kite kara kenkō ni nattayo* would be used to say the same thing in standard Japanese.

In addition, *Uchinaa-Yamatoguchi* has two ways to indicate possibility (in contrast to one in standard Japanese) and there is a distinction in their meaning. The auxiliary *rareru* is used when external conditions make something possible, and means 'it's possible to ...', while *kireru* is used to express individual capability, and means 'be able to ...'. In *Uchinaa-Yamatoguchi*, *taberareru* ('We can eat [now]') is used when food is ready to eat, while *tabekireru* ('We can eat it [all]') is used when people are capable of consuming the food (because they have large enough appetites). In standard Japanese, the auxiliary *rareru* would be used in both cases.

Particles and demonstratives

Another difference between standard Japanese and *Uchinaa-Yamato-guchi* is seen in the use of particles and demonstratives. For example, the particle *kara*, which usually means 'from' or 'since' in standard Japanese, is used to mean 'as' or 'because' in Okinawa where it would not be needed in standard Japanese: e.g. *Ijimerarete kara naite ita* (She cried because she was bullied) in contrast to *Ijimerarete naita* (Being bullied, she cried) in mainland Japanese.

Moreover, *kara* is sometimes used in Okinawa where *wo* or *de* would be used in standard Japanese, as in the following sentences: *Michi kara aruku* (walk in the street), which would be *michi wo aruku* in standard Japanese, and *hikōki kara kita* (came by plane), which would be *hikōki de kita* on the mainland.

Double particles are sometimes heard in Okinawa where only one would be used on the mainland. For example, an Okinawan might say *Doko ni ga ii ka* (Where should I put it?) where a Tokyoite would say *Doko ga iika*. Similarly, an Okinawan might say *Yaa ga wa ie kara deta* (You left your house) where mainland Japanese would say *Anata wa ie wo deta*.

Another difference between *Uchinaa-Yamatoguchi* and standard Japanese lies in the usage of such verb pairs as *iku* (go) and *kuru* (come), or *ageru* (give) and *kureru* (receive), in which perspective is important. In standard Japanese, the choice of which verb to use is based on the speaker's perspective (whether the action is moving/directed towards the speaker or away from the speaker). Thus, in standard Japanese the verb *kuru* (come) is used only when someone or something moves toward the speaker, or more precisely, toward the speaker's domain. If the speaker is going to visit the listener, s/he would say, *Ima kara ikuyo* (I'm going now). However, Okinawans can say *Ima kara kuruyo* (I'm coming [to your place or where you are] now), an expression which is not acceptable in standard Japanese.

Words used with different meanings

As was mentioned above, there are many words in Okinawan languages that are the same as or similar to words in standard Japanese, but that have slightly different meanings. In much the same way, there are many words in the Okinawan variety of Japanese (*Uchinaa-Yamatoguchi*) that are used with slightly different meanings. A list of some of these terms, most of which are close enough to standard Japanese to make the difference barely noticeable, is provided in Table 4.

New Developments in *Uchinaa-Yamatoguchi*

The above examples of differences in pronunciation, lexicon and usage between Okinawan Japanese and standard Japanese are indicative of the residual influence Okinawan languages exert on the community as it is undergoing language shift. Although I have explained these differences in

Table 4 Words with different meanings in *Uchinaa-Yamatoguchi* and Japanese

Word	Meaning in Uchinaa-Yamatoguchi	Meaning in Standard Japanese	Actual Japanese Equivalent
aruku	go around, commute, work	walk	*iku*
*hizamazuki**	sit properly	kneel	*seiza*
katai	strong taste	hard	*koi*
amai	weak taste	sweet	*usuaji*
yagate	almost, dangerously	eventually	*ayauku*
korosu	hit	kill	*tataku*
awateru	hurry	panic	*isogu*
*yomu***	count	read	*kazoeru*
haku	put on (clothes)	put on (trousers or socks)	*kiru*
yabureru	break	tear	*kowareru*
yasui	easy	cheap	*yasashii; yasui* means easy only in a compound with a verbal stem, as in *tabeyasui* (easy to eat).

*Follows usage of Okinawan term *fishamanchishun*.
**Editor's note: The author is contrasting Okinawan usage with standard Japanese. However, it should be noted that many of Japan's 'dialects' share expressions and usages. For example, even as far north and east as the Kansai area, the verb *yomu* is used to mean 'count' as well as 'read', just as it is in *Uchinaa-Yamatoguchi*.

great detail, it must be stressed that language use in Okinawa today is far from stable. *Uchinaa-Yamatoguchi* is subject to assimilation to standard Japanese through the effects of the standardised education system, the mass media, and expanding contact with mainlanders.

This phenomenon resembles the process of de-creolisation, which can be observed when a creole and the colonisers' language (generally a European language) are in a continued state of contact and the creole continues to become increasingly like the latter, which is seen as the more prestigious language. We can observe a similar continuum of languages along the line extending from the Okinawan vernaculars through *Uchinaa-Yamatoguchi* to standard Japanese.

Although the language in Okinawa is approaching standard Japanese, movement is not entirely one-directional. Young Okinawans have also coined many expressions using Okinawan morphological devices. As indicated in the survey, many feel a strong attachment to their parents' language and wish to learn it. However, few have the ability to use it freely, as attested to by the fact that none of the respondents in my survey claimed much proficiency in it. The study by Ono and Hokama (explained above and reported in Ono, 1995) also suggested a lack of confidence on the part of young Okinawans in speaking Okinawan languages as well as standard Japanese. Perhaps to relieve this tension between their attachment to their heritage language and their inability to speak it, young Okinawans have created their own version of *Uchinaa-Yamatoguchi*, one that older people say 'isn't Okinawan', but which nonetheless reflects the young people's desire to assert their identity as Okinawans.

The survey questionnaire elicited examples of this type of expression. It asked subjects to 'give words or expressions heard around you which you think are different from standard Japanese but not Okinawan either.' It also asked the respondents to distinguish between 'special expressions used among young people' and those 'used by everybody'. Finally, it instructed subjects to explain the origins of these words if they 'know or can guess' them. The responses indicated that the respondents recognised the existence of certain expressions that are used among the youth. It was also clear that they sometimes use these expressions without really knowing what they mean.

This new language mixture is growing rapidly, continually adding new vocabulary. Some of the new words are absorbed from the mass media. Some English expressions are acquired from the American military personnel stationed in Okinawa. Other words are introduced by mainlander students, whose presence is continually increasing at Okinawan universities.[9] Thus the language of Okinawan youth today includes a lot of the slang that is popular on the mainland, while maintaining an Okinawan tint. One of its distinctive features is the creation of a variety of hybrids including standard Japanese words with Okinawan inflections. Examples of some of the new developments in the language used by Okinawan youth are presented below.

Suffixes: *-aa* and *-gwaa*

As explained above in the section 'Okinawan Words and Expressions in Use Today', many of the Okinawan expressions still in use contain the suffix *-aa*, which means 'a person who . . .' One of the ways Okinawan youth are developing new expressions with an Okinawan flavour is by adding this suffix to standard Japanese words to create new nouns that describe various types of people. Some examples of this trend are: *hattaraa* ('lier', from the Japanese word *hattari*, which means 'bluff'), *shittakaa* ('someone who pretends to know', from the Japanese word for pretending: *shittakaburi*), *kusaraa* ('a sulker', from *kusaru*, which means 'to feel depressed or blue'), *inchikaa* ('a trickster', from *inchiki*, the Japanese word for trickery or deception), *kuruma mucchaa* ('a car owner', from *kuruma* and *motsu* the Japanese words for 'car' and 'own', respectively), and a*merikaa* ('an American').

It is interesting to note that the 'wannabe' fans of Amuro Namie, an Okinawan native who has become one of the mainland's most popular female pop vocalists, are known as *'Amuraas'* in the mainland Japanese mass media. This naming was possibly derived in the same way as the expressions above, the Okinawan suffix *-aa* having been added to a truncated version of the singer's family name, Amuro, to create the term for 'a person who (wants to be) Amuro'. If this is indeed the origin of this term, it would be a case of reverse linguistic influence, moving from Okinawan languages into standard Japanese.

In either case, another Okinawan suffix mentioned above in the section 'Okinawan words and expressions in use today', the diminutive suffix *-gwaa*, is also attached to many Japanese nouns to create new terms used by Okinawan youth. Among those reported by the survey subjects were: *amegwaa* ('little rain', from *ame*, the standard Japanese word for rain); *orikoogwaa* ('a good little boy', from *orikō*, a good boy), and *sukoshigwaa* ('a tiny bit', from *sukoshi*, the standard Japanese word for a little).

Okinawan verbs and adjectives with Japanese morphology

Another way Okinawan youth are creating words is by using the stems of Okinawan verbs and adjectives and adding Japanese inflections. A list of such expressions gathered from the survey and other research appears below, followed by the English equivalent in parentheses.

abishiteiru (shout)	*wajiwajiisuru* (get irritated)
yuntakusuru (have a group talk)	*chanpuruu* (mix)
hingasu (let escape)	*niriru* (get tired)
shikabu (be surprised)	*sugaru* (dress up)
kanihanjiru (grow senile)	*yaasagamiisuru* (eat like a glutton)
daaru (that's right; it is so)	*yamasu* (hurt)
ihuuna [*henna*] (strange)	*yaasai* (hungry)
hogasu (dig a hole)	*duugurushii* (feeling uneasy)
anmasai (troublesome, tiring)	*hiisai* (cold)
umusai (interesting)	*chimui* (pitiful)

Other borrowings

Although Japanese itself has a great many words it has borrowed from English, there are a few English loan words that are unique to Okinawa. Among these are *paaraa* (the word 'parlor' used to mean 'a stall'), *biichi paatii* (beach party — used to connote a barbecue on the beach), and *takoraisu* (rice with tacos). One interesting new term actually combines the

English word 'rich' with the Okinawan suffix *-aa*: many young Okinawans use *ricchaa* to refer to 'a rich person'.

Okinawan youth also use many words borrowed from mainland slang. These include *chō* ... (super ...), *mecchaa* (very), *habuu* (ostracise, an outcast), *dasadasa* (country bumpkin, boorish), *kebai* (meritricious), *nanigeni* (in a casual manner), *mukatsuku* (feel angry – literally 'feel nauseous'), *maji* (really, [I] mean it), *misudō* (Mr Doughnuts [the fast food chain]), and *takuru* (take a taxi).

Resurgence of Ethnic Identity and Language

At the same time that the youth of Okinawa have been developing their own creative mixture of Okinawan languages, standard Japanese and a sprinkling of English words, the image of Okinawa has been undergoing a major transformation.

Since the reversion of Okinawa to Japan in 1972, there has been a gradual resurgence of Okinawan identity and pride. The mass media, especially the Okinawan branch of Japan's public broadcasting network, NHK, have played a major role in highlighting the distinctiveness of Okinawan culture and giving it respectability in the eyes of mainland Japanese as well as Okinawans.

Another source of ethnic pride has been the return of overseas Okinawan emigrants. During the early years of this century, vast numbers of Okinawans emigrated to other countries. It is now estimated that about 270,000 people (Okinawan natives and their offspring) live abroad (Okinawan Prefectural Government, 1996). Recently, many of these expatriates have either returned themselves or are sending their children back home. Universities and local Japanese language institutions in Okinawa admit dozens of such students, mainly from South America, each year.

In 1990, the First International Convention for Overseas *Uchinaanchu* was held to commemorate the 90th anniversary of the beginning of emigration from Okinawa. Seeing 'Okinawans' from around the world, many wearing the national costumes of their adopted countries, boosted Okinawan pride and made the Ryukyuans feel less isolated (Taira, 1997: 167).

I personally witnessed the effect of these return visits during the Second International Convention for Overseas *Uchinaanchu*, which was held in 1995. Approximately 3500 visitors came from 29 countries and areas from around the world to attend this event (Okinawan Prefectural Government, 1996). The whole of Okinawa enthusiastically welcomed them, with tens of thousands of participants in different events. Students, especially those from overseas, as well as learners of Spanish and Portuguese, all worked together to make this convention successful. This occasion helped build pride in both local and overseas Okinawans. I was impressed, at the same time, by the very 'authentic' Okinawan language spoken by these returnees.

Another boost to Okinawan pride came in 1992 when NHK began airing shows on Okinawan culture to commemorate the 20th anniversary of the reversion of the islands to Japan. In addition to traditional art forms, these programmes introduced Okinawan pop music to mainland audiences. As a result, several well-known Okinawan groups achieved national fame, including Kina Shokichi and the Nenes. The most well-known of these groups is the Rinken Band, which sings songs written in an Okinawan language and incorporating the traditional Okinawan musical scale. One of its songs with Okinawan lyrics, *Haru-dee-mun*, was included in a Japanese language textbook for second year junior high school students published in 1993 (*Japan Times*, Naito, 1992).

The use by these pop groups of the Okinawan lute called the *sanshin* led to mainland concerts by traditional Okinawan musicians, including sanshin master Kadekaru Rinsho, who is known as the 'godfather of island songs' (*Japan Times*, Fisher, 1994).

In addition to this boom in Okinawan music, people on the mainland have become increasingly interested in Okinawa as it is introduced through literature, comics, artifacts, arts and various other Okinawan products. Okinawa has produced a number of prominent scholars or writers, including Iha Huyu and Yamanoguchi Baku. The area and its culture have also been introduced through mainland literature by writers such as Yanagita Kunio, Orikuchi Shinobu, and Nobel Prize winner Oe Kenzaburo. In recent years, Okinawan writers have been especially successful, with Oshiro Tatsuhiro, Matayoshi Eiki and Medoruma Shun winning the Akutagawa Prize, the nation's highest award for literature.

In 1997, the Third International Symposium on Okinawan Studies was held in both Naha and Sydney on the occasion of the 25th anniversary of Okinawa's reversion to Japan. The success of the symposium proved that interest in Okinawan culture, language, and environment extends far beyond the prefecture's borders.

In addition to such positive evaluation of its culture and talent, Okinawa also attracted attention after frequent crimes and accidents related to American forces stationed there were unveiled, starting in 1995 with international coverage of the rape of a 12-year-old Okinawan girl by three American soldiers stationed in the prefecture. Concern developed nationwide when it was pointed out that the islands house 75% of the US military facilities in the country.

Okinawans began demanding that the mainland provide relief from this heavy burden by getting the US to move some of its military facilities out of the prefecture. As the protests continued and former Governor Ota of Okinawa succeeded in getting concessions from the national government and plenty of attention from the mass media, people in Okinawa seemed to gain confidence in expressing what they feel and want.

Revival of cultural activities, success of popular musicians

Renewed confidence – culturally and politically – on the part of the Okinawan people has led to a revival of traditional arts and culture that has spread beyond the borders of the prefecture. In addition to well-known Okinawan-born martial arts such as karate, and the fame of Okinawan world champion boxer Gushiken Yoko, the Okinawan *kachaashii* folk dance, *eisaa*[10] dance and drum music, and Ryukyu *Buyo* (dance) have been introduced on TV and by other media. Ryukyu *Buyo* and traditional Okinawan martial arts were also performed at the Sydney Opera House in 1997 in connection with the International Symposium on Okinawan Studies. These artists are now increasingly receiving invitations to perform both within and outside Japan.

Traditional crafts such as *bingata* dyeing and exotic Okinawan foods have also been introduced to mainland Japanese through Okinawan fairs held at department stores and other venues throughout Japan.

Moreover, while the popularity of Okinawan music remains high on the mainland, a number of new-age pop singers from Okinawa have also become popular. Among those claiming the greatest success are Amuro Namie (mentioned earlier in connection with the Okinawanised term for her fans), Chinen Rina, Ishimine Satoko, South-American born Diamantes, Speed and Max. The music of these national rock icons does not bear any hint of Okinawa; in fact, they are not generally even recognised as being from Okinawa. They have gained national recognition without relying on their 'difference'. However, their success, in its own way, has also boosted the confidence of young Okinawans.

Language as expression of identity and pride

The increased self-assurance discussed so far has also given Okinawans a chance to reconsider the importance of their language. In many parts of Okinawa, including Miyakojima, Okinawan speech contests and recitations of Okinawan folk tales are held to encourage the use of Okinawan languages.

There are also radio programmes featuring talks in Okinawan languages: either chats mixed with standard Japanese, or 'let's learn *Uchinaaguchi*' type lessons. An Okinawan comedy group, Shochiku Kagekidan, attracts both Okinawan and mainland audiences by comically mixing Japanese with Okinawan language.

Okinawan literature has also taken a new direction. Where earlier Okinawan writers opted to use standard Japanese in their works, even in stories with Okinawan settings and themes, more recent authors like Matayoshi Eiki show less inhibition in using vernacular expressions in their writings. Ikegami Eiichi even used Okinawan in a fantasy novel. In doing so, however, these authors have to wrestle with the questions of how much

Okinawan language they can use without hindering their readers' comprehension and what devices they can develop to facilitate understanding. They need to decide whether to put Japanese *kana* alongside Okinawan words to impart their meaning, provide annotations in footnotes, or offer no support at all.

One way around this dilemma was developed by Nakaima Tsuyoshi: he tells stories of Okinawan baseball players in comic books. Although his characters use Okinawan vernaculars, the language is fairly readable and the meaning easy to guess, as it is accompanied by illustrations and also includes many interjections such as *akisamiyoo* (Oh, my god!).

Such use of Okinawa's vernacular languages, whether spoken or written, is significant, as it carries the essence of the people's lifestyle and feelings, which cannot really be translated into standard Japanese.

Conclusion

Perhaps it is inevitable that many languages in the world are used less frequently than in the past. However, the survival of a language depends largely on how conscious its speakers are of their language and how hard they strive to preserve their culture and traditions and maintain their identity.

In the case of Okinawa, the language generally spoken now is no longer the same as the vernaculars spoken by earlier generations. Older Okinawans felt inferior to mainland Japanese and tried hard to catch up with them, in part by switching to standard Japanese. The result was the onset of language shift, with a continuum of language use extending from the original Okinawan vernaculars, through the Okinawanised version of standard Japanese known as *Uchinaa-Yamatoguchi*, and on to standard Japanese. In a phenomenon resembling the process of de-creolisation, *Uchinaa-Yamatoguchi* was seen to be moving towards standard Japanese due to the effects of the standardised education system, the mass media, and expanding contact with mainlanders.

However, the older generation is being replaced by a younger generation who have greater assurance in their ethnic identity, even though they did not have their heritage language transmitted to them. This may well be the result of the more positive image of Okinawa and its culture that has developed during the nineties. The language of Okinawa has therefore entered a new phase, reflecting greater self-confidence. It expresses the feelings of young people, strongly attached to Okinawan traditions and culture but aware of the changing nature of society — young people who are striving to forge a new identity as Okinawans. Though many traditional words and expressions have died out, their *Uchinaa-Yamatoguchi* still maintains a strong flavour of Okinawan vernaculars. By creatively mixing standard Japanese with elements of Okinawan languages and a sprinkling of English, they have given their *Uchinaa-Yamatoguchi* great vitality. This new style of speaking serves to unite people of various backgrounds and make them feel 'Okinawan'.

Acknowledgements

This is a revised version of 'Languages in Changing Societies: New Caledonia and Okinawa', which was published as a working paper in *Tokyo Joshi Daigaku Kiyo*, No. 48, 1998. I would like to thank Mary Goebel Noguchi for her valuable suggestions and her help in rewriting it to fit this volume. I would also like to thank Ms Miyagi Shizu of Ogimi, Ms Tonaki Kazue of Nakijin, Mr Kamiya Yoshimasa of Itoman, my students at Meio University, especially Mr Nagahama Munetaka, and the many others who helped me during my research in Okinawa.

Notes

1. Hanihara (1994: 50) reported that recent studies comparing ancient bones and modern Japanese on the basis of anatomy, specific viruses, DNA and other factors revealed their basic similarity. According to him, Okinawans and Ainu retain the prototypical characteristics of Jomon people, while people of eastern Japan, especially from Hokkaido and the Tohoku area, as well as those of southern Kyushu, also show higher rates of retention of these ancient characteristics. In contrast, people of western Japan generally have mixed features, probably gained through intermarriage with later immigrants who came from China and Korea between around 300 BC and 700 AD. These later arrivals, generally refugees from frequent warfare on the continent and the Korean peninsula, immigrated to western Japan in several waves (Hanihara, 1994: 52). Hanihara calls the division between these people of mixed genes in the west and the people with older characteristics in the east 'bipolarization' (Hanihara, 1994: 57–58). According to him this dual structure is also observed in the distribution of animals (e.g. dogs and mice) in Japan.

2. For example, [ha] (tooth) in standard Japanese has the following cognates: [ha] in Amami, [ha:] in Shuri, [p'a:] in Nakijin, [hwa:] in Kakeroma. Cognates of [hune] (boat) include: [huni] in Shuri, [p'uni] in Nakijin, [funi] in Miyako, [uni] in Ishigaki (Uemura,1994; Hokama, 1989: 101–102).

3. Dixon (1997: 7–8) refers to the two different senses of the word 'language'. Okinawan languages are dialects 'in the political sense', but languages 'in the linguistic sense'.

4. There were also active exchanges of people between Okinawa and China. Many Chinese scholars, politicians, artists, and scientists left their names in Okinawan history, contributing to the society and its cultural and scientific progress (Takara and Dana, 1993).

5. In 1940 there was a big controversy over the standardisation of language in Okinawa. A delegation from the mainland expressed their concern over the disappearance of the traditional Okinawan languages, but the Okinawan prefectural government reportedly asked for the thorough standardisation of the language anyway (Hokama, 1989).

6. A comprehensive dictionary, *Okinawa nakijingo jiten* was compiled in1983 by Nakasone Seizen and published by Kadokawa shoten. The Shuri and Nakijin dialects (as well as some others) show a high number of honorific expressions that had developed because of social class distinctions formed under the warrior class.

7. The words in this section were collected by the writer in Nakijin.

8. The data are based on Uemura (1989).
9. Around 42% of the freshmen at the University of the Ryukyus are from outside Okinawa.
10. *Eisaa* is traditionally performed during the Bon Festival. Since around 1956, it has been recognised as an independent performing art (Terauchi, 1992).

Appendix

Questionnaire (translated into English)

Please check where it is appropriate, or fill in the blank.
Age: _____

You were born in:
Okinawa _____, Kyushu _____, Other parts of Japan _____,
Overseas _____

You can speak Okinawan (*Uchinaaguchi*):
very well _____, fairly well _____, well _____,
a little _____, only very little _____, not at all _____

You can understand Okinawan (*Uchinaaguchi*) when spoken to:
very well _____, fairly well _____, well _____,
partly _____, hardly _____

You use generally at home:
Okinawan (*Uchinaaguchi*) _____, Uchinaa-Yamatoguchi _____,
Yamatoguchi (standard Japanese) _____

You use generally with friends:
Okinawan (*Uchinaaguchi*) _____, Uchinaa-Yamatoguchi _____,
Yamatoguchi (standard Japanese) _____

When you hear Okinawan (*Uchinaaguchi*) spoken, when is it?

What do you feel about Okinawan (*Uchinaaguchi*)?
Okinawan should be spoken more often. _____
I am interested in Okinawan, and would like to learn and use it if I could. _____
Okinawan is the language of elderly people. _____
We had better learn standard Japanese rather than Okinawan. _____
It is not useful any more in modern society. _____

When you use Okinawan expressions or *Uchinaa-Yamatoguchi*, what is the reason?
Okinawan is our traditional language that should be maintained. _____
We can express ourselves better using them. _____
I feel I am an Okinawan. _____
It keeps people together; we feel we are comrades. _____

What do you feel about recent *Uchinaa-Yamatoguchi* expressions used by young people?

_____

Please give words or expressions in Okinawan which you use or hear sometimes.
If possible, please explain the meanings of them, too.

_____

Please give words or expressions heard around you which you think are different from standard Japanese but not Okinawan either. Are they special expressions used among young people, or used by everybody? If you know or can guess the origins of these words, please write them.

Please give your opinions about the use of Okinawan or *Uchinaa-Yamatoguchi*, and the recent expressions used among Okinawan young people.

Thank you very much for your cooperation.

References

Chamberlain, B.H. (1895) Essay in aid of a grammar and dictionary of the Luchuan language. *Transactions of the Asiatic Society of Japan*, Vol. 3 Supplement.

Dixon, R.M.W. (1991) The endangered languages of Australia, Indonesia and Oceania. In Robert H. Robins and Eugenius M. Uhlenbeck (eds) *Endangered Languages* (pp. 229–55). Oxford, UK: Berg.

Dixon, R.M.W. (1997) *The Rise and Fall of Languages*. Cambridge, UK: Cambridge University Press.

Fishman, J.A. (1991) *Reversing Language Shift*. Clevedon, UK: Multilingual Matters.

Hanihara K. (1994) *Okinawa no hito* [The People of Okinawa]. In Committee for the International Symposium on Okinawa Studies on the Occasion of the 20th Anniversary of Okinawa's Reversion to Japan (ed.) *Okinawa bunka no genryū wo saguru* [In Search of the Root of Okinawan Culture] (pp. 49–60). Naha: Bunshin insatsu.

Hokama, S. (1989) *Okinawa no rekishi to bunka* [The History and Culture of Okinawa]. Tokyo: Chuko shinsho.

Hokama, S. (1995) *Nanto no jojo* [Lyric Poems of the Southern Islands]. Tokyo: Chuko bunko.

Japan Times
    (articles with by-lines)
    Fisher, P. (1994) Island songs discover new urban audience, *Japan Times* Kansai Edition, October 4.
    Naito Y. Roots vital to Rinken Band, *Japan Times*, Kansai Edition, December 31.

Kyan K. (1996) *Okinawago to kozumorojii* [The Okinawan Language and Cosmology]. *Edge* 1, 30–1.

Matsumori A. (1995) Ryukyuan: Past, present and future. In J.C. Maher and Yashiro K. (eds) *Multilingual Japan* (pp. 19–45). Clevedon, UK: Multilingual Matters.

Nakamoto M. (1992) *Tōkyō bunka to okinawa bunka* [Tokyo Culture and Okinawa Culture]. *Gengo dokuhon 1972–92* (pp. 181–187). Tokyo: Taishukan [*Gengo* special publication].

Nakamoto M. (1988) *Nihongo no genkei* [The Origins of Japanese]. Tokyo: Rikitomi shobo.

Nakasone S. (compiled) (1983) *Okinawa nakijingo jiten* [Dictionary of the Nakajin Language of Okinawa]. Tokyo: Kadokawa shoten.

Okinawan Prefectural Government (ed.) (1996) *Okinawa-ken shiryō* [Information on Okinawa Prefecture].

Ono M. (1995) *Chūkan hōgen toshite no uchinaa-yamatoguchi no isō* [Aspects of *Uchinaa-Yamatoguchi* as an Interdialect Form]. In *Henyōsuru nihon no hōgen* [Changing Japanese Dialects] (pp. 178–91). Tokyo: Taishukan [*Gengo* special publication].

Serafim, L.A. (1991) Prospects for the survival of the Ryukyuan language through standardisation. *The Ryukyuanist* 13 (Summer), 5–8.

Taira, K. (1997) Troubled national identity: The Ryukyuans/Okinawans. In M. Weiner (ed.) *Japan's Minorities: The Illusion of Homogeneity* (pp. 140–177). London and New York: Routledge.

Takaesu Y. (1994) *Uchinaa-yamatoguchi no kenkyū* [Study of Okinawan-standard Japanese]. *Okinawa gengo kenkyū sentā shiryo 117* [Okinawan Language Research Center Monograph117]. Naha: Ryukyu University.

Takara K. and Dana M. (ed.) (1993) *Ryūkyū ōkoku* [The Ryukyu Kingdom]. Tokyo: Kawade shobo shinsha.

Terauchi N. (1994) Trans-contextualization and stylistic changes of *Eisaa*. Paper presented at The Third International Symposium on Okinawan Studies, Sydney.

Uemura Y. (1989) *On'in henka wa donoyō ni shite hikiokosareruka* (2) [How phonological changes arise]. *Okinawa gengo kenkyū sentā shiryō* 79 [Okinawan Language Research Center Monograph 79]. Naha: Ryukyu University.

Uemura Y. (1994) *Ryūkyū shohōgen kara ippan gengogaku e* (From Okinawan Dialectology to General Linguistics). Paper presented at the 109th Conference of the Japan Linguistic Society. Nago, Japan.

Chapter 5

Affiliation, Not Assimilation: Resident Koreans and Ethnic Education

ANN B. CARY

Introduction

Koreans are the largest and most stable group of foreign residents of Japan. The Ministry of Justice (which controls immigration) reported that 676,793 Koreans were registered as resident foreigners in 1994. Another source indicates that the nation is home to around 700,000 Korean nationals, plus an additional 200,000 to 300,000 ethnic Koreans who have become naturalised Japanese.[1]

Most of these people are living in Japan as a direct result of Japan's pre-war policies. Japan's colonisation of the Korean peninsula and use of its people to fill labour shortages brought large numbers of Koreans to the Japanese mainland. At the end of World War II, close to 2.4 million ethnic Koreans were in the country (Ko, 1996: 83), and approximately a fifth of them remained in Japan for various reasons. Today, in addition to these 'first-generation' immigrants, many of their children, grandchildren and great-grandchildren are permanent residents of Japan.

The third- and fourth-generation Korean residents of Japan are in many ways no different from their Japanese contemporaries. Many choose to live like the Japanese. More than 91% use *tsūshōmei* (or *tsūmei*) – Japanese names similar to those which were required of Koreans during Japan's colonial control over Korea (Harajiri, 1998: 172). Moreover, their language of choice is often Japanese.

However for quite a few resident Koreans, affirming their rights as non-Japanese and valuing their heritage culture and language are a high priority. In fact, fourteen percent of the Korean children in Japan today receive their education in Korean ethnic schools, and the Korean education system is firmly rooted in the country. Almost as soon as World War II ended and Korea was liberated from imperial Japan, Koreans residing in Japan set about establishing schools to teach the Korean language. By 1948, six hundred Korean schools were reportedly operating in the country (Lee, 1981: 163). In the early years, these schools were viewed as preparation for eventual repatriation to the homeland, but more recently, their purpose appears to have shifted to helping Koreans establish their identity. The Chongryun organisation for North Korean overseas nationals in Japan and its schools continue to resist assimilation as they adjust to legal and political changes within Japan and reform the curriculum in their schools in accordance with global developments.

To provide a better idea of how the ethnic Korean education system developed in Japan and what its aims and accomplishments are, I will begin by presenting an overview of the history of Koreans in Japan, with a particular focus on postwar political groups and ethnic education, as well as an examination of Japanese attitudes towards resident Koreans. I will then report on a study of the Shikoku Korean school and suggest that the Chongryun school system has offered Koreans in Japan a way to retrieve and maintain their heritage language and assert their identity and rights within Japanese society.

Historical Overview

Status and identity of ethnic Koreans in Japan

From the earliest years of the 20th century there were Koreans in Japan, including street vendors, labourers working in the mines and on the railroads, and students (Fukuoka, 1993: 22; Ryang, 1997: 6). After Japan annexed Korea in 1910, however, the number of ethnic Koreans coming to work and live in Japan steadily increased, with migration facilitated by their newly acquired (second-class)[2] Japanese citizenship. By 1924 there were 120,238 ethnic Koreans residing on the mainland (Home Ministry Security Office figures quoted in Ko, 1996: 83). Most came from the southern part of the Korean peninsula, while people from northern Korea seeking work tended to go to Manchuria, which was also controlled by Japan at the time. The descendants of the latter group now comprise the 1.8 million Korean-Chinese in China (Fukuoka, 1993: 23). As Japan expanded its military movement in China from 1937 on, Korean labourers and military draftees were forced to work as subjects of imperial Japan and support its war efforts. For some, this meant forced migration to factories, mines and construction worksites on the mainland. By 1945, there were 2,365,263 ethnic Koreans in Japan (Home Ministry Security Office figures quoted in Ko, 1996: 83).

Immediately after World War II, these Koreans faced a choice of returning to their homeland or staying in Japan. By early 1946, around 1.9 million (approximately 80%) had returned to Korea (Ryang, 1997: 80). At that time, the rest were made to register their wishes concerning return to their homeland. According to a memorandum issued by the allied occupation forces GHQ regarding the registration of natives of Japan's former colonies, Koreans, Chinese, Ryukyuans and Taiwanese not wishing to return to their home country and not registering their ethnicity would lose the right to repatriation, and even those who registered a desire to be repatriated had to abide by the regulations dictated by the Japanese government or lose their right to return to their home country (Nada, 1995: 47).

Of the 657,000 ethnic Koreans in Japan at the time of registration, almost 80% (514,000) indicated their desire to return to southern Korea (Nada, 1995: 47–48) and just under 10,000 (approximately 1.5%) to northern Korea (Ryang, 1997: 80). Around 80,000 were actually repatriated between April and December 1946, when the Japanese government issued a directive that the repatriation of Koreans was complete and that those ethnic Koreans remaining in Japan were to be regarded as Japanese citizens and treated as Japanese (Nada, 1995: 49).

By 1948 the number of Koreans in Japan amounted to 588,170 (Ryang, 1997: 80). Reasons given for staying included that they had already established their base of livelihood in Japan and that conditions in Korea were highly unstable at that time (Nada, 1995: 47–49). Thus, between 500,000 and 600,000 Koreans lived in Japan with Japanese nationality until 1952, when the San Francisco peace treaty removed Korea from Japanese influence (Ryang, 1997: 120), and the Alien Registration Law was enacted, stripping Koreans and natives of other former colonies of their Japanese citizenship.

The Japanese government's decision to position Koreans as legal aliens apparently

> did not meet strong resistance from Koreans themselves. … To retain Japanese nationality for Koreans was out of the question, as they assumed it meant becoming Japanese in all senses; a change of nationality was generally taken as an alteration of one's essence. (Ryang, 1997: 121)

It is interesting to note that both Japan and Korea claim a high degree of homogeneity – a stance that is relatively rare among the nations of the world. For both populations, nationality is equated with ethnicity. In Japan, one's ethnicity is one's identity and one's identity is one's nationality. Children born in Japan are therefore not granted citizenship unless one of their parents is Japanese.[3] Thus Koreans 'resident in Japan' (*zainichi*) are exactly that unless they become naturalised.

This tendency to equate ethnicity with nationality permeated Japan's postwar naturalisation policy. The process of naturalisation in Japan was seen as the granting of eligibility to gain citizenship after strict background checks, including whether the applicant was ever a member of the Japanese Communist Party or Chongryun (the residents' association affiliated with North Korea). Regulations were highly arbitrary and the final decision rested with the Justice Minister (Ryang, 1997: 121). Until recently, assimilation into Japanese society was considered a prerequisite for naturalisation, and the use of names that did not sound Japanese was discouraged (Ryang, 1997: 122). Thus from the Korean point of view, naturalisation meant assimilation into Japanese society, becoming Japanese and forfeiting all Korean identity (Harajiri, 1998: 93; Ryang, 1997: 121).

As a result of this strong identification of ethnicity with nationality, annual naturalisation figures for resident Koreans averaged only about 2000 in the 1950s. This figure increased to approximately 4600 in the 1980s after changes in the naturalisation process eliminated the need to give up un-Japanese sounding names (Ryang, 1997: 122). Nonetheless, as of 1988, only 145,572 Koreans had received Japanese citizenship (Ryang, 1997: 122), meaning that the vast majority of ethnic Koreans in Japan had not been naturalised.

The status of Korean nationals in Japan has changed several times since the signing of the peace treaty, reflecting developments in the relations between Japan and South Korea as well as between Japan and the rest of the world. Between 1952 and 1965, Koreans were legal aliens in Japan. When the normalisation treaty between the Republic of Korea and Japan was signed in 1965, it was accompanied by an agreement that granted permanent residence to Koreans who had lived continuously in Japan since August 15, 1945 and those who were born in Japan after August 16, 1945 and who could prove that they were South Korean nationals (Ryang, 1997: 124). The status of permanent residence conferred rights and benefits, including national health insurance.

In 1979, Japan ratified the International Covenant on Human Rights, and in 1981, joined the United Nations Convention Relating to the Status of Refugees.

> The implication of the ratification was immense, since the Japanese government had much to change before it reached the standards required by the covenant. The status of women, Burakumin (Japan's untouchables), Ainu people, disabled people, the elderly, and children had to be considerably improved ..., as did the status of Koreans. (Ryang, 1997: 125)

A number of these changes concerned resident Koreans who viewed themselves as nationals of North Korea or were associated with Chongryun, a group historically affiliated with the Democratic People's Republic of Korea (DPRK). One improvement was the 1982 granting of 'exceptional permanent residence' for Koreans who had not been eligible for permanent residence under the 1965 treaty (in many cases because they identified themselves as North Koreans). Also, single re-entry permits were issued by the Justice Ministry after that time to allow Koreans associated with Chongryun to travel abroad and visit North Korea to be reunited with family and relatives (Ryang, 1997: 125; Harajiri, 1998: 116). A decade later reforms were made to the Alien Registration Law and the Immigration Control Act, giving all Korean permanent residents, including most Chongryun (North) Koreans, 'special permanent residency' and making them eligible to apply for social benefits such as pension schemes (Ryang, 1997: 125).

As we have seen, the status and treatment of resident Koreans in Japan varied according to whether the Koreans themselves were affiliated with North or South Korea. I would therefore like to briefly introduce the main organisations that reflect these affiliations and explain how they provide ethnic education for children of Korean residents of Japan, focusing in particular on the North Korean-affiliated institutions, since the majority of resident Koreans receiving ethnic education attend these schools.

Resident Korean associations

Although the Korean population in Japan has formed many organisations (Ryang, 1997: 5; Shin, 1995: 194), the two largest and best-known are Chongryun (or in Japanese, *Chōsen sōren*; full name: *Zai-nihon chōsenjin sō rengō kai* – the General Federation of Korean Residents in Japan) and Mindan (full name: *Zai-nihon daikanminkoku-min dan* – the Association for Koreans in Japan).[4]

Chongryun was founded in 1955 and is historically affiliated with and aligned to the Democratic People's Republic of Korea (DPRK). Since its formation, this organisation has been committed to providing its own education for Korean children in Japan.[5] It sponsors and operates nearly 150 schools and one university where the emphasis is on teaching Korean ethnic cultural values and the Korean language. Under Japanese law, Chongryun schools are recognised as special schools (*kakushu gakkō* in Japanese, which is sometimes rendered in English as 'miscellaneous schools').

Sonia Ryang, author of *North Koreans in Japan: Language, Ideology and Identity*, claims that 'Chongryun has never been the subject of serious academic scrutiny' (Ryang, 1997: 11). In her 1997 book, she analyses the position of overseas nationals of North Korea (*zaigai kōmin* in Japanese), the identity which replaced that of colonial subject for Koreans in Japan who chose to align themselves with North Korea in political opposition to the South Korean regime. She asserts that Chongryun 'required a specifically political identity, labeling its members overseas nationals of North Korea, even though the majority of its members came from southern Korea' (p. 115). Focusing on the physical and temporal space Chongryun Koreans inhabit within Japanese society, Ryang shows how the association

> adjusts and readjusts North Korean identity to keep pace with change within Chongryun and conditions surrounding it. It involves the development of a body of knowledge and pedagogical technology that give rise to legitimate discourse used within the organisation. This is a process that crosses time and space, various sites and managements. (Ryang, 1997: 2)

In the identity formation of North Korean overseas nationals, language is 'socially and culturally given through training and learning' (Ryang, 1997: 2). Ryang's analysis of the Korean language taught in Chongryun schools explains how it is a language taught for the continuation and survival of the organisation.

The second major organisation of Korean residents in Japan, Mindan, is aligned to the Republic of Korea (ROK). Founded in 1946, Mindan operates four schools, two of which have full legal status as private schools (Ko, 1996: 54). The two Mindan schools in Osaka accorded private school status must follow the curricular guidelines of the Ministry of Education and conduct instruction in Japanese in order to maintain this status. The other 'special category' schools are free to design their own curriculum in which the language of instruction is Korean (Ko, 1996: 54). Thus, in most cases, students educated at the schools operated by these two groups are instructed in their heritage language, although, as indicated above, the language taught in the Chongryun schools is highly politicised in nature.

Out of approximately 150,000 school-age Korean children in Japan in 1986, 135,000 (about 86%) attended Japanese schools, 19,500 (about 13%) attended Chongryun schools, and 1600 (about 1%) attended Mindan-affiliated schools (Fukuoka, 1993: 55). Although 92% of the students opting for Korean ethnic education chose Chongryun schools, the number of students at these institutions is said to be declining in recent years, whereas the number of students at Mindan schools is said to be increasing because of the growing number of South Korean businesses assigning employees to Japan who send their children to these schools.

The reasons most often heard for declining enrollments at Chongryun institutions are the high cost of sending children to unsubsidised schools and the fact that until recently, the Ministry of Education categorically denied graduates of special schools the eligibility to sit for entrance exams to Japanese high schools and universities.[6] Yet despite these drawbacks, 13% of the school-age Korean children in Japan choose to attend Chongryun schools. Many are motivated by their attitude toward the political ideology of their homeland, as well as by their rejection of pressures to assimilate into Japanese society (Umakoshi, 1991: 283).

Since the vast majority of the resident Korean children who attend ethnic schools are enrolled in Chongryun institutions, it might be said that the number of resident Koreans who can speak both Korean and Japanese will be determined primarily by enrollment in Chongryun schools. However, whether or not these bilinguals will maintain their active bilinguality as they grow up and live and work in Japan will depend on that society's willingness to confer full participatory status to non-Japanese residents. Unfortunately, in the years since the end of World War II, the policy of the Japanese government toward the Koreans residing in Japan can be summarised by two words: exclusion and assimilation

(Harajiri, 1998: 77). In the next section, I would like to examine this policy and the attitudes towards ethnicity it reveals.

Japanese attitudes

Issues pertaining to Koreans in Japan have often been labeled 'ethnic issues' or 'ethnic problems', or even in one instance, the 'Korean problem' (Reischauer and Jansen, 1995: 35). However, attempts to define ethnicity have shown that

> there is something elusive about the phenomenon of ethnicity or ethnic identity – and, by extension, also about ethnic group – which explains the reluctance of some writers to commit themselves to a statement of meaning. (Hoffman, 1991: 194)

This ambiguity is further compounded in Japan by language differences. One researcher pointed out in her writing on resident Koreans in Japan and their ethnicity and education that not only is there no clear definition of *ethnicity*, there is no adequate equivalent for it in Japanese. According to Nakajima, discussion of issues involving resident Koreans in Japan requires a new conceptual format and a borrowing of the English word 'ethnic', which points to groups of persons sharing the same origins and cultural identities. In contrast, the Japanese word *minzoku*, used historically in describing the various issues relating to the Koreans in Japan, indicates common blood lineage, language, territory, culture and lifestyle. With more and more Koreans intermarrying with Japanese, changing over to a Japanese lifestyle, and living throughout Japan with the greatly increased expectation since the 1970s of permanent residence in Japan, a new perspective or approach is required in talking about the resident Korean population (Nakajima, 1994: 29). Elsewhere, a historian notes that the term *minzoku*, 'whose most apt translation is the German word *Volk* ... has powerful overtones of communal solidarity, but is equivocal about the basis of that solidarity' (Morris-Suzuki, 1996: 88).

Though difficult to define, ethnicity can be discussed from several angles. It is often illogically equated with minorities, but as Edwards (1995) asserts, '*all* people are members of some ethnic group or other,' so even dominant, majority groups are ethnic (p. 125). However boundaries, or group content, can help define ethnicity. Various traits of a group, including language, may change across generations, but to the extent that such traits constitute a 'valued symbolic feature of group life', they contribute to the maintenance of the boundaries (Edwards, 1995: 126). We may also consider the objectively observable traits of ethnic groups or consider how members perceive their own sense of belonging. An ethnic group can thus be defined along racial or ancestral or linguistic lines or by the power of ethnic symbols within the group, such as language, religious holidays and rites of passage, special foods and festivals. To be sure, there is also an ascribed group membership which has had 'historical relevance, particularly for persecuted populations' (Edwards, 1995: 127–129).

For Koreans in Japan one of the most visible markers of ethnicity is the traditional style of costume for women, especially as reflected in the cut of the school uniforms worn by female students attending ethnic schools. On occasions when there have been outbursts of attacks of a discriminatory nature, they have often been directed at schoolgirls wearing these uniforms (*Asahi shimbun*, September 10, 1998).

Language has also been closely tied to issues of Korean ethnicity. During the colonial era, use of the Korean language was prohibited, both on the Japanese mainland and on the occupied peninsula. After World War II, identity formation for Koreans in Japan revolved first around retrieving their language, then teaching it to their children in preparation for the hoped-for future repatriation to a reunified home country. In more recent years, teaching the language to the younger generations has been important as a vehicle to impart their ancestral culture and affirm their affiliation with Korea, and to resist being assimilated into Japanese society. First-generation Koreans know from experience that loss of language destroys a sense of identity. Establishing schools and classes immediately after the end of World War II, Korean communities in Japan consciously chose to revalue and actively sought to retrieve and maintain their language. They exhibited a strong 'collective volition' to revitalise their language and culture (Hoffman, 1991: 185).

Japanese attitudes and government policy regarding minority groups, on the other hand, centre on Japan's neglect in giving equal treatment to non-Japanese. A number of scholars have commented on this neglect. According to Mabuchi Hitoshi (1995), 'Generally, in making their comparisons, Japanologists fail to recognise sub-cultures among the Japanese' (p. 43); as a result, '... little or nothing is said about women, ethnic minorities, or part-time workers' (p. 45). Failing to recognise sub-cultures which indeed exist as a part of the Japanese social fabric is one manifestation of how Japanese see themselves and their society. Self versus other, or insider versus outsider, is a construct often used to explain the Japanese sensibility which sees foreignness or difference as intrinsically unacceptable. Anthropologist Millie Creighton points out that 'the imagination of a national Japanese identity has emphasised, indeed insisted upon, a homogeneous, unified self' and this imagination 'has been capable of denying the realities of those on the margins, Japan's minorities, including Burakumin, Okinawans, resident Koreans, indigenous Ainu' (Creighton, 1997: 213).

The emphasis placed on internationalisation (*kokusaika*) in Japan since the 1980s has done little to include other national groups within Japan. *Kokusaika* does not necessarily imply an increase in understanding and valuing that which is culturally diverse within Japan. In the words of Gavan McCormack, internationalisation:

did not necessarily imply the internal transformation of Japanese society; rather, it was accompanied by a continued, perhaps growing Japanese insistence that economic success demonstrated the unique qualities of the Japanese way (McCormack, 1996: 274–275).

In fact, Japan continued to deny the existence of diversity within its borders. Creighton (1997: 227) points out that:

> the Japanese government's response to the United Nations' call for the elimination of discrimination against minorities was an official statement that no minorities exist in Japan and that therefore there is no discrimination against minorities in Japan.

This mindset extends to the field of education. Internationalisation was one of the issues discussed by the Ad Hoc Council on Education Reform (*Rinji kyōiku shingi-kai* or *Rinkyō shin*) and included in their final report in 1987. From this document, it would appear that the three major areas of concern for the Japanese public and government related to the internationalisation of education are (1) the education of foreign students in Japan, (2) the education of and readjustment to Japan by children whose families have resided overseas (returnees, or *kikoku shijo*), and (3) the employment of foreign teachers. Educating Japan's resident Korean population was not included. 'Although the council's several reports mention international schools in Japan, they fail to acknowledge the problems associated with the nation's more than 150 *minzoku gakkō* (ethnic schools) and the problems of resident Koreans' (Umakoshi, 1991: 281). Moreover, the Ministry of Education has not shown much interest in or willingness to promote bilingual or immersion education (Bostwick, 1995; Maher & Kawanishi, 1995b: 168).

It is evident, then, that supporting ethnic schools where resident Koreans can become bilingual by learning their heritage language is not perceived as part of 'internationalisation' in Japan. By refusing to confer full-fledged school status to Korean ethnic schools and to recognise and support the existence of a well-developed Korean-language school system operating throughout Japan, the government reinforces the view that diversity is not valued in Japanese society. In this context, Maher & Kawanishi (1995b: 168) wrote, 'The guiding concept of cultural pluralism which positively welcomes ethnic and linguistic diversity hardly exists in Japan.' Yet despite this lack of support, ethnic Korean education has a long history in Japan.

Education of Koreans after 1945

Korean ethnic education started to flourish immediately following the end of World War II. The League of Koreans, the first association for Koreans in Japan, was founded in October 1945 and was admittedly an interim organisation to facilitate eventual repatriation and contribute to the construction of a new Korea, [thus] the teaching of the Korean language to Korean children in Japan was a matter of considerable importance. (Ryang, 1997: 84)

At its third general meeting in October 1946, the League adopted a core philosophy for its schools aimed at 'education and enlightenment' to retrieve the history, culture, and language of which Koreans had been deprived by imperial Japan (Nada, 1995: 55). Initially, the Korean schools had only three early elementary grades; then in April 1947, the 6-3-3 schooling format was adopted, making it conform to the Japanese educational system.

The weekly curriculum first adopted in October 1946 combined Korean language instruction with a fully developed course of social studies, mathematics, science, music, art, and physical education. In first grade, pupils were to receive five hours of Korean language instruction, in Grades 2 and 3, six hours, and then in Grades 4 through 6, seven hours of Korean plus two hours of Japanese. Thus the schools offered what could be called an immersion programme in Korean. By October 1946, the League had established 525 elementary level schools, four middle schools, and ten 'youth schools' with a total of 1100 teachers and a total enrollment of more than 42,000 students (Nada, 1995: 55).

A major aim of these schools was to undo the effects of Japan's prewar assimilation policy. Lee (1981) asserts that the 'primary goal of the Korean ethnic studies programmes that Koreans established immediately after the war was to de-japanise the Koreans and their children in Japan' (p. 162).

Such a goal was not easily accepted by the Japanese government. It soon acted to:

> limit Korean ethnic studies to discourage further ferment. For many Japanese, ethnic diversity was intolerable in a land proud of its mythological founding as a homogeneous culture. (Lee, 1981: 166)

Rather than directly attack ethnic education in the name of cultural homogeneity, the government focused on the political ideology of the schools operated by the League of Koreans. As Lee (1981: 166) points out, they tended to be Communist-leaning and anti-American:

> ... the curriculum in schools operated by the [League of Koreans] was heavily slanted toward Communist doctrine as advocated by the North Korean regime. Schoolchildren were taught to pledge allegiance to North Korean Premier Kim Il-sung and to embrace a revolutionary spirit against the United States and the 'element of reactionary forces' in Japan. Ethnicity was politicised and exploited as a political weapon.

This gave the government the excuse it needed to take action against a rapidly expanding alternative educational system:

> The mounting tension of the cold war provided a convenient excuse for the Japanese government to suppress political and educational diversity. (Lee, 1981: 166).

In October 1947, a directive was issued by the Civil Information and Education Section of the Supreme Command for the Allied Powers (SCAP) stipulating that Korean children in Japan must comply with the School Education Law of 1947 (Lee, 1981: 163; Nada, 1995: 87). A short while later, on January 24, 1948, the Ministry of Education issued a communication to the prefectural governors directing that (1) Korean children must enroll in Japanese schools upon reaching school age; (2) privately operated schools had to be approved by the governors of each prefecture – however, 'miscellaneous schools' would not be recognised for the education of school-age children; and (3) extracurricular Korean language instruction would not be prohibited (Nada, 1995: 87).

SCAP's directive was followed by immediate protest. The League of Koreans proposed four conditions to enable the continuation of ethnic education under government control: (1) instruction in Korean; (2) use of textbooks written by a Korean committee but censored by SCAP's Civil Information and Education Section; (3) administration of the schools by the Korean school management union; and (4) compulsory instruction of Japanese (Lee, 1981: 165; Nada, 1995: 88). None of these conditions was accepted.

Prefectural governments made broad application of the clause that allowed for the closing of schools that contravened a governor's orders. Orders were mechanically issued to close Korean school programmes that used classroom space in Japanese school buildings. During February and March of 1948, each prefectural government notified Korean children that they were to enroll in Japanese schools. Korean schools that were operating in Japanese school buildings were ordered to vacate the premises by the end of March (Nada, 1995: 88). Tension ran high, especially in Yamaguchi, Okayama, Hyogo, Osaka and Tokyo prefectures. In Yamaguchi and Okayama, the governors agreed to postpone the closing of the Korean schools. In Hyogo, however, there was violence and 2000 Koreans were arrested (Ko, 1996: 91).

In September 1949, the government cited the Organisation Control Law (precursor of the Subversive Activities Prevention Law enacted in 1952) in ordering the dissolution of the League of Koreans; this order covered 370,000 members, including leaders and staff (Ko, 1996: 96). All 48 prefectural headquarters plus 620 branch offices and 1214 local centres were ordered to close. The youth league was also ordered to close its 48 prefectural headquarters, 458 branch offices and 308 local centres. The government also put restraints on Mindan at this time, but to a much lesser degree. It was ordered to close one of its prefectural headquarters, two branch offices, and one local centre, and its youth organisation was ordered to close one of its prefectural headquarters; 230 people were affected (Nada, 1995: 98).

These closure orders were enforced. Needless to say, suppression of the organisations running the Korean schools in the nation constituted a major blow to the pursuit of ethnic education in Japan. However, the attack on Korean education did not stop with the dissolution of the League of Koreans and the paring of the Mindan organisation. The month after the government issued that order, the Ministry of Education moved to forcibly close Korean ethnic schools that were still in operation. The Ministry's reasons for doing so were that Korean schools had taken a combative attitude in ignoring the directive to conform to Japan's education laws, and the Korean schools still operating were mostly under the organisational control of the League, which had been legally dissolved because of its resistance to the government's education policy and its political education supporting the use of violence to protest Occupation policies (Nada, 1995: 99).

There were two stages in the forced closing of schools. First, on October 19, 1949, 92 schools thought to have been under League jurisdiction were ordered closed. Armed police arrived in trucks, clubbed protesters and threw out resistant children, then boarded up the doors and windows of the schools. The remaining Korean schools were ordered to reorganise by applying for private school status within two weeks' time. The second wave of forced closures was carried out just after the deadline for reorganisation, when 117 schools that had not complied with the order to apply for private school status were automatically closed on November 4th. The 128 schools that had applied for private school status were reviewed but none was granted approval, with the single exception of Hakuto Gakuin in Osaka, a neutral or unaffiliated school with elementary, middle and higher school divisions. This school alone was given private school accreditation; the rest were ordered to shut down (Nada, 1995: 100; Ko, 1996: 97).

The most famous of the forced closings of Korean schools occurred in Hyogo Prefecture when the governor ordered ethnic schools to close. About 40,000 Koreans gathered nearly every day in front of the prefectural government office demanding that the school closing order be rescinded. On November 27, 1949, 4000 armed police were mobilised to arrest 30,000 Korean protesters and effectively end the protest demonstrations (Lee, 1981: 166).

Other protests arose throughout the country in areas where Korean schools had been operating. At the prefectural level, authorities generally avoided making independent decisions; rather, decisions were taken along the lines of official Ministry of Education policy to eliminate distinctions between Japanese and Koreans (Nada, 1995: 111). All Korean schools were ordered incorporated into the Japanese public school system, to be supervised directly by the prefectural government, which would appoint Japanese principals to head the schools. Korean ethnic studies were to be taught only after school hours. Administrative expenses would be borne by the Japanese public, as Korean children were now pupils in the Japanese compulsory educational system (Lee, 1981: 167). In this way, the Japanese government sought to effectively halt Korean ethnic education conducted in schools run by Korean organisations and thus to deprive the Korean community in Japan of the right to pursue its own educational goals.

Yet the community held fast to its desire to teach the children the language and culture of their homeland. Leadership was found by turning to the women's unions and student leagues which had escaped dissolution (Nada, 1995: 114), and ethnic education for Koreans continued in three main forms.

First, some independent Korean schools continued to operate. From the viewpoint of the Japanese government, these schools were illegal, but a number of ethnic schools nonetheless continued functioning on their own without accreditation or approval. Most of these schools were located where strong ethnic education movements had existed and where the schools owned the land and buildings. There were 44 such schools as of April 1952, including three in Ehime Prefecture: an elementary and a middle school in Matsuyama and a school in Niihama (Nada, 1995: 112). Thus, while there were 88,524 Korean children attending Japanese public schools according to a report by the Ministry of Education for the 1951–1952 school year, there were also a total of 17,678 Korean children attending the remaining ethnic schools as of April 1952.[7]

The second type of ethnic education occurred at Japanese public schools that had only Korean students enrolled, even after the clampdown. This exceptional format was allowed in 15 schools (13 elementary, one middle, and one high school) in Tokyo, five elementary schools in Kanagawa Prefecture, three elementary schools in Aichi Prefecture, one middle school in Osaka Prefecture, eight elementary schools in Hyogo Prefecture and three elementary schools in Okayama Prefecture (Ko, 1996: 98).[8]

Thirdly, ethnic education classes which were considered extracurricular by the government were conducted in some Japanese public elementary schools. Seventy-seven such classes were established in 13 prefectures (Ko, 1996: 98), with Shiga Prefecture offering 18 ethnic education classes taught by full-time Korean teachers (Nada, 1995: 113). In other areas, afternoon and night classes were organised at the initiative of Korean parents. As of April 1952, there were 21 such schools or classes: nine in Kyoto, five in Gifu, and seven scattered in four other prefectures (Nada, 1995: 113). The number of this type of class increased in later years. In Ehime Prefecture, such programmes were operated in Imabari, Shuso, Yawatahama and Uwajima, but the difficulty of finding instructors was a constant problem (Nada, 1995: 113).

This threefold system of ethnic education did not last for long, however. Korean children were permitted to receive compulsory education in Japanese schools for only a short while. After the Peace Treaty was signed in April 1952, 'Koreans in Japan were no longer considered to be Japanese nationals ... since the Japanese government had abandoned its claim of sovereignty over Korea' (Lee, 1981: 167). The Japanese government therefore refused to continue financing the education of resident Koreans.

Strong protest by Koreans led the government to declare that Korean students already enrolled in public schools would not be affected but from then on students would be allowed entry into public schools only if certain conditions were fulfilled, including provisions that: (1) space and facilities were available, (2) a pledge was made not to disturb public order, (3) Korean ethnic studies were not demanded, and (4) the students agreed to be taught the curriculum set forth by the Japanese government (Lee, 1981: 167). Finding it too difficult to enforce these complex provisions regarding education for Koreans, Japanese education officials decided to eliminate the Korean schools from the Japanese public school system altogether (Lee, 1981: 167).

In Tokyo, the prefectural authorities 'announced that all matters concerning Korean education would be transferred back to the hands of Koreans effective as of April 1955, and that the expense of Korean schools would no longer be defrayed by the prefecture' (Lee, 1981: 167). Further protests by Koreans claiming that they were full taxpayers led to a compromise in which the Tokyo prefectural government agreed to provide financial support for currently enrolled Korean students for five more years so that they could complete their schooling, but refused to give support for new students. The prefecture also granted permission for the legal incorporation of the Korean Education Institute to oversee Korean education in Tokyo (Lee, 1981: 168).

Other prefectures followed Tokyo's lead in refusing to provide public education funds for Korean students who were not already enrolled in the public school system. The Korean community found itself in the position of once again having to establish schools for its children. However, this turn of events also allowed the community to renew its commitment to teaching its heritage language and culture. 'Now that Korean schools existed as private institutions, ethnic studies programmes again flourished, especially after the formation of the [Chongryun] in 1955' (Lee, 1981: 168).

Six years after the government ordered the dissolution of the League of Koreans, the Chongryun, or General Federation of Korean Residents in Japan, was born in May 1955. Its purpose was to reaffirm that North Koreans in Japan are expatriate citizens of the Democratic People's Republic of Korea and that ethnic schools are necessary in order to provide ethnic democratic education as long as Koreans live in Japan (Nada, 1995: 171–172). The possibility of repatriating was still alive in 1955, and it was felt that if and when a Korean resident of Japan returned to the homeland, s/he needed to be prepared to be a useful member of that society. (See Nada, 1995: 170–176.)

Ethnic democratic education as espoused by the Chongryun was defined to mean an education that was ethnic in style and democratic in content. The elements of ethnic democratic education that were considered most important were fully learning the Korean language and also becoming aware of and proud to be citizens of an independent state, learning to love one's country and fellow citizens and to respect all other peoples in the world. Towards that end, Korean language, history, geography and social studies were taught. The expressed desires of Chongryun Koreans for their children were to become Koreans who speak the Korean language, who know the history of their homeland, who take responsibility for its future development, and who live successfully in Japanese society. (See Nada, 1995: 170–176.)

Once the Chongryun was established in 1955, there was a rush of construction of Chongryun schools throughout Japan: Between 1955 and 1959, 37 new schools were built (Nada, 1995: 175). This construction drive was accompanied by a strengthened resolve to teach more effectively on the part of the teachers given the responsibility for 'democratic ethnic education'. The Korean teachers' league, a fraternal as well as professional organisation devoted to raising educational standards and results, to which teachers of the Korean schools in Japan generally belong, was also reorganised in 1955 (Nada, 1995: 176).

Koreans in Japan gained the right to freely return to their home country as of April 1952 when they became legal aliens, but it was not until 1959 that the North Korean and Japanese Red Cross organisations concluded negotiations on repatriation to North Korea for humanitarian reasons. Repatriation was permitted to those at least 16 years of age, which in the DPRK is the age when one can legally vote and work. The first ship carrying returning Koreans departed Japan in December 1959. The agreement between the two Red Cross organisations resulted in 154 ships crossing the Japan Sea, transporting a total of 88,360 persons over a period of eight years (Nada, 1995: 191). From October 1967 to May 1971, however, the repatriation programme was interrupted by the Japanese government's decision to suspend an agreed extension of the programme. After that, the programme resumed and continued to the end of 1982, when the status of 'exceptional permanent residence' was granted to all Koreans living in Japan. Records show that a total of 93,344 persons returned to their homeland between 1959 and 1982. (See Nada, 1995: 190–3; Ryang, 1997: 113–15.)

When the repatriation programme to the Democratic People's Republic of Korea began in 1959, there was a surge in the number of students whose families wished for their children to at least know the language and history of their homeland before return. In the early 1960s, with increased numbers of Koreans repatriating to their homeland, 46,000 students were attending Korean schools, double the figure for 1955, when Chongryun was formed (Nada, 1995: 201). There was a need to build new schools and to expand existing ones. Between the years 1960 and 1964, 93 new schools were built (Nada, 1995: 175).

In 1991 there were 219 Korean educational institutions in Japan: 67 kindergartens, 83 elementary schools, 56 junior high schools, 12 senior high schools and one university (Shin, 1995: 167). Since that time, financial difficulties and declining enrollments have forced some schools to close or merge with nearby Korean schools. For example, four schools in Hiroshima Prefecture have recently joined to form one school. At present, no new schools are being founded because of administrative costs. In some cases, such as in Gumma Prefecture, an incorporated Korean school operates businesses such as stores or pachinko or pinball parlors, where graduates can find employment after graduation (Kim Sun-jon, 1996).

This general history of Korean schools in Japan is reflected in the history of the Shikoku Korean school, the focus of the present study. Interviews, observation and a survey of parents were conducted there to determine the current aims of this Chongryun school, the curriculum used to achieve those goals, and parental attitudes about the language and identity of resident Koreans today.

The Shikoku Korean School

History

The first Korean school building in Matsuyama, the capital of Ehime Prefecture on Shikoku island, was completed in July 1947 and was called *Matsuyama chōsen shōtō gakuin* (Matsuyama Korean Elementary Academy); it had four teachers and an enrollment of 28 students (Nada, 1995: 72).

At the time of the government's dissolution of the League of Koreans two years later in 1949, the League headquarters in Matsuyama, six branch offices on Shikoku (in Niihama, Imabari, Hinode-cho, Nagahama, Yawatahama, Uwajima) and 12 local centres, as well as the youth league's prefectural headquarters, were ordered to close. Official staff members were forced out, organisational funds were confiscated and the closing of the schools was enforced (Nada, 1995: 99).

Police came to the school in Matsuyama early in the morning of October 19, 1949. The following day, *Ehime shimbun* newspaper reported the forced closing of League-affiliated schools on its front page. Coverage included the government warning to Korean schools to apply for accreditation and the seizure of two schools in the prefecture: 'Thirty-eight students of the Matsuyama Korean elementary school and 120 students in the Niihama school were ordered to disband. Property was confiscated.' (Quoted in Nada, 1995: 101; English translation by the author).

When the loss of Japanese citizenship in 1952 forced members of the Korean community to reassume the responsibility of educating their young people, the Matsuyama school expanded by adding a middle school. New facilities comprising a one-storey frame structure with four classrooms, a dormitory for middle school students and a playing field were built two years later, the result of painstaking fund-raising efforts on the part of students, parents and the Korean community. In April 1954, the school had 55 students; three years later enrollment had burgeoned to 81, and three new classrooms were added.

With the establishment of the repatriation programme in 1959, increased interest in ethnic education was reflected in Ehime Prefecture as well. In April 1960, the Matsuyama school had 156 students at the start of the school year, nearly twice as many as three years earlier, resulting in a pressing need for dormitory space.

Five thousand Korean residents of Ehime Prefecture therefore resolved to build a new school. Lengthy discussions concerning the optimal location focused on two cities: Matsuyama, which was the seat of the prefectural government and the location of the headquarters of the prefectural Chongryun office, and Niihama, in the vicinity of which more than two-thirds of the prefecture's Korean population resided. In the end, the political centre of Matsuyama was chosen. The building was completed in November 1964 and still stands today. The school is named *Shikoku chōsen shō-chū-kyū gakkō* (The Shikoku Korean Elementary and Junior High School). It is the only Chongryun school on Shikoku, which is the smallest of Japan's four main islands. The nearest Korean high school lies in Hiroshima on the main island of Honshu, across the Seto Inland Sea.

While the repatriation programme was in full swing, numerous inquiries came from Korean parents about enrolling their children in the sole Korean school on the island. Sixty-three graduates or former students of the Korean school on Shikoku are known to have repatriated by April 1967 (Nada, 1995: 193).

The school's history reveals the treatment it has received from the municipal, prefectural and national governments. Recognition as a legally incorporated educational institution is required for a school to carry on its instruction. In Ehime Prefecture, even with all the requirements properly met in order to gain legal status, official recognition was not forthcoming. The process stretched out over three years, with legal incorporation finally accorded in January 1969 (Cary, 1997: 181).

The Shikoku school is at present (1997) the only Korean school in Japan that does not receive any financial aid from the government of the prefecture wherein it is located. The government of metropolitan Tokyo has given financial support from its private school subsidy funds to Korean schools in its precincts since 1970, and Okayama Prefecture began providing financial aid to the Korean school there as of February 1996. Among the 29 prefectures where Korean schools exist, Ehime Prefecture alone does not allot any funds for the Korean school located therein.[9] The prefecture bases its refusal to provide financial support on the condition given at the time of legal incorporation in 1969 that the school would not accept any financial aid. An annual subsidy of ¥300,000 is paid to the school by the city of Matsuyama; this amounts to 0.5% of the operational cost of the school. According to printed information distributed by the school and obtained in June 1996, annual tuition and fees come to ¥1,181,250 per student.

Financial difficulties are compounded by unfavourable demographic trends. As of March 1996 the number of registered foreigners in the city of Matsuyama (population 463,730) was 1608, of whom 796 (49.5%) are Korean (*Ehime-ken tōkei nenkan*, 1997: 24). Of the 4175 registered foreigners in Ehime Prefecture, 1778 (42.5%) are Korean (*Ehime-ken tōkei nenkan*, 1997: 24). As of July 1996, the Shikoku Korean school had 12 teachers and 36 pupils. However in 1997 there were three students each from two neighboring prefectures in Shikoku: Kagawa and Kochi. At its current location since November 1964, the school has seen the number of pupils dwindle since the 1988 completion of the Seto Ohashi bridge between Shikoku and the main island of Honshu, enabling students from neighboring Kagawa Prefecture to commute to the Korean school in Okayama. A marked reduction in the size of the student body was seen in March 1996 when a class of 14 junior high school students graduated.

Mission and curriculum of Chongryun Schools: 'If we lose ethnic education, we cannot live as Koreans'

The staff and supporters of the Chongryun school in Matsuyama are dedicated to providing ethnic education for Korean children in their community. Their conviction is based on the Universal Declaration of Human Rights, which asserts that such education shall be free, that parents have a right to choose the kind of education that their children receive, and that the rights of ethnic, religious or language minorities shall not be denied to them.

According to the staff of the Shikoku Korean school, the purpose of ethnic education for Koreans in Japan today is to educate persons whose self-realisation and creative ability enables them to interact in a positive way with the changes in today's world, including those of Japanese society. The goal is to equip students with broad-ranging knowledge and well-developed physical skills, to cultivate individuals who love their DPRK homeland and their fellow nationals, and who can relate living in Japan to their native country and its destiny. In order to fulfill this goal, there is constant effort to tailor the curriculum of Chongryun schools.

The education offered is based on independence, scientific correctness, and realistic objectivity. Independence means to have an independent world view and a sense of history and to cultivate an autonomous ethnic consciousness based on an accurate body of knowledge concerning the Korean people. Scientific correctness means learning truths about nature and society based on modern scientific and studied results. Realistic objectivity is defined as the acquisition of sufficient knowledge to live as Koreans in Japan, to have a better command of both Japanese and English, as well as a better grasp of world history, than what is taught at Japanese schools.

The curriculum and textbooks are designed and written in light of the philosophy and principles described above. Texts used at the Chongryun schools have been produced in Japan since 1946, first by the League of Koreans, and since 1955 by Chongryun. Japanese textbooks published by the nation's five or six printing houses that deal in school materials are reviewed and content deemed most appropriate and effective is selected and translated into Korean. In the past, textbook material was censored by authorities in the DPRK and the Chongryun schools in Japan waited for the approved versions. Now, approval is pro forma with all writing, editing and publishing, including layout and design, done by Chongryun's Education Department (Ryang, 1997: 58). The texts are distributed to the students as a gift from the home country. In an interview with the author on May 14, 1996, then head teacher Kim Sun-jon stressed,

'Our textbooks are better, of a higher level than those for the same grades used in Japanese schools. We design our own texts one or two years after the changes occur in Japanese textbooks. Our texts are uniform throughout the Korean schools in Japan, and changes are made every year if all concerned agree.' [English translation by the author]

As mentioned above, Chongryun currently operates some 200 educational institutions, from kindergarten up through Korea University. The most important task in the elementary division years is seen to be teaching the basic elements of the Korean language. According to both parents and teachers at the Matsuyama school, it takes about two years for the students to learn Korean to the extent that all instruction can take place in that language. In junior high school, ethnic studies centreing on Korean language, natural sciences and math, and foreign language education are stressed. In Chongryun high schools, further concentration in areas taught in junior high school and cultivation of the proper world view are emphasised. From high school, students can elect whether to major in humanities or sciences, and in schools in Tokyo, Osaka, and Aichi prefectures, commercial courses are also offered. At Korea University, in addition to traditional academic majors, training is available for those seeking employment in the Chongryun organisations.

Chongryun curriculum and textbooks have undergone two major revisions over the years. Until 1976, the courses of study and textbooks were based on the assumption that the students would eventually return to their homeland. However in the 1980s, with the ageing and passing of the first generation and the rise of second generation leaders, Koreans in Japan became more assertive about their rights to live permanently in Japan. Therefore, in 1983, a shift was made in the curriculum reflecting the understanding that students would most likely live permanently in Japan.

The most recent curricular revision was made in 1993. Like the 1983 curriculum, the new one is also based on 'living in Japan', but there is a significant shift in emphasis. Where the 1983 curriculum was based on a recognition of the *possibility* of remaining in Japan, the revisions for the 1993 curriculum were based on the realisation that these students would *most likely* remain in Japan. The assumption that the students might move to and live in North Korea has now been 'abandoned' (Ryang, 1997: 53).

These revisions involved virtually no change in the curriculum for the elementary grades, but significant changes are seen in the courses of instruction for the junior high school years. There has been a reduction of two hours per week of Korean language in the first year and another hour in the second and third years. On the other hand, one extra hour of English has been added per week in the second and third years, and instruction in Japanese language has been increased by one hour in the second year. The addition of a Korean writing class one hour a week is new for all three years, while computer courses have been added in the second year.

According to Cho Song-ho, principal of the Shikoku Korean school from 1990 to 1996 and head of the education office of the prefectural Chongryun organisation since 1996, the current curriculum reflects a change in thinking about ethnic education in the context of the post-Cold War era. It is based on assessing the position of Koreans in Japan from a global standpoint.

> 'How we are to live as Koreans in Japan remains central to continuing to protect our self-reliance as Koreans in Japan. Thus, the focus of the most recent revision is pointed toward the cultivation of our self-awareness and self-reliance. It means maintaining the dignity of being Korean and adjusting to the reality of life in Japanese society.' (Nada, 1995: 251) [English translation by the author.]

Although the curriculum is national, tests are developed by the Korean schools of the district. The mid-term tests administered at the Shikoku Korean school on May 21–23, 1996, for example, were written by teachers and staff of the Korean schools in Hiroshima, Okayama and Ehime prefectures, who meet annually to discuss curricular and other issues. Nationwide meetings are held every three years. The students at the Shikoku Korean school are then evaluated individually according to a relative scale.

Extracurricular activities and sports are intended for the development and discipline of the whole person and to heighten cultural achievement. Participating and competing in athletic meets is, for the Shikoku Korean school, a way to help the students know that they have the same opportunities as students of other schools. For although it is often said there are no national boundaries where sports is concerned, in Japan obstacles still remain. The Japan Athletic Association traditionally excluded all non-Japanese from its competitions, but began allowing the participation of resident foreigners (except students from abroad who are only studying in Japan temporarily) in high school competitions as of the 36th national meet in 1981, in junior high school meets starting with the 43rd national meet in 1988, and for university competitions starting with the 45th national meet in 1990 (Nada, 1995: 256).

Barriers do exist on the local level. In Matsuyama there is a soccer league for elementary school students. The Korean school pays full dues to the league but has been given only affiliate status. Korean school students are not officially allowed membership in the junior high school athletic association either. Participation in tournaments that might lead to national-level competition is not allowed.

Head teacher Kim Sun-jon told me:

> 'Competing in athletic meets is not our primary goal; we encourage and value sports for self-discipline. The school chooses to participate in order to give the students the same opportunity as students of Japanese schools. We don't want to have to continue saying that if you are *zainichi* [Koreans resident in Japan], you have to be resigned to the fact that you will not be treated the same. We have continually asked for the right for our team to participate.'

He does question why full dues must be paid by the school when it is not a full member, but adds,

> 'Our ethnic education is not just for schooling and teaching our students to be upright citizens, but also for maintaining a consciousness about our rights.'

Through sports and other activities, the Shikoku Korean school elementary division has contact with four local Japanese primary schools and the junior high school division with more than ten junior high schools in the area. The volleyball, soccer, traditional dance, drama, and journalism clubs interact with members of similar clubs at other junior high schools and joint music and dance performances have been staged in one of the city's major performance halls. The faculty and students of the Korean school feel they are contributing to deepening international understanding in the city in this way. A teacher from Mitsuhama elementary school in Matsuyama reported on the contact and interaction between his school and the Korean school at a teachers' seminar held on January 18, 1995. As a result, students from the Korean school were invited to participate in the opening parade of a city-wide human rights festival in April 1996.

The school and its supporters in the community plan to continue working toward gaining further support from the city, as well as from the prefectural and national governments.

Parental attitudes about language and ethnic identity

Learning takes place in the family, community and school. Because there is no geographically distinct Korean community in Matsuyama, the Korean school is the only place where children can learn the Korean language. As noted above, the teachers at the Korean school in Matsuyama suggest that it takes two years for the language to be learned and the curriculum is designed with that in mind. All instruction takes place in Korean, and Chongryun school students are said to master Korean nearly perfectly. It has been reported that they have no trouble understanding the language of Koreans from their homeland (Fukuoka, 1993: 56). Nonetheless, interference from their first language, Japanese, is inescapable, and their speech patterns contain some expressions which appear to be based on Japanese language patterns or intonation (Fukuoka, 1993: 56; Maher & Kawanishi, 1995a: 92).

What is the nature of the language instruction taking place in Chongryun schools? As mentioned above, establishing identity is one of the goals of ethnic education at Chongryun schools. Ryang (1997) asserts that 'the North Korean identity is primarily a political one, not an ethnic one' (p. 62). Since for the children enrolled in Chongryun schools and for the majority of their parents, Japanese is their first language, the Korean acquired at school is that which is used for Chongryun's public life, learned and used in order not to lose that political identity.

North Korean ideology, including praise for Kim Il-sun (who died in 1994) and his son Kim Jong-il (head of the DPRK since his father's death), is reflected in the curriculum and lexicon of the Chongryun-operated schools (Maher & Kawanishi, 1995a; Umakoshi, 1991; Rohlen, 1981). Indeed, the government of the DPRK has continuously sent money to support the Korean schools in Japan since 1957. It is interesting to note that despite the severe flooding in North Korea and the dire problems the country had in feeding its own people in 1995, the government nevertheless continued to provide aid to the schools in Japan.[10]

Ryang analysed the language used and taught at Chongryun schools and reported that it has the following characteristics: (1) The Korean language of Chongryun is limited in the settings in which it is used: mainly within the schools and offices of the organisation; (2) Korean is reserved for discussion of matters related to the organisation and to North Korea, leading to a concentration on political vocabulary; (3) It is marked by the formal form and dependency on the written version in speech; (4) It is marked by fixed metaphors and idioms (Ryang, 1997: 43–44).

To explore how the parents of the students in this education system felt about their languages and identity, I mailed questionnaires to
22 families introduced to me by the Shikoku Korean school in May 1996.
All were families with children attending the Chongryun school in
Matsuyama. My purpose was to investigate the attitudes about speaking
Korean and Japanese held by the parents of the students attending the
Korean school in Matsuyama, and to examine their language use within
the home. (See appendix for an English translation of the survey
instrument.) The rate of response was 54.5% (12 responses).

The questionnaire began with a family profile to determine the number
of people living in the household, their sex, age, relationship, nationality
and the languages they spoke. Among the 12 responses received, the
average number of persons in the family or household was 5.25. There were
three single-parent families and three households that were comprised of
three generations. The number of children averaged three. Three couples
indicated that the parents had different nationalities (i.e. DPRK and ROK)
and the remaining six couples indicated both parents had DPRK nationality. There were no naturalised Japanese among the family members in
this sample.

In general, everyone in the respondents' families were reported to
speak both Korean and Japanese, the only exceptions being two fathers
who spoke only Japanese, very young children ages three and five who
had not yet learned Korean, and a one-year-old who did not speak yet.

The next section of the questionnaire explored language use between
family members.[11] Japanese was reportedly used at least part of the time
for communication between all family members in all of the respondents'
families. One respondent reported that Korean was used more frequently
between the two children (ages 14 and 12) who were attending the
Korean school. Another family reported more frequent use of Korean
between the mother (age 41) and grandparents (grandmother 73,
grandfather 74). Ten out of 12 (83%) mothers spoke both Korean and
Japanese to their children but used Japanese more frequently; one mother
indicated she used Korean more frequently, and one mother indicated she
used only Japanese with her children. Similarly, eight out of the nine (88%)
fathers used Japanese more frequently with their children, while one father
(11%) indicated he used primarily Korean when speaking to his children.
Among the 22 school-age children (ages 6 to 14) in the 12 families, only
two seven-year olds were listed as speaking only Japanese in the home.

In these families then, we see that Japanese is most often the language
used and that children in the youngest grades at school speak only
Japanese, whereas older school-age children speak both Korean and
Japanese. This supports the teachers' suggestion that it takes around two
years for the students to learn Korean. Through the school's immersion-
style instruction in Korean, the children are trained to be bilinguals, acquiring their heritage language after they have already acquired the majority

language as their first language. Thus, we see here the phenomenon of school bilingualism rather than natural bilingualism, as distinguished by Skutnabb-Kangas (reported in Hoffmann, 1991: 19). This is also called consecutive childhood bilinguality (Hamers & Blanc, 1989).

The next section of the questionnaire was designed to elicit attitudes towards the Korean and Japanese languages, as well as towards bilingualism. Question 4A (see appendix) asked, 'Do you think it is beneficial or detrimental to be able to speak both Japanese and Korean?' All respondents (100%) indicated they felt it was beneficial. All 12 responses were written in Japanese and are introduced here (English translation by the author).

(1) First of all, though I don't live in my own country, by being able to speak the language of my country, I can be aware of myself as a Korean. It makes me happy to be able to communicate smoothly with visitors from my home country. As for Japanese, as long as I'm living here, I think it's necessary and right to make the effort to speak it correctly and well. Because we are Koreans living in Japan, we should first know Korean and then study Japanese.

(2) Understanding one's mother tongue allows for the proper understanding of one's tradition, culture, etc., so it's only right to speak Korean; and in reality I live in Japan, so I need to speak Japanese, therefore it's beneficial.

(3) In our family, the children have naturally come to realise what's most important – who they are (Koreans living in Japanese society) – and have true pride in their roots. Having been to other countries (the USA and other countries) and speaking to lots of people in English as well as in Korean, I truly feel that language serves as an important bond between people.

(4) It is only natural for me to speak Japanese because I was born in Japan, and it is only proper as a Korean to speak Korean.

(5) As a Korean, it is only proper to speak Korean. It is indispensable to speak one's mother tongue for communication with other Koreans. That we can speak the two languages is not a conscious choice but because it is necessary in order to live as Koreans in Japan.

(6) I think the younger you are the easier it is to learn the language and culture of the yet unseen country of your grandparents' birth and then to weave it into Japan's culture.

(7) It's a matter of course to speak Korean because it's my mother tongue. As for Japanese, it's better to be able to speak it because I live in Japan.

(8) Of course I speak Korean because it's my country's language. I need Japanese because I live in Japan. Language is culture. If I didn't know my own culture, I would be assimilated into Japan. I think it's beneficial to speak Korean.

(9)   Speaking Korean means knowing one's mother tongue, which is
      equivalent to knowing and being aware of one's own country.
      Speaking Japanese is a matter of course because we live in Japan.
      I have never thought about whether it is beneficial or not but
      I would say that speaking two languages can't be bad and if pos-
      sible, I would like to learn to speak a third language, such as English.
      In order to do so, one must learn, so I think it is beneficial from the
      point of view of learning.
(10) I want to know the culture and history of my own country even
      though I was born and am living abroad.
(11) Since I live in Japan, my life is centred here. It's probable that I will
      never return to our ancestral land, so I must continue to live in this
      country; therefore I need to speak Japanese. But more importantly,
      my mother tongue is my heritage, I need it like the blood running
      through my veins. I need a language that I can have in common
      with my family and relatives and friends in our ancestral land. If you
      want to really understand the situation of Korean and Japanese
      bilinguals, I think you have to understand the history of resident
      Koreans in Japan which is unknowable through Japanese education.
      (Please come to our open house on June 16th.) Language is very
      important in order to live with confidence as a Korean in Japan.
      That's how much I myself am my mother tongue.
(12) It is only right to speak the language of one's own country.

The above responses explaining the positive aspects of being able to
speak both Korean and Japanese focus on the importance of proficiency in
Korean for one's self-awareness as a Korean living in Japan and as a means
of resisting assimilation – resisting becoming Japanese. The respondents'
stress on the appropriateness or necessity of being able to speak Korean
in order to live as a Korean in Japan is a reflection of the stated purpose
of Chongryun's ethnic education. The comments referring to the joy of
communicating with others (on trips to other countries or with visitors
from the home country) and positive language learning experiences
suggest that the respondents feel that the school education they support is
worthwhile.

Question 4B (see appendix) was designed to elicit the subjects'
perceptions of societal attitudes towards their bilinguality. In response to
the question 'How is being able to speak Korean and Japanese regarded in
Japan?', five respondents (41.6%) indicated they thought the ability to
speak Japanese and Korean was valued very positively in Japan, two
(16.6%) rated it rather positively, four (33.3%) as neutral, and one (8.3%)
very negatively.

The final question tried to further probe the respondents' perceptions of
societal attitudes to determine if they thought bilingualism would be more
highly valued if the minority language were a language other than

Korean. The term *bairingaru* (bilingual) was used for the first time in the latter part of this question, which asked, 'Do you think being a speaker of Japanese and another language other than Korean (i.e. being bilingual) is also regarded in the same way? Why do you think so?' Three (25%) respondents indicated that they thought other language combinations are regarded similarly to Japanese and Korean, while eight (66.6%) indicated there is a difference, and one was non-committal.

The reasons given are presented in translation below. The brackets at the end of the responses indicate how the subject responded to the previous question about how the ability to speak Japanese and Korean is regarded in Japan. The first three responses were written by subjects who indicated speakers of Japanese and Korean are regarded similarly to bilinguals with other language combinations.

(1) Being able to speak a language opens up an entire world. If you can speak two languages, another world is added onto what you know. It isn't strange for foreigners not to be able to speak Japanese, but it would be embarrassing not to be able to speak the language of one's own country. [Very positively]

(2) When one lives in Japan for a long time, since Japanese and Koreans are racially so close and indistinguishable, being able to speak our mother language is what allows for others to tell the difference in our ethnic origins. Also, people will see that we have our pride as an ethnic group. [Very positively]

(3) So many different people live in Japan and they all have their own cultural customs; being able to speak two languages shows that you are smart. [Very positively]

Responses four through eleven are the comments of respondents who felt that there is a difference in the way Japanese and Korean bilinguals are perceived as compared to bilinguals with other combinations of languages.

(4) There are still a great many Japanese who feel that Japan is the best in every respect among the countries of Asia. If the language in question is English or French, people are impressed; but if it's an Asian language, people dismiss it by saying, 'Oh, that's nice.' [Somewhat positively]

(5) There is discrimination and lack of understanding about Korea and Korean because of past history. [Neutral]

(6) We are different from what is generally called *bairingaru* [bilingual]: our Japanese was learned naturally, as a matter of course, as the language of the country and culture where we were born, while our Korean is an acquired language, part of our ethnic education, in order to be proper Koreans. [Very positively]

(7) If the languages were Korean and English, Japanese people would place a different value on it. I think the image of the country gets in the way. [Neutral]

(8) There's much discrimination against Korea in Japan and I think that Japanese feel it's much more international to be a speaker of English or other European languages. In reality, lots of effort is put into English language education because English is the foremost language in the world. [Neutral]

(9) I think speakers of English and another language are considered very positively. Myself included, we feel that a person who can speak English is cool. That's most likely due to the mystery of why I can't really speak English even though I've studied it from junior high through college ... but essentially I think it's because of the social climate in Japan. [Somewhat positively]

(10) I think it's different because there's discrimination. [Neutral]

(11) Unlike in our parents' time, we weren't forced by the whip to learn Japanese. Having been born in Japan, we have naturally learned the language that surrounds us and have accepted it. Yet, as we grow up and learn about our history, we see what our position is in Japanese society and it's there that we encounter our mother tongue. We learn history. That is, we come to understand that Japanese language is necessary for the purpose of living in Japan, and then in turn Korean takes on much more weight. Japanese dominates because we have been using it longer but Korean controls our soul. It is not just a matter of using two languages – Korean offers a way to look at oneself, guide oneself, like a light. This consciousness is thinning among second- and third-generation Koreans in Japan. For me, because I depend almost entirely on Japanese in my everyday life, Korean language education is a very important bond for me and my children. [Very positively]

Comment 12 was written by the subject who did not commit him/ herself to an answer to the question about the relative value of different language combinations in terms of general attitudes towards bilinguals. S/he wrote:

(12) Among Japanese there's a strong sense of yearning for greatness. I think the question could be answered either way – for example, there are many English conversation schools but very few for other languages. [Very negatively]

The above comments show that even though all of these individuals perceive their own bilinguality and bilingualism positively (as indicated by their responses to Question 4A), most feel that Japanese do not value the bilinguality of speakers of Korean and Japanese, even though they value speakers of another language and Japanese. The reasons suggested for this are discrimination and ignorance of the history of the two countries. [Editor's note: For evidence of this kind of discrimination, see Chapter 2, 'Japanese Attitudes Towards Bilingualism: A Survey and Its Implications', by Yamamoto Masayo.]

For the respondents, knowing and understanding the language of their 'own country' is directly connected to self-awareness. At the same time bilinguality is considered a matter of course, a natural necessity to live as Koreans in Japan. The language itself serves as a bond between generations, as expressed by the writer of Response 11, reflecting the importance of the language as a vehicle in constructing their identity as Koreans.

Ethnic education today

In the chapter entitled 'Education: Policies and Prospects' in *Koreans in Japan: Ethnic Conflict and Accommodation*, Thomas Rohlen regarded 'much of the ethnic education movement as well intended but historically limited. The forces producing cultural assimilation seem far more powerful' (Rohlen, 1981: 221). Rohlen's research in the 1970s was noteworthy because he focused his attention on ethnicity and worked with experiential data. However, he never visited a Chongryun school:

> Before discussing the [Chongryun] school system today, I must indicate the limits of my knowledge. I have walked by but have never been permitted in one of their schools. I have talked to Japanese and Koreans with acquaintances who are teachers in these schools. I have read the few written accounts available and have looked briefly at [Chongryun] textbooks, but as an American with no special credentials or contacts I have been unwelcome in schools fiercely loyal to a nation that has considered the United States its greatest enemy. (Rohlen, 1981: 206)

This was not my experience. On June 16, 1996, I attended the open house the Shikoku Korean school held for visitors to observe classes in session. The guests at the school that day included parents and grandparents, university students and faculty, municipal government workers, community leaders. The media were present too.

Grades three, four and five had the fewest students, with only two in each class. The first year junior high school class was the largest, with eight students. In the fourth grade art class I visited, a video was shown of the grand civic buildings in Pyongyang and the students drew what they saw in watercolour. In the first year junior high school science class, experiments were being conducted and reviewed with key terms introduced in Japanese as well as Korean. In the third year junior high school English class, a vocabulary building activity was taking place.

All of the instruction occurred in Korean; occasionally Japanese terms were introduced, especially in history and science. We were treated to some well-rehearsed performances of songs and dances with traditional Korean instrumental accompaniment, followed by a Korean-style lunch in the school cafeteria. It was clear that this small school values ethnic education.

School status

Students of the school do pay a price for this commitment to ethnic education, however. According to the *Asahi shimbun* newspaper of September 1, 1995, among Ehime Prefecture's 17 private high schools, junior colleges and colleges, 12 do not permit graduates of Korean schools to sit for their entrance exams. None of the schools has citizenship requirements *per se*; rather, this refusal is due to the fact that Korean schools are classified as 'miscellaneous schools' by the School Education Law. The *Asahi shimbun* article reported that among the ten high schools, four junior colleges and three colleges that responded to a survey conducted by the *Ehime gendai chōsen mondai kenkyūsho* [Ehime Center for Current Korean Issues], only four high schools permitted Korean school graduates to sit for their entrance exams. Because the Ministry of Education stipulates that only graduates of junior high schools and comparable schools are eligible to take public high school entrance examinations, the prefectural office for private schools in Ehime maintains the perspective that graduates of the miscellaneous status Korean schools are not eligible to take those entrance exams (*Asahi shimbun*, September 1, 1995). However, some improvement in eligibility to take entrance examinations for public universities in Japan have been made recently. (See Note 6.)

Moreover, as mentioned above, the Shikoku Korean school does not receive any subsidies from the national or prefectural government because of its status as a miscellaneous school. In contrast, overseas Japanese receive considerable government support in educating their children: Textbooks are distributed free of charge to students enrolled in the 91 full-time Japanese schools overseas and 167 'Saturday schools' where the purpose is indeed Japanese ethnic education (Ko, 1996). The course of instruction in the Shikoku Korean school, adapted to the generation of Koreans growing up in Japan today, is as fully developed, if not more so, than at overseas Japanese schools. At the Korean school, Japanese language is taught at the same level as in Japanese schools, and there may possibly be greater emphasis on practical skills in English than in Japanese schools.

However, if full status recognition and subsidisation were obtained, the Korean school in Matsuyama would have to submit to Ministry of Education censorship of textbooks and follow a curriculum nearly identical to that of the Japanese schools. The desired ethnic education would most certainly be undermined. Therefore, rather than striving to acquire such accreditation, the Shikoku Korean school seeks to gain the status of private school for foreigners with the same rights as a fully accredited school. Accredited private schools in Japan receive yearly subsidies of ¥222,366 per elementary school student and ¥236,859 per junior high school student (Ko, 1996: 32). Resident Koreans contribute to these subsidies by paying taxes. It would seem fair that they receive support for ethnic education for their children in return. If Korean schools were given the same treatment accorded private international schools, the burden of educational costs for the school and parents of the children would be alleviated.

Conclusion

Korean ethnic education in Japan has served as the vehicle for the resident Korean community to resist the assimilationist policies of the Japanese government, assert their identity and establish a measure of self-esteem in the face of societal discrimination. The main provider of this ethnic education has been Chongryun, the organisation of resident Koreans affiliated with North Korea (DRPK). Chongryun operates a well-organised, integrated school system, including the only Korean university in Japan. As Kim Sun-jon, head teacher of the Shikoku Korean school clearly stated, the schools and Chongryun are mutually dependent on each other. Their purpose is to teach the Korean children in Japan the Korean language, history and culture, and impart an awareness about their rights.

My survey of parents of Shikoku Korean school students and direct observation of classes suggest that to a large extent, the Chongryun school system succeeds in fulfilling these goals. Although Japanese is used in most of the respondents' families, the immersion-style Chongryun education system appears to foster consecutive binguality, a positive view of the Korean language and bilingualism, and a consciousness of ethnic identity.

In the 1980s and '90s, Japanese studies and publications began to recognise the value of multicultural education and need to recognise cultural and ethnic diversity in modern Japanese society. There is a visible cultural and economic vitality among some Korean communities in Japanese cities, especially in Osaka, where the population of Koreans is most dense. (See Maher & Kawanishi, 1995b.) In 1982 'the third annual Meeting on Educational Research for Koreans in Japan was attended by 595 teachers and scholars involved in efforts to develop ethnic awareness and bilingualism among Korean children' (Hirasawa, 1991: 203). Many critics and writers advocate full recognition and rights for Koreans in Japan, calling for an end to the discriminatory policies of the Ministry of Education against Koreans in Japan and for the arrival of a truly multicultural society. (See, for example, Ko, 1996.)

The Chongryun organisation has kept its identity as an association of North Korean overseas nationals and its schools have served as a key location for such identity formation. Chongryun Koreans have exhibited strong resistance to being assimilated into Japanese society. However, by seeking support from and becoming involved in the communities where they live, Koreans in Japan have demonstrated their desire to be fully affiliated with Japanese society as resident citizens who will live permanently in Japan.

Notes

1. Shin, 1995: 159. According to the *Asahi shimbun* newspaper of July 8, 1996, as of the end of 1995, the number of registered Koreans living in Japan was reported to be 666,376 out of the record number of 1,362,317 registered foreigners; this was the first time Koreans accounted for less than half of all registered foreign residents.

2. Ryang (1997: 129) explains that although Koreans became Japanese citizens after the annexation, they were treated differently from mainland Japanese in terms of the household registration documents (*koseki*) that serve as identity papers for employment, education and marriage. When Japanese moved, they could move their place of registration, but Koreans and other natives of Japan's colonies were not allowed to bring their registration along with them to Japan. Their registration documents were called *gaichi koseki* (outland registration) and had to remain in their native land, in contrast to those of native mainlanders, who had *naichi koseki* (inland registration). Weiner (1997: 84) also notes that 'Koreans were not guaranteed the rights of full citizenship ... economic, social and educational policies of the colonial administration ... [gave Koreans] a subordinate identity ....'

3. Until the mid-eighties, children were considered Japanese only if their father was Japanese; the child of a Japanese mother and foreign father was not normally granted Japanese citizenship.

4. At its regular general meeting on April 20, 1994, Mindan decided to delete *kyoryū*, or resident, from their name and to invite as guest members Koreans who had obtained Japanese nationality.

5. An earlier association of Koreans in Japan, called the League of Koreans, was founded in October 1945 in Tokyo. The League's purpose was to prepare for repatriation and protect the interests of Koreans in Japan. Shortly, it became affiliated with the Japanese Communist Party and was forced to dissolve in 1949; however, from the time of its founding, the League dedicated itself to establishing schools and educating Korean children for eventual repatriation. (See Harajiri, 1998: 40; Ryang, 1997: 79–80). Today, there are many smaller organisations which concentrate on the better integration of Koreans into Japanese society rather than toward North or South Korea. Some are 'explicitly opposed to North Korea and Chongryun' (Ryang, 1997: 126–127).

6. In the 1990s, more and more colleges and universities in Japan started disregarding the Ministry of Education's rules. As of 1997, 30 publicly-funded and 219 privately-funded universities allowed 'miscellaneous school' (*kakushu gakkō*) graduates to sit for their entrance exams, 13 and 57 more, respectively, than in 1994. No national university recognised such eligibility at that time (*Asahi shimbun*, September 21, 1997). However, it was reported that the graduate school of Kyoto University had accepted a graduate of Korea University in violation of Ministry of Education policy (*Asahi shimbun*, September 5, 1998). Finally, on July 8, 1999, the Ministry of Education announced a change in policy starting in the year 2000 which will allow graduates of Korean and international high schools in Japan to take entrance examinations for public universities. Students taking such entrance exams, however, will still have to pass a qualifying examination because ethnic and so-called international schools are not accorded full certification under the Education Law. In addition to the easing of university entrance requirements, graduate school entrance requirements will also be eased so that Korea University and foreign university graduates can further their studies at Japanese universities (*Asahi shimbun*, July 9, 1999).

7. Of the 88,524 Korean children attending Japanese public schools, 70,273 were in elementary schools, 15,409 in middle schools, and 2842 in high schools. Of the 17,678 in ethnic schools, 14,204 were in elementary, 2903 in middle, and 571 in high schools. The combined total for these two figures – 106,202 – should represent the total number of school age Korean children in Japan at that time. It must be remembered, however, that some families were financially unable to send their children to school at all. A realistic count would have to be higher (Nada, 1995: 113–114).

8. The three Korean elementary schools in Okayama Prefecture closed in 1950 (Ko, 1996: 98).

9. *Zai-nichi chōsen-jin no minzoku kyōiku no kenri: nijū-isseiki ni mukete chō-nichi yūkō to kokusaika no naka de* [Ethnic Education Rights for Resident Koreans in Japan: Internationalisation and Korean-Japanese Friendship in the 21st Century], edited by *Zai nihon chōsen-jin kyōiku kai* [Association for Education for Koreans in Japan], p. 180.

10. The first such funds were sent in April 1957 in the amount of ¥21,099,086; payments have been made 132 times, usually twice a year. In September 1995, ¥97,750,000 was remitted. The total across the years has amounted to ¥42,494,432,433. (See Lee, 1981: 171–172; Nada, 1995: 180.)

11. The survey instrument I sent was adapted from a questionnaire distributed by Yamamoto Masayo in April 1996. The results of Yamamoto's survey are reported in her 1997 publication *Kokusai kekkon katei ni okeru gengo shiyō no jittai: nigengo shiyō no jōkyō chōsa* [Research on Language Use in International Families: Survey on Bilingual Language Use], The Ministry of Education, Science and Culture: Grant-in-Aid for Scientific Research (C)/ Project number: 07610517. Osaka, Japan.

Appendix

Survey of Families with Children Attending the Shikoku Korean School
(English translation by author)

1. Family Composition
Who lives in your household? (Include children who might not be living in your home now.)

Parents   Mother _____   Father _____

Grandparents   Grandmother _____   Grandfather _____

Number of Children   One _____ Two _____ Three _____ Four_____

Other   _____ (Relationship) _____ Persons

2. Background
Fill in sex, age, nationality, place of domicile and languages spoken.

	Sex	Age	Nationality	Place of domicile	Languages spoken
Mother					
Father					
Child 1 F/M					
Child 2 F/M					
Child 3 F/M					
Grandmother					
Grandfather					
(Other) _____ F/M					

3. Languages Spoken at Home

What language is used between family members? If more than one language is used, please indicate that used more frequently.

	Mother	Father	Child 1	Child 2	Child 3	Grand-mother	Grand-father
Mother: speaking to	X	___	___	___	___	___	___
Father: speaking to	___	X	___	___	___	___	___
Child 1: speaking to	___	___	X	___	___	___	___
Child 2: speaking to	___	___	___	X	___	___	___
Child 3: speaking to	___	___	___	___	X	___	___
Grandmother: speaking to	___	___	___	___	___	X	___
Grandfather: speaking to	___	___	___	___	___	___	X

4. Attitudes Toward Korean and Japanese

A. Do you think it is beneficial or detrimental to be able to speak Korean and Japanese?
Mark with an x and explain why.

_____ Beneficial _____ Detrimental _____ Both _____ Neither

Why do you think so?

B. How is being able to speak Korean and Japanese regarded in Japan?
Mark with an x.

_____ Very positively _____ Somewhat positively _____ Neutrally

_____ Somewhat negatively _____ Very negatively

Do you think being a speaker of Japanese and another language other than Korean (i.e. being bilingual) is also regarded in the same way? Why do you think so?

_____ Same _____ Different
Why?

References

Asahi shimbun
   Ken'nai no watakushiritsu kō tandai daigaku no uchi yon kōkō dake mitomeru [Only four high schools among all private high schools, junior colleges and colleges in the prefecture accept (graduates of Korean school)]. *Asahi shimbun*, September 1, 1995.
   Gaikokujin no tōrokusha saikō no 136 mannin — kankoku chōsenjin 50% waru [Registered foreigners peak at 1.36 million — Koreans less than 50%]. *Asahi shimbun*, July 8, 1996.
   Chōsen kōkō sotsu e no monko kaihō — kō shiritsu dai kahansū de [Over half of public and private colleges open their doors to graduates of Korean schools]. *Asahi shimbun*, September 21, 1997.

Kyōdai daigakuin ni chōsen dai sotsugyōsei [Korea University graduate accepted at Kyoto University Graduate School]. *Asahi shimbun*, September 5, 1998.

Chōsen gakkō ni iyagarase [Harassment directed at Korean schools]. *Asahi shimbun*, September 10, 1998.

Gaikokujin gakkō ni daigaku monko kakudai [Eligibility for university entrance extended to international school graduates]. *Asahi shimbun*, July 9, 1999.

Bostwick, R.M. (1995) After 30 years: The immersion experiment arrives in Japan. *The Language Teacher* 19 (5), 3–6.

Cary, A.B. (1997) An introduction to the Shikoku Korean School: From its beginnings to accreditation. *The Annual Bulletin of the Faculty of the Humanities*, 171–184. Matsuyama Shinonome College.

Creighton, M. (1997) *Soto* others and *Uchi* others: Imaging racial diversity, imagining homogenous Japan. In M. Weiner (ed.) *Japan's Minorities: The Illusion of Homogeneity* (pp. 211–238). London and New York: Routledge.

Edwards, J. (1995) *Multilingualism*. London: Penguin Books.

Ehime-ken tōkei nenkan 1997 [Ehime Prefecture Statistical Yearbook] (1997) Ehime Prefecture, Japan.

Fukuoka Y. (1993) *Zainichi kankoku chōsenjin* [Koreans in Japan]. Tokyo: Chuo koronsha.

Hamers, J.F. and Blanc, M.H.A. (1989) *Bilinguality and Bilingualism*. Cambridge, UK and New York: Cambridge University Press.

Harajiri H. (1998) *'Zainichi' toshite no korian* [Koreans as 'Japanese Residents']. Tokyo: Kodansha.

Hirasawa Y. (1991) The education of minority group children in Japan. In B. Finkelstein, A.E. Imamura and J.J. Tobin (eds) *Transcending Stereotypes: Discovering Japanese Culture and Education* (pp. 197–204). Yarmouth, Maine: Intercultural Press.

Hoffmann, C. (1991) *An Introduction to Bilingualism*. New York: Longman.

Kim S.J. (1996) Personal interview. Matsuyama, Japan, May 14, 1996.

Ko C.Y. (1996) *Kokusaika-jidai no minzoku kyōiku* [Ethnic Education in the Age of Internationalization]. Osaka: Toho shuppan.

Lee, C. (1981) Ethnic education and national politics. In C. Lee and G. De Vos (eds) *Koreans in Japan: Ethnic Conflict and Accommodation* (pp. 159–181). Berkeley, CA: University of California Press.

Mabuchi H. (1995) The problem of Japanology. In Kitao K. (ed.) *Culture and Communication* (pp. 33–47). Kyoto: Yamaguchi shoten.

Maher, J.C. and Kawanishi Y. (1995a) On being there: Korean in Japan. *Journal of Multilingual and Multicultural Development* 16 (1 & 2), 87–101.

Maher, J.C. and Kawanishi Y. (1995b) Maintaining culture and language: Koreans in Osaka. In J.C. Maher and G. Macdonald (eds) *Diversity in Japanese Culture and Language* (pp. 160–177). London: Kegan Paul International.

McCormack, G. (1996) *Kokusaika*: Impediments in Japan's deep structure. In D. Denoon, M. Hudson, G. McCormack and T. Morris-Suzuki (eds) *Multicultural Japan: Paleolithic to Postmodern* (pp. 265–286). Cambridge, UK and New York: Cambridge University Press.

Morris-Suzuki, T. (1996) A descent into the past: The frontier in the construction of Japanese history. In D. Denoon, M. Hudson, G. McCormack, and T. Morris-Suzuki (eds) *Multicultural Japan: Paleolithic to Postmodern* (pp. 81–94). Cambridge, UK and New York: Cambridge University Press.

Nada T. (1995) *Non'namu wa miteita: Shikoku chōsen sho/chūkyū gakkō gojū-nen* [The Laurel Tree Was Watching: Fifty Years of the Shikoku Korean School]. Matsuyama, Japan: Saramu saran-sha.

Nakajima T. (1994) *Zainichi kankoku-chōsen-jin no esunishitii to kyōiku* [The education and ethnicity of North and South Korean residents in Japan]. *Kyōikugaku kenkyū* [The Japanese Journal of Educational Research] 61 (3), 233–241.

Reischauer, E.O. and Jansen, M.B. (1995) *The Japanese Today: Change and Continuity*. Cambridge, MA: Harvard University Press.

Rohlen, T. (1981) Education: Policies and prospects. In C. Lee and G. De Vos (eds) *Koreans in Japan: Ethnic Conflict and Accommodation* (pp. 182–222). Berkeley, CA: University of California Press.

Ryang, S. (1997) *North Koreans in Japan: Language, Ideology, and Identity.* Boulder, CO: Westview Press.

Shin S. (1995) *Kankoku, kita-chōsen, zainichi-korian ga wakaru hon* [Understanding South Korea, North Korea and Resident Koreans and Japan]. Tokyo: KK Bestsellers.

Umakoshi T. (1991) The role of education in preserving the ethnic identity of Korean residents in Japan. In E.R. Beauchamp (ed.) *Windows on Japanese Education* (pp. 282–290). Westport, Connecticut: Greenwood Press.

Weiner, M. (1997) The representation of absence and the absence of representation: Korean victims of the atomic bomb. In M. Weiner (ed.) *Japan's Minorities: The Illusion of Homogeneity* (pp. 79–107). London and New York: Routledge.

Yamamoto M. (1997) *Kokusai kekkon katei ni okeru gengo shiyō no jittai: nigengo shiyō no jōkyō chōsa* [Research on language use in international families: Survey on bilingual language use], The Ministry of Education, Science and Culture: Grant-in-Aid for Scientific Research (C)/Project number: 07610517. Osaka, Japan.

Zai nihon chōsen-jin kyōiku kai [Association for Education for Koreans in Japan] (ed.) (1996) *Zainichi chōsen-jin no minzoku kyōiku no kenri: nijū-isseiki ni mukete chō-nichi yūkō to kokusaika no naka de* [Ethnic Education Rights for Resident Koreans in Japan: Internationalization and Korean-Japanese Friendship in the 21st Century] Tokyo: *Zai nihon chōsen-jin kyōiku kai chūo jōnin riji-kai.*

Chapter 6

Japan's Hidden Bilinguals: The Languages of 'War Orphans' and Their Families After Repatriation From China

TOMOZAWA AKIE

Introduction

The normalisation of Sino-Japanese relations in 1972 led to large-scale repatriation of the so-called Chinese 'War Orphans' (Japanese children who had been abandoned in China during the Japanese retreat in the closing days of World War II), as well as their spouses, children, grandchildren and other relatives. The total of those 'repatriated' at government expense stood at approximately 17,093 people in 5484 households as of October, 1997 (Ministry of Public Welfare, 1997). Still others have 'returned' at their own expense. When the first groups of 'war orphans' arrived in search of their relatives, they received wide-scale media coverage, but interest in them in Japan has waned as the novelty wore off.

Statistics on income, livelihood, degree of adaptation to their new environment, and so on for those 'war orphans' who repatriated at government expense have been compiled, but these figures hardly give a complete picture. Though the government is trying to develop a comprehensive programme aimed at promoting the returnees' independence, including acquisition of the Japanese language and permanent living quarters, there is little tolerance for the development of a distinct cultural niche for these people within Japanese society, which still has a strong assimilationist tendency.

Much has been made of the need for 'war orphans' and their families to learn Japanese. However, little attention has been given to maintenance of their first language (Chinese) or to provisions for educational institutions to make use of the knowledge and cultural heritage the 'war orphans' acquired during their years in China. Moreover, the longer these families live in Japan, the greater the problems that arise between the children, who rapidly acquire Japanese, and their parents and grandparents, for whom Chinese continues to be the dominant language.

133

While a great deal of attention has been given to bilinguals whose minority language is English or a European language, such as *kikoku shijo* (Japanese 'returnees' whose parents are Japanese businessmen and who were educated in public schools in developed countries or in international schools in developing countries), the returnees from China have not received much notice. This paper will focus on these 'hidden' bilinguals in Japan, reporting on a survey of their use of Chinese and Japanese, including when each language is used, the subjects' attitudes towards maintaining their Chinese proficiency, and differences in language use according to the area in which these returnees are residing. Before describing the survey and presenting the results, however, we need to take a closer look at who the 'war orphans' are, as well as why and when they began 'returning' to Japan.

Historical Background

After the Manchurian Incident – the seizure of the Manchurian city of Mukden by Japanese troops, followed by the Japanese invasion of all of Manchuria and the establishment of the Japanese-dominated state of Manchukuo in the area – in 1931, the Japanese government started sending Japanese colonists to the Manchuria area, in what is now the north-eastern part of China. It is estimated that more than one and a half million Japanese were living in this area at the end of World War II, and that 270,000 of these settlers were farmers. It was for the most part these farming families who left behind the children who became known as 'war orphans' when the Japanese were forced to retreat in the waning days of the war. More than 200,000 Japanese are said to have died in the turmoil of the retreat, while thousands of children and women were simply left behind, receiving no help from the Japanese government until very recently (Sakamoto, 1994).

Yet it was Japanese government policy that sent the settlers to Manchuria in the first place. Japanese settlement of Manchukuo, which was regarded as a 'paradise' of opportunity, was seen as a means of absorbing the growing number of farmers living in poverty on the Japanese mainland after the great depression of the 1930s. Establishing settlements was also considered a vital means of support for the Japanese army, which anticipated a fierce battle against the USSR and was hoping that soldiers could easily be recruited from civilian families living near the border. However, as the war dragged on, the men from the colonist villages were siphoned away to fronts in the Pacific and southern Asia, where Japan was losing battles. Only women, children and the elderly were left in the Japanese villages in Manchuria as the end of the war approached.

The tragedy is that those who were left unarmed in Manchuria were not informed of Japan's real situation, so they were not prepared to do anything when Soviet troops advanced on August 9, 1945. Many were killed; some killed their own young children whom they felt would be a burden in their difficult repatriation journey, and others were compelled to sell their children in exchange for food. Many women who had been left behind married Chinese men in order to survive. Many children whose parents were killed or who got separated from their parents were picked up by Chinese (many of whom became their foster parents) and managed to survive. Often these children were not told that they were Japanese or even that the people who raised them were not their biological parents until these foster parents were on their deathbed many years later.

In contrast to the tragic situation of the farming families, the professional soldiers stationed in Manchuria were in a position to know Japan's exact situation and had already started sending their families back to Japan via the military railway by the beginning of 1945. The Ministry of Public Welfare admits that no members of the families of professional soldiers are to be found among the 'war orphans' (Kunitomo, 1986).

Those who were abandoned in China by their nation had to wait more than a quarter of a century before they could announce their identity as Japanese and express their will to return to Japan with their families.

Settlement of the 'War Orphans' and Their Families in Japan

Official status

As defined by the Japanese government, *zanryū koji* (literally, 'stranded or remaining orphans') are Japanese who were under 13 years of age when they lost their parents in the confusion after the advancement of the Soviet army, while the term *zanryū fujin* (literally, 'stranded or remaining women') are Japanese who were over 13 years old at the end of the War and who 'could have returned' to Japan when the repatriation programme restarted in 1953 but 'intentionally remained' in China. The latter are thus put into a different category of expatriates, for whom the Japanese government does not necessarily acknowledge responsibility to support their return to Japan. *Nisei* (second generation) and *sansei* (third generation) are the children and grandchildren of these stranded Japanese and their Chinese spouses.

After the normalisation of Sino-Japanese relations in 1972, the Japanese government agreed to provide moving expenses for the 'orphans' and 'remaining women', as well as their spouses and children under 20 years of age, so that they could come to Japan. However, because the government placed restrictions on the number of such returnees who could be repatriated annually and also strictly regulated conditions for recovering their legal status as Japanese citizens, the 'orphans' and 'remaining women' have generally been put on a long waiting list before finally coming to Japan. Until recently, an 'orphan' needed the consent of a blood relative to come back to his/her own country, and in many cases this was not forthcoming because families in Japan were embarrassed to admit they had left family members behind.

In 1994, a bill to lay the responsibility on the government to promote the return and self-sufficiency of the remaining Japanese in China was passed by the Diet. The Ministry of Public Welfare set up a plan to complete the repatriation of approximately 2000 'remaining' Japanese and their families (estimated to be four to five times the number of 'orphans') over the next few years.

Those who come back at government expense are provided temporary residence and Japanese language training for four months at one of three reception centres specially built for returnees from China. Three more centres were supposed to be built in 1995 to bring the total capacity of the centres to 402 households or 1000 people.

After four months at a centre, the returnees have to leave and start supporting themselves, although they do receive a modest one-time grant (*shitaku-kin*; e.g. ¥500,000, or approximately $4000, for a family of four) to help them move out of the centre and set up new living quarters. The returnees usually start their new life in a place where their Japanese relatives or guarantors live, but many families soon move to larger cities where there are more job opportunities. Many municipal governments give scrupulous care, providing public housing and assistance in finding jobs. For the following eight months, the returnees may continue to learn Japanese free of charge at language schools located in 15 major cities. Some local governments provide special services for a maximum period of three years, including providing a consultant who gives guidance about work, children's education and social life in general, as well as a translator for communication with doctors and school teachers when requested.

Settlement and identity problems

The government (through the Ministry of Public Welfare) has conducted surveys and taken measures to meet the needs of the returnees. However, these initiatives are not necessarily sufficient; moreover, the government confines its consideration to those who were repatriated at government expense. Those not included in the limited quota of orphans and remaining women entitled to come to Japan at government expense — the majority of whom are *nisei* and *sansei* and their spouses who are over 20 years old — came to Japan at their own expense and had to start a new life with no knowledge of the language or cultural orientation.

The Ministry admits that the actual number of returnees who have come to Japan at their own expense is not precisely known. Moreover, although it is expected that thousands (some anticipate tens of thousands) of Japanese and their families will come to Japan in the coming years, there is no government section in charge of promoting the settlement of these descendants of Japanese, who will surely need appropriate assistance in the process of their acculturation in a new environment.

In that sense, these returnees are far more neglected and insecure than the other ethnic minorities in Japan. 'Old comers' like Korean residents (about 700,000, excluding those who have been naturalised) and overseas Chinese (about 50,000 permanent residents) have already established organisations which represent their political and economic interests and cultural solidarity, and operate their own ethnic schools, ranging from a four-year university and 150 primary and secondary schools throughout Japan enrolling 40,000 students for Koreans (Maher & Kawanishi, 1995: 89) to several elementary and secondary schools in major port cities for Chinese (Maher, 1995: 126), which provide education with ethnically oriented curricula to the coming generations. [See Chapter 5 of this book for more on Korean ethnic education.] Among the 'newcomers', the approximately 10,000 Indochinese refugees in the nation (*Asahi shimbun*, October 17, 1994) are handled by a specifically assigned section of the national government with higher ranking officials that was established mainly in response to international pressure.

Besides the dearth of government assistance for returnees from China, the very complex nature of their ethnic identity also makes resettlement difficult for the war orphans and their families. Various degrees of self-identification, from 'firm' to 'ambivalent' can be observed, even among the 'orphans' themselves. Some who have firmly kept their identity as Japanese and long hoped to come back to Japan are to some extent satisfied, but others who were informed of their true ethnic origin at the very last moment of their foster parent's life are confused by having to shift to being Japanese. Their children and grandchildren are even more troubled. Though they are categorised in one big group as 'returnees' and the government takes measures to promote their prompt 'adaptation' as Japanese, they were born, brought up and spent most or all of their lives in China and came to Japan for the first time accompanying a grandmother, parent or spouse. In any sense, they are first-generation immigrants with a firm ethnic identity as Chinese (especially those who came to Japan after their adolescence), not real *nisei* (people of Japanese ancestry born in a foreign country to parents born in Japan) nor *sansei* (children born to *nisei* parents).

Interestingly enough, their Chinese identity is not necessarily allied with that of other Chinese who have settled in Japan. In interviews, many returnees confessed that they would not count on any job offers from the rather prosperous *kakyō* (overseas Chinese) business community. This is because the returnees themselves feel that they do not belong to the overseas Chinese network because they are partly Japanese. Moreover, the *kakyō* admit that they consider these returnees to be Japanese, not compatriots, and feel that the responsibility for their betterment should be shouldered by the Japanese government and Japanese society. To make matters worse, the apathy or insular mentality of Japanese society, which denies full societal participation to those who are perceived to be 'different' from the norm in any way, hinders the painstaking transition of ethnic identity from Chinese to Japanese, particularly for those who came to Japan in their youth or those who were born in Japan.

Language education for returnees

In striking contrast to the sensational media coverage expended on the reunion of long-lost families after nearly a half century, the slow but steady efforts of the returnee families to settle in their new environment does not receive much attention, except for negative reports when returnees commit crimes or get involved in trouble, and many of these problems are attributed to their insufficient Japanese language ability.

As mentioned above, many (but unfortunately not all) 'war orphans' and their families who came to Japan at government expense receive four months' adjustment training, including 500 hours of Japanese language instruction and very basic cultural orientation. However, one study showed that their language competency after four months of study was so low that only 2% could smoothly perform such tasks as going shopping or running an errand at the post office (Ministry of Public Welfare, 1987). This does not necessarily mean the instruction at the centre is a failure, but many admit that there is room for developing a specifically prepared curriculum and teaching materials aiming at more communicative competency.

Free language education is available in major cities for those who want to continue learning for the following eight months, but not all returnees from China can attend these classes because the class hours are set during the daytime when most of the adults are working and the school-age children are attending primary or junior high schools in their local community. In many cases, children are placed one or two grade levels lower than usual for their age because of their lack of language competency and 'scholastic ability'. A few schools do assign a special teacher (who generally does not speak any Chinese) to teach Japanese language and content subjects in a pull-out class, but in most cases Chinese returnee students are dealt with in Japanese submersion (or sink-or-swim) classes.

To investigate more closely the linguistic situation and identity issues related to this neglected group of bilinguals, a survey was conducted between late 1994 and March 1995. This survey is described and the results presented below.

Survey

Purpose

The purpose of the survey was to investigate the language use of returnees in their family, school and work environments, focussing mainly on second- and third-generation family members whose language shift from Chinese to Japanese tends to be particularly rapid and extreme. Returnees living in two different localities were surveyed: one was the city of Sakai (population 800,000) in Osaka Prefecture (population 8.8 million), and the other was the city of Takamatsu (population 330,000) and surrounding areas in Kagawa Prefecture (population 1 million) on the island of Shikoku.

One reason why these two localities were chosen was that the author was acquainted with several school teachers in each city who are actively engaged in Japanese language education and in the betterment of living conditions for returnees from China, and who could therefore be asked to distribute questionnaires. Among these teachers is a Chinese woman who is married to the son of a 'remaining woman' and who is striving to bring up her children as bilinguals with a Chinese identity. It would have been quite difficult to collect questionnaires, especially from returnees who came at their own expense, without the cooperation of these acquaintances. Thus this was a convenience sample, but it was nevertheless seen as important since the national government does not even have a grasp of the actual numbers of returnees who have come back from China at their own expense, much less their language situation.

The other purpose of this survey was to examine whether there were any differences in the linguistic transition patterns of the returnees in these two cities, which differ greatly in terms of the effort made to provide services for the returnees. Sakai is the second largest city in Osaka Prefecture and lies adjacent to the prefectural capital, Osaka (population 2.6 million), where a national reception centre for returnees and three Japanese language schools recognised by the government are situated. According to a detailed survey conducted by the Osaka Prefectural Government, of the total of 4463 returnees living in the prefecture as of August 1994, 1028 were living in the city of Sakai. This was the second largest number in the prefecture after the city of Osaka, which was home to 1287 returnees at that time (Osaka Prefectural Office, 1994).

Among the 346 returnee families living in Sakai, only 78 (23%) came to Japan at government expense. Of the 1028 individual returnees, only 258 (25%) were 'orphans' and 'remaining women'; the other 770 (75%) were their children or grandchildren who were born and brought up in China. These ratios are similar in the prefecture as a whole: 26.6% of the returnees in the prefecture came to Japan at government expense, and 65.8% were second- and third-generation family members. Therefore, issues related to returnees – especially ethnic identity and language maintenance or shift – tend to be more focused on the children and grandchildren of the 'orphans' there – that is, the second- and third-generation family members whose cultural and linguistic background is distinctly Chinese.

The Osaka Prefectural Government has extended its services to promote the settlement of returnees irrespective of how they came to Japan, so that they will reach all returnees, including those excluded from the assistance of the national government. These services include preferential allotment of public housing, provision of counselors and translators, distribution of a bilingual (Japanese and Chinese) guidebook to daily life in Osaka (*Nihon no kurashi*), and subsidised Japanese language education for adults. The prefecture has also implemented extensive support policies in its school system, appointing four schools to develop special programmes for the returnee students, providing JSL (Japanese as a Second Language) classes in most of the schools with some returnee students enrolled, hiring teachers specialising in the acculturation problems of returnee students, developing Japanese language textbooks, organising extracurricular activities to maintain returnees' Chinese language ability and so forth. Prefectural education guidelines also stipulate special treatment for returnees in entrance examinations to public high schools. Voluntary associations of teachers concerned with returnee students hold regular meetings to exchange information. Some volunteer groups teach Japanese to adults and hold get-together meetings for the returnees and Japanese in their communities. These positive attitudes may be related to the fact that Osaka has the largest number of Korean residents in Japan and is relatively enthusiastic about and receptive to 'multicultural' education and maintenance of an ethnic identity.[1]

In contrast, there were only 286 returnees from China living in all of Kagawa Prefecture in 1995.[2] The prefecture has no special facilities for returnees (in fact, there are none on the island of Shikoku) and there are almost no opportunities for returnees to learn Japanese, except for JSL classes in a few elementary and junior high schools. Services like preferential arrangement for public housing and sending out counselors and translators are offered only to those returnees who came back from China at government expense. Most returnees in the Takamatsu area are living in close proximity to each other, and chose to live in the area because their Japanese parent or grandmother was originally from the region and as a natural consequence they expected assistance from their Japanese relatives.

In short, there are more returnees living in Sakai but they are widely dispersed and have no specific bond to relatives or a community of their own ethnic group in the area, which they live in because they have better opportunities to learn Japanese and find jobs. In contrast, Takamatsu is home to only a small number of returnees who live close together in a rather small community and receive little in the way of preferential treatment.

Method

To investigate the language use of returnees in various environments, a series of questions was composed concerning language choice in communication among the different members of the returnees' families and with returnee friends. An English translation of these questions is provided in the Appendix. The idea of creating a series of questions on language choice depending on the interlocutor came from Joshua A. Fishman's work, 'Who speaks what language to whom and when?' (Fishman, 1972). However, as the present study was intended to be an initial probe and the survey was meant to be very general, questions concerning the 'particular kinds of occasions to discuss particular kinds of topics' which Fishman describes as 'domains' of language behaviour were not included.

The questions were translated into Chinese and sets of both questionnaires (one written in Japanese and the other in Chinese) were directly handed to returnees' families between the end of 1994 and March 1995 by teachers and volunteers who knew the families very well and were very much trusted by them. The only specification the author gave to these teacher acquaintances about whom the questionnaire should be given to was that the subjects should to be old enough to answer the questions by themselves. Respondents could choose either the Japanese or Chinese version of the questionnaire and fill it in using either of their languages.

Though a detailed explanation of the purpose of the survey and the assurance of confidentiality was given in the introductory part of the questionnaires, according to the teachers who distributed them, many returnees were reluctant to cooperate at first because they were not accustomed to being asked about their private life either in China or in Japan; there was also anxiety and skepticism about expressing their true opinions for fear that they might suffer some adverse effects if they gave negative answers.

Thus, questionnaires were distributed to only those who agreed to cooperate, and even then, some questions were left unanswered.

Subjects

Questionnaires were collected from 117 returnees: 53 in Sakai and 64 in Takamatsu; 64 men (54.7%), and 53 women (45.3%). Their ages at the time of the survey ranged from 13 to 68 years of age. The age distribution of the subjects is presented in Table 1.

The majority of the respondents must have been *nisei* and *sansei* (children and grandchildren of the Japanese stranded in China after the war), as 94.9% were younger than 50 years old at the time the survey was conducted, which was 50 years after the end of the war.

Table 1 Subjects' ages $(N = 117)$

Locality	Age in Years					
	13–19 n (%)	20–29 n (%)	30–39 n (%)	40–49 n (%)	50–59 n (%)	60–68 n (%)
Sakai (n = 53)	23 (43.4%)	7 (13.2%)	9 (17.0%)	11 (20.8%)	3 (5.7%)	0 (0.0%)
Takamatsu (n = 64)	18 (28.1%)	8 (12.5%)	22 (34.4%)	13 (20.3%)	1 (1.6%)	2 (3.1%)

Survey Findings

As mentioned above, some of the respondents did not answer all of the questions. In presenting the survey results, then, the total number of responses for each question (N) as well as in each category (n) are indicated.

Subject profiles

The questionnaire asked the subjects to indicate whether they were students, and if so, what level of school they were attending, or whether they were working or not. The responses are presented in Table 2.

Overall, the numbers of students (43.4%) and workers (46.2%) were almost equal. However this breakdown differed in the two localities: the lower average age of the returnees in Sakai meant that 53.8% were students, compared to only 33.3% in Takamatsu.

Table 2 Subjects' occupational status in Japan $(N = 106)$

Locality	Junior High Students n (%)	Senior High Students n (%)	College Students n (%)	Working n (%)	Not Working n (%)
Sakai (n = 52)	7 (13.5%)	17 (32.7%)	4 (7.7%)	18 (34.6%)	6 (11.5%)
Takamatsu (n = 54)	10 (18.5%)	8 (14.8%)	0 (0.0%)	31 (57.4%)	5 (9.3%)

Table 3 Age on arrival in Japan $(N = 117)$

Age in Years	Under 10	11–20	21–30	31–40	41–50	Over 50
n (%)	7 (6.0%)	48 (41.0%)	18 (15.4%)	32 (27.4%)	8 (6.4%)	4 (3.4%)

Table 4 Length of residence in Japan ($N = 116$)

Locality	Less Than 1 Year n (%)	1–3 Years n (%)	3–5 Years n (%)	5–10 Years n (%)	Over 10 Years n (%)
Sakai ($n = 52$)	3 (5.8%)	21 (40.4%)	18 (34.6%)	8 (15.4%)	2 (3.8%)
Takamatsu ($n = 64$)	6 (9.4%)	20 (31.3%)	18 (28.1%)	14 (21.9%)	6 (9.4%)

The subjects' ages upon arrival in Japan are presented in Table 3. Nearly half (47%) were younger than 20 years of age when they came to this country.

The data on the subjects' length of residence in Japan is presented in Table 4. Although a few of the respondents had been living in Japan for more than 10 years, the majority (74.1% overall; 80.8% in Sakai and 68.8% in Takamatsu) had lived in Japan for less than five years at the time of the survey.

The data collected on the education the subjects had received in China and their occupations there are presented in Figures 1 and 2. 35.6% had graduated from elementary school, 34.6% from junior high, 21.2% from senior high, and 4.8% from college in China. Before coming to Japan, 21.5% were farmers, 33.8% factory workers, and 29.2% engineers, teachers and other professionals in China.

These two sets of figures on the subjects' educational background and occupation in China do not necessarily coincide with the prevalent image in Japan of 'war orphans' as victims of the war who had been engaged in farming and had little chance to receive formal education. There is no doubt that many went through hardships, but that does not mean that they should be regarded as people who need only protection and supervision. Especially in the case of their descendents, they should instead be

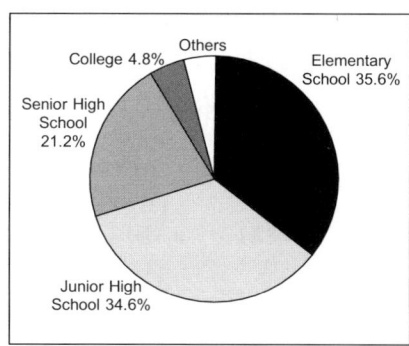

Figure 1 Highest level of education received in China

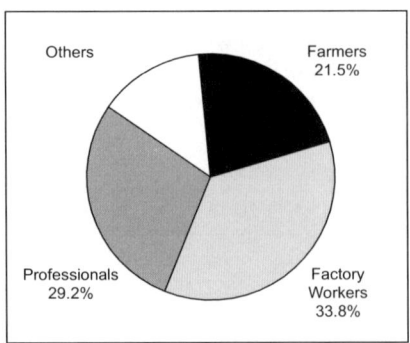

Figure 2 Subjects' occupations in China

viewed as respectable constituents of the community with backgrounds not much different from the average Japanese.

In response to the question on whether they had studied Japanese before coming to the country, and if so, how they had done this, only 14.5% of the subjects indicated that they had previously studied the language, and many of them reported that they had learned it by themselves, not at school.

After they arrived in Japan, however, 66.7% reported receiving Japanese language education at an institution, with 25.3% of these indicating that they had been taught at a reception centre, 29.3% at a language school, and 36.0% in a JSL class in their school. (Presumably most of the subjects giving the last answer were students.) The reports of the subjects' Japanese language education in Japan, broken down by occupation and locality, are presented in Table 5.

The fact that as many as 84.9% of the Sakai group had received some kind of Japanese language education, in contrast to only 51.6% of the Takamatsu group, deserves attention. The gap was especially large for the workers: All of the workers in Sakai had received some instruction in Japanese, while only about a third (32.3%) of the workers in Takamatsu had.

Table 5 Japanese language education received in Japan ($N = 106$)

Occupation	Student		Worker		Not Working	
JSL Instruction Received?	*Yes n (%)*	*No n (%)*	*Yes n (%)*	*No n (%)*	*Yes n (%)*	*No n (%)*
Sakai ($n = 52$)	22 (78.6%)	6 (21.4%)	18 (100%)	0 (0%)	5 (83.3%)	1 (16.7%)
Takamatsu ($n = 54$)	15 (83.3%)	3 (16.7%)	10 (32.3%)	21 (67.7%)	3 (60.0%)	2 (40.0%)

In response to the query as to whether they were studying Japanese now, 52.6% of the respondents indicated that they were (59.6% in Sakai vs. 46.8% in Takamatsu). Among the reasons given for not studying Japanese now, 23.9% said they did not have time, 19.7% said no classes were available, and 6% said there was no need; none indicated that they did not want to study Japanese.

The respondents were also asked to assess their Japanese language ability. Although a few rated their proficiency 'ordinary' (2%), the vast majority (86%) reported that it was very poor, with some (12%) deeming it poor. These evaluations did not differ much between the two localities. As for reading and writing competency, it is estimated that the majority of the respondents understood Japanese to some extent, since 54.7% filled in the questionnaires only in Japanese and 41% used both Japanese and Chinese, while only 4.3% used Chinese alone.

Language(s) used in daily communication

After the initial questions on subject profile, the questionnaire moved on to the series of questions on language use. Question 12 asked respondents to indicate the language (Japanese, both Japanese and Chinese, or Chinese) they use when speaking to their parents, spouse, grandparents, siblings, and returnee friends, as well as the language these interlocutors use in speaking to the subjects. The results are presented in Tables 6 through 14.

Table 6 Language used with grandparents, sorted by age of respondent

	Language Used When					
	Respondent Speaks to Grandparents (N = 69)			Grandparents Speak to Respondent (N = 72)		
Respondents' Ages	Japanese	J&C*	Chinese	Japanese	J&C*	Chinese
13–19 years old	12 (34.3%)	16 (45.7%)	7 (20.0%)	9 (27.3%)	19 (57.6%)	5 (15.2%)
20–29 years old	5 (45.5%)	5 (45.5%)	1 (9.1%)	5 (45.5%)	3 (27.3%)	3 (27.3%)
30–39 years old	7 (38.9%)	2 (11.1%)	9 (50.0%)	6 (31.6%)	2 (10.5%)	11 (57.9%)
40–49 years old	1 (20.0%)	0 (0.0%)	4 (80.0%)	2 (22.2%)	2 (22.2%)	5 (55.6%)
Total	25 (36.2%)	23 (33.3%)	21 (30.4%)	22 (30.6%)	26 (36.1%)	24 (33.3%)

* J&C: Mixing Japanese and Chinese.
Subjects older than fifty years of age (*n* = 3) were excluded from this table.

Within the returnee families, the respondents reported using Japanese most in communicating with their grandparents. As shown in Table 6, 36.2% of the 69 respondents who answered the question on the language they used with their grandparents said they used Japanese, while 30.6% of the 72 respondents who answered the question on which language their grandparents spoke to them said the grandparents used Japanese. A full 80% of the teens and 91% of the respondents in their twenties reported using some Japanese in speaking to their grandparents.

The high proportion of Japanese used with grandparents may be related to the fact that many of the grandparents in these families are *zanryū fujin* (Japanese 'remaining women') who managed to maintain their Japanese during their residence in China and soon recovered full command of the language after coming back to Japan.

This contrasts with the high percentage of Chinese used by the respondents in speaking to their parents (66.3%) and used by the parents in speaking to the respondents (71.7%). As can be seen in Table 7, 82.1% of the respondents in their teens and 73.3% of those in their twenties who answered the question on the language used by their parents in speaking to them reported that their parents spoke to them only in Chinese.

This can be attributed to the parents' desire for their children to maintain their Chinese language ability (discussed in the following section) rather than to insufficient proficiency in Japanese. In interviews, many teenage students said that their parents insisted on speaking in Chinese whenever possible.

Table 7 Language used with parents, sorted by age of respondent

Respondents' Ages	Language Used When					
	Respondent Speaks to Parents (N = 104)			Parents Speak to Respondent (N = 99)		
	Japanese	J&C*	Chinese	Japanese	J&C*	Chinese
13–19 years old	0 (0.0%)	14 (34.1%)	27 (65.9%)	0 (0.0%)	7 (17.9%)	32 (82.1%)
20–29 years old	0 (0.0%)	4 (26.7%)	11 (73.3%)	0 (0.0%)	4 (26.7%)	11 (73.3%)
30–39 years old	1 (3.4%)	9 (31.0%)	19 (65.5%)	1 (3.4%)	9 (31.0%)	19 (65.5%)
40–49 years old	0 (0.0%)	7 (36.8%)	12 (63.2%)	1 (5.9%)	7 (41.2%)	9 (52.9%)
Total	1 (1.0%)	34 (32.7%)	69 (66.3%)	1 (1.0%)	27 (27.3%)	71 (71.7%)

*J&C: Mixing Japanese and Chinese.
Subjects older than fifty years of age (*n* = 4) were excluded from this table.

Table 8 Language used with parents, sorted by respondents' length of residence in Japan

Respondents' Length of Residence in Japan	*Language Used When*					
	Respondent Speaks to Parents (N = 107)			*Parents Speak to Respondent (N = 103)*		
	Japanese	*J&C**	*Chinese*	*Japanese*	*J&C**	*Chinese*
Under 1 year	0 (0.0%)	2 (22.2%)	7 (77.8%)	0 (0.0%)	4 (44.4%)	5 (55.6%)
1–3 years	0 (0.0%)	6 (16.2%)	31 (83.8%)	0 (0.0%)	5 (14.3%)	30 (85.7%)
3–5 years	0 (0.0%)	9 (27.3%)	24 (72.7%)	0 (0.0%)	6 (18.2%)	27 (81.8%)
5–10 years	0 (0.0%)	12 (60.0%)	8 (40.0%)	1 (5.6%)	6 (33.3%)	11 (61.1%)
Over 10 years	1 (12.5%)	5 (62.5%)	2 (25.0%)	1 (12.5%)	6 (75.0%)	1 (12.5%)

* J&C: Mixing Japanese and Chinese.

However, when we examine the relationship between parent-child language use and length of residence in Japan, as presented in Table 8, we see that even the parents tend to start using some Japanese in speaking to their children as the length of their residence in Japan increases.

The only subjects who said their parents spoke to them solely in Japanese had resided in Japan more than five years. Moreover, use of a mixture of Japanese and Chinese by parents rose to 75% among respondents who had lived in Japan more than ten years. In fact, many returnees admitted that they had to switch to speaking in Japanese when the topic of conversation was related to things that happened after they came to Japan, and that the longer they stayed in the country, the more frequently their topics of conversation had to do with their experiences in Japan, especially those related to their school or work.

Nonetheless, Chinese appears to be the dominant language of communication between spouses in the returnee families. Of the 61 respondents who answered one or both of the questions on language used with their spouse, a large majority (81.8%) reported that Chinese was the only language they used in speaking to their spouse, as well as the language used by the spouse in speaking to the respondent in most cases (75.4%). This was not affected by the age of the respondent, as seen in Table 9, or the length of the respondents' residence in Japan, as shown in Table 10.

No respondents reported speaking only in Japanese to their spouse – even those who had already been living in Japan for more than ten years. This might be explained by the fact that the couples, who most probably

Table 9 Language used with spouse, sorted by age of respondent

| Respondents' Ages | Language Used When | | | | | |
| | Respondent Speaks to Spouse (N = 59) | | | Spouse Speaks to Respondent (N = 61) | | |
	Japanese	*J&C**	*Chinese*	*Japanese*	*J&C**	*Chinese*
13–19 years old	0 (0.0%)	0 (0.0%)	1 (100.0%)	0 (0.0%)	1 (50.0%)	1 (50.0%)
20–29 years old	0 (0.0%)	1 (25.0%)	3 (75.0%)	0 (0.0%)	2 (50.0%)	2 (50.0%)
30–39 years old	0 (0.0%)	6 (20.7%)	22** (75.9%)	0 (0.0%)	6 (20.7%)	23 (79.3%)
40–49 years old	0 (0.0%)	3 (13.6%)	19 (86.4)	0 (0.0%)	6 (41.2%)	16 (52.9%)
50–59 years old	0 (0.0%)	0 (0.0%)	3 (100.0%)	0 (0.0%)	0 (0.0%)	3 (100.0%)
Over 60 years old	0 (0.0%)	0 (0.0%)	1 (100.0%)	0 (0.0%)	0 (0.0%)	1 (100.0%)
Total	0 (0.0%)	10 (16.7%)	49 (81.8%)	0 (0.0%)	15 (24.6%)	46 (75.4%)

* J&C: Mixing Japanese and Chinese.
** Total is less than 100% because of one ambiguous response.

Table 10 Language used with spouse, sorted by respondents' length of residence in Japan

| Respondents' Length of Residence in Japan | Language Used When | | | | | |
| | Respondent Speaks to Spouse (N = 59) | | | Spouse Speaks to Respondent (N = 60) | | |
	Japanese	*J&C**	*Chinese*	*Japanese*	*J&C**	*Chinese*
Under 1 year	0 (0.0%)	2 (33.3%)	4 (66.7%)	0 (0.0%)	2 (33.3%)	4 (66.7%)
1–3 years	0 (0.0%)	3 (15.0%)	17 (85.0%)	0 (0.0%)	4 (20.0%)	16 (80.0%)
3–5 years	0 (0.0%)	0 (0.0%)	15 (100.0%)	0 (0.0%)	1 (6.3%)	15 (93.8%)
5–10 years	0 (0.0%)	3 (25.0%)	8** (66.7%)	0 (0.0%)	5 (41.7%)	7 (58.3%)
Over 10 years	0 (0.0%)	2 (33.3%)	4 (66.7%)	0 (0.0%)	3 (50.0%)	3 (50.0%)

* J&C: Mixing Japanese and Chinese.
** Total is less than 100% because of one ambiguous response.

belong to the same age group, share many experiences and topics in common, so their personal communication is carried out most smoothly in the more familiar language (Chinese).

In contrast to this tendency of returnee couples to use Chinese, the children in the returnee families reportedly used a great deal of Japanese in their communication with each other. The answers of the 105 subjects who answered one or both of the questions on language used with their siblings were sorted by age and length and residence, and the results are presented in Tables 11 and 12, respectively.

As seen in Table 11, the tendency of the returnees to speak Japanese with their siblings is particularly conspicuous among the young.

No less than 83.8% of the teenage respondents reported using at least some Japanese with their brothers and sisters, including 35.1% who said they use only Japanese with their siblings. Likewise, 73.3% of the respondents in their twenties indicated that they use some Japanese with their siblings, including 13.3% who use only Japanese with them. In contrast, none of the respondents over 30 indicated that they spoke to their brothers and sisters exclusively in Japanese, while the proportion of those relying exclusively on Chinese in communication with their siblings generally increased with age.

Table 11 Language used with siblings, sorted by age of respondents

Respondents' Ages	Language Used When					
	Respondent Speaks to Siblings (N = 104)			Siblings Speak to Respondent (N = 105)		
	Japanese	J&C*	Chinese	Japanese	J&C*	Chinese
13–19 years old	13 (35.1%)	18 (48.6%)	6 (16.2%)	14 (36.8%)	18 (47.4%)	6 (15.8%)
20–29 years old	2 (13.3%)	9 (60.0%)	4 (26.7%)	3 (20.0%)	9 (60.0%)	3 (20.0%)
30–39 years old	0 (0.0%)	10 (34.5%)	19 (65.5%)	1 (3.4%)	7 (24.1%)	21 (72.4%)
40–49 years old	0 (0.0%)	3 (15.8%)	16 (84.2%)	0 (0.0%)	6 (31.6%)	13 (68.4%)
50–59 years old	0 (0.0%)	0 (0.0%)	2 (100.0%)	0 (0.0%)	0 (0.0%)	2 (100.0%)
Over 60 years old	0 (0.0%)	1 (50.0%)	1 (50.0%)	0 (0.0%)	1 (50.0%)	1 (50.0%)
Total	15 (14.4%)	41 (39.4%)	48 (46.2%)	18 (17.1%)	41 (39.0%)	46 (43.8%)

*J&C: Mixing Japanese and Chinese.

Table 12 Language used with siblings, sorted by length of respondents' residence in Japan

Respondents' Length of Residence in Japan	Language Used When					
	Respondent Speaks to Siblings (N = 103)			Siblings Speak to Respondent (N = 104)		
	Japanese	J&C*	Chinese	Japanese	J&C*	Chinese
Under 1 year	0 (0.0%)	5 (55.6%)	4 (44.4%)	0 (0.0%)	5 (55.6%)	4 (44.4%)
1–3 years	0 (0.0%)	14 (41.2%)	20 (58.8%)	1 (3.0%)	12 (36.4%)	20 (60.6%)
3–5 years	9 (27.3%)	10 (30.3%)	14 (42.4%)	8 (23.5%)	11 (32.4%)	15 (44.1%)
5–10 years	5 (26.3%)	7 (36.8%)	7 (36.8%)	8 (40.0%)	7 (35.0%)	5 (25.0%)
Over 10 years	1 (12.5%)	5 (62.5%)	2 (25.0%)	1 (12.5%)	6 (75.0%)	1 (12.5%)

* J&C: Mixing Japanese and Chinese.

In addition to age, length of residence in Japan was also found to be related to the language choice of returnee siblings, the use of Japanese increasing with the passage of time in this country. As shown in Table 12, the shift to speaking exclusively in Japanese occurred within as little as three years in some cases, while more than a quarter of the respondents had shifted to speaking only Japanese with their siblings within five years of moving to Japan.

Japanese was also used by the respondents, especially the youth, in communicating with returnee friends. The responses of the 110 subjects who answered one or both of the questions on language use with friends, sorted by age and length of residence in Japan, are presented in Tables 13 and 14, respectively.

It is interesting to note that age is a factor in language choice among returnee friends, with teenagers more likely to use Japanese with returnees outside of their family — most probably, their classmates. A quarter of the respondents in their teens reported that they speak only in Japanese with their returnee friends and more than 80% indicated that they use some Japanese with such friends, suggesting that their communication activities depend heavily on Japanese in both the private and public domain.

However, the proportions of returnees who used some Japanese or exclusively Japanese in speaking with their returnee friends were not as high and the shift to speaking exclusively in Japanese did not advance as quickly as it did in communication between siblings, as can be seen by comparing Tables 12 and 14. Where 40% of the siblings of respondents

Table 13 Language used with returnee friends, sorted by age of respondents

Respondents' Ages	Language Used When					
	Respondent Speaks to Siblings (N = 110)			Siblings Speak to Respondent (N = 108)		
	Japanese	J&C*	Chinese	Japanese	J&C*	Chinese
13–19 years old	10 (25.6%)	21 (53.8%)	8 (20.5%)	9 (23.7%)	20 (52.6%)	9 (23.7%)
20–29 years old	1 (6.7%)	6 (40.0%)	8 (53.3%)	0 (0.0%)	7 (46.7%)	8 (53.3%)
30–39 years old	0 (0.0%)	5 (17.2%)	24 (82.6%)	0 (0.0%)	5 (17.2%)	24 (82.6%)
40–49 years old	0 (0.0%)	4 (17.4%)	19 (82.6%)	0 (0.0%)	4 (19.0%)	17 (81.0%)
50–59 years old	0 (0.0%)	0 (0.0%)	2 (100.0%)	0 (0.0%)	0 (0.0%)	3 (100.0%)
Over 60 years old	1 (50.0%)	0 (0.0%)	1 (50.0%)	0 (0.0%)	1 (50.0%)	1 (50.0%)
Total	12 (10.9%)	36 (32.7%)	62 (56.4%)	9 (8.3%)	37 (34.3%)	62 (57.4%)

* J&C: Mixing Japanese and Chinese.

Table 14 Language used with returnee friends, sorted by respondents' length of residence in Japan

Respondents' Length of Residence in Japan	Language Used When					
	Respondent Speaks to Friends (N = 109)			Friends Speak to Respondent (N = 107)		
	Japanese	J&C*	Chinese	Japanese	J&C*	Chinese
Under 1 year	0 (0.0%)	3 (33.3%)	6 (66.7%)	0 (0.0%)	3 (33.3%)	6 (66.7%)
1–3 years	1 (2.7%)	11 (29.7%)	25 (67.6%)	1 (2.6%)	9 (23.7%)	28 (73.7%)
3–5 years	6 (17.6%)	10 (29.4%)	18 (52.9%)	7 (20.6%)	10 (29.4%)	17 (50.0%)
5–10 years	4 (18.2%)	9 (40.9%)	9 (40.9%)	1 (5.3%)	12 (63.2%)	6 (31.6%)
Over 10 years	1 (14.3%)	3 (42.9%)	3 (42.9%)	0 (0.0%)	3 (42.9%)	4 (57.1%)

* J&C: Mixing Japanese and Chinese.

who had lived in Japan between five and ten years were reportedly speaking to them exclusively in Japanese, only 5.3% of the friends of respondents who had lived in Japan that long spoke to them in Japanese only. Moreover, the proportion of subjects who said they spoke Chinese to their friends and who said their friends spoke Chinese to them was higher than that of those who reported using Chinese with their siblings, regardless of length of residence.

The reason why returnees use less Japanese with returnees outside their family than they do with their brothers and sisters may lie in differences in the length of their residence in Japan and the resulting differences in their Japanese proficiency. Siblings normally would have spent the same amount of time in Japan and their command of Japanese would be approximately the same, so they could be fairly sure of each others' Japanese ability. This would not be the case with returnees who had lived in Japan for less time, especially if they had come to Japan recently and had not yet acquired a good command of the language. In that case, Japanese would not be likely to be chosen as a medium of communication.

It may be appropriate to infer from this data that a shift to speaking only in Japanese – or at least not speaking only in Chinese – occurs among returnees as the length of their residence in Japan increases. This shift appears to occur no matter who the interlocutors are, except for spouses, who do not seem to communicate with each other using only Japanese no matter how long they have lived in Japan.

Chinese language: Domain, ability and maintenance

Another series of questions was asked about the respondents' use of their first language (Chinese), including the setting in which it is used. More than half of the respondents (53.3% overall; 46.8% in Sakai and 58.3% in Takamatsu) indicated that they have an environment outside their home where they can speak Chinese in their daily life. Among the places where subjects said they speak Chinese were friends' houses (43.9%), schools, including language schools and evening classes (28.1%), the work place (15.8%), and relatives' homes (8.8%). However, for nearly half of the respondents, opportunities for Chinese language communication were very limited, with conversation partners generally confined to family members.

Unlike many newly-arrived immigrants in the US who gravitate towards a community where many opportunities are found to use their ethnic language, these returnees are dispersed, especially in cities where their domiciles depend on vacancies in public housing. The group is so small and the society so monolingually oriented that there are no prominent community resources, such as periodicals, radio and TV stations, ethnic schools, and local religious institutions, which would help the ethnic language 'survive in any sociofunctional sense' (Fishman, 1984: 83).

One noteworthy fact suggested by this survey is that these returnees are not inclined to establish contact with other returnees who came from different regions in China. This tendency prevents their limited language resources from being effectively mobilised.

Thus, in response to Question 14, which asked, 'Do you think your Chinese proficiency declined after you came to Japan?', 28.4% (30.6% in Sakai and 26.4% in Takamatsu) indicated that it had, while 65.7% (59.2% in Sakai and 71.7% in Takamatsu) felt it was unchanged.

Loss of Chinese proficiency appeared to be related to the respondents' length of residence in Japan. Those who had been living in the country for less than a year reported no decline in their Chinese ability, but after three years of residence, the decline began and appeared to accelerate as their stay became longer. Moreover, the younger the age at which the respondents came to Japan, the more they tended to feel that their first language ability had declined. 45.5% of the teenagers in Sakai and 53.8% of the teens in Takamatsu responded that they thought their Chinese proficiency had deteriorated.

Those who indicated that they thought their Chinese proficiency had declined were asked if they thought this was related to acquiring Japanese; 89.7% felt that that Japanese language acquisition had contributed to the decline in their Chinese.

Research on bilingualism shows that the acquisition of a second language does not necessarily entail the replacement of the first. However, it has also been claimed that a second language gradually undermines proficiency in the first language when the development of that language is disrupted or incomplete, as in the case of children who are educated in second language submersion programmes (Romaine, 1995: 246). It has even been claimed that it is possible for adults to be 'semilingual' if their first language was not fully acquired and education in the second language was not sufficient (Romaine, 1995: 264). There have been no assessments done on the competency of the returnees' first and second languages except for the school examinations the students have to take in Japanese, but the conditions the young returnees are facing are close to those that are thought to produce 'semilinguals' or at least to induce the loss of the first language.

Nonetheless, most respondents indicated both a desire to maintain their first language and a belief that this will be possible. As shown in Tables 15 and 16, 79.6% strongly desire to maintain their own Chinese ability and 87.5% consider it possible. Interestingly, more respondents (85%) expressed a strong desire for their children and grandchildren to maintain their Chinese ability, but fewer (56.5%) considered it possible for their descendants to do so.

As seen in Table 15, the respondents' desire to maintain their own and their descendants' Chinese does not weaken as their residence in Japan lengthens. However, as shown in Table 16, the anticipated possibility of

Table 15 Desire to maintain Chinese, sorted by respondents' length of residence in Japan

Respondents' Length of Residence in Japan	For Oneself (N = 103)			For Descendants (N = 80)		
	Strong Desire	No Desire	Can Not Say	Strong Desire	No Desire	Can Not Say
Under 1 year	6 (75.0%)	0 (0.0%)	2 (25.0%)	3 (60.0%)	1 (20.0%)	1 (20.0%)
1–3 years	30 (83.3%)	0 (0.0%)	6 (16.7%)	26 (89.7%)	0 (0.0%)	3 (10.3%)
3–5 years	21 (63.6%)	1 (3.0%)	11 (33.3%)	19 (79.2%)	0 (0.0%)	5 (20.8%)
5–10 years	18 (100.0%)	0 (0.0%)	0 (0.0%)	13 (92.9%)	0 (0.0%)	1 (7.1%)
Over 10 years	7 (87.5%)	0 (0.0%)	1 (12.5%)	7 (87.5%)	0 (0.0%)	1 (12.5%)
Total	82 (79.6%)	1 (1.0%)	20 (19.4%)	68 (85.0%)	1 (1.3%)	11 (13.8%)

* One respondent's answer was excluded from this table because the subject did not answer the question on length of residence in Japan.

Table 16 Expectation of maintaining Chinese, sorted by length of residence in Japan

Respondents' Length of Residence in Japan	For Oneself (N = 88)		For Descendants (N = 69)	
	Possible	Impossible	Possible	Impossible
Under 1 year	5 (100.0%)	0 (0.0%)	0 (0.0%)	3 (100.0%)
1–3 years	28 (93.3%)	2 (6.7%)	16 (69.6%)	7 (30.4%)
3–5 years	26 (83.9%)	5 (16.1%)	13 (56.5%)	10 (43.5%)
5–10 years	13 (81.3%)	3 (18.8%)	7 (53.8%)	6 (46.2%)
Over 10 years	5 (83.3%)	1 (16.7%)	3 (42.9%)	4 (57.1%)
Total	77 (87.5%)	11 (12.5%)	39 (56.5%)	30 (43.5%)

* One respondent's answer was excluded from this table because the subject did not answer the question on length of residence in Japan.

Table 17 Desire to maintain Chinese, sorted by respondents' place of residence

Respondents' Place of Residence in Japan	For Oneself (N = 89)			For Descendants (N = 70)		
	Strong Desire	No Desire	Can Not Say	Strong Desire	No Desire	Can Not Say
Sakai	32 (69.6%)	1 (2.2%)	13 (28.3%)	24 (72.7%)	1 (3.0%)	8 (24.2%)
Takamatsu	51 (87.9%)	0 (0.0%)	7 (12.1%)	45 (93.8%)	0 (0.0%)	3 (6.3%)

language maintenance, especially for descendants, appears to decrease as the returnees' residence in Japan is prolonged.

When the subjects' responses were sorted by place of residence, an interesting trend came to light. As shown in Table 17, a lower proportion of the returnees living in Sakai indicated a desire for the maintenance of their own (69.6%) or their descendants' Chinese (72.7%) than did the respondents living in Takamatsu (87.9% and 93.8%, respectively). Moreover, fewer of the Sakai respondents felt that it would be possible to maintain their own Chinese proficiency (82.6%), or for their descendants to do so (46.9%), than did the respondents living in Takamatsu (93% and 65.8%, respectively), as shown in Table 18.

The responses on the desire to maintain Chinese and the expected probability of doing so were further sorted by age, and are presented in Table 19. As mentioned above, respondents under the age of 49 are presumed to be *nisei* or *sansei*, since the war ended 50 years ago and the actual 'war orphans' (*zanryū koji*) and 'remaining women' (*zanryū fujin*) were alive at that time. When the results are examined in terms of age group and location, we find that more than half of the *nisei* and *sansei* subjects in Sakai felt it would be impossible for the next generation to maintain proficiency in Chinese, with the highest proportion of those deeming it impossible found among respondents in their thirties living in Sakai (62.5%). Their

Table 18 Expectation of maintaining Chinese, sorted by respondents' place of residence

Respondents' Place of Residence in Japan	For Oneself (N = 89)		For Descendants (N = 70)	
	Possible	Impossible	Possible	Impossible
Sakai	38 (82.6%)	8 (17.4%)	15 (46.9%)	17 (53.1%)
Takamatsu	40 (93.0%)	3 (7.0%)	25 (65.8%)	13 (34.2%)

Table 19 Expectation of maintaining Chinese, sorted by age and place of residence

Respondents' Age	Sakai				Takamatsu			
	For Oneself (n = 46)		For Descendants (n = 32)		For Oneself (n = 43)		For Descendants (n = 37)	
	Possible	Impossible	Possible	Impossible	Possible	Impossible	Possible	Impossible
13–19 years	14 (70.0%)	6 (30.0%)	4 (44.4%)	5 (55.6%)	10 (83.3%)	2 (16.7%)	4 (66.7%)	2 (33.3%)
20–29 years	6 (85.7%)	1 (14.3%)	2 (40.0%)	3 (60.0%)	5 (100%)	0 (0%)	1 (50.0%)	1 (50.0%)
30–39 years	8 (88.9%)	1 (11.1%)	3 (37.5%)	5 (62.5%)	14 (100%)	0 (0%)	10 (58.8%)	7 (41.2%)
40–49 years	7 (100%)	0 (0%)	3 (42.9%)	4 (57.1%)	11 (91.7%)	1 (8.3%)	10 (83.3%)	2 (16.7%)
50–59 years	3 (100%)	0 (0%)	3 (100%)	0 (0%)	–	–	–	–
Over 60 years	–	–	–	–	–	–	0 (0%)	1 (100%)

prognosis may be viewed as realistic when we consider that those in their thirties are the parents of young children who were either born in Japan or at least have been educated in kindergartens and schools in this country, and have therefore been immersed in the Japanese language and culture from infancy.

The difference in attitude to language shift between the returnees living in Sakai and those in Takamatsu was also evident in answers given to Question 17, which asked subjects what they do when they realise that their children and/or grandchildren are speaking more in Japanese than in Chinese. Subjects were asked to indicate which of five responses they made: (1) forcing the children or grandchildren to use Chinese, (2) continuing to speak Chinese to them, (3) trying to convince them of the importance of being able to speak Chinese, (4) giving up and taking no measures against the shift to Japanese, or (5) welcoming the shift to Japanese. The results are presented in Table 20. The most frequently chosen answer in Takamatsu was to continuing to speak Chinese (46.5%), but in Sakai, it was to welcome the shift (38.1%).

The average age of the respondents in Sakai was younger and their average length of residence was also shorter than the respondents living in Takamatsu. The Sakai returnees seemed less likely to persist in maintaining their own Chinese proficiency and more accepting of the attrition of Chinese in their children. In contrast, the respondents living in Takamatsu tended to adhere to the hope of maintaining Chinese despite the absence of specific measures to do so beyond defending the family domain by speaking in Chinese to the best of their ability.

Since no conspicuous difference was found between the respondents in the two cities in terms of their language choice when speaking with family

Table 20 Response to children's shift to speaking mainly in Japanese

Respondents' Place of Residence in Japan	Response to Children's Language Shift				
	a	*b*	*c*	*d*	*e*
Sakai (*n* = 21)	2 (9.5%)	6 (28.6%)	3 (14.3%)	2 (9.5%)	8 (38.1%)
Takamatsu (*n* = 43)	2 (4.7%)	20 (46.5%)	9 (20.9%)	4 (9.3%)	8 (18.6%)
Total (*N* = 64)	4 (6.3%)	26 (40.6%)	12 (18.8%)	6 (9.4%)	16 (25.0%)

Responses to Children's Language Shift
(a) I force them to use Chinese.
(b) I continue speaking Chinese to them.
(c) I try to convince them of the importance of being able to speak Chinese.
(d) I give up and take no measures against the shift to Japanese.
(e) I welcome the shift to Japanese.

members and friends, this clear difference in their desires and expectations concerning Chinese language maintenance is worthy of attention. Though it may be going too far to directly relate the returnees' reception in the community, including opportunities to learn Japanese and administrative support services for the returnees offered in Sakai, to the swift shift to speaking only in Japanese, the correlation should not be underestimated.

Question 19 asked the subjects which of five factors they thought was most important in being able to maintain Chinese language proficiency in Japan: (1) places to speak in Chinese and people to speak it with, (2) easy access to information in Chinese, (3) Chinese language education in public schools in Japan, (4) elevating the status of the Chinese language in Japan, or (5) developing independent-study textbooks and materials. In response, 65% chose the existence of places to speak the language and people to speak it with, 48.7% chose easy access to information and language (TV, radio, newspaper, magazines etc.), 29.9% chose teaching Chinese language in public schools, 23.9% selected elevating the status of Chinese language in Japanese society and 23.1% chose developing textbooks and teaching materials. The responses were not affected by the length of residence in Japan except that the longer the respondents had lived in Japan, the more they tended to place importance on access to information.

In response to Question 18 about the information source from which they receive the latest news or literature on China, 59% selected television and radio as their most important source of information. Many parents noted that they have their friends and relatives send programmes recorded on video and cassette tapes from China especially for their children. After that, the responses, in descending order of frequency, were conversation with relatives both in Japan and China (46.2%), conversation with returnee friends (41.6%), newspapers and magazines (26.5%), and colleagues in their place of work (22.2%). These answers suggest the scarcity of human interaction, except with relatives and friends, as well as efforts on the part of the returnees to obtain new language resources which are not easily available in Japan.

Ethnic identity

It should be mentioned that many of these returnee families still have not been naturalised as Japanese, a process that would automatically be followed by the loss of their Chinese nationality and of the possibility of going back to China. Thus, they still have Chinese passports and presumably, Chinese names. Nonetheless, much as many resident Koreans use Japanese-sounding names [see Chapter 5], many of these returnees from China also use Japanese-style names. Though the Chinese and Japanese languages use the same characters (*kanji*) to write names, Chinese and

Japanese names are easily distinguished because of differences in pronunciation as well as in the selection of characters for a name. In much the same way that Europeans can easily tell that the name 'Smith' is English and 'Schmidt' is German or 'Victor' is English or French and 'Vittorio' is Italian, Japanese can look at names and tell whether they are Japanese or Chinese.

The questionnaire did not specify the type of name respondents should use. The name each respondent used when filling in the questionnaire was therefore examined as a clue to the subject's ethnic identity, in that it shows at least how the respondent desires to be seen by others. It was found that 45.3% filled in a Japanese name, 44.4% a Chinese name and 10.3% wrote both Japanese and Chinese names. However, a full 60.9% of the students wrote their Japanese names and only 26.1% wrote Chinese names, whereas only 40% of the workers wrote Japanese names and 53.3% wrote Chinese names.

The high proportion of students who chose to write a Japanese name needs to be explained. According to their teachers, many students prefer to be called by their Japanese name and some even request that nothing be said or done to reveal their Chinese ethnicity in the classroom. One reason for this choice of names among the students might be that the young came to Japan while they were in the middle of developing their ethnic identity. Another more serious possibility, however, is comformist pressure. They may be trying to protect themselves from being ignored or bullied by their Japanese classmates for 'being different'. Therefore, it is too hasty to conclude that those who chose Japanese names are denying their ethnic identity as a Chinese or trying to acculturate themselves to Japanese society.

Conclusion

Language shift from Chinese to Japanese is occurring rapidly among the young returnees from China, especially those who are receiving their elementary and secondary education in Japan. The possibility of their becoming Japanese monolinguals is high considering that domains for using Chinese are restricted to the family and/or returnee friends, and there is a scarcity of opportunities for them to learn Chinese (especially reading and writing). Many of the respondents expressed a desire to maintain their own Chinese proficiency and that of their descendants, but they seemed to be skeptical about the possibility of being able to do so, and had no effective measures to ensure that they retained their Chinese language.

In response to the final open-ended question, 'Write about any problems related to language acquisition and maintenance that you've experienced in Japan', many of the parents complained about their inability to teach Chinese to their children, while the young students expressed chagrin at their Chinese language attrition.

The respondents apparently accept the priority of learning Japanese over the maintenance of Chinese because they consider Japanese proficiency indispensable for full participation in Japanese society. It would seem, then, that they disregard the fact that they are losing their ethnic language, and consequently, the possibility of becoming bilingual.

It is putting a great burden on the returnees to make them shoulder the full responsibility for maintaining their Chinese, yet they can expect no assistance from schools, which focus on teaching Japanese only as a remedial measure and mainstream returnee children in Japanese monolingual classrooms as soon as possible. Nor can they expect to receive help from local and national governments, who see no necessity for Chinese language maintenance. In this linguistically homogeneous society, the chances are low for minority language speakers (especially newly immigrated groups from developing countries who tend to be in lower socioeconomic classes) to assert their right to maintain their language or to request public recognition of their language as an asset to society.

It seems that the returnees cannot even count on special treatment because they are dealing with two languages. Many say that one of their biggest motives in coming to Japan was to send their children to a high school or to a college.[3] However, it is very difficult for their children to pass the competitive university entrance examinations on equal terms with other Japanese students. Thus, entry is essentially barred unless some kind of preferential treatment such as a special admission quota or a time extension for the examination is offered. Foreign students who wish to study in a college or a technical school in Japan usually take at least one year of intensive language education before they take an entrance examination which is specially arranged for them. Linguistically, returnee students should be treated in the same way as foreign students in the sense that they learn Japanese as a second language.

I would like to conclude by introducing a ray of hope: one small endeavour by a group of high school teachers in Osaka who acknowledge the rich resources of these returnee students and are trying to incorporate their language skills and literacy in Chinese into socially and academically meaningful tasks. These teachers regularly organise extracurricular activities for returnee students, one of which is a cooking party where about fifty returnee students from several junior and senior high schools in the vicinity gather in the school kitchen at a senior high school and cook Chinese home-style meals. The students are divided into several groups with 'heterogeneous' members: boys and girls, senior and junior high students (seniority is an important cultural element), students who have been living in Japan for different amounts of time (directly reflected in their Japanese language competency), and students who originally came from different regions in China.

When I visited one of these gatherings, I witnessed very lively interaction among the students. Some insisted on the 'legitimacy' of their own recipe and tried to explain and convince the others that they knew best, while others showed off their skill at cooking. They frequently codeswitched between Chinese and Japanese (something that does not often occur in mainsteam Japanese classrooms). They laughed and made jokes. According to the teachers, who were guests at the 'dinner', the students are never this lively and expressive in the classroom. They seemed full of joy and confidence to be able to present their knowledge from home and the outcome of their efforts (delicious Chinese dishes) to their teachers.

After the meal, the students freely discussed their problems in school and at home. The junior high students posed many questions to the senior high students about how to pass entrance examinations. The senior high students tried to be as informative and helpful as possible. Some newly-arrived students poured out their frustrations and uneasiness over adjusting to their new environment. The teachers told me that only in this way could they approach these students and know what they really wanted.

Another occasion for more open interaction is provided by a Chinese reading club held every weekend at a senior high school. There ten returnee students gather to read Chinese literature with the help of a Chinese lecturer who is a visiting researcher at a university nearby. The time I visited the club, they were reading a novel by Lu Xun, one of the most prominent writers of the twentieth century. Students who struggle with Japanese textbooks could read the novel with ease and discuss the theme and symbolism in fluent Chinese. Japanese teachers accompanying the students and trying to learn some Chinese for their own educational purposes confessed that the level was too high for them and admitted that they realised the academic competence of these students every time they came to this reading club. Through use of Chinese, the students were teaching their teachers and both groups were happy about this 'cooperative' relationship. Here I see convincing evidence to support the implementation of bilingual education (at least transitional bilingual education) utilising the students' first language to promote their academic and cognitive development as well as to ensure the maintenance of their language, culture and ethnic identity.

It is difficult to depict the actual language situation of the returnees because their competency and usage depend on many factors, including their age when they came to Japan, the duration of their residence, their occupation and educational background, whether and what kind of Japanese language education they had before and after coming to Japan, their place of residence, their intention to settle in Japan, and their ethnic identity. However, if we fail to recognise that these fellow countrymen offer rich linguistic resources and have a high potentiality of becoming bilingual, and we allow a shift to Japanese monolingualism, it will be a great loss to Japanese society and there will be little chance left to accommodate other more linguistically and ethnically different minority groups residing in Japan.

Notes

1. As of June 30, 1997, a total of 212,229 foreigners were registered residents of Osaka Prefecture; among them, Koreans (167,999) are the largest in number, followed by Chinese (23,151), and Brazilians (6358) [Osaka Prefectural Office, 1997].
2. The number of returnees from China living in Takamatsu City and its vicinity was not available. Among 286 returnees living in Kagawa Prefecture, 89 (31%) came to Japan at government expense and 197 (69%) came at their own expense but with the confirmation of the prefectural office. The prefectural office was rather reluctant to reveal detailed information on the returnees in Kagawa and regretfully admitted that the assistance provided for these returnees was not sufficient.
3. In the latest survey of foreign students in junior high schools who need Japanese language education, 82.3% of the Chinese students (returnee students are categorised in this group) said that they want to go on to a senior high school, and only 2.6% said they intended to go back to their country. By contrast, only 23.3% of the Brazilian students (many of whom are Japanese-Brazilian) said they wanted to go on to a senior high school while 17.3% indicated that they intend to go back to their country (*Asahi shimbun*, 1997).

Appendix

Questionnaire on Language Background and Use

Q1   Name   Q2 Sex (Male, Female)   Q3 Age
Q4   When did you come to Japan?
Q5   Your Occupation
     (Junior High School Student, Senior High School Student, College Student, Working: What kind of work?, Not working)
Q6   Educational Background in China
     (Elementary School, Junior High School, Senior High School, College)
Q7   What was your occupation in China?
     (Farmer, Factory worker, Engineer, Teacher, Professional, Other)
Q8   Did you study Japanese before you came to Japan? (If 'Yes', where and how long?)
Q9   How would you assess your Japanese language proficiency? (Good, Fair, Poor)
Q10 Have you studied Japanese after you came to Japan? (If 'Yes', where and how long?)
Q11 Are you studying Japanese now? (If 'No', explain the reason.)
Q12 What language do you use (Japanese, both Japanese and Chinese, Chinese) when you speak to the following interlocutors? What language do these interlocutors use in speaking to you?
     (a) Your parents, (b) Your spouse, (c) Your grandparents, (d) Your siblings, (e) Your returnee friends.
Q13 Do you have any places you can use Chinese other than your home? (If 'Yes', where?)
Q14 Do you think your Chinese proficiency declined after you came to Japan? (If 'Yes', do you think the decline is related to acquiring Japanese?)
Q15 Do you want to maintain the ability to speak the Chinese language for yourself and your descendants?
     (Strongly desire, Do not desire, Can not say)
Q16 Do you think that it will be possible for you and your descendants to maintain Chinese language proficiency in the future? (Possible, Impossible)
Q17 To those who have children and/or grandchildren:
     What is your reaction when you realise that your children and/or grandchildren are speaking more in Japanese than in Chinese? (Pick one of the reactions below.)
     (a) I force them to use Chinese.
     (b) I continue speaking Chinese to them.

(c) I try to convince them of the importance of being able to speak Chinese.

(d) I give up and take no measures against the shift to Japanese.

(e) I welcome the shift to Japanese.

Q18   How do you obtain information in Chinese?

(a) TV/radio, (b) Newspaper/magazines, (c) Returnee friends at school/work, (d) Returnee friends in the community, (e) Friends and relatives living in China.

Q19   What do you think is the most important factor in being able to maintain Chinese language proficiency in Japan?

(a) Places to speak in Chinese and people to speak it with, (b) Easy access to information in Chinese, (c) Chinese language education in public schools in Japan, (d) Elevating the status of the Chinese language in Japan, (e) Developing independent-study textbooks and materials.

Q20   Write about any problems related to language acquisition and maintenance that you've experienced in Japan.

References

Asahi shimbun (1994) *Indo-shina nammin teijūsha* [Permanent Resident Indochinese Refugees], October 17.

Asahi shimbun (1997) *Gaikokujin no shingaku kibō* [Foreigners' Hopes for Higher Education], May 14.

Fishman, J.A. (1972) Who speaks what language to whom and when? In J. Prides and J. Holmes (eds) *Sociolinguistics* (pp. 15–33). Harmondsworth: Penguin.

Fishman, J.A. (1984) Mother tongue claiming in the United States since 1960: Trends and correlates related to the 'revival of ethnicity'. *International Journal of Sociology of Language* 50, 21–99.

Kunitomo T. (1986) *Haikei nakasone yasuhiro shushō-dono* [An Open Letter to Prime Minister Nakasone Yasuhiro]. *Asahi Journal* July 4, 88–91.

Maher, J. (1995) The *Kakyō*: Chinese in Japan. In J. Maher and Yashiro K. (eds) *Multilingual Japan* (pp. 125–38). Clevedon, UK: Mutilingual Matters.

Maher, J. and Kawanishi Y. (1995) On being there: Koreans in Japan. In J. Maher and Yashiro K. (eds) *Multilingual Japan* (pp. 87–102). Clevedon, UK: Multilingual Matters.

Ministry of Public Welfare (1987) *Chūgoku zanryū koji* [Chinese War Orphans]. Cited in Yashiro K., *Imin no bairingarizumu* [Bilingualism of immigrants]. In J. Maher and Yashiro K. (eds) *Nihon no bairingarizumu* [Bilingualism in Japan] (pp. 177–209). Tokyo: Kenkyusha.

Ministry of Public Welfare (1997) *Chūgoku kikokusha no nendobetsu kikoku jōkyō* [Annual Trends in Arrivals of Chinese Returnees]. Tokyo: Ministry of Public Welfare.

Osaka Prefectural Office (1994) *Chūgoku kikokusha no teichaku jōkyō no gaiyō* [Report on the Settlement of Chinese Returnees in Osaka Prefecture]. Osaka: Osaka Prefectural Office.

Osaka Prefectural Office (1997) *Osaka-fu gaikokujin tōrokusū* [Registered Number of Foreigners in Osaka Prefecture]. Osaka: Osaka Prefectural Office.

Romaine, S. (1995) *Bilingualism* (Second Edition). Oxford, England: Basil Blackwell.

Sakamoto T. (1994) *Sokoku sōshitsu* [The Loss of the Mother Country]. *Sekai*, September, 61–67.

Chapter 7

On the Language Environment of Brazilian Immigrants in Fujisawa City

HIRATAKA FUMIYA, KOISHI ATSUKO AND KATO YOSUKE

Introduction

The number of officially registered foreign residents of Japan exceeded 1% of the total population of the country for the first time in 1992. Compared to European countries, where foreigners comprise approximately 7% to 8% of the total population, 1% is a small proportion. However in Japan, which is often called a 'mono-racial nation', it was viewed as surprising that the proportion of foreign residents rose to such an extent. Nonetheless, both the number of foreigners living in the country and their percentage of the nation's population have continued to rise every year since that time, as shown in Table 1.

This remarkable rise in the foreign population in Japan was due to a large influx of immigrants that began in the 1980s. There were three

Table 1 Increase of foreign residents in Japan[1]

Year	Foreign Residents (n)	(% of Japan's Total Population)	South Americans (Including Brazilians) (n)	(% of Japan's Foreign Residents)
1985	850,612	(0.70%)	3,608	(0.4%)
1986	867,237	(0.71%)	3,961	(0.5%)
1987	884,025	(0.72%)	4,134	(0.5%)
1988	941,005	(0.77%)	6,872	(0.7%)
1989	984,455	(0.80%)	21,899	(2.2%)
1990	1,075,317	(0.87%)	71,495	(6.6%)
1991	1,218,891	(0.98%)	153,099	(12.6%)
1992	1,281,644	(1.03%)	187,140	(14.6%)
1993	1,320,748	(1.06%)	196,491	(14.9%)
1994	1,354,011	(1.08%)	203,840	(15.0%)
1995	1,362,371	(1.08%)	221,865	(16.3%)
1996	1,415,136	(1.12%)	248,780	(17.6%)
1997	1,482,707	(1.18%)	284,691	(19.2%)
1998	1,512,116	(1.20%)	296,659	(19.6%)

main factors underlying this increase in immigration: (1) a general lack of manpower in Japan, (2) high wages in comparison to other countries, and (3) Japanese reluctance to engage in tedious manual labour (Shimada, 1993: 34–36; Kajita, 1994: 50).

Revision of the Immigration Control Law in June 1990 spurred further rises in immigration, especially from South America, as evident in Table 1. Many of the South American immigrants are *Nikkei-jin* — people of Japanese ancestry. This is because the new immigration law allows Nikkei to work in Japan, while other foreigners are prohibited entry if the purpose is to engage in simple manual labour. Formerly, only Nikkei with Japanese nationality could live and work legally in Japan, but under the new immigration law, Nikkei down to the third generation, as well as their spouses, can legally stay and work in Japan even if they do not have Japanese nationality. In addition to these favourable revisions in the Immigration Control Law and the three factors mentioned above that served to 'pull in' labourers to Japan, economic stagnation and social unrest in their home countries also served as 'push-out' factors for many South Americans (Watanabe, 1995, Vol. 1: 20).

After the 1990 revision of the immigration law, the city of Fujisawa, where our university is located, experienced a rapid rise in the number of South American residents, as shown in Table 2. Fujisawa is situated south of Tokyo, about one hour away by train, and has a population of approximately 370,000, including some 5500 foreigners. Many major manufacturers, including Sony, Panasonic, IBM and Isuzu, have factories in this city, and the number of immigrant workers in these factories has been growing. The countries of origin of these labourers are quite varied; however in April 1997, the six largest groups were Brazilians, Peruvians, Koreans, Chinese, Argentinians, and Vietnamese (*Fujisawa shiyakusho*

Table 2 Increase in South American residents in Fujisawa City[2]

Year	Brazilians (n)	South Americans (Including Brazilians) (n)	(South American Proportion of All Foreign Residents)	Foreign Residents (n)
1987	7	9	(0.6%)	1430
1988	27	36	(2.3%)	1549
1989	219	436	(21.2%)	2058
1990	588	1270	(41.0%)	3095
1991	1270	2321	(54.9%)	4226
1992	1843	3270	(59.8%)	5470
1993	1846	3423	(60.1%)	5692
1994	1561	2975	(56.9%)	5232
1995	1375	2781	(54.1%)	5140
1996	1493	2874	(54.4%)	5287
1997	1491	2935	(51.7%)	5672

gaikokujin sōdanshitsu, 1996). The largest single group was the Brazilians (26.3% of all foreigners in Fujisawa), and the total number of South American immigrants including Brazilians represented 51.7% of all foreign residents in the city. As can be seen by comparing Tables 1 and 2, the proportion of South Americans in Fujisawa City is much larger than the national average.

This rapid increase of immigrant workers during the last decade has given rise to various social problems, and measures are being taken to deal with many of these concerns. However, the immigrants' language problems are seldom among those that are actively addressed. Nonetheless, language issues are a major concern for the immigrants themselves. For example, a 1992 survey taken in Hamamatsu, an industrial city with many immigrant workers like Fujisawa, shows that Japanese language courses stand first among administrative services desired by immigrants.[3]

Similarly, even though there are many studies concerning the social situation of immigrant workers, the language issue, which is most important in promoting intercultural understanding and communication, is rarely the subject of research. The object of this paper, therefore, is to examine the language problems of immigrant workers in Japan through a case study of Fujisawa City, a typical industrial city with many immigrants, and to analyse these problems from the viewpoint of language rights. We will begin with a brief discussion of language rights for immigrants so that we will have a theoretical basis for reflection on the situation in Fujisawa. We will then describe a survey we made of the language situation of Brazilian residents of this city and present the results. Next we will describe the public services offered to immigrants by Fujisawa City. Finally, we will discuss the necessity of improving the language environment of Brazilian immigrants in the city, as well as in Japan as a whole, and make concrete suggestions for doing so. We would be happy if our study contributes not only to the improvement of the language situation for immigrant workers in Japan, but also to a re-examination of commonly-held views of the purpose of foreign language teaching in Japan.

Language Rights for Immigrants

Compared to the attention given to the language rights of other minorities, immigrants' language rights are seldom referred to. In 'Some provisional generalizations about linguistic human rights in the UN Framework', Skutnabb-Kangas & Phillipson (1995: 78–79) point out that, 'Immigrant minorities were deliberately excluded from consideration in the Capotorti Report, hence from the main thrust of UN efforts to end discrimination against minorities.'

Moreover, in the International Convention on the Protection of the Rights of All Migrant Workers and Members of Their Families, a resolution from the 69th UN Plenary Meeting on the 18th of December, 1990, which covers nearly the whole range of human rights for migrant workers and members of their families, there are only a few passages which refer to language rights. Article 16 mentions language rights in case of arrest, Article 22, in relation to expulsion, and Article 18, in case immigrants are brought before courts and tribunals. However these cases are relatively rare in the daily life of most migrant workers.

For more day to day situations, the Convention refers to language rights only indirectly. For example, Article 43.1 provides that, 'Migrant workers shall enjoy equality of treatment with nationals of the State of employment in relation to' access to 'educational institutions', 'social and health services', and other benefits. Although we can easily imagine that migrant workers need a certain degree of fluency in the host country's language in order to get access to 'educational institutions' and 'social and health services', the word 'language' cannot be found in this article.

One reason why immigrants' language rights are not mentioned often is that there are factors which differentiate immigrants from national or regional minorities. One is that immigrants sometimes do not stay in a country for very long, making it difficult to take their language rights into consideration.

Nonetheless, the Convention does make some mention of language rights for immigrants in everyday situations. For example, the three sections of Article 45 shown in Figure 1 clearly refer to the language rights of children of immigrant workers.

Article 45

2. States of employment shall pursue a policy, where appropriate in collaboration with the States of origin, aimed at facilitating the integration of children of migrant workers in the local school system, particularly in respect of teaching them the local language.

3. States of employment shall endeavour to facilitate for the children of migrant workers the teaching of their mother tongue and culture and, in this regard, States of origin shall collaborate whenever appropriate.

4. States of employment may provide special schemes of education in the mother tongue of children of migrant workers, if necessary in collaboration with the States of origin.

Figure 1 Language Rights and the Convention on the Protection of the Rights of All Migrant Workers and Members of Their Families

These provisions suggest that there are two aspects to the language rights of the children of immigrant workers. Following Skutnabb-Kangas

& Phillipson (1995), we will define these two types of language rights as follows:

(1)   The right to learn and use one's mother tongue.
(2)   The right to learn an/the official language in the country of residence.

Although it remains to be proven whether the same rights apply to adults as well, this does not affect the validity of the twofold nature of language rights as the basic assumption and the starting-point of our paper. A close examination of the two types of language rights is therefore called for:

(1)   The right to learn and use one's mother tongue.
      We have the right to learn and use our mother tongue in order to protect our basic human rights. This right has two facets: the first is practical and the second is psychological. We use the word 'practical' to refer to, for example, the right to receive public services offered by the municipal government, including the right to communicate with the help of an interpreter, if necessary. The second facet is psychological: we have the right to protect and maintain our identity.[4]

(2)   The right to learn an/the official language in the country of residence.
      In order to lead a life in which minimum requirements can be fulfilled, a language environment to facilitate the learning of an/the official language of the country of residence must be created for all immigrants.

To determine the extent to which these two rights are perceived to have been met by Brazilian immigrants in the city of Fujisawa, we conducted a survey between late 1995 and early 1996. The results are presented and discussed below.

Research Survey

Object and methodology

The main object of our study was to investigate the language environment and language use of Brazilian residents of Fujisawa. Prior to this survey, a pilot study had been conducted in 1994 on the language situation of Peruvian immigrants living in Fujisawa (mentioned in LAPO, 1998). However we opted to focus on Brazilians in our main survey for the following reasons:

(1)   Brazilians constitute the largest group of foreign residents in the city.
(2)   Japanese language maintenance is reputed to be more successful among Nikkei Brazilians than Nikkei groups from other countries.
(3)   We knew of a Japanese-speaking Brazilian couple from whom we could expect help in conducting our survey.
(4)   A survey had already been conducted on Peruvian immigrants in Fujisawa and the Kanto area which could be used for comparison (Nakajima, 1996).

After deciding on the target group, we developed our own questionnaire containing 29 questions in Portuguese. (An English translation is provided in the appendix.) From November 1995 to January 1996, 451 questionnaires were distributed to Brazilians in Fujisawa, mainly in the northern part of the city, which is an industrial area. Most were distributed through our collabourator to Brazilian workers in factories, but others were distributed through restaurants, ethnic grocery stores, travel agencies, churches, and so on.

Perhaps because the researchers had no direct communication with the subjects, only 183 of the questionnaires were returned and there were problems with four of these. This left a total of 179 valid questionnaires, for a response rate of 39.7%. Moreover, some of the respondents left some questions unanswered or their answers were deemed invalid.

Although this was not a random sample and the response rate was low, it was felt that the large number of responses can contribute to our understanding of the language situation of Brazilian immigrants in Fujisawa, and by extrapolation, in the rest of Japan. The results are presented and discussed below, with the number of valid responses for each question (N) indicated on the data tables.[5]

Subjects

Reflecting the general makeup of the Nikkei Brazilian population in Japan,[6] 64% of our subjects were men and 36%, women. Only 9% of our informants had been living in the country for more than six years; the rest had been in Japan for five years or less. Thus, most of our subjects had come to Japan after the new Immigration Control Law was enacted.

The questionnaire revealed that our subjects had a fairly high level of education compared to the average educational level in Brazil. As can be seen in Table 3, 79% of our respondents went to high school, university or a polytechnic school. In contrast, only 17% of Brazil's total population had finished primary school in 1990 (Watanabe, 1995, Vol. 1: 413).

When asked to describe their profession in Japan, however, almost two thirds of our subjects indicated that they were doing unskilled labour;

Table 3 Educational background (N = 176)

Educational Background	n	(%)
No formal education	1	(0.6%)
Primary school	29	(16.5%)
High school	77	(43.8%)
University	41	(23.3%)
Polytechnic school	21	(11.9%)
Other	7	(4.0%)

Table 4 Nationality (*N* = 177)

Nationality	n	(%)
Brazilian	173	(97.7%)
Japanese	2	(1.1%)
Dual nationals	2	(1.1%)

59 (32.2%) wrote that they were labourers, 6 (3.3%) said they were migrant workers, and 52 (28.4%) indicated that they were factory workers (including various areas of speciality). Thus, there was a gap between their educational background and the work they were doing in Japan.

We also discovered a gap between the respondents' nationality and their self-perceived ethnic identity. As shown in Table 4, 97.7% had Brazilian nationality, 1.1% were Japanese, and the remaining 1.1% were dual nationals with both Japanese and Brazilian nationality. However, when asked whether they perceived themselves to be Brazilians, Japanese, Nikkei or something else, more than 80%, regardless of their nationality, responded that they saw themselves as Nikkei (Table 5). These results indicate that most of our subjects, in spite of their Brazilian nationality, regard themselves as people of Japanese descent rather than as Brazilians *per se*.

This tendency was also noted by Mita (1995), who reported that in Brazil, where a multicultural policy has been adopted since the 1960s, different ethnic groups are allowed to maintain their own ethnic identity. In this context, Nikkei consider themselves to be 'japonês' or 'japonesa' in Brazil.

In Japan, however, they are seldom treated as 'Japanese', mostly because of their poor proficiency in the Japanese language. Instead, they tend to be treated as 'foreigners' or 'foreign workers'. This gap between the Nikkei's perception of their own identity and the way they are perceived in Japan sometimes causes serious identity crisis problems among the Nikkei Brazilians living in Japan.

The root of the tension appears to be language proficiency. Although over 80% of the respondents based their identity on their Japanese ancestry, only 11.9% declared Japanese to be their mother tongue. Most of the remainder indicated that Portuguese was their mother tongue, as shown in Table 6.

Table 5 Ethnic identity (*N* = 176)

Self-Perceived Ethnicity	n	(%)
Nikkei	142	(80.7%)
Brazilian	31	(17.6%)
Japanese	3	(1.7%)

Table 6 Mother tongue ($N = 177$)

Language	n	(%)
Portuguese	154	(87.0%)
Japanese	21	(11.9%)
Other	2	(1.1%)

Table 7 Japanese language learning experience in Brazil ($N = 177$)

Experience	n	(%)
Did not learn at all	88	(49.7%)
Used at home	44	(24.9%)
Learned someplace other than at home	45	(25.4%)

Moreover, almost half of our subjects indicated that they had not learned any Japanese before coming to Japan, as shown in Table 7.

Nonetheless, almost a quarter of the respondents said that they had used Japanese to some extent at home in Brazil and about the same percentage had studied Japanese to a certain extent in language schools or in private lessons. Thus, approximately half of our subjects were somewhat familiar with Japanese before their arrival in this country.

Results and Discussion

Language use at home

Our subjects were asked to indicate whether they were currently living alone, with their Japanese family and/or relative(s), friend(s) and/or colleague(s), or with their Brazilian family and/or relative(s), friend(s) and/or colleague(s). Only 7 (4%) said they live with Japanese, whereas 148 (81%) reported living with other Brazilians (LAPO, 1998: 28–29).

Nonetheless, when asked to indicate what language or combination of languages they used at home, more than 20% indicated that they use Japanese to some extent (both languages equally, usually Japanese, or only Japanese), as shown in Table 8.

Table 8 Language used at home in Japan ($N = 178$)

Language(s)	n	(%)
Only Portuguese	92	(51.7%)
Usually Portuguese	45	(25.3%)
Both equally	33	(18.5%)
Usually Japanese	2	(1.1%)
Only Japanese	6	(3.4%)

We can say that this 'familiarity' with the Japanese language, though modest, both prior to and after their arrival in Japan, is one of the distinctive characteristics of the Brazilian immigrants in Japan. This is a marked contrast to Peruvian immigrants, for example, who reportedly do not have much familiarity with Japanese at all before coming to Japan. According to a similar study conducted in Tokyo and Kanagawa from 1994 to 1995, 88% of the Peruvian immigrants surveyed said they rarely used Japanese in Peru, in spite of their perception of themselves as Nikkei (Nakajima, 1996).

The Brazilian's familiarity with Japanese can be explained as follows. As pointed out by Skuttnab-Kangas & Phillipson (1989), it is not easy to define and determine one's mother tongue in many cases. Especially for Nikkei immigrants, this is a very delicate question. Among the four criteria (origin, competence, function and identification[7]) proposed by Skuttnab-Kangas & Phillipson for mother tongue determination, the first three would seem to justify the designation of Portuguese as the mother tongue of Nikkei Brazilians, at least for adults. However when using the criteria of *identification*, particularly *internal identification*, we hesitate to declare Portuguese to be their mother tongue because, as seen above, they perceive themselves to be *Nikkei-jin* – people of Japanese origin – rather than Brazilians. Thus, their familiarity with the Japanese language may perhaps be explained in this context.

As to other differences between Brazilian and Peruvian Nikkei immigrants, they are due to historical and geographical causes which space limitations do not allow us to discuss here.[8]

Language use at work

The respondents' reports of the language they used to communicate with their Japanese colleagues are presented in Table 9. Over 77% said they use Japanese. Since most of the respondents were involved in manual labour, a high level of Japanese language proficiency was probably not required. A few words would suffice to conduct work-related conversations with Japanese colleagues.

For complicated matters, employers may ask for assistance from interpreters. We therefore asked our subjects, 'Who serves as interpreter at

Table 9 Language used with Japanese colleagues ($N = 171$)

Language(s)	n	(%)
Do not talk with Japanese	20	(11.7%)
Japanese	132	(77.2%)
Portuguese	18	(10.5%)
Other	1	(0.6%)

Table 10 Interpreters at the work place (*N* = 173)

Interpreters' Ethnicity	n	(% Total)	(% of Interpreters)
None	47	(27.2%)	–
Japanese	8	(4.6%)	(6.3%)
Nikkei	63	(36.4%)	(50.0%)
Brazilians	45	(26.0%)	(35.7%)
Others	10	(5.8%)	(7.9%)

your work place?' Their answers are presented in Table 10. Forty-seven respondents (27.2%) indicated that they had no interpreters at their work place, while 126 subjects (72.8%) picked one of the other answers: Japanese, Nikkei, Brazilian or Other. Of those who indicated that there was an interpreter at their workplace, 50% (63 subjects) said the persons who serve as interpreters were Nikkei and 35.7% (45 subjects), Brazilians. Only a very small number of subjects said they had Japanese interpreters. In any case, these interpreters are apparently never professionals. As a general rule, it is the minority group that provides the interpreter, with one of the workers who is relatively more proficient in Japanese serving in that capacity.

Japanese language proficiency and learning conditions

We asked our subjects to evaluate their Japanese language proficiency, both before they came to Japan and their current level, in terms of their ability in each of the four language skills: listening, speaking, reading and writing. Their evaluations of their current Japanese proficiency are presented in Table 11.

We can see from this table that the subjects' oral proficiency is far superior to their written proficiency in Japanese. When asked whether they felt their Japanese proficiency was sufficient, 20.3% of our subjects answered 'yes'. However, some of those who said that they had no problems in daily conversation admitted that they either could not write at all (17%) or that they could not write Chinese characters (*kanji*). This suggests that the Nikkei do not encounter major difficulties in everyday life in Japan even when they do not have a high level of written proficiency in Japanese. Possible reasons for this may be: (1) they are doing unskilled labour which does not require high levels of written language proficiency, and (2) they are living within a Brazilian community which provides them with all the information they need in Portuguese.

Only 35.6% of our subjects indicated that they had actually studied Japanese since their arrival in Japan, although 88.1% reported that they would like to improve their Japanese. These two results suggest that in spite of a desire to learn Japanese, the immigrants encountered obstacles

Table 11 Self assessments of current Japanese language proficiency

Listening Ability (N = 177)	*n*	*(%)*
Cannot understand at all	10	(5.6%)
Can understand only greetings	38	(21.5%)
Can understand daily conversations	110	(62.1%)
Can understand TV news programs	19	(10.7%)
Speaking Ability (N = 176)		
Cannot speak at all	10	(5.7%)
Can say only greetings	43	(24.4%)
Can conduct daily conversations	82	(46.6%)
Can converse on the telephone	41	(23.3%)
Reading Ability (N = 177)		
Cannot read at all	57	(32.2%)
Can read only *hiragana* or *katakana*[9]	72	(40.7%)
Can read short memos	36	(20.3%)
Can read letters	12	(6.8%)
Writing Ability (N = 176)		
Cannot write at all	50	(28.4%)
Can write *hiragana* or *katakana*[9]	80	(45.5%)
Can write short memos	27	(15.3%)
Can write letters using Chinese characters (*Kanji*)	19	(10.8%)

to language study. Possible problems might be: (1) they are too busy with their work to find time to study Japanese, or (2) they cannot take Japanese lessons at a time convenient for them. On the other hand, some immigrants may not be motivated to study Japanese because they can manage daily life without a high level of Japanese proficiency.

We asked those who had studied Japanese after their arrival in Japan where they took their lessons. The largest percentage (8% of the total subjects) studied with volunteer teachers at community centres, and only 6.3% at their workplace. It appears that little opportunity is offered at the workplace.

On the whole, it can be said that our subjects could manage daily life one way or another with their current Japanese proficiency. However, in spite of their desire to make progress in Japanese, their living and working environment was not ideal for improving their Japanese proficiency.

Usage of Portuguese

Brazilian communities are being formed in Fujisawa: Beside the networks the immigrants form through their workplace, religious services and meetings organised regularly by religious groups, both Christian and Shintoist, provide good opportunities for Brazilians to come into contact with others from their country. Within these local groups, active information exchange appears to take place.

There are also a number of Latin-American food restaurants, grocery stores and travel agencies in Fujisawa where Brazilian people have access to newspapers[10] and community newsletters written in Spanish or Portuguese, as well as videos and CDs. Through these media, Brazilian people can keep in touch with the Portuguese language as well as with other South Americans.

However, support networks to help Nikkei Brazilian children learn their mother tongue are far from sufficient. Occasionally it is arranged for bilingual 'Japanese Language Tutors' (explained below) to teach the children's mother tongue as well, especially when the children are planning to go back to Brazil. Portuguese language courses organised by Brazilian volunteers are offered at a community centre once a week and in a primary school every Saturday. However these attempts rely entirely on private initiative and are therefore not sufficient. Consequently, communication problems between children and parents are reported. Some children speak Japanese and know very few Portuguese words, while their parents do not understand enough Japanese to communicate with them. Therefore, many Brazilian parents wish to have Portuguese lessons taught at community centres.

Public Services Offered by the City

The city of Fujisawa offers a number of services for foreign residents, especially for children of school age. As shown in Table 2, there were 5672 registered foreign residents of Fujisawa in 1997, of whom 1491 were Brazilians. According to data published by the City Board of Education (*Fujisawa-shi kyōiku iinkai*, 1997), as of May 1 of that year 296 of these foreign residents were children attending primary schools (including 56 Brazilian children), while 96 were students attending secondary schools (with 21 Brazilians among them). Widely dispersed, these foreign children were enrolled in 29 of the city's 35 primary schools and 15 of the city's 19 secondary schools. One hundred and thirty-four of these children needed to be taught Japanese as a second language. [See Chapter 8 for more on the education of language minority children in Japan.]

Japanese language education

Language support for the city's foreign children began with the 'Japanese Language Tutor' programme that was established for Chinese children in 1989. [See Chapter 6 for background information on these children.] These bilingual tutors speak the children's mother tongue and help them learn Japanese. As mentioned above, they are occasionally enlisted for mother tongue support as well. There are currently six Japanese Language

Tutors in Fujisawa: three Japanese nationals and three non-Japanese. Two speak Spanish, two Portuguese, one Chinese, and one Vietnamese.

In 1992 the first Japanese as a Second Language (JSL) class in Fujisawa was established at the Shonandai Primary School. Called '*Nihongo kyōshitsu*' (Japanese Language Class), this class is currently run by two full-time teachers and two part-time Japanese Language Tutors, all of whom speak Spanish or Portuguese. The instructors teach 'pull-out' type JSL classes (where children are released from their regular lessons for special instruction in Japanese) for Shonandai Primary School children in the morning, and for junior high school students who live in the area in the afternoon. Some Keio University students also work in the school as volunteers to provide the children with language support in their academic work.

Also since 1992, schools with more than five students from different language backgrounds needing JSL lessons have been able to add one extra teacher to create a *kokusai kyōshitsu* (International Class). Under this system, the additional teachers, sometimes assisted by a bilingual Japanese Language Tutor, teach Japanese in a 'pull-out' type class two or three times a week to non-Japanese students who need individual JSL lessons. This measure has been provided by Kanagawa Prefecture, in which the city of Fujisawa is located. At present, seven primary schools and six junior high schools in Fujisawa benefit from this system.

In 17 other primary schools and two junior high schools, special Japanese lessons are offered by Japanese Language Tutors who travel from school to school. When necessary, they sometimes teach the children's mother tongue to those who are already fluent in Japanese.

In addition to these support programmes for the children of immigrants, there are also Japanese courses for adults taught by volunteers. Fujisawa City often provides the classroom space, mostly at community centres. At present, there are approximately ten courses of this kind.

In spite of these services, our study suggests that several problems remain, especially in relation to Japanese courses for adults. First, we found that many Brazilian workers are not aware of opportunities for studying Japanese free of charge. Second, even if they know about these opportunities, they often do not take advantage of them because they are not accustomed to using public services to improve their life. Third, the Japanese courses are not offered at times that are convenient for the workers. Many of the immigrants work overtime in order to earn as much money as possible, so they do not have time to study on weekdays, when the classes are usually offered.

Mother tongue support

In contrast to the variety of Japanese language classes provided for immigrants in Fujisawa, little is being done to support mother tongue education. The only service offered at present is to employ people who speak the children's mother tongue as 'Japanese Language Tutors'. As mentioned above, these tutors sometimes teach children their mother tongue as well.

Some efforts are being made to communicate with immigrant workers and their families in Portuguese, however. For example, the Japanese Language Tutors translate notices and information sent from schools to the children's parents. Moreover in 1991, Fujisawa's Board of Education prepared a guide for foreign students in six languages and distributed it to schools with non-Japanese students. The Spanish and Portuguese editions were revised in 1993. With the collaboration of Keio University students, the Board of Education also produced a video introducing Japanese primary school life in three languages: Spanish, Portuguese, and Japanese. Furthermore, for the last several years the Board of Education has organised five-day summer schools at which teachers and school employees can study Spanish, Portuguese and English so that they can better communicate with foreign students.

Other services

In the Fujisawa City Hall there is an advisory office for foreigners whose staff includes one Brazilian, one Argentinian and one Paraguayan. Since its opening in 1991, the number of foreigners who have come in for consultation has steadily increased, with the office handling 3821 cases in 1994. A breakdown of the cases by type is presented in Table 12.[11]

In addition to these services, community centres in Fujisawa occasionally organise cultural exchange meetings such as multinational cooking classes and language lessons.

Table 12 Topics of consultation at Fujisawa Municipal Advisory Office for Foreigners (1994)

Topic	*n*	*(%)*
Registration	886	(23.2%)
Taxes	655	(17.1%)
Insurance & Health Concerns	520	(13.6%)
Education	313	(8.2%)
Employment	264	(6.9%)
Housing	136	(3.6%)
Japanese Language	54	(1.4%)
Others (Traffic Accidents, Translation, Moving, etc.)	993	(26.0%)
Total	*3821*	*(100.0%)*

Conclusion

Compared to the average municipal government in Japan, Fujisawa City is making considerable efforts to integrate non-Japanese students into its schools. Yet, on the whole, municipal services, including education programmes, are rather focused on teaching Japanese, not the mother tongue. This is the general tendency in Japan, where only monolingual education has traditionally been offered.

However, Cummins and Swain (1986) point out the theoretical basis of the importance of bilingual education:

> ... there may be threshold levels of linguistic competence which a bilingual child must attain both in order to avoid cognitive disadvantages and to allow the potentially beneficial aspects of becoming bilingual to influence his cognitive functioning. (p. 18)

They recommend striving to develop 'an additive form of bilingualism' at school, 'if optimal development of minority language children's academic and cognitive potential is a goal' (p. 18).

In a previous study (LAPO, 1998), we found that foreign children experience much less difficulty in the classroom after living in Japan for five years. In other words, it takes at least five years for language minority children to acquire 'Cognitive Academic Language Proficiency' (Cummins, 1981; Cummins, 1984), in contrast to 'Basic Interpersonal Communication Skills', which children appear to acquire rather quickly (Cummins, 1981).

Cummins and Swain suggest that instruction for language minority children should start in the children's mother tongue and shift to the majority language later in cases like those of the Brazilian children in Fujisawa and other towns in Japan where many minority children go to school:

> ... when the home language is different from the school language and the home language tends to be denigrated by others and selves, and where the children come from socio-economically deprived homes, it would appear appropriate to begin initial instruction in the child's first language, switching at a later stage to instruction in the school language. (Cummins & Swain, 1986: 18–19)

It is therefore important for all municipal governments to be more aware of the importance of mother tongue education, and to study support programmes developed in other countries with many immigrants.

To conclude our study, we will summarise the reasons why the language environment of Nikkei Brazilians in Japan must be improved. Our starting point was that all immigrants have two language rights: 'the right to learn and use one's mother tongue' as well as 'the right to learn an/the official language in the country of residence'. With respect to

Nikkei Brazilians, we have seen that neither right is fully guaranteed, especially the right to maintain their mother tongue.

However, we have to take into account the following characteristics of Nikkei Brazilian immigrants when we consider their language environment. Though they declare Portuguese to be their mother tongue, their familiarity with the Japanese language is very marked. This can be explained by the fact that most of them identify themselves as Nikkei, not as Brazilians.

This gap between nationality and self-perceived ethnic identity should lead us to develop a flexible solution to their language problems. What is necessary is a detailed analysis of their linguistic needs, for adults as well as for children, and the provision of several options so that individuals can choose what is best for them. It is from this point of view that we would like to make the following suggestions:

(1) We should provide immigrants and their children with opportunities to study the languages they need—whether Japanese or their mother tongue—in their own environment, for example, at the workplace or at school. In particular, the immigrant children's need for mother tongue education appears to be urgent given the findings of Cummins & Swain (1986).

To obtain the understanding of the Japanese government and society at large concerning the need for mother tongue education, they must be informed of the importance of such language issues. Since Japanese society depends on immigrant workers, the Japanese national government should also give support at least to those immigrants who are granted legal status. This support can be provided in the form of financial assistance to companies or schools that offer language courses for Japanese or the mother tongue.

(2) As mentioned earlier, the public services offered by the city of Fujisawa are focused on Japanese learning and not on mother tongue education. One reason for this is the very limited number of teachers who can teach the languages of the city's minority groups. Since the Meiji Restoration in 1868, three Western languages – English, German and French – have been considered important in Japan because these languages were necessary for the modernisation of the country. Consequently, very little effort has been made in this country to teach other languages such as Spanish, Portuguese and various Asian languages. Therefore, although the demand for minority language instruction is increasing today, we do not yet have the means to satisfy it.

It is time now to change this limited view of foreign language education and to emphasise the importance of teaching minority languages. In order to implement this idea and to support mother tongue education for immigrant children, more minority language teacher training programmes must be established. This will be a step toward internationalisation in the true sense of the word, moving beyond the current trend to think of 'internationalisation' as synonymous with mastering of the English language, and instead, embracing multiple languages, cultures and peoples.

Acknowledgements

This is a revised version of a paper presented at the International Conference on Language Rights held at the Hong Kong Polytechnic University, June 22–24, 1996. We would like to thank Sato Hatie and Helio de Moraes e Silva Filho for their help in our survey and for giving us insight into the Brazilian community in Fujisawa; Matsunaga Minoru for the statistics on foreigners in Fujisawa City; Koike Mari and Viviane Dauge for reading and revising our paper; Mary Goebel Noguchi, Florian Coulmas, Phil Benson and Krzysztof Batorowicz for their helpful comments. We also thank Kikuchi Hiroyuki, Hirata Maki, Nagae Chikayo, Okuno Miki and Yasuda Ryo for their cooperation in conducting our survey.

Notes

1. Compiled from data from *Hōmusho nyūkoku kanrikyoku* [Ministry of Justice, Immigration Bureau], 1996 and *Hōmu daijin kanbō shihō hōsei chōsabu* [Research Group in the Secretariat of the Ministry of Justice], 1999.
2. Compiled from data from the Fujisawa Municipal Office. The figures given for each year represent the total as of March 31 of the following year. However, those for 1997 stop at December 1, 1997.
3. *Hamamatsu-shi kikakubu kokusai kōryūshitsu* [Hamamatsu City International Exchange Section], 1993: 24.
4. In 'relation to the mother tongue(s)', Skutnabb-Kangas & Phillipson (1995) refer to 'the right to identify with it/them, and to education and public services through the medium of it/them' (p. 71).
5. On the data tables that follow, the total number (N) sometimes varies. This is because the number of valid answers for each question varied.
6. Watanabe (1995), Vol. 1: 26.
7. These terms were defined as follows. *origin*: the language(s) one learned first; *competence*: the language(s) one knows best; *function*: the language(s) one uses most; *internal identification*: the language(s) one identifies with; *external identification*: the language(s) one is identified as a native speaker of by others (Skutnabb-Kangas & Phillipson, 1989: 452–453).
8. In brief, we can explain the difference as follows. Historically, Japanese immigration to Peru was organised earlier (1899) than to Brazil (1908). Moreover, compared to Japanese settlements in Peru, which were dispersed geographically, the Japanese immigrants in Brazil lived in ethnic communities, at least at first. These factors may have contributed to the better maintenance of Japanese language skills among Japanese immigrants to Brazil. We also have to keep in mind the fact that among Nikkei Peruvian immigrants who live in Japan, there are a considerable number of people who have made false claims of Japanese ancestry (Seki & Hirataka, 1997: 146–149; LAPO, 1998: 54; Nakajima, 1996: 6).
9. *Hiragana* and *katakana* are both phonetic alphabets which are used along with Chinese characters (*kanji*) in Japanese writing.

10. Three newspapers written in Portuguese are easy to get in the Fujisawa area: *International Press, Tudo Bem* and *Nova Visao. International Press* has a circulation of 57,000 and has also a Spanish Version (LAPO, 1998: 137).
11. Compiled by Fujisawa City's Advisory Office for Foreigners (*Fujisawa shiyakusho gaikokujin sōdanshitsu*, 1996).

Appendix

Questionnaire on Language Situation of Brazilian Immigrants Living in Fujisawa City
(Translated from Portuguese)

Please choose the number(s) which correspond(s) to your answer. When there is ( ), please fill in your answer.

(1) Gender: 1. M   2. F
(2) Age: 1. Under 19   2. 20–29   3. 30–39   4. 40–49   5. 50–59   6. 60 or older
(3) What is your nationality?: 1. Japanese   2. Brazilian   3. Dual nationality
    (and   )   4. Other (   )
(4) Which are you? 1. Nikkei (*sei*)   2. Japanese   3. Brazilian   4. Other
(5) And your spouse? 0. Single   1. Nikkei (*sei*)   2. Japanese   3. Brazilian
    4. Other (   )
(6) What is your mother tongue? 1. Japanese   2. Portuguese 3. Other (   )
(7) What is your educational background? 0. No formal education
    1. Primary school   2. High School   3. University   4. Polytechnic school
    5. Other (   )
(8) With whom are you living now? 1. Alone   2. With Japanese family and/or
    relative(s)   3. Brazilian family and/or relative(s)
    4. Japanese friend(s) and/or colleague(s)   5. Brazilian friend(s) and/or colleague(s)
    6. Other (   )
(9) How long have you been in Japan in all? (   ) year(s) and (   ) month(s)
(10) How long are you going to stay in Japan? 0. Not decided yet
    1. Less than 1 year   2. Between 1 and 3 years   3. Between 3 and 5 years
    4. More than 5 years   5. Permanently
(11) What is your profession in Brazil and in Japan?
    In Brazil: (   )
    In Japan: (   )
(12) What was your Japanese language ability level before coming to Japan?
    Listening Ability: 0. Could not understand at all   1. Could understand only greetings
    2. Could understand daily conversations   3. Could understand TV news programmes
    Speaking Ability: 0. Could not speak at all   1. Could say only greetings   2. Could
    conduct daily conversations   3. Could converse on the telephone
    Reading Ability: 0. Could not read at all   1. Could read only *hiragana* or *katakana*
    2. Could read short memos   3. Could read letters
    Writing Ability: 0. Could not write at all   1. Could write *hiragana* or *katakana*
    2. Could write short memos   3. Could write letters using Chinese characters (*kanji*)
(13 Where did you learn Japanese before coming to Japan? 0. Did not learn at all
    1. Used at home   2. Japanese language school
    3. Nippo-Brazilian Cultural Association   4. Private teacher 5. Friend(s) or
    acquaintance(s)   6. Company   7. Alone   8. Church 9. Other (   )
(14) For how long did you learn Japanese before coming to Japan?   0. Not at all
    1. Less than 1 week   2. Less than 1 month   3. Less than 6 months
    4. Less than 1 year   5. Less than 2 years   6. More than 2 years
(15) What is your Japanese language ability level now?
    Listening Ability: 0. Cannot understand at all   1. Can understand only greetings

2. Can understand daily conversations   3. Can understand TV news programmes
Speaking Ability: 0. Cannot speak at all   1. Can say only greetings 2. Can conduct daily conversations   3. Can converse on the telephone
Reading Ability: 0. Cannot read at all   1. Can read only *hiragana* or *katakana*
2. Can read short memos   3. Can read letters
Writing Ability: 0. Cannot write at all   1. Can write *hiragana* or *katakana*   2. Can write short memos   3. Can write letters using Chinese characters

(16) Where have you learned Japanese after your arrival in Japan?
      0. Have not learned at all   1. Japanese language school 2. Nippo-Brazilian Cultural Association   3. Private teacher   4. Friend(s) or acquaintance(s)   5. Company
      6. Alone   7. Church   8. Other (   )

(17) For how long have you learned Japanese after your arrival in Japan? 0. Not at all
      1. Less than 1 week   2. Less than 1 month   3. Less than 6 months
      4. Less than 1 year   5. Less than 2 years   6. More than 2 years

(18) After your arrival in Japan, about how many hours per month have you learned Japanese? About (   ) hours per month

(19) Please write down your opinions on contents and methods of Japanese learning in Japan.
      (   )

(20) At your workplace, from which country are the people you see almost everyday from?
      1. Brazil (   ) person(s)   2. Japan (   ) person(s)   3. South-American country(ries) other than Brazil (   ) person(s)   4. Other country(ries) (   ) person(s)

(21) Which language do you use at home in Japan? 1. Only Portuguese 2. Usually Portuguese   3. Half and half   4. Usually Japanese   5. Only Japanese
      6. Other language(s) (   )

(22) Which language do you use most frequently at your workplace with Japanese colleague(s)? 0. Do not talk with Japanese   1. Japanese   2. Portuguese
      3. Other language(s) (   )

(23) Which language do you use most frequently at your workplace with Brazilian colleague(s)? 0. Do not talk with Brazilian   1. Japanese   2. Portuguese
      3. Other language(s) (   )

(24) Which language do you use most frequently at your workplace with your colleague(s) other than Japanese or Brazilians? 0. Do not talk with them   1. Japanese
      2. Portuguese   3. Other language(s) (   )

(25) Who serves as interpreter at your workplace? 0. No one   1. Japanese 2. Nikkei
      3. Brazilian   4. Other (   )

(26) Do you have opportunities to speak in Japanese outside of your workplace? Which occasions are they?
      1. Yes. On which occasions? (   )
      2. Do not have such opportunities.

(27) Do you find your Japanese proficiency sufficient? 1. Yes   2. No

(28) Would you like to make progress in Japanese? 1. Yes   2. No

(29) If you answered 'Yes' to question 28, tell us why, please.
      (   )

Thank you very much for your collaboration. If you have comments about our questionnaire, please do not hesitate to let us know. Thank you.

References

Cummins, J. (1981) The role of primary language development in promoting educational success for language minority students. In California State Department of Education (ed.) *Schooling and Language Minority Students: A Theoretical Framework* (pp. 3–49). Los Angeles, CA: Evaluation, Dissemination and Assessment Center, California State University.

Cummins, J. (1984) *Bilingualism and Special Education: Issues in Assessment and Pedagogy.* Clevedon, UK: Multilingual Matters.

Cummins, J. and Swain, M. (1986) *Bilingualism in Education.* London and New York: Longman.

Fujisawa-shi kyōiku iinkai [Fujisawa City Board of Education] (ed.) (1997) *Fujisawa-shi ni okeru gaikokuseki jidō seitosū ni tsuite* [Data on Foreign Students in Fujisawa City]. Fujisawa, Japan: Fujisawa Municipal Government.

Fujisawa shiyakusho gaikokujin sōdanshitsu [Fujisawa City Advisory Office for Foreigners] (ed.) (1996) *Gaikokujin sōdan tōkei* [Statistics on Consultation for Foreigners]. Fujisawa, Japan: Fujisawa Municipal Government.

Hamamatsu-shi kikakubu kokusai kōryūshitsu [Hamamatsu City International Exchange Section]. (ed.) (1993) *Hamamatsu-shi ni okeru gaikokujin no seikatsu jittai, ishiki chōsa hōkokusho – Nanbei-nikkeijin wo chūshin ni* [Report on Foreign Workers' Life in Hamamatsu City – Focussing on South American Nikkei). Hamamatsu, Japan: Hamamatsu Municipal Government.

Hōmu daijin kanbō shihō hōsei chōsabu [Research Group in the Secretariat of the Ministry of Justice] (ed.) (1999) *Dai 38-ji shutsunyūkoku kanri tōkei nenpō: Heisei 11-nen ban* [38th Annual Report on Immigration Control: 1999 Edition]. Tokyo: Ministry of Finance Printing Office.

Hōmusho nyūkoku kanrikyoku [Ministry of Justice, Immigration Bureau] (ed.) (1996) *Heisei 7 nen-matsu no gaikokujin tōkei* [Statistics on Alien Registration at the End of 1995]. http://www.moj.go.jp/PRESS/960707-1.htm

Kajita T. (1994) *Gaikokujin rōdōsha to nihon* [Foreign workers and Japan]. Tokyo: Nihon hoso shuppan kyokai.

LAPO (Koishi A. and Hirataka F. Research Group on Language Policy) (ed.) (1998) *Fujisawa-shi oyobi fujisawa-shi shūhen zaijū no burajiru-shusshinsha no gengo shiyō jōkyō ni kansuru chōsa* [A Survey on the Language Situation of Brazilian Immigrants in Fujisawa City and Its Vicinity]. Fujisawa, Japan: *Keio gijuku daigaku, shōnan fujisawa gakkai* [Keio SFC Academic Society].

Mita C. (1995) *Futatsu no hainichi wo koete – burajiru no imin seisaku to nihon imin* [Transcending Two Anti-Japanese Movements: Brazilian Immigration Policy and Japanese Immigrants]. In Nakagawa F. and Mita C. (eds) *Raten-amerikajin to shakai* [Latin-Americans and Society] (pp. 297–321). Tokyo: Shin-hyoron.

Nakajima S. (1996) *Zainichi perūjin no gengo kankyō* [Linguistic Environment of Peruvian Immigrants in Japan]. MA thesis, Keio University, Fujisawa, Japan.

Seki M. and Hirataka F. (eds) (1997) *Nihongo kyōikushi* [History of Japanese Language Teaching]. Tokyo: ALC.

Shimada H. (1993) *Gaikokujin rōdōsha mondai no kaiketsusaku* [Solving the Problems of Immigrant Workers]. Tokyo: Toyo keizai shinposha.

Skutnabb-Kangas, T. and Phillipson, R. (1989) 'Mother tongue': The theoretical and socio-political construction of a concept. In U. Ammon (ed.) *Status and Function of Languages and Language Varieties* (pp. 450–477), Berlin, New York: Walter de Gruyter.

Skutnabb-Kangas, T. and Phillipson, R. (eds) (1995) *Linguistic Human Rights: Overcoming Linguistic Discrimination.* Berlin: Mouton de Gruyter.

Watanabe M. (ed.) (1995). *Dekasegi nikkei burajirujin* [Nikkei Brazilian Migrant Workers], 2 vols. Tokyo: Akashi shoten.

Chapter 8
Language Minority Students in Japanese Public Schools

SHARON SEIBERT VAIPAE

Introduction

As explained in Chapter 1, the economic boom that began in the 1970s made Japan an attractive destination for a wide range of immigrants. One magnet for foreigners was a labour shortage that began in the mid 1980s, particularly in the construction and manufacturing industries, where jobs were deemed too 'difficult, dirty or dangerous' (the 'three 'k's': *kitsui, kitanai, kiken*) to attract young Japanese. Large numbers of men from Pakistan, Bangladesh, Iran, the Philippines and other Asian nations began entering the country on tourist visas to find work doing jobs that Japanese did not want. Revision of the immigration control law in 1990 made it easier for *Nikkei-jin* (people of Japanese ancestry) and their families to obtain work visas, and as a result, the large-scale influx of illegal Asian workers during the 1980s tapered off due to the legal immigration of South American Nikkei during the 1990s. The 1994 enactment of a bill that eased restrictions on the return of Chinese 'War Orphans' and their families further increased the pool of unskilled labour, as many of the 'returnees' from China either lacked professional skills or could not make use of them because of language barriers. [See Chapter 6, 'Japan's Hidden Bilinguals: The Languages of "War Orphans" and Their Families After Repatriation From China'].

Nonetheless, Japan continues to attract unskilled workers of other nationalities despite immigration restrictions. As of January 1st, 1998, there were 276,000 foreigners who had overstayed their visas in the country, and most of them were believed to be working illegally (*Japan Times*, June 17, 1998). By country, roughly equal numbers of illegal workers come from South Korea, Thailand, the Philippines and China, with fewer coming from Peru, Iran, Malaysia, Taiwan, Bangladesh, Myanmar and Pakistan.[1]

In addition to these groups, many young North Americans and Europeans came to study Japanese business practices or learn about the highly acclaimed education system, while others relied on their status as 'native speakers' of their language to get jobs as language teachers and copywriters. Japan also attracted large numbers of Korean and Chinese students hoping to master Japanese technology or to learn the Japanese language so that they could get jobs in companies that dealt with Japan after they returned to their country. The foreign student population has therefore increased substantially since 1983, when the Ministry of Education launched its '100,000 Foreign Students Plan'. Where students from overseas numbered only 10,428 in that year, they reached 53,847 as of May 1, 1995, with 91.5% (49,212) coming from Asian countries, predominantly China and South Korea.[2]

As a result of these immigration trends, the total number of foreign residents in Japan rose to 1.48 million by mid 1998 (*Japan Times*, June 29, 1998). This dramatic growth in the population of foreign residents led to an explosive increase in children of foreign nationals studying in Japanese schools. The number of students in Japanese public schools identified by the Ministry of Education as 'needing Japanese language instruction' doubled between 1991 (5463) and 1995 (11,553). Another increase of nearly 50% was seen between 1995 and 1997, when it exceeded 17,000.[3]

Questions regarding the sociocultural conditions, second language acquisition, and academic achievement experienced by language minority (LM) students during the important primary years of education arose as the author's children moved through Japanese elementary school, and these questions prompted a study of the schooling provided to LM students. The purpose of this investigation was to determine the type(s) of language education and support offered to LM students in Japanese schools and to explore the effects of this education on the students in terms of academic achievement and social well-being.

It should be noted that the number of children needing Japanese language instruction reported by the Ministry of Education is thought to represent only a portion of the actual number of language minority students in Japanese schools, since the term 'children who need Japanese language instruction' is not strictly defined, and students who have daily conversation skills in spoken Japanese are not generally considered to 'need Japanese language instruction'. For the purposes of this study, language minority students were defined as 'children who do not have a native Japanese speaking parent and do not use Japanese as the primary home language'.

Starting with pilot studies of her own children, the author began to collect longitudinal data in 1990. In 1994, case studies on another six LM students commenced, with observation of the two pilot students and the six other cases continuing until 1997. To get a broader picture of the situation throughout the country, parent, student and teacher question-naires in English, Spanish, Portuguese, Chinese and Japanese, as well as teacher questionnaires, were widely distributed. Further information was gathered through visits to schools and government offices, collection of materials related to Japanese language instruction in the public schools, coincidental interviews with other parents and LM children, and a range of other sources.

This paper attempts to compile the information gathered during the course of this investigation into a broad, qualitative description of the situation of LM students in Japan in the 1990s, including their classroom and overall school experience and their linguistic and academic achievement.

Overview of Japan's LM Population and Educational Setting

Numbers and national origin

Every two years since 1991, the Ministry of Education has made a count of the number of students attending Japanese public elementary, junior and senior high schools who need Japanese language instruction, the number of schools at which they study, and the native language of each student. Figure 1 shows the number of such students for each language group for 1991, 1993, 1995, and 1997, the most recent year in which complete figures for the biannual survey were available.

LM children in Japan can be grouped into three relatively distinct populations according to who their parents are: foreign academics and professionals, working class immigrants, or Chinese 'War Orphans' and their families. The first, and smallest, group includes teachers, students, and other professionals whose educational and economic background put them into a relatively elite class. This group has maintained a small but stable and steadily increasing population in Japan. The teachers are most often from English-speaking countries, and the students, from other Asian countries.

The majority of the working class families are South Americans of Japanese descent (Nikkei) who came to Japan with three-year work visas available after the 1990 Immigration Control and Refugee Recognition Law revision eased immigration restrictions for ethnic Japanese of other nationalities in order to help alleviate the labour shortage. [See Chapter 1, 'Introduction', and Chapter 7 'On the Language Environment of Brazilian Immigrants in Fujisawa City' for more information on this group.] By nationality, Brazilians form the largest group of Nikkei Latin Americans who accepted this implicit invitation to fulfill Japan's need for manufacturing labour.

The second largest group of LM students are children of Chinese 'War Orphans' (Japanese who were left in China after World War II) and their families. [See Chapter 6, 'Japan's Hidden Bilinguals: The Languages of "War Orphans" and Their Families After Repatriation From China'.]

When grouped by their L1, native speakers of Portuguese comprised 43.1%, Chinese, 30.8%, and Spanish, 10.1% of the LM students in Japan in 1997 (Figure 1). These three language groups account for four-fifths of the nation's LM students.

Whether or not the number of immigrants and LM children will remain at these levels or in these proportions in the future cannot be predicted

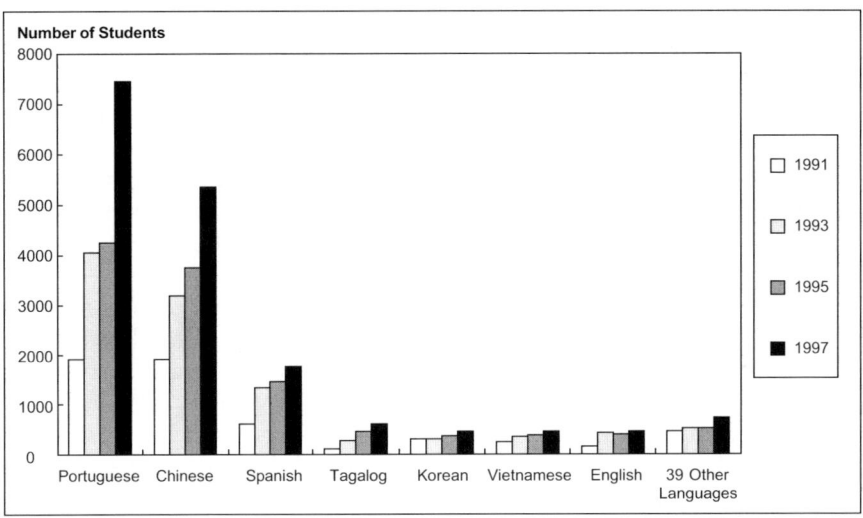

	1991	*1993*	*1995*	*1997*
Portuguese	1,932	4,056	4,244	7,462
Chinese	1,624	3,171	3,726	5,333
Spanish	596	1,347	1,423	1,749
Tagalog	121	284	494	618
Korean	326	328	362	482
Vietnamese	263	346	405	475
English	155	429	391	443
39 other languages	446	489	497	734
Total	**5,463**	**10,450**	**11,553**	**17,296**

Figure 1 Students needing Japanese language instruction in Japanese public schools, categorized according to native language

with any certainty, as their presence depends on the nation's immigration policies, which may well tighten if the current prolonged recession continues. There are indications, however, that there will be an increasing foreign presence, as demonstrated by the Osaka City call in July 1997 (*The Daily Yomiuri*, July 14, 1997) for the hiring of additional skilled foreign labour. The Immigration Bureau of the Ministry of Justice also reported that the demand for foreign workers remains high, and cited the continuing need for foreign language skills in explaining a major category of visas granted for expertise in 1995 (*Yomiuri shimbun*, June 5, 1996).

Educational setting

According to the report of the Ministry of Education's 1997 survey of children needing Japanese language education, there were 17,296 such

students studying at 5209 different public schools scattered throughout the nation. About 70% – 12,302 – of these children attended public
elementary schools, 4533 (about 25%) were in public junior high schools,
and 461 (approximately 5%) were studying in public high schools as of
September 1st of that year. The report indicated a 317% increase in the
number of students and a 552% increase in the number of schools at which
they were studying over the first such census in 1991, when 5463 LM
students were reported to be attending 943 Japanese schools concentrated
in industrial zones near Tokyo and Osaka.

The Ministry of Education's report of a similar survey made in 1995
indicated that just over half (52.4%) of the foreign students lived in the
prefectures of the industrial belt along the southern coast of Honshu:
Aichi, Shizuoka, Tokyo, Osaka and Kanagawa (Ministry of Education,
1996). The remainder of the students were scattered around the rest of the
country, with no prefecture left out of the picture. The prefecture with the
lowest number of LM students was Akita in northern Japan, which had
only four LM students attending four different schools. The highest
concentration of LM students outside of the industrial belt was in Gunma
Prefecture in the Kanto area (not far from Tokyo), where 513 were
studying in 122 schools.

The presence of a student who was not a native speaker of Japanese
was still considered an isolated event in at least 1785 Japanese classrooms – the number of schools that had only a single LM student
enrolled in 1995. The wide dispersion of LM students throughout the
country is underscored by the fact that 3368 schools, or 87.5% of the
3848 host schools, had five or fewer LM students. This means that four-
fifths of the students were so located that planning and implementation of
appropriate language and academic assistance were a greater administrative and resource challenge than would be true were they more concentrated in fewer schools.

Japan's problem of dealing with LM students is further illustrated by
other figures from the 1995 Ministry of Education report. Of the 850
municipalities in which LM students resided, only 171 (20%) staffed
schools with assistant Japanese language instructors, 74 (8%) provided
educational counselling, 56 (6%) had set up liaison councils, and 41 (5%)
had training programmes for teachers of LM students. A comparison of
the 1995 survey figures with those of the previous (1993) report show
no increase of measures designed to assist the students or their teachers.
Data from the 1997 survey reveal that there are 3535 LM children
who need Japanese language instruction but are not getting it: 2394 in
elementary schools, 1416 in junior high schools and 95 in high schools.
Of the 5209 schools with LM students, 1566 (30.1%) do not offer special
Japanese language training.

The Ministry of Education's reports also categorised the LM students
according to their average length of residence in Japan. As of September

1st, 1995, 32.5% of the elementary school and 45.6% of the junior high school LM students had lived in the country for two years or longer, while 28% of the elementary students and 32.4% of the junior high school LM students had been in Japan for six months or less.

However, these Ministry of Education surveys are limited to the numbers which have been reported to the Ministry; there is no in-depth analysis of the collected data. The government accepts teachers' subjective estimations of students' Japanese language ability in compiling the data. This approach hinders reliable identification of genuine needs because the reporting teachers are generally untrained in second language teaching or assessment (Takahashi and Vaipae, 1996b). The case studies reported below gave clear evidence that teachers often failed to accurately estimate their students' language proficiency. Frequently, they believed that the LM student's social language skills (discussed below as BICS) were indicative of their competency for academic content learning (discussed below as CALP), and so mistakenly deemed the LM students to be equals of native Japanese speakers for instructional purposes.

Previous Studies

Theoretical background

Hamers and Blanc (1989) argued that, while bilinguality is generally a positive experience, negative consequences are possible under certain conditions:

> ... when negative consequences are reported for bilingual experience, they invariably refer to a sociocultural setting which has the following characteristics: the child (1) comes from a socially disadvantaged subordinate group; (2) speaks a mother tongue which is little valorized in the society at large; and (3) is schooled through a prestigious L2 while the school system tends to ignore or denigrate the mother tongue (pp. 78–79).

Ruiz (1984, cited in McKay & Freedman, 1990) categorised government policies regarding minority languages as falling into one of three categories: language as problem, language as right, and language as resource. A 'language as problem' policy generally leads to 'submersion' majority language schooling, which tends to result in subtractive bilingualism – the replacement of the first language during incomplete acquisition of the second. A 'language as right' policy sets up adversarial positions between majority and minority viewpoints. In contrast, implementing a 'language as resource' strategy encourages schooling which is supportive of the maintenance and development of minority languages and cultures for the benefit of the individual as well as the advantage to the country. Since the latter two approaches require planning, the 'language as problem' outlook is the default setting.

Skutnabb-Kangas and Toukomaa (1976) examined the academic achievements of immigrant children in Sweden and found that students need more than conversational competence to cope with a school or college curriculum in their second language. They also suggested that the level of the development of immigrant children's mother tongue prior to contact with their second language was strongly related to how well the second language was learned.

In 1978, Cummins proposed the developmental interdependence hypothesis, which suggests that a child's second language competence is partly dependent on the level of competence already achieved in the first language (summarized in Cummins & Swain, 1986). Cummins (1984) went on to draw a distinction between Basic Interpersonal Communication Skills (BICS), which is the level of language needed to carry on conversation when there is ample contextual support in the form of feedback, gestures, and other forms of nonverbal communication, and Cognitive/Academic Language Proficiency (CALP), which is the level of language skills required in context-reduced academic settings in which language is the main or only conveyor of meaning and the focus is on more abstract content and advanced thinking skills. He suggested that the reason language minority students often failed when assigned to mainstream classes was that their L2 CALP was not highly enough developed for them to comprehend the academic curriculum. Cummins stressed that the foundation on which academic achievement is built is the 'common underlying proficiency', which needs to be developed through the language minority child's first language, or through both languages simultaneously.

Support for Cummins' theory was provided by Canadian studies of bilingual immersion programmes taught in French and English, which found that the students' literacy level in their first language was the strongest predictor of academic success in a third language (Swain *et al.*, 1990).

Research in this area was summarised by Collier, who initially (1989) reviewed over 25 basic and evaluation research studies to determine the length of time required for foreign students to reach the average level of performance of native English speakers in all academic subjects in their second language (English). Studies reviewed (Collier, 1995) now cover the progress of 700,000 students, primarily in American school settings, including ESL and bilingual programmes.

The first of Collier's findings is that non-native English speaking children arriving in English-speaking countries between the ages of eight and 12 with at least two years of L1 (native language) schooling in their home country will take five to seven years to reach the level of average performance by native speakers in English reading, social studies, and science, while it may take them as little as two years to reach the average performance level in math and language arts.

Second, Collier found that young arrivals with no experience of schooling in their first language took as long as seven to ten years to reach average performance levels in reading and social studies, if indeed, they ever did. This finding stands in spite of the very rapid development of social language skills often seen in pre-schoolers during peer play and interaction, and is consistent with the distinction between BICS and CALP and the 'developmental interdependence hypothesis' advanced by Cummins (Cummins & Swain, 1986).

Collier's third finding was that adolescent arrivals who were unable to continue academic work in their L1 may never reach literate levels in their L2 and may drop out before completing high school. Collier suggests:

> During the initial years of exposure to English, continuing cognitive and academic development in the first language is considered to be the key variable for academic success in the second language (Baker, 1988; Bialystok, 1991; Collier, 1989; Cummins & Swain, 1986; Cummins & Dolson, 1985; Garcia, 1993, 1994; Genesee, 1987, 1994; Hakuta, 1986; Lessow-Hurley, 1990; Snow, 1990; Tinjero & Ada, 1993).

She further notes,
> ... when I examined patterns of long-term achievement of LM students who enter U.S. schools below grade level in their academic work, these students can much more efficiently catch up and keep up by receiving intense academic instruction in their first language, all of which will eventually transfer to their second language.

Official reports on LM students in Japan

Turning to Japan, we find a series of reports by the Ministry of Education on the practical problems faced daily by schools with LM students and the specific educational measures taken. These reports were based on records submitted by 36 'Schools Cooperating in Research on the Education of Foreign Children' (*Gaikokujin shijo kyōiku kenkyū kyōryoku kō*) that were designated by the Ministry of Education since 1990 and were asked to keep such records for two-year periods. The reports contain heartwarming as well as heart-rending stories, but as research data, they do not provide the objective descriptions of problems and solutions which could be used for comparison in a controlled study. In general, they focus on the difficulties the students presented to the schools and teachers, without indicating that the situations were problematic for the students themselves, and thus did not recommend sociocultural or educational support for the students.

The extent of Japanese language acquisition by LM children in Japanese elementary and junior high schools was explored in a large-scale survey (*Kyōiku no kokusai kōryū ni kansuru jittai chōsa*) conducted by the Ministry

of Education in 1991. The Ministry asked the teachers of 3978 foreign
students who had been enrolled in Japanese schools for five years or less
to evaluate the students in terms of their proficiency in Japanese listening,
speaking, reading and writing skills. Students were to be rated in each skill
as '*mattaku dekinai*' (can't do at all), '*sukoshi dekiru*' (can do a little, or can
get by) or '*ōmune dekiru*' (adequate). It should be noted that the teachers in
this survey may well have been describing all non-native students using
Japanese as a second language and currently present in their classrooms.
There is no way to ascertain what percentage were identified as 'needing
Japanese language instruction' in the biannual Ministry of Education
survey. It is possible that students rated by teachers as having 'adequate'
Japanese skills in this survey were not included among the students
reported to the Ministry of Education.

The results of this survey, which are in the public domain, are
reproduced in Table 1. As can be seen in this table, the teachers rated
roughly half of their LM students as having listening and speaking skills
good enough to benefit from academic instruction at their grade level, and
approximately one fifth of the students as having the prerequisite reading
and writing skills. The fact that half of the students were deemed to have
sufficient oral skills may be partly attributed to the fact that the majority
of the respondents were lower elementary school teachers, and much of
the curriculum in the first years of school is taught through high-context
oral methods. By the beginning of fourth grade in elementary school,
however, the literacy demands, including full mastery of the *hiragana* and
katakana syllabaries and knowledge of hundreds of *kanji* (Chinese characters used in Japanese writing), are much greater. Thus, unless combined
with knowledge of all scripts used in reading and writing Japanese,
sufficient levels of listening and speaking proficiency are of limited value
beyond the first three years of elementary school.

In contrast to this optimistic Ministry of Education report, a recent
newspaper article by Sato G. (*Daily Yomiuri*, July 14,1997) on the language
proficiency of LM students in 953 junior high schools showed only 31%

Table 1 Teachers' evaluations of LM students' general Japanese language skills

Functioning Level	Skill			
	Listening	*Speaking*	*Reading*	*Writing*
Not at all	15%/13%	32%/27%	43%/34%	47%/34%
Can get by	50%/47%	45%/47%	42%/50%	41%/53%
Adequate	34%/40%	21%/25%	14%/16%	11%/12%

Elementary school students/Junior high school students
No answer: remainder of 100% in skill categories.
Combined figures for 3978 LM students enrolled in Japanese schools for 5 years or less.
Statistics from *Kyōiku no kokusai kōryū ni kansuru jittai chōsa* (Ministry of Education, 1991).

reporting their skills at a level where they felt they could keep up with their Japanese classmates in all subjects. Another 27% of the students said they could keep up in some subjects, while the remaining 42% described themselves as merely functional or less so at a conversational level.

Independent research on LM students in Japan

In the last decade, a number of books have also been published on the topic of foreign students in the Japanese schools (e.g. Ezaki & Moriguchi (ed.), 1988; Nakanishi *et al.*, 1991; Harada & Akabori, 1992; Sakai, 1992; Tada & Honda, 1993; Iwasaki, 1995). These works are mainly anecdotal, however, and omit contextualizing incidents.

One exception is Watanabe's work (1996) on Brazilian immigrant workers of Japanese descent (Nikkei). One chapter (pp. 331–490) of this book is devoted to the educational problems faced by the workers' children. Data was gathered through extensive interviews with Brazilian families, their children, and their Japanese school teachers living in the city of Hamamatsu in Shizuoka Prefecture. These Brazilians generally expressed favourable opinions of the Japanese schools and the Japanese education system. It was not clear, however, whether they were genuinely satisfied, or if instead, they were simply too busy making a living for close involvement in their children's education. It should also be noted that the community context in this case was relatively favourable, with the high concentration of Brazilian immigrants in Shizuoka ensuring the support of a large number of families in a similar in-migration situation which led to the establishment of JSL programmes in the prefecture's schools.

An examination of a broader scope of LM situations was provided by Murata (1994) in the final report of research funded by a Ministry of Education Scientific Research Grant. Murata's research team compared LM in four cities: the industrial centres of Moka (Tochigi Prefecture) and Toyohashi (Aichi Prefecture), and the cultural centres of Kyoto and Tsukuba, which both have well-known universities. The research team found that the families of the LM children in these four cities could be categorised as falling into two groups: (1) immigrant labourers (mostly Nikkei of South American origin) and (2) Asians and academics. There was a sharp contrast in the educational background of the parents in these two groups: while only 30% of the immigrant labourer parents are university graduates, 94% of the Asian and academic parents have university degrees. The research team also found that the children of the Asians and foreign academics displayed a higher level of eagerness to learn Japanese (94.3%) than the children of the immigrant labourers (78.4%). Murata's team examined the parents' and children's stated reasons for learning Japanese and interpreted them as indicating that the immigrant labourers felt more social pressure to adapt to the Japanese way of life than the foreign academics did. The team saw this pressure displacing parental concern over the children's educational well-being.

Thus, research on Japan to date is incomplete and rife with contradictions. The teacher assessments of LM students in the Ministry of Education study are so optimistic as to give the impression that the Japanese language is quickly mastered, while Sato's *Daily Yomiuri* report suggests many LM students face serious problems, and independent research suggests that parents are reluctant to complain.

Research Focus

The present study was designed to gather more extensive information on the situation of LM students in Japan. The educational experience of a wide range of LM students was examined to determine the prevalent government policies towards the minority language (categorised according to Ruiz, 1984), to analyse special educational programmes for LM students, and to check whether the academic achievement of the LM students was as remarkable as the Ministry of Education's 1991 survey suggests, or whether it was more in accord with predictions based on Cummins' (1984, 1986) theories. Longitudinal data from two pilot studies and six case studies is also presented to assess the impact of current policies and programmes on individual LM students.

Method

Development of the research project

As was mentioned in the introduction to this paper, the investigation of educational opportunities for LM students in Japan was prompted by observation of the author's two daughters, who were then attending a public elementary school in Niigata. Both children arrived in Japan during their preschool years and began attending elementary school from first grade. Longitudinal data on their participation and functioning in the Japanese education system was collected between 1990 and 1997, following them through moves to two other municipalities and schools.

Funding from the Japan Association for Language Teaching (JALT) in the form of a 1993 Research Scholar Grant made it possible to begin a nationwide survey of LM students, their parents, and teachers. A Toyota Foundation Grant (94B1-108) received in 1994 enabled continuation of the project and the formation of a research team composed of members specialising in different disciplines, having three different nationalities and capable of speaking several languages. During the period covered by the JALT grant, several inquiries indicated a deeper interest in the education of LM students. One of them was from Evelyn Sasamoto, a community volunteer and University of Maryland graduate student who offered to help in the data collection. Ms Sasamoto recommended expanding the team to include Kawamura Takeo, an elementary teacher who worked with LM students in the city of Fussa in the Kanto area. It was Mr Kawamura who facilitated arrangements for five of the six case studies. Dr Barbara Merino, Director of Bilingual Teacher Education at the University of California, Davis, was added to the team as a consultant because of her expertise in research on the education of LM students. Professor Takahashi Masao of Niigata University took on the responsibilities of coordinating school site contacts and administering the budget after translating the Toyota grant proposal into Japanese. Other team members included contacts made during inquiries at the Ministry of Education and the National Language Research Institute, as well as contacts at the university and in the community who were able to serve as translators and/or consultants because of their ties to immigrant communities.

Data collection

A 14-page questionnaire, originally composed in English and later translated into Spanish, Portuguese and Chinese, was prepared to collect data on LM students from their parents as well as from the children themselves. The questionnaire, which contained a total of 36 questions, began with two pages of questions on the student's age, grade in school, gender, proficiency in each language, and history of schooling in Japan and prior to arrival. Duplicate questions for the second and third child in the family appeared on pages 3 to 6. The next two pages contained questions about parental concerns, parent-school communication, parental involvement in the PTA, and the language use in the home, and also asked for the parent's evaluation of the student's schooling in Japan. Pages 9 through 11 formed the student questionnaire: one sheet was provided for each of three children to fill in themselves or for the parent to fill in for the child. The questions concerned the child's favourite and least favourite subjects, what s/he liked and did not like about school life, how much the student understood of what the teacher said, and the amount of time spent daily on various activities in Japanese and in the student's native tongue. Page 13 asked for parental evaluation of how well the Japanese school system was serving their children's needs in each of five areas (intellectual, social, physical, emotional, communication skills), and collected demographic information about the mother and father, as well as information on their proficiency in Japanese. The final page of the questionnaire asked the parents to write additional information or comments about their children's schooling.

A separate five-page questionnaire for teachers was composed in Japanese. The final version of the questionnaire contained 23 questions that focused on five areas: the teacher's background and training, the teacher's assessment of his or her experience with the LM student, the teacher's evaluation of the LM student, the school's provision of special programmes for LM students, their teachers and parents, and the teacher's perception of the LM student's parents. Teachers were asked to write their name and the name of the school for later publication.

Packets containing both questionnaires, two stamped and addressed return envelopes, a cover letter and a stamped blank post card addressed for return to the researcher were prepared. The parent/student questionnaire was designed to be anonymous, and the cover letter stated, 'All information you provide will be treated in accordance with American university human subjects research standards of confidentiality.' Parents willing to answer additional questions were asked to write contact information on the front of the questionnaire or on the post card that was included in the packet.

These packets were distributed in several ways. At the 1993 International Japan Association for Language Teaching (JALT) Conference, a request for cooperation was made at the Colloquium on Bilingualism and survey packets were given out to people identifying themselves as parents of LM students. Respondents were asked to give the teacher questionnaire and its return envelope to their children's teachers. Personal contacts continued to be one source of respondents throughout the duration of the project.

Next, the education boards of several municipalities were contacted and asked to serve as intermediaries to distribute the questionnaires to LM students and their teachers. Three municipalities agreed to cooperate: Yokohama, Osaka and Niigata. However, city-level school authorities in five other instances did not give permission to distribute the questionnaires, saying this was a 'highly sensitive political area' or that it called 'undue attention to minorities' when they declined to cooperate.

A third method used to locate subjects was a classified advertisement in a national English language newspaper. This system greatly extended the geographical range and number of students covered. Questionnaires were returned from as far as Hokkaido to the north and Wakayama to the south. Moreover, approximately three-fourths of the total number of respondents in this study were located in this manner. The mailed return rate for the questionnaires remained steady at 20% over the four years of distribution.

Approximately 400 teacher questionnaires and 325 parent questionnaires were distributed in these three ways. Of these, a total of 187 teacher questionnaires and 121 parent questionnaires were returned, with data on 156 children.

Respondents who provided contact information on the survey instrument or the post card enclosed in the packet were contacted to arrange in-depth interviews. Extensive interviews with 18 parents were conducted, providing detailed descriptions of their children's reactions to school, language use, concerns, attitudes, situations, and experiences.

In addition to the information and contacts made through the questionnaires, case studies of six LM students from five different countries were made between 1994 and 1997, with initial and exit interviews, including assessment of their L1 and L2 narrative abilities. Native language interviews with their parents were also conducted, with interpreters on the team used as necessary. Repeated classroom observations with time/behaviour-coded protocols of the two pilot students and six case studies as well as five other LM children were made by two to four observers and two video cameras in schools in Niigata and Tokyo. Follow-up interviews of the students and teachers were made after each observed class.

Administrators in the children's schools were also interviewed when they were available. Informal interviews allowed exploration of the school personnel's reactions to the study. Access was gained to seven additional schools in Yokohama, Osaka, Niigata, Kanuma and Tokyo, allowing in-depth formal interviews with more classroom teachers of LM students. Visits to government offices and interviews with educational administrators were conducted at the municipal governments of Tokyo, Osaka, Niigata and Utsunomiya, and the prefectural governments of Tokyo, Niigata, Osaka and Tochigi. In addition, four meetings were held with officials of the Overseas Children's Education Division of the Ministry of Education. Other information was gathered through collection of materials related to Japanese language instruction in the public schools, communication with JSL (Japanese as a Second Language) teachers and teacher training professors at five universities, coincidental interviews with 28 other parents and LM children between 1992 and 1997, and a range of other sources.

Limitations

Although the survey sampling was originally intended to be conducted so as to reflect the proportion of each native language in the total LM population in Japan, the difficulties in distributing the questionnaire outlined above forced the research team to settle for a convenience sample rather than a random sampling. Lack of cooperation from the authorities in five municipalities led to geographical skewing of the results. Moreover, the most effective method of distributing the survey instrument (the newspaper advertisement) skewed the response in terms of native language representation. Subjects whose native language was English or Chinese provided approximately half of the returns from the advertisement, although Chinese students account for only 30.8% of the LM students in Japan and English is not even the native language of one of the major LM student groups. Nonetheless, responses were obtained from families representing the other three major language groups during the survey period (Portuguese, Spanish and Korean) and seven smaller ones (Tagalog, Urdu, Vietnamese, Malaysian, German, Swedish and Indonesian) in addition to English. Thus, although the respondents come from a representative range of language groups, the number of respondents from each native language group is not representative of its proportion of the LM population in the nation, nor does the geographical distribution of the respondents faithfully correspond to the distribution of LM students in the country. The self-selected nature of many of the respondents further calls the reliability of the results into question.

Nonetheless, a total of 121 parent/student questionnaires from respondents with 12 different native languages, as well as 187 teacher questionnaires were returned and tabulated. Multiple revisions of the questionnaire complicated statistical analysis and necessitated adjustments in grouping the responses. However, extensive observation, interviews and collection of materials provided supporting information. When viewed together, this data provides a broad qualitative overview of the experience of LM students and their teachers in Japan — a picture that, it is hoped, will be brought into clearer focus by more rigorous research in the future.

Results and Discussion

In presenting the data gathered during this four-year project, I will start with the national and move toward the personal, beginning with an overview of the situation based on national policy and nationwide statistics and looking at the manifestations of this policy (or lack of it) in programmes implemented in three localities: Tokyo, Niigata, and Osaka. I will then report selected results of the teacher survey, the parent survey and the student questionnaires. Finally, I will summarise the stories of the pilot and case studies. In this way, I hope to present the wider picture as well as the impact it has on individual lives.

National policy and local programmes

Four meetings with officials of the Overseas Children's Education Division of the Ministry of Education, interviews with educational administrators at the municipal governments of Tokyo, Osaka, Niigata and Utsunomiya, and the prefectural governments of Tokyo, Niigata, Osaka and Tochigi, interviews with personnel at seven schools in Yokohama, Osaka, Niigata, Kanuma and Tokyo, and contacts with JSL (Japanese as a Second Language) teachers and teacher training professors at five universities provided repeated opportunities to verify the fact that the approach to minority languages in Japan is Ruiz' (1984) 'default setting' — language as problem, which was mentioned above.

There is no legal mandate that non-Japanese children must attend school, nor is there an official national language policy. The closest statement to an official policy on LM student education was found among recommendations in a publication by the 1996 Ministry of Education Study Group called 'Newest Questions and Answers About School Administration':

> There is no difference in enrolling foreign students; no need of tuition or payment for school texts, and the same procedures will be followed for financial and school records. Teaching should be done according to the Japanese curriculum. There is no need for their native language education. It is desirable for educational considerations that an appointment of a teacher who understands the student's native language should be made as long as possible.

To interpret the impact of the final sentence in this policy statement, it is necessary to understand the meaning of the term 'as long as possible'. The gap between the number of students speaking each of 47 different languages represented in the nation's schools (Ministry of Education, 1994) and the number of teachers in Japanese schools who speak these languages is so great that the above recommendation can have no impact upon instructional practices. For example, there were only 31 teachers in the entire country identified as fluent in Portuguese to serve the 4056 students whose native language was Portuguese and who were dispersed among 813 schools nationwide in 1992 (Noyama, 1992). In fact, neither bilingual education nor native language support is offered in Japanese schools (Noyama, 1992).

Without policies and pedagogical imperatives in place, initiatives by the Ministry of Education relating to LM children are strictly voluntary. Overlooking the specific linguistic and educational needs of LM students requires few administrative changes, and thus is the norm nationwide. Because there is no codified policy, there are no standards to meet, and no challenges to administrators to produce effective programmes and provide supporting personnel. Special education measures were found to be at a minimum during this investigation, and those that were implemented were found to have been given impetus primarily by teacher needs rather than by student needs.

The only language education model apparent in our observation was submersion with the goal of assimilation. LM students were either kept in regular classrooms for the entire school day ('mainstreamed') or 'pulled out' for limited JSL instruction several hours a week. Schools that had more than ten LM students were assigned a full-time teacher to run a pull-out programme for Japanese language instruction partially funded by the national government.

In Tokyo, in addition to such schools with full-time JSL teachers, centralised JSL programmes were offered to students in schools with only a few LM students. This necessitated considerable travel for some students and left others unserved despite parental requests for support.

The system in Niigata was similar to that in Tokyo, but there were very few schools with a full-time JSL instructor. The number of LM children in any one school also tended to be much smaller than in Tokyo. The foreign children in this large city (population approximately 475,000[4]) generally stayed in regular classrooms and were not usually given special Japanese language training.

Like Tokyo, Osaka has a centralised pull-out JSL programme. The city designated four schools to serve as 'Centre Schools' to which LM students from nearby areas commute two or three times a week for Japanese language instruction. However, the Osaka programme does not allow children below the fourth grade to travel long distances to reach these Centre Schools. LM students in first to third grade who live outside the boundaries of the areas served by these schools must wait until they reach fourth grade before they are eligible to travel to the JSL classes.

At a Centre School in Osaka that was visited by the research team, 25 LM students who were enrolled in mainstream classes were pulled out to attend JSL classes one to five periods a week. As with most programmes observed, there was no evidence of coordination between the JSL teacher and the homeroom teacher in terms of curriculum classroom tasks. In addition to these 25 students, this programme also served two LM students from other schools who travelled 45 minutes on a subway to attend twice-weekly JSL classes at the Centre School.

Osaka school authorities indicated that there was a time limit of six months for JSL class attendance. However, a JSL teacher at one of the Centre Schools said that this was only a general rule and that a decision on when children were ready to give up the JSL classes was made on a case-by-case basis according to 'when the child felt comfortable and confident to do so.'

Interviews with authorities and JSL teachers suggested that frequently the teachers selected to teach Japanese to the LM children were ordinary teachers from the school faculty, often those whose teaching schedules were not full or teachers who were not in charge of a homeroom, including those who teach special subjects such as Japanese calligraphy (*shūji*), cooking, art and music. These teachers may never have even had an LM student in one of their classes before being assigned to teach JSL, and may not want to teach LM children. Moreover, we found that these teachers generally received little or no JSL training or guidance, and that their achievements with their foreign charges depended almost entirely upon their own initiatives.

In Tokyo, the research team did not meet a single professionally-trained JSL instructor assigned to teach LM students in public schools, even though some of the schools that the team visited had more than the ten LM students required to warrant a full-time JSL teacher for a pull-out programme.

In Osaka, however, Japanese language teachers assigned to the Centre Schools were generally chosen by the Osaka Board of Education because they had experience teaching in Japanese schools abroad. Authorities expressed a belief that the international awareness gained while teaching abroad and the experience of having lived in a foreign country would make such teachers more sensitive to the needs of LM students.

The one professionally-trained JSL instructor encountered during the research project taught at a Centre School in Osaka. This school had a bright, inviting JSL classroom with lots of posters and pictures from around the world. The researchers were told that the professionally-trained JSL instructor's predecessor had initiated some very innovative learning modules for all the children at the school in an effort to integrate the LM students more completely into the student body and to help all children – foreign and Japanese – develop a healthy sense of self-esteem and thus eliminate bullying. In addition, he had started an annual festival in which the foreign students could share aspects of their homeland's culture, including dances, songs, foods and native costumes. This reportedly created a great deal of interest in and respect for other cultures in the student body at large and reinforced the pride of the LM students in their cultural and linguistic background. This school, however, appeared to be the exception rather than the rule.

A second Centre School the research team visited in Osaka stood in stark contrast to the first. The JSL classroom in this school was devoid of posters and artifacts of other cultures. Books were hidden away in cupboards. The lesson the team observed seemed as sterile as the room. Although it was a private lesson, the teacher rigidly followed the text despite the fact that the lone LM student obviously already knew the rudimentary material being covered – the names of colours.

The team had been informed by the Osaka Board of Education that this second Centre School was considered a model for the other Centre Schools, while the one at which innovative programmes had been observed had not even been mentioned as having a good programme. This discrepancy underscores the bureaucracy's narrow focus on language needs to the exclusion of the sociocultural needs of the LM students.

In addition to the absence of minority language support, the paucity of JSL programmes, the short-term nature of the programmes that are provided, and the tendency to assign the teaching work to untrained instructors, another problem uncovered during observation was the single-minded focus of the existing JSL programmes upon teaching communication skills. As mentioned above, the biggest problem for LM children is generally not Basic Interpersonal Communication Skills (BICS), but rather, Cognitive/Academic Language Proficiency (CALP) in the L2. If this is true for immigrants to countries where the L2 writing system is similar to the L1 writing system, as it is for Spanish and English or Finnish and Swedish, then how much more of a problem academic language must be for immigrants who have to learn Japanese, with its unique writing system.

Mastery of written Japanese is a difficult task even for native speakers: almost one-third (30.5%) of the time in the elementary school curriculum set out by the Ministry of Education is devoted to reading and writing Chinese characters (*kanji*) and the two syllabaries (*hiragana* and *katakana*) that are combined in written Japanese. In addition, a large portion of the daily homework assigned is devoted to learning reading and writing of the 1850 *kanji* used in newspaper Japanese. Students in elementary school learn between 160–200 *kanji* each year after first grade (when they learn the two syllabaries plus 80 *kanji*), and by the end of elementary school, they are expected to know 1006 *kanji* (Itoh and Miyashita, 1994). An LM student entering the Japanese school system in late elementary or junior high school would be at a considerable handicap in 'catching up' on literacy skills, yet no help in this area is provided by JSL classes offered by the schools.

In fact, the principals and teachers interviewed acknowledged little understanding of the LM students' educational and sociocultural needs, and evidenced anxiety about how to effectively manage various aspects of their enrollment and instruction. There was also a consistent denial of the special needs of the LM students, from the Ministry of Education Study Group statement presented above, to individual teachers dealing with LM students. For example, when the research team observed a homeroom teacher in Niigata whose teaching style was very helpful to the LM students in her class, the researchers praised her approach during a post-observation interview. However, the teacher vehemently denied that she was doing anything special for the foreign students and insisted that all teachers at the school taught in this manner and that all children there were the same. This strong emphasis on 'equality' in terms of treating all students in the same way no matter what their capacities or problems are was a recurring theme in the Japanese schools the team visited.

It was also reflected in the 1992 Ministry of Education report on LM children in Japanese schools. In response to a question about instruction for LM children 'during classes', 89.7% of the 1437 elementary and 84.1% of the 536 junior high schools surveyed gave the following answers, all of which emphasise mainstreaming LM students: 'Conduct class with ordinary pupils, with no special consideration given', 'Instructor adds explanations as needed in classes with ordinary students', and 'Depending upon the subject, individual instruction including Japanese language instruction given'. Only 1.9% of the elementary schools and 3.3% of the junior high schools chose the answer 'Special classes were arranged exclusively for foreign students'. As a prevailing value in Japanese society at large, this emphasis on absolute equality works to the detriment of LM children and others with special needs.

Nonetheless, some progress was evident during the course of the research project. According to the Ministry of Education's September 1, 1995 survey, 171 out of the 850 municipalities and three of the 47 prefectural governments which had LM students attending school in their precincts were sending Japanese language teaching personnel to schools where LM students were concentrated (Ministry of Education, 1996). This same Ministry of Education survey showed that 74 municipalities and three prefectures had organised counselling for LM students. Teacher training was being given in 51 municipalities and 11 prefectures. Thirteen prefectures provided a guidebook for teachers in charge of LM students. These figures were up from the Ministry survey made two years earlier, and indicate that local and prefectural boards of education were beginning to respond to the larger concentrations of LM students in their schools.

However, while these statistics show that additional administrative entities have taken steps towards meeting LM students' needs, as well as those of their teachers, the majority of both students and teachers remain unserved. Moreover, the quality of the programmes and measures initiated have not yet been evaluated for their effectiveness, nor was the research team made aware of any efforts to conduct preprogramme needs analysis and set appropriate programme, teacher and student goals. A start has been made, but there is a long way to go.

Teacher survey

The five-page teacher questionnaire was filled in and returned by 187 teachers who were either currently teaching or had previously taught LM children in Japan. The questionnaire contained 23 questions that focused on five areas: (1) the teacher's background and training, (2) the teacher's assessment of his or her experience with the LM student, (3) the teacher's evaluation of the LM student, (4) the school's provision of special programmes for LM students, their teachers and parents, and (5) the teacher's perception of the LM student's parents.

The first section of the questionnaire investigated the profile of the Japanese language teachers. It asked for the teacher's previous training and/or research on teaching foreign students, proficiency in English and/or any other foreign language, and experience living and travelling abroad. Question 1 was, 'Have you had some kind of training to work with LM students?' In response, the majority of the respondents (116, or 62.2%) answered 'No' or did not answer the question (25, or 13.1%). The 46 (24.5%) who answered this question 'Yes' cited short local workshops or Ministry of Education-sponsored seminars as their preparation.

Question 2 asked if the teacher had 'attended an LM-related seminar sponsored by the Ministry of Education or some other institution.' Only 13 (7%) of the repondents answered 'Yes', while the other 174 (93%) answered 'No.' In fact, at the time this paper was written only 580 teachers and administrators nationwide had attended the six previous five-day LM student seminars sponsored by the Ministry of Education each year in August, although from the Ministry's 1995 figures, it can be calculated that there were between 10,000 and 15,000 teachers in the country with LM students in their classes (Ministry of Education, 1996). This would make the proportion of such teachers nationwide who had attended seminars related to LM students approximately 4%–6%.

Question 3 asked the teachers to rate their foreign language skills in English and in any other foreign language using a 5-letter scale in which (A) signified 'excellent' and (E), 'very poor or none'. The results are presented in Table 2 below. The level of foreign language skills claimed by the respondents is comparable to that of the general Japanese populace. A survey of 2318 university graduates made by the Japan Association of College English Teachers in 1989 found that only 7% felt that their English skills were adequate for communication, while approximately one-third evaluated their skills as considerably inadequate, and 8% declared that their English was totally inadequate for communication purposes.

Similarly, the respondents' foreign travel experience was within the range expected of the general Japanese populace. In response to Question 4, 'Have you lived in a foreign country more than one month?', 150 (80.2%) of these teachers answered 'No', while 24 (12.9%) responded 'Yes' and 13 (6.9%) did not answer this question. Question 5 was, 'How often do you travel in foreign countries?' 64 (33.7%) respondents indicated that they had never been outside of Japan, 53 (28.4%) wrote that they only travelled abroad once every four to six years, 22 (11.8%) said they went abroad once every two or three years, 16 (8.8%) reported that they went abroad annually, and 32 did not answer this question. None of the respondents claimed to travel abroad more than once a year.

While these figures are not intended to be an accurate measure of natural dispositions towards foreigners and/or foreign cultures, they are offered as crude indicators of the depth and breadth of the teachers' experiences with cultural others. As explained above, the research team found no evidence of teachers being selected to teach LM students because of their experience or expertise except in the centralised pull-out programmes in Osaka.

Table 2 Teachers' self evaluation of their foreign language skills

Language	A		B		C		D		E		No Answer	
	n	*%*	*n*	*%*	*n*	*%*	*n*	*%*	*n*	*%*	*n*	*%*
English	3	1.6%	7	3.7%	38	20.3%	81	43.3%	47	25.1%	11	5.9%
Any other foreign languages	1	0.5%	2	1.1%	0	0.0%	6	3.2%	147	78.6%	31	16.6%

A = Excellent
E = Very poor or none

The survey teachers also admitted that they had little knowledge of the culture of their LM students' native countries. Question 7 was, 'How good is your knowledge of your LM student's native culture?' Using a scale of 1 to 5, in which (1) indicated 'no knowledge' and (5) signified 'extensive knowledge', only four teachers (1.9%) rated themselves (5), 12 (6.6%) gave themselves a (4), 59 respondents (31.7%) gave themselves a (3), another 59 (31.7%) a (2), 23 (12.5%) rated themselves (1), and 30 (15.9%) did not answer.

In the third section of the questionnaire, the teachers were asked to evaluate their LM students. Question 11 asked them to rate the students' Japanese language for academic purposes. Their evaluations, which are presented in Table 3 below, correlated well with the rosy results of the large-scale survey conducted by the Ministry of Education (1991), which was presented as Table 1 above. Over half of the respondents (56.7%) saw the LM students' listening skills as 'Good enough' and almost as large a proportion (49.3%) viewed the students' speaking skills to be adequate as well. Over three quarters of the LM students were not seen as 'Deficient' in any Japanese language skill, even though, according to Sato's report in the July 14, 1997 *Daily Yomiuri*, which was described above, only 31% of the junior high school students Sato surveyed reported having skills at a level where they felt they were learning academic content, and a full 42% described themselves as only capable of understanding daily conversation or not even capable of that.

Moreover, the teachers' overly generous evaluations of their students' academic Japanese proficiency stood in striking contrast to their evaluations of their LM students' academic work, which are presented in Table 4 below. There is a public school bias against standardised testing in Japan which, for the purposes of this study, eliminated the possibility of more objective achievement comparisons between native and non-native students. Question 12 therefore asked the teachers, 'How do you rate the LM student's school work by subject compared with other students?' The subjects in which they were to compare the students were the four main academic subjects: Japanese language arts, math, science, and social studies.

Table 3 Teachers' evaluation of LM students' Japanese fluency for academic purposes

Functioning Level	Skill			
	Listening	*Speaking*	*Reading*	*Writing*
Deficient	8.6%	11.1%	23.4%	23.4%
Minimum	34.5%	34.5%	49.3%	51.8%
Good Enough	56.7%	49.3%	27.1%	22.2%

Percentages shown above are for those who gave answers. 25.6% of the respondents (48) did not rate the students' listening, speaking and reading skills, and 28% (52) did not give an evaluation of the students' writing skills.

Table 4 Teachers' evaluation of LM students' work compared to Japanese students in their class

Evaluation	Japanese	Mathematics	Science	Social Studies
Above Average	2.6%	6.6%	3.2%	4.9%
Average	23.6%	37.5%	17.4%	28.5%
Below Average	48.6%	33.7%	42.6%	37.0%
No Answer	25.0%	22.0%	18.3%	27.4%

Academic progress is primarily reported subjectively in Japanese elementary schools, with only three grades given: 'above average', 'average' or 'below average' (or A, B and C, which are considered equivalent). While the degree of achievement reported by the teachers for the pilot and case study students was much higher than that actually observed, the actual evaluations the teacher survey respondents gave their LM students were not very high. Only about one-fifth to one-half of the LM students were considered to be doing average or above average work in any of the major subjects. Even in math (one of the subjects in which Collier found LM students catch up most quickly), more than a third were deemed to be doing 'below average' work, while another 22.0% were not evaluated.

Question 13 asked, 'To what cause do you attribute their below-average or above-average achievement?' Since no attempt was made to substantiate the teachers' judgements of the LM students' intelligence (by using standardised intelligence tests, for example), this question has little value other than to gain an assessment of the LM students by individual teachers. It may not be surprising, then, that more than three quarters of the respondents (76.3%) did not answer this question at all. However, it is interesting to see that of those who did respond, the same percentage (9.8%) attributed the children's academic performance (or lack of it) to the student's 'General intelligence level' as saw it to be the result of his or her 'Japanese language proficiency'. Another 3.9% saw the problems to be a result of the student's 'general attitude to school life'. What is important here is that more teachers attributed the LM students' scholastic problems to non-linguistic factors than to language difficulties.

This difficulty in pinpointing the source of their LM students' difficulties is most likely due to the fact that few elementary school teachers have an understanding of second language acquisition theory and practice, and most are therefore unaware of the distinction between more highly contextual social communication and less contextual academic language (Cummins, 1984). Younger LM students were often described by their teachers as 'just like the Japanese children', without reference to defining characteristics. Such orally-proficient children were very frequently assumed to be ready for instruction similar to that given to native speakers of Japanese, so when the children did not make native-like progress, factors other than their languages skills were often cited.

Table 5 Teachers' assessments of student adaptation to school life

Degree of Adaptation	1	2	3	4	5	No Answer
Life outside school	1.7%	9.5%	39.8%	14.2%	8.3%	26.1%
Friendship within homeroom class	0.0%	8.9%	35.0%	22.2%	14.6%	19.1%
Friendship outside homeroom class	1.1%	17.8%	34.5%	14.8%	8.3%	23.2%
General attitude toward study	2.3%	16.5%	28.4%	17.1%	11.2%	24.1%
Perceived student satisfaction with school	1.2%	7.7%	50.6%	20.1%	1.9%	25.9%

5 = very well adapted
1 = complete lack of adaptation

Question 14 asked the teachers to assess how well the LM student had adapted to school life in each of five different areas. The results are presented in Table 5. While few of the teachers had an experiential basis for understanding the LM students' dual cultural experiences and reduced home exposure to Japanese cultural knowledge, most were able to recognise that adjusting to school life presented major problems for the LM students in their classes. In particular, over 60% of those who answered this question recognised the fact that the LM students were not very satisfied with their schooling.

Question 16 asked, 'How strongly do you feel that the LM students' need to succeed in each of the following areas: (1) Adaptation to school life in general, (2) Skill in Japanese language for academic work, (3) Communication between the parents and teacher, (4) Communication between the LM students and teacher, and (5) Cultivation of native culture and mother tongue?' Answers were to be given on a scale of 1–5, with (1) indicating 'not at all important' and (5) signifying 'very important'. The breakdown of the responses to this question is presented in Table 6.

The Japanese education system places a great deal of emphasis on social skills and community building as a support for individual academic growth (Lewis, 1995). It is therefore not surprising that the survey teachers identified adaptation to school life as the most important priority for their LM students. Since friendships with classmates and participation in non-academic events would be facilitated by better Japanese language skills and better understanding of the Japanese school culture by the LM students' parents, these were given second and third priority by the responding teachers. The need for LM students to communicate with their teachers and to develop their first language and culture were viewed as less important by the respondents.

Table 6 Teachers' evaluation of factors important to LM students' success

Perceived Degree of Importance	1	2	3	4	5	No Answer
Adaptation to school life in general	0.0%	1.9%	8.2%	26.1%	36.9%	26.7%
Skill in Japanese language for academic work	0.0%	0.5%	11.6%	30.9%	33.9%	22.8%
Communication between parents and teacher	0.0%	1.1%	15.2%	27.4%	32.1%	23.9%
Communication between student and teacher	1.1%	2.9%	21.7%	30.5%	19.4%	24.1%
Cultivation of native culture and mother tongue	0.0%	3.7%	21.3%	28.3%	21.9%	24.5%

5 = very important
1 = not at all important

As noted, however, second language acquisition studies have demonstrated that students with more highly developed first language skills show stronger academic performance in all second language skill areas (Skutnabb-Kangas & Toukomaa, 1976; Cummins, 1981; Collier, 1989, 1992, 1995). This strengthening of second language skills and academic performance is a result of skill transfer, especially general literacy connections between the spoken word and the corresponding printed word, and the awareness of and readiness to use schema. Mother tongue proficiency also allows LM students to communicate more fully with their parents, who can in turn provide more support for their children's schooling. The fact that the respondents in this survey did not appreciate the importance of their LM students' first language development serves as a further argument for greater preparation of and training for teachers who will have LM students in their classrooms.

The fourth section of the questionnaire contained two questions on school support for LM students. Question 17 asked, 'Does the LM student have some kind of special instruction?' 51.8% of the teachers answered 'Yes', 21.7% replied 'No', and 26.8% did not answer the question. Question 18 tried to pinpoint the type of programmes that are provided. It asked, 'In which of the following areas does your school have special programmes to meet LM student needs: (1) to facilitate adaptation to school life, (2) to help learning Japanese, (3) for parents who do not speak Japanese, (4) special consideration for teachers in charge of LM students, (5) to help learning LM student's mother tongue and native culture, and (6) to help parents understand events and school life?' The results are given in Table 7.

Table 7 Provision of special support programmes in respondents' schools

Type of Programme	Yes	No	No Answer
To facilitate adaptation to school life	53.7%	15.1%	31.0%
To help learning Japanese	51.5%	17.4%	31.0%
For parents who do not speak Japanese	42.3%	25.3%	32.3%
Special consideration for teachers in charge of LM students	21.5%	43.0%	35.3%
To help learn LM students' mother tongue and native culture	46.2%	21.2%	23.5%
To help parents understand events and school life	49.4%	15.3%	35.1%

More than half of the respondents (53.7%) said that their school had a programme to facilitate the LM students' adaptation to school life. More than half of the teachers surveyed (51.5%) also reported that a programme was in place to help students learn Japanese more quickly. However, none of the parents who responded to the survey (summarised below) reported that their children had school-based JSL instruction. This discrepancy may be explained by the concentration of the returned teacher questionnaires in urban areas with larger populations of LM students that make pull-out programmes more common, while the majority of the returned parent questionnaires were from people living in more rural areas.

Almost half of the respondents (46.2%) also claimed that a programme was in place to help them learn their LM students' mother tongue and native culture. However, the nature of these programmes remains unclear, especially since in response to Question 7 of the questionnaire (reported above), over 60% of the respondents rated their knowledge of their LM student's native culture (2) or (3) on a scale of 1–5, where (5), indicated 'extensive knowledge'.

These discrepancies aside, the most striking figure in Table 7 is the low percentage of teachers in charge of LM students who are given special consideration. As explained above, teachers put in charge of JSL classes for LM students are generally not selected because of their educational or personal experience, but rather, because of flexibility in their teaching schedule. Moreover, as reported above, few had special training. Thus, the teacher survey supports the impression given by the Ministry of Education's report on its 1995 survey that while administrative entities are making increased efforts to provide training for teachers and support for LM students, the majority of teachers are still not being trained (Ministry of Education, 1996).

The fifth section of the teacher questionnaire focused on the LM students' parents. Question 19 asked, 'Do you think the parents understand information supplied by the school?' A full 65% of the teachers answered affirmatively, 14.6% answered negatively, and 20.2% did not answer this question. This contrasts with the high number of parents who complained on their questionnaire (reported below) about the difficulty of understanding messages from school and reports on their children's academic progress.

Question 20 asked, 'Do you think the parents are satisfied with the present state of communication with them?' 23.8% of the respondents answered affirmatively, 13.8% answered negatively, and 62.2% did not answer. The high percentage of those who did not answer this question may be explained by the comment frequently added: 'Impossible to gauge parents' satisfaction.'

The response to Question 21, 'Are you satisfied with the present state of communication with the parents?', was overwhelmingly negative, with 46.6%% of the teachers answering 'No', 17.4% not answering at all, and only 35.9% marking 'Yes'. Answers to Question 22 on the language(s) used to communicate with the parents give some clue as to why the respondents were generally dissatisfied: 34.4% said they used 'Mostly Japanese', 36.8% didn't answer, and 28.8% marked 'Others', which included Japanese and the parents' native tongue. None of the respondents indicated that they used 'Mainly the LM student's native tongue'.

Question 23 asked, 'Is your contact with the LM student's parents more frequent than with Japanese parents?' 18.3% of the teachers answered 'Yes', 22.1% said 'No', 21.5% didn't answer, and 37.9% responded that the amount was 'The same for both groups'. The large percentage that stressed equality may be interpreted to indicate stress on equality in the Japanese education system.

The final section of my report on the teacher questionnaire analyses the results for questions which focused on the teachers' evaluation of their experience with LM students. Question 15 asked, 'To what degree do you consider the LM students in your class beneficial to Japanese students' understanding of foreign cultures?' Question 6 inquired, 'To what degree is teaching the LM students beneficial to your professional experience?' Question 8 was, 'Do you think there are many problems in teaching the LM students?' Each of these three questions was answered using a 5-point scale. For the first two, (5) signified 'very beneficial' while (1) was defined to mean 'no benefit'. For Question 8, an answer of (5) indicated 'many problems', while an answer of (1) meant 'no problems'. The answers to these three questions are presented in Table 8.

It is disturbing that some 10% of the respondents rated the benefits of having LM students in class for the Japanese students' understanding of foreign cultures as only (1) ('no benefit') or (2). The popular wisdom in Japan is that frequent contact with foreign students promotes international understanding. Perhaps these teachers had negative classroom and personal experiences with the LM students, and thus saw their presence as

Table 8 Teachers' assessment of experience with LM students

Perceived Degree of Benefit or Number of Problems	1	2	3	4	5	No Answer
Degree LM students benefit Japanese students' understanding of foreign cultures	3.2%	7.4%	19.8%	30.5%	20.9%	15.9%
Degree teaching LM students beneficial to teachers' own professional experience	0.0%	4.6%	32.0%	22.6%	25.3%	15.2%
Number of problems in teaching LM students	4.8%	15.2%	36.1%	13.1%	14.5%	15.9%

5 = very beneficial/many problems
1 = no benefit/no problems

counterproductive. This supports asssertions that unsought cultural contact and familiarity do not necessarily result in better understanding of the other culture. The teachers' response to Question 8 shows that some of the teachers were in fact encountering problems in teaching their LM charges.

Nonetheless, 20% indicated that they were having few or no problems with their LM students and over 50% of the respondents saw the LM students' presence as beneficial. Nearly 50% saw teaching LM students as beneficial to their own professional experience. Moreover, the respondents were even more positive in response to Question 9: 'Do you consider your experiences in teaching LM students beneficial to your teaching career?' 74.5% answered 'Yes', only 16.8% replied 'No', and 9% did not answer this question. Comments accompanying the affirmative responses included, 'It has widened my perspectives,' 'It brings better international understanding', 'It encourages me to learn another language', 'It gives me the chance to learn better instruction techniques', and 'It helps me realise the common human nature that transcends national boundaries'.

Question 10 asked teachers who had been in charge of LM students in the past, 'Do you want LM students in your class again?' The majority of the respondents (52%) answered 'Yes'. Nonetheless,12% clearly marked 'No', 27% did not answer, and another 9% chose, 'Yes, on certain conditions'. Some of the reasons that accompanied the negative responses were, 'Adequate training should precede the actual assignment', 'I have no preparation for such students', 'I have no knowledge of the students' native languages' and 'I have to sacrifice the Japanese students to care for the LM students.' Comments given by the 9% of the respondents who answered with a conditional yes included, 'It depends upon the type of student', 'If I am given the additional time needed to teach the LM student', and 'I am ready to accept any assignment from the principal.'

These comments reflect differing experiences teachers are having with LM students, as well as differences in the teachers' own attitudes towards accommodating the varying needs of LM students.

Parent survey

As mentioned above, a total of 121 parent questionnaires were received from respondents with 12 different native languages. The results of this survey have already been reported in 'Language Minority Students in Japanese Elementary and Junior High Schools, Part 1' (Takahashi and Vaipae, 1996a), so only the major findings will be summarised here. Additional comments and concerns voiced by 28 other parents in letters and coincidental interviews will also be presented to give additional perspectives on foreign parents' perceptions of their children's experiences in the Japanese education system.

The survey instrument began with questions on the student's age, grade in school, gender, proficiency in each language, whether the parent(s) consider the child to be bilingual, and the child's history of schooling both in Japan and prior to arrival. The average age of the children when they arrived in Japan was 9 years, 8 months, and their average grade when they entered school was 1.5. Their current grade level average was 3.9. Approximately one-third of the children had attended pre-schools, kindergartens or elementary schools in their native countries and the average length of their study there was two years, while the average length of time they had attended school in Japan at the time the survey was completed was 2.3 years. Ninety-five percent of the parents considered their children to be bilingual in Japanese and their native language, although they noted that development of the native language had decreased, especially among the younger arrivals.

The last section of the survey instrument, which appeared on the pages after the student questionnaire, asked parents to indicate the degree of their concern with 23 issues related to their children's attendance at a Japanese school. Only 67 of the parents completed this section, and of those 67, some did not fill in all of the blanks. The results are presented in Table 9.

Before trying to discuss the figures in Table 9, it is important to note the limitations of this data. Parents' concerns regarding their children's schooling in a foreign language and foreign culture cannot adequately be expressed in numbers nor are they fully covered within the framework of this question. However, the relative degree of concern about specific areas can be identified. Inasmuch as the majority of the questionnaires returned by parents were from locales representative of 85% of the LM student population (in which there were fewer than six LM students in a school), it is possible to accept the results as representative of parents living outside areas where there is a sizeable concentration of LM students in a single

Table 9 Degree of parental concern about issues related to LM students' school life (Listed in order of average concern indicated by parents)

	Issue	Average Degree of Concern
1.	Your child's development of communication and academic skills in two languages.	4.17
2.	Little or no time with peers of child's own culture.	4.12
3.	Host culture's impressions of or attitudes towards your child's ethnicity, culture or country.	3.52
4.	Accuracy of your native country's history as taught in Japanese schools.	3.45
5.	Delayed native language skill development.	3.33
6.	No school-based instruction in the native language.	3.30
7.	Amount of practice in problem-solving, critical thinking and logical reasoning skills.	3.26
8.	Lack of training in critical thinking.	3.17
9.	Amount/quality of Japanese school language instruction your child receives at school.	3.14
10.	Amount of independent action and thought encouraged by school activities.	3.10
11.	Pressure to conform to behavior of Japanese peers.	2.98
12.	Corporal punishment.	2.97
13.	Your child's development of creativity.	2.93
14.	Different treatment on gender.	2.88
15.	Emphasis on passing examinations.	2.86
16.	School regulation of personal habits.	2.81
17.	Lack of acceptance for, or isolation of, your child.	2.78
18.	Appropriate individualisation of instruction.	2.75
19.	Teacher's attitudes	2.75
20.	More time required by child's school activities than fits your family's life patterns.	2.68
21.	Communications with teacher and/or school regarding child's academic progress or social welfare.	2.64
22.	Teasing child as foreigner ('*gaijin*').	2.61

5 = very much concerned, 4 = quite a bit concerned, 3 = somewhat concerned, 2 = not much concerned, 1 = not at all concerned
Adapted from Takahashi and Vaipae, 1996a.

school. Further caution regarding these results is necessary because the questionnaire was translated from English into Spanish, Portuguese, Japanese and Chinese, although back-translation procedures were employed to ensure equivalency.

Most importantly, for all of the issues raised by the questionnaire, there is an underlying ambiguity about what the question really means. The variety of mindsets possible became obvious as questionnaires were returned with comments. One parent wrote, 'I have no concern about my child being teased as a *gaijin* because my daughter is not teased, but if she were I would have great concern'. Another commented, 'Our son is enrolled in an overseas correspondence school, so first language academics is not a problem for us.' These parents both indicated a degree of concern of (1) about these issues. The indicated lack of concern in the second case was not due to a lack of priority placed on instruction in the native language, but due to the fact that the parent was already addressing this concern and therefore did not need the school to do so. The fact that the parent who wrote the second answer was investing considerable family time and money on a native language academic programme can be taken as evidence that this issue was in fact important to the parent.

These considerations may explain why the respondents expressed low levels of concern about the traditional characteristics of Japan's nationally-controlled school system (issues 7, 8, 10 and 13 in Table 9). However, language education was a major concern for the survey parents: Three-fourths of the parents from all language groups indicated a high priority for their children learning to study in both of their languages, with this issue having the highest average degree of concern expressed by the parents. Other areas of concern were for the little amount of time spent with peers of the child's own culture (4.12), delayed native language skill development (3.33) and lack of school-based instruction in the native language (3.30). These concerns suggest the importance that the respondents placed on their children maintaining contact with their native culture and continuing to develop their native language skills. Unfortunately, the survey also revealed that less than a third of the LM children were receiving specific mother tongue literacy instruction beyond casual reading at home. However, as noted above, neither bilingual education nor native language support is offered in Japanese schools (Noyama, 1992).

Parents in the elite Asian and foreign scholar group generally accepted the unavailability of school-based native-language instruction, giving one or both of the following reasons in their comments: (1) They were anxious to have their children learn Japanese as a second language; (2) Many were already tutoring their children in their first language at home or had them enrolled in distance education programmes. The working-class parents were more concerned about their children's loss of skills and lack of progress in their mother tongue. This concern was understandably most pronounced among those parents who intended to return within a few years to their homelands, where the children would once again attend schools conducted in their L1. Neither group of parents expressed awareness of the important relationship between first and second language literacy (Cummins, 1981).

Many of the parents seemed to expect more help from their schools than their children actually received. Approximately one-third of the parents' comments and interviews mentioned unkept promises by school personnel to provide special assistance in the form of language instruction or academic tutoring. Two examples from comments on the parent survey illustrate this problem.

One American junior high school boy was already bilingual and biliterate in Spanish and English when he arrived in Japan as an eighth grader. He had not been able to participate in his junior high school classes because he did not know Japanese and received no school-based JSL instruction. He was then lured by a promise of intensive tutoring in Japanese to a high school that wanted to take advantage of his basketball skills. The parent questionnaire was filled in at the end of his first term at the high school, and at that time, the promised instruction had not yet begun. Ironically, he received a failing grade in English because he could not read the Japanese instructions on the term test. Although his parents had requested that the readings of the Chinese characters be provided in the easily-mastered *hiragana* syllabary, the English teacher refused to provide this linguistic support, pointing out that it would be unfair to the other students if the tests were not identical.

The second instance of schools and teachers being unaccommodating to the needs of LM students occurred in an elementary school. An American first grader was not able to keep up with his class, and unlike his classmates, could not properly read and write the *hiragana* and *katakana* syllabaries by the third (final) term of the school year. Through a translator, the child's mother requested help for her son from his teacher, but the instructor replied, 'I do not have time.' The mother reported feeling thoroughly confused by this response, and said she was left wondering exactly what the priorities were at Japanese schools.

Although the schools were not prepared to give the LM children 'extra' support and the children's low Japanese CALP led to below-average academic achievement, many parents did not appear to fully comprehend the difficulties their children were facing. Over one-fourth of the parent responses suggested a limited understanding of the considerable cultural and social adjustments required of their children as they began attending school in Japan. Despite the difficulty of achieving academically in a second language, many survey parents expressed confidence that their children would 'catch up' within one or two years. In this respect, the foreign parents were not adequately prepared for the rigours their children faced. Moreover, without accurate information, they were less able to support their children in their efforts to integrate socially or to undertake the considerable task of becoming literate in Japanese.

The results in Table 9 are also intriguing in that issues of a serious nature, such as teasing a child as a foreigner ('*gaijin*') and physical bullying by schoolmates, appear to be of relatively little concern, but were very frequently mentioned in the free comment column on the questionnaire. Moreover, bullying and teasing were the most common problems referred to in parents' letters and interviews. Despite Japan's reputation for maintaining a safe public environment, the problem of bullying in schools is common and is widely reported in the media in Japan. In a survey by the Ministry of Education Junior High School Section Student Guidance Study Group (1994), 47% of the elementary school children and 34% of the junior high school students said there were children in their class who were being bullied. Although the survey parents did not appear to be particularly concerned about this problem, as evidenced by the fact that it had the lowest average degree of concern rating, in questionnaires and interviews, there were reports of physical bullying by other students as well as reports of physical violence visited by teachers upon students.

Survey parents whose children who had experienced some form of teasing or bullying voiced uncertainty about the school's determination to deal with the incidents. In one case, a boy was kicked and groped repeatedly and pushed into a pond on several occasions during a six-month period, yet the school did nothing about it even though the boy asserted that several of the teachers were aware of his situation. Similar reports of teachers ignoring bullying of Japanese children have appeared in the media frequently in the past few years, so this type of treatment can not be attributed solely to discriminatory attitudes towards foreigners. Nonetheless, two children in the surveyed families were removed from public schools because of bullying by other students, and a third child was removed after an incident of teacher violence. All three were subsequently enrolled in private schools.

It should also be noted that the degree of concern over different issues varied somewhat according to the native language of the parents. On the issue of physical bullying, one-third of the Spanish and Portuguese speaking parents expressed very much concern, in contrast to only slightly over 10% of the Chinese parents and less than 5% of the English speaking parents. Interestingly, another third of the Spanish and Portuguese speaking parents were only slightly concerned about physical bullying or said they had no concern about it at all. This evidence of extremes in the degree of concern within a language group may reflect only the particular environment of each family.

Another issue for which the degree of concern differed according to the language group was 'lack of acceptance for, or isolation of, your child'. Although the average degree of concern indicated by all parents was only 2.78, making this issue 17th in terms of average degree of concern, English speaking parents tended to give this issue a higher priority. One fourth responded with the highest possible mark of (5). It should be noted, however, that English speakers tend to be more scattered geographically, and for some, the isolation may be primarily due to location rather than any perceived deliberate isolation or lack of acceptance.

Two questions on the parent survey concerned parental satisfaction with their children's schooling. The first question was, 'Indicate how well you believe your child's needs are being served by his/her school experiences according to the following five goals of student well-being generally fostered by schools: Intellectual, social, emotional, physical, and communication skills.' The breakdown of the ratings by language group are presented in Table 10.

The second question dealing with parental evaluation of their children's schooling asked parents to 'indicate your overall satisfaction with your child's school experiences' on a scale of five, where (5) signified 'highly satisfied' and (1), 'not satisfied at all'. The breakdown of the mean ratings for each language group are presented in Table 11.

Although Table 10 showed that the parents had differing perceptions of various aspects of their children's Japanese schooling, their overall mean evaluation of 2.91 in Table 11 indicates moderate satisfaction. The combined total of parents who graded their children's schools as 'satisfactory', 'very satisfactory' or 'excellent' was 57%. This finding was particularly surprising given the poor grades the children were getting (Figure 2 above) and the *Daily Yomiuri* article by Sato (1997) which

Table 10 Parental perception of fulfillment of LM children's needs

Language of Response	Educational Goal	Degree Served					Average Rating
		1	2	3	4	5	
Chinese	Intellectual well-being	20%	20%	40%	20%	0%	2.60
	Social well-being	8%	20%	44%	24%	4%	2.96
	Emotional well-being	0%	20%	72%	0%	8%	2.96
	Physical well-being	25%	36%	24%	14%	1%	2.30
	Communication skills	24%	36%	32%	8%	0%	2.24
Spanish/ Portuguese	Intellectual well-being	0%	0%	60%	0%	40%	3.80
	Social well-being	0%	10%	50%	10%	30%	3.60
	Emotional well-being	0%	10%	50%	30%	10%	3.40
	Physical well-being	0%	0%	40%	20%	40%	4.00
	Communication skills	0%	10%	40%	20%	30%	3.70
English	Intellectual well-being	0%	48%	40%	8%	4%	2.68
	Social well-being	0%	32%	64%	4%	0%	2.72
	Emotional well-being	4%	60%	28%	8%	0%	2.40
	Physical well-being	4%	32%	36%	28%	0%	2.88
	Communication skills	0%	52%	40%	8%	0%	2.56

5 = highly served
1 = almost none
Adapted from Takahashi and Vaipae, 1996a.

Table 11 Overall parental satisfaction with LM children's schooling

Language of Response	Chinese	Spanish/Portuguese	English	All
Mean Satisfaction Rating	2.58	3.84	2.72	2.91

reported that only about a third of the LM students surveyed in junior high schools felt adequately prepared to do satisfactory work at their grade level.

We do see major differences between the language groups in Table 11. The Spanish and Portuguese speakers appear to have evaluated their children's Japanese schooling more highly than the Chinese or English speakers did, giving it a mean rating of 3.84 compared to 2.58 by the Chinese and 2.72 by the English speakers. This favourable appraisal by the Nikkei is similar to the high evaluations of Japanese education given by the Nikkei Brazilians in Watanabe's (1996) study.

These figures could be misleading, however. The limited number of responses from each group and the fact that it is not a random sample threaten their reliability. Morever, the different language groups are living in different areas. In addition, the higher appraisals by the Spanish and Portuguese parents may be partly explained by the ethnic identity of the respondents, since most were Nikkei (people of Japanese descent). The economic hardships faced by these parents and their demanding work schedules may also have left them with less time and energy for more active evaluation of their children's educational environments.

In fact, some of the more positive ratings seen in Tables 10 and 11 stood in sharp contrast to vehement comments made by some of the parents on their questionnaires and in personal interviews. The final page of the questionnaire asked the parents to write additional information or comments about their children's schooling. The depth of the frustrations parents voiced here and in interviews and letters cannot be expressed in tables, graphs or percentages. The frequency of specific criticisms, complaints, and misgivings, and the documentation of incidents and situations identify problematic areas, some of which were not touched upon by the questions in the survey instrument itself. Ironically, it was the Spanish and Portuguese speakers who wrote the harshest comments, with the Nikkei students seeming to be especially distainful of their school experiences. I will therefore conclude my summary of the parent questionnaire by outlining some of the major areas of concern expressed in the free comments on the questionnaires and in letters from and interviews with parents.

Before discussing these concerns, however, I should note that although 90% of the survey respondents had children in the lower primary grades, the majority of parents who wrote letters and were interviewed had children in the upper grades of elementary school or in junior high school, where the curriculum is harder and the difficulties in dealing with the Japanese writing system, greater.

The concern most often mentioned by parents in comments on the questionnaires and in letters and interviews was communication problems with the schools. Their complaints appeared to mirror the teachers' dissatisfaction with parent-teacher communication reported above. Those unable to read *kanji* expressed a desire for easier access to translation and mentioned unhappiness with having to repeatedly bother neighbours and friends for help in understanding school notes and report cards. Most parents had only recently arrived, did not intend to stay long, and were busy with work, making the expectations of Japanese educators that they become literate in Japanese unrealistic. As only one of Japan's 47 prefectures and 14 municipalities has even produced a multilingual guidebook (Ministry of Education, 1996), it was not surprising that none of the survey respondents had received school information in their native language.

Parents specifically cited the difficulty of understanding teacher's descriptions of their children's academic progress. One American parent stated she had learned that when a teacher said to her, 'Don't worry, everything is fine', it was her clue to start worrying. She became nervous because Japanese parents continually asked her if her daughter was being bullied; the ongoing nature of the inquiries made her feel as though they might be aware of something she did not know about. Dissatisfaction with the educational conditions encountered during the first three years of her daughter's schooling encouraged the family's earlier-than-planned departure from Japan.

Approximately two-thirds of the parents also lamented their inability to assist their children with homework and wanted to be better informed about the content matter being presented to their children.

Other facets of home-school relations seen as problematic included various routines and regulations peculiar to Japanese schools. Although the survey indicated a mean degree of concern of 2.81 (not much concern) about 'school regulation of personal habits', several parents were thoroughly distressed by the detailed directions and specifications for items the children were required to bring to school, including handkerchiefs, small packets of tissue paper, name tags, writing paper, pencils and erasers. The difficulty of making the standard kind of boxed lunches (*bento*) that children needed to take on sports days and outings, the high prices of the large array of regulation school equipment, checks on whether the children wore name tags and brought handerchiefs and tissue paper to school, and classroom practices such as reading language texts out loud in unison were among the aspects of school life about which some foreign parents complained. Not knowing how Japanese schools differ from those in other countries makes it difficult for school personnel to anticipate areas of probable difficulty for foreign parents and may make them mistakenly assume that foreign parents understand the school requirements.

Many of the misunderstandings were described as distressing to the children as well as the parents, as they made the children aware of their parents' inadequate communication skills. Parents mentioned efforts their children made to avoid being seen with them by schoolmates, as well as requests by the children to refrain from speaking their native language to them outside of the home. Several incidents in which children witheld information that would have led the parents to come to school were also reported. Other parents noted their children's reluctance to translate for them in public meetings.

The immense pressures on the LM students were revealed in two other forms of behaviour. One-fourth of the parents described various subterfuges their children took to avoid school or believed that their children were disguising their emotions as they feigned hearty involvement. The latter strategy — 'hyperparticipation' in classroom activity — was observed in one of the pilot studies and two of the case study students. It is a strategy LM students use to avoid attracting attention and detection of their lack of understanding of material presented in class. This phenomenon involves intense surface production using the few skills the child has in order to cover up for others s/he lacks. In these cases, the LM students were bravely attempting to blend in with the Japanese students by not calling attention to their deficiencies. None of the teachers reported instances of this, but it is, after all, a strategy applied to fool teachers and classmates.

Thus, the comments received from parents tended to stand at odds to the more positive image gleaned from the statistical results of the survey. However, they may not be considered representative of the overall situation of LM students in Japan because many of them came from American or European professional educators living in relatively isolated areas where there were few other LM students. Nevertheless, these comments reveal aspects of some LM students' lives which were unnoticed by many Japanese teachers and educational authorities.

Student comments

The questions on the student survey instrument concerned the child's favourite and least favourite subjects, what s/he liked and did not like about school life, how much s/he understood of what the teacher said, and the amount of time spent daily on various activities in Japanese and in the student's native tongue. Space limitations do not allow a full presentation here, so only general trends will be reported.

The students indicated that Japanese and math were their least favourite subjects. Memorizing *kanji* (Chinese characters used in Japanese writing) was cited as particularly difficult. Math story problems, which require the ability to read and sometimes to interpret cultural nuances, were singled out as highly problematic. Social studies also presented considerable difficulties, although the children were not able to articulate the reasons for this. EFL learners, however, frequently have problems with social studies because of the specialised vocabulary used (Collier, 1995).

Problems in school life mentioned by older elementary and junior high school students who had begun their schooling in their home cultures included regimentation of social activities and discouragement of self-expression in and out of class. About half of the students indicated that they were reluctant or even afraid to ask clarifying questions of the teacher, and instead, would try to obtain missing information or achieve understanding by asking their fellow students.

Varying degrees of student adjustment to Japan's culture and education system were reported. Some elementary school LM children were well-accepted and functioning well, socially and emotionally, within the system. Others were in great personal pain, as illustrated by the following student comments.

> *American third-grader*: It's hard to live in Japan. People make fun of me. No one understands English, and I don't speak enough Japanese to say what I want. The teachers are kind of nice, kind of mean. When I don't understand in class, I am too scared to ask the teacher to explain it again. Japan is like a stranger. I can't get used to it.

> *Peruvian sixth-grader*: In my country I had a good life. After I came to this country, I was discouraged by my feelings of being insulted and ashamed. I could do everything when I was in my own country, but now I can't do anything good. I really feel as if I cannot speak. In my country, everything goes as I like, for instance, soccer, volleyball, swimming, running, talking and studying. I was really good at these things and I also had many friends. Now I am good at nothing. (*Translated from Spanish.*)

Some junior high students who had completed most of their elementary school education in Japan were succeeding or at least holding their own; others were just spending the day at school.

Case studies

The author's two children, who served as the pilot cases, attended school in Niigata, as did one of the case study LM students. The other five case studies were selected from a group of 14 LM students attending a suburban school in the Tokyo area that had a special JSL teacher for its pull-out language programme. They were chosen to represent a variety of grade entry levels in school as well as nationality, native language and gender. The classroom teachers, students and parents were interviewed over a two-year period, and repeated protocol-based classroom observations were also videotaped and transcribed. Narratives and vocabulary measures were administered by six members of the research team having three different nationalities and capable of speaking several languages. Heritage language translators provided assistance with the parent and student interviews.

Space limitations allow only brief summaries of the pilot and case studies. Vital statistics for each of these children are provided in Table 12.

Table 12 Pilot and case study students

Student (Gender)		Locale	Country of Origin	L1	Age on Arrival	Entry Grade	Grades Obs.	Length of Res.	Preschool J. Exp.
Pilot Studies									
Christa	(F)	Kanuma Niigata Osaka	USA	English	3;7	PS	PS–5	7;9	1.4
Mele	(F)	Kanuma Niigata Osaka	USA	English	5;5	K	K–7	7;2	1.0
Case Studies									
Okusay	(F)	Tokyo	China	Chinese	10;10	4	6–7	2;8	None
Okime	(F)	Tokyo	Peru	Spanish	9;1	2	6–7	4;7	None
Willy	(M)	Tokyo	USA	English	8;7	3	3–4	0;1	None
Carol	(F)	Tokyo	USA	English	7;10	2	2–3	0;8	None
Ayako	(F)	Tokyo	Philippines	English	5;3	1	2–3	1;4	1.0
Ygun	(F)	Niigata	Vietnam	Vietnam	12;10	6	6–7	0;6	0.5

Grades Obs. = Grades children were in while they were under observation
Length of Res. = Length of Residence (years; months) * Preschool J. Exp. = Length of exposure to Japanese language before entering Japanese school (in years)

Christa had a joyful entry into preschool life in Japan and easily made friends as she gained communicative skills in Japanese. The young American was active in a figure-skating club and competitions until her family moved from Niigata to Osaka. Her first and second grade teacher (she had the same teacher for both grades – a common practice in Japan) was a severe disciplinarian with no knowledge of second language acquisition and no willingness to devote extra time or effort to needs which she did not perceive. There were several periods, ranging from a few days to six weeks during second, third and fourth grades, when Christa refused to go to school, but specific reasons for her refusal were never determined.

The move to Osaka between her third and fourth grade school years was a major setback to her adjustment and progress, as she had to leave her friends and familiar environment behind. Nonetheless, teachers consistly reported that she was 'doing fine', and her term grades were always average or above average. Her fourth grade teacher actually gave Christa higher grades for the second quarter than were warranted by her skills. This boost to Christa's confidence resulted in increased efforts both at home and school in all subjects. However, from the middle of fourth grade, she was experiencing anxiety bordering on depression and began weekly visits to a clinical psychologist for play therapy.

At the start of fifth grade, Christa was switched to her third new teacher and set of classmates in three years. By the end of the first term she was severely stressed by her struggle to keep up with her classmates academically. At this point, it became apparent that Christa had for years been expending considerable effort to hide her academic deficiencies, especially from her parents. The school's lack of responsiveness to Christa's educational needs in the face of her own and her parents' expectations became a source of constant and increasing anxiety. At the end of the first term of fifth grade, she was withdrawn from school on the counsellor's advice.

Mele, Christa's older sister, was a kindergartener upon arrival in Japan. She quickly learned to communicate with Japanese friends, and throughout her time in Japan, participated frequently in cultural activities with neighborhood families. Musically talented, Mele performed frequently in regional events, placing second in a national folk song (*minyō*) competition when she was in fifth grade.

Yet at the end of elementary school, after seven years in Japan, her sixth grade teacher described Mele as inadequately prepared for the academic rigours of junior high school. No previous teacher had suggested that Mele was considerably behind native peers in skill levels. Her adjustment and ease within classroom routines encouraged teachers to treat her exactly as a native student, and no JSL instruction had been given. In addition to her lack of skills, the sixth grade teacher noted Mele's lack of enthusiasm for schoolwork. Mele herself declared that she did not enjoy school in Japan, but only went to be with her friends.

In her first term examinations in junior high school, Mele received failing grades in all academic subjects except English. Since her parents had taught her to read English at home, Mele was already reading it at a fourth grade level. In response to her parents' request that the junior high school English teacher give her more challenging materials than learning the alphabet, Mele was given pages of written English to be translated into Japanese. Deciding that continuing school in Japan would not contribute further to Mele's education, the family sent her to the United States to live with an aunt. There, she began attending summer ESL classes prior to entry into regular school.

Okusay came to Japan from China when she was almost 11 years old and entered an elementary school in Tokyo in the fourth grade. Receiving little support from her classroom teachers and no extra JSL instruction outside of class during elementary school, she had not reached a literacy level in Japanese that allowed academic class participation three years later when she entered junior high school. Her teacher for fifth and sixth grades ran an entirely teacher-fronted lecture class with minimal student participation. Throughout the two years and six sessions in which the research team observed her, Okusay never volunteered nor responded to indirect teacher prompts in class.

Although her social integration was unsatisfactory during elementary school, she made friends quickly after she moved on to seventh grade. The sullen and withdrawn demeanour that had been observed in fifth and sixth grades was transformed into cheerful, open smiles and increased ease in social contacts observed at the time of her interview during her second term in middle school.

One factor in this transformation may have been the commencement of JSL instruction. A community volunteer came to the junior high school for two hours once a week and tutored Okusay and her cousins in a pull-out programme. Her spoken Japanese had improved, especially in terms of vocabulary and ease of delivery. It was observed, however, that she still often did not know alternative meanings of homonyms, mistaking 'change' (*kaeru*) for 'return' (*kaeru*) even when they were used in context. She continued to speak Chinese at home, but reported that she had forgotten all the written Chinese characters she had known.

Okime was nine years old when she came to Japan from Peru and entered second grade in a Tokyo elementary school. Her early production in Japanese was ridiculed by some Japanese children, and frequent reoccurrences of this embarrassment resulted in her almost total refusal to use the language. Her social language was therefore extremely slow to develop. Okime also demonstrated low motivation and effort to become literate in Japanese. The special JSL class teacher reported that her third and fourth grade teacher frequently complained of her lack of attention to work in class. However, her limited Japanese vocabulary precluded any meaningful participation in lessons. On the other hand, Okime eagerly attended her JSL classes, where she was able to converse with the special class teacher in her limited Japanese and his limited Spanish.

Fifth grade saw a change of class and teacher. The new instructor used more student-centreed, small-group, cooperative learning activities. This encouraged Okime to renew her efforts to make friends. During fifth and sixth grades, she developed more rewarding peer relationships and improved her strategies for appearing more productive in class. However, she lacked so much core vocabulary that her interactions in class were primarily social. Once she became comfortable in fifth grade, she became reluctant to leave her classroom to attend the pull-out JSL class, saying that she wanted to study with her new friends.

Okime was unable to catch up with her classmates by the end of sixth grade and entered junior high school unprepared for academic work. Although she received passing grades in her second term academic classes, a brief questioning about the subject content by the research team revealed that she had little comprehension of the material. Okime could not, for example, name the basic shapes (circle, square, triangle, etc.) from her geometry class handouts.

Willy moved to Tokyo from the US when he was eight and a half and had just started attending Japanese third grade when we first observed him. A very shy boy, he made few efforts to communicate or play with classmates. His slow progress in learning to read and write Japanese could be attributed in part to his delayed rate of vocabulary building, a process normally enhanced by peer conversation and exchanges in play. His isolation also affected his in-class interactions, and he was unable to benefit from the higher-context academic exchanges of Japanese classmates to assist himself in understanding the teacher's presentations. During the course of our observations over two school years, he remained apparently overwhelmed by his new environment, and his adjustment to class and school routines was very slow. Without intensive intervention and assistance, it appeared unlikely that he would be able to get to a point where he could learn academic content in class before he finished elementary school.

Carol was almost eight years old when she moved to Tokyo from America and began second grade. She did not receive JSL instruction until she was in third grade. She demonstrated a high level of interest and participation in her Japanese lessons, although at the beginning of third grade, she knew only half of the words in the first grade textbook. Her attention to the classroom teacher's presentations was limited to that which she was able to comprehend. If the material was not within her vocabulary range, she distracted herself by playing with her pencils, doodling, or laying her head on her desk. She received little classroom support to integrate her tentatively-acquired skills into the subject matter tasks.

Carol was observed to have but a tenuous hold on her beginning literacy skills. She needed careful monitoring to maintain her initial gains. As with all the case study students, careful placement with an encouraging and mindful teacher would have been a considerable boost to her own efforts.

Ayako moved to Tokyo from the Philippines and lived in Japan for a full year before entering Japanese school in the first grade. Her entry into school was not accompanied by rapid acquisition of social language, although her high energy level and friendliness attracted attention. Her vocabulary expanded slowly, while she developed strategies to facilitate communication. Japanese classmates sought out contact with Ayako and adopted her imperfect use of the language, thus delaying even longer her acquisition of correct usage.

Despite fairly intensive training over several months in a pull-out JSL class, Ayako persisted in reading words written in the *hiragana* syllabary symbol by symbol rather than recognizing combinations as words that she already had in her vocabulary. The support of her JSL special class teacher and instruction did not appear to compensate for her classroom teachers' inattention to her language needs for academic purposes.

Despite her limited skills, Ayako had the appearance of being actively involved in class activities and aggressively pursued peer and teacher interaction. Toward the end of our observation period, she developed a friendly rivalry with two other Filipinas recently enrolled in other grades that could possibly provide additional impetus for more rapid acquisition of the language skills necessary for even minimally successful elementary education.

Ygun was already almost 13 years old when she came to Niigata from Vietnam with her family. She was placed in the sixth grade, although she was ready to begin eighth grade in Vietnam. Within three years, she had mastered the *kanji* normally learned in the first six years of Japanese schooling, had absorbed the subject matter for her grade level, and kept up with her Vietnamese textbooks.

An exceptional example of an LM child with an elite background and strong parental moral and academic support, Ygun appeared likely to progress successfully through high school despite her late start in the Japanese education system. Her father was a doctoral candidate who could speak French, German, English and Japanese in addition to his native Vietnamese. He shared his knowledge of language-learning strategies with Ygun and had high expectations of her. Her motivation, hard work, and intellectual acuity, complemented by intensive private and parental tutoring, led to a level of accomplishment that may have ensured a good chance of academic success were she to continue in the Japanese education system.

Socially, however, Ygun appeared to be less successfully integrated. Despite the outward evidence of integration through swimming club activities, her outspokenness distanced her from friendships during her first year of junior high school.

At the end of seventh grade, Ygun returned to Vietnam to take entrance examinations for high school there.

Discussion of case studies

The pilot and case studies investigated the students' sociocultural adjustment and its impact upon their academic achievement in their second language. The eight LM students described above represented a variety of entry ages and entry levels in schools, differing schooling options and teachers, varying home situations and community contexts, diverse personalities and four different native languages. It is therefore understandable that they achieved varying levels of communicative and academic competence in Japanese and comfort in their schools and in Japanese society at large.

No one factor seemed to determine the degree to which these students experienced success or failure in terms of second language growth, academic achievement, and social and emotional adjustment. The variables involved appeared to be far more complex than the language itself. The combination of psychological and social influences singled out by Freeman and Freeman (1994) include family, community and school perceptions of the student, the level of acceptance by mainstream society, background knowledge and experience, the view of language learning held by the students' teachers, the curricular approach used, teacher and peer response to the student, the value of education to the family and community, and the students' own expectations of what education is. Freeman and Freeman assert that all of these factors interact to permit or prohibit students' access to the acquisition of a new language and the academic content of subjects within it. The effects of many of these factors were evident in the pilot and case studies. However, it could be argued that in the case of the child who displayed the most second language development and academic achievement, the student and her parents never appeared to question the prevailing assimilation model; they simply worked hard within its confines.

Although a wide range of communicative and academic competence in Japanese was achieved, considered together, the pilot and case studies highlight the undesirable aspects of mainstream submersion schooling for children with no systematic instruction in their second language. Wong Filmore (1991) suggests that the two to five years normally required to develop social language for use in everyday situations may be prolonged if such necessary components to language acquisition as motivation, helpful and competent target language speakers, and an appropriate setting are lacking. Yet classroom submersion under the conditions observed in Japan did not provide LM students with these requisite components.

Moreover, the pull-out programmes provided for four of the case study children were not seen to be much more effective, supporting Cummins & Swain's assertion (1986) that pull-out classes are counterproductive because students are often removed from core curriculum classes such as social studies and language arts, and because the students are often socially stigmatised by these special instructional arrangements.

The speed with which LM students often develop basic social language skills tends to compound barriers to receiving needed assistance for academic language, as seen in the case of the pilot study sisters. The fact that teacher evaluations of the LM students' linguistic competence for academic learning (Cognitive/Academic Language Proficiency, or CALP) were not always accurate was first noticed in the case of these sisters. Teachers in general were neither knowledgeable nor aware of various language learning strategies used by the LM students in classroom environments, and thus could employ no techniques of their own to assist them (Takahashi and Vaipae, 1996b). Moreover, efforts by parents or JSL teachers to deliberately place students in classes taught by teachers whose styles, personalities and JSL awareness might have been more suitable to their needs were ignored by administrators for reasons such as 'staff harmony' which were unrelated to the LM students' best interests.

The prevalence of non-individualised instruction in elementary schools was detrimental to the LM students' progress; even native Japanese students are seldom given additional assistance when experiencing difficulty, thus leading to the perception that special attention for LM students is 'unfair'. Moreover, approaches by some of the case study children to indicate their need for teacher or peer assistance were frequently interpreted by the classroom teachers as inappropriate classroom behaviour.

Although one of the case study children was able to make remarkable progress despite her late entry into the Japanese school system, this was done with a level of support that is not available to the vast majority of the LM students in Japan. Other cases showed that even after years of residence, and with an entry level of first grade, LM students may continue to experience social and cultural discomfort while making little academic progress. Moreover, regardless of the length of residence or school attendance in Japan, none of the case study students reached academic achievement levels on par with their Japanese classmates during the years they were under observation.

Conclusion

The number of language minority students in Japan has increased dramatically during the 1990s. This qualitative overview of four years of informal and three years of formal research could only paint the situation of LM students in Japan with the broadest of strokes. It has, however, suggested that Japan's LM students, like many other LM students worldwide, are seriously underserved both socially and educationally.

The research team found that the Japanese egalitarian philosophy of education, coupled with an absence of a national language policy, has resulted in a tendency for educational institutions and government authorities to minimise their efforts in dealing with LM students. With assimilation as the goal, foreign children are 'mainstreamed'. Japanese language instruction is provided in only about 20% of the schools that host LM students nationwide, and then it is limited to short-term pull-out programmes that focus on communication skills and are taught by untrained, occasionally unwilling teachers with little or no outside support. Innovation and student-centred programmes evolve only when individual teachers take the initiative.

The limited language assistance given to approximately one-fifth of the LM students in the country may contribute to increased levels of social communication skills, but stops far short of providing the instruction necessary to build academic language skills (CALP). Younger students, in particular, lacked an inventory of language learning strategies which would have enabled more independent progress. If the classroom teacher did not know how or chose not to provide the necessary monitored language assistance, the student often struggled to meet expectations, and, as was seen in the reports of the case studies, was seldom successful.

Since bilingual programmes and minority language support are not provided by Japanese schools and most teachers were found to place little importance on the maintenance and/or development of the LM children's native language, their bilingual experience meets one of the conditions Hamers and Blanc (1989) linked to negative consequences: they are 'schooled through a prestigious L2 while the school system tends to ignore or denigrate the mother tongue'.

The parents of the LM students were found to be highly concerned about their children's development of communication and academic skills in both of their languages, but in many cases, they did not appear to appreciate the rigours their children faced or the considerable effort required to become literate in Japanese. Many thought their children would 'catch up' within one or two years, and in general, the parents evaluated the schooling their children were getting in Japan fairly highly. Greater formal knowledge of the difficulties faced by language minority children in general and of the difference between Basic Interpersonal Communication Skills (BICS) and Cognitive/Academic Language Proficiency (CALP) might help them make more informed decisions, make them better able to support their children's efforts, and stimulate them to put pressure on education authorities in Japan to provide more assistance to their children.

Investigation of in-progress programmes for teacher training and student Japanese language instruction revealed no instances of first, needs analysis; second, the setting of goals for teachers and/or students; or third, evaluation of programme effectiveness. Reforms of stifling institutions, uninformed practices, misguided assumptions and counterproductive and rigid instructional approaches look to research for direction. Uncontexted language research alone is an inadequate basis for change. Understanding and unravelling heirarchical relations among a culture's interpretive schemas are necessary in refining structures and processes in which the participants are inextricably bound. Participant action research and programme development involving native and non-native researchers and stakeholders are recommended for meaningful improvement.

A quote from Collier (1995: 28) sums up the hopes of this investigator for the future, not only of language minority students, but for all students in the Japanese education system:

> 'Schools reflect the community and the broader society. But they do not have to be limited by existing societal patterns. Schools can be agents of change....'

Acknowledgements

Portions of this paper are revised versions of a working paper published in two parts under the title 'Language Minority Students in Japanese Elementary and Junior High School' (Takahashi and Vaipae, 1996a and Takahashi and Vaipae, 1998).

Toyota Foundation Project Team Members

Takahashi Masao, Niigata University, Teacher Educator
Kawamura Takeo, Special Teacher, Tokyo Daiichi Elementary School

Dr Barbara Merino, University of California, Davis, Director of
Bilingual Teacher Education
Furukawa Chikashi, National Language Research Institute, JSL Teacher
Education
Evelyn Sasamoto, University of Maryland, Graduate Student in Second
Language Acquisition
Sharon Vaipae, Niigata University, *Gaikokujin kōshi* (Foreign Lecturer)

Consultants and Translators

Nagaoka Aya, Niigata University, English Education graduate
Sun Le Bing, Niigata University, Faculty of Economics graduate
Dr Angelo Iishi, Tokyo University
Ricardo Misuki, Niigata University, Faculty of Law
Rosa Higa, parent and community member

Notes

1. Ministry of Justice figures presented in an article by Yamagiwa Hiroshi in the *Japan Times* Kansai edition of June 13, 1996.
2. Statistics from an article by Nagoya Satoru in the Kansai edition of the *Japan Times*, July 3, 1996.
3. Every two years since 1992, the Ministry of Education has published this information under the title, *Nihongo kyōiku ga hitsuyōna gaikokujin jidō seito no ukeire jōkyō ni kansuru chōsa no kekka* [Survey on the Acceptance and Instruction of Foreign Children and Students Needing Japanese Language Education]. The figures have also been widely published in vernacular and English-language newspapers in Japan.
4. *Nihon daihyakka zensho* [Encyclopedia Nipponica 2001], Vol. 17: 651. Tokyo: Shogakukan.

References

Baker, C. (1988) *Key Issues in Bilingualism and Bilingual Education*. Clevedon, UK: Multilingual Matters.
Bialystock, E. (ed.) (1991) *Language Processing in Bilingual Children*. Cambridge, UK: Cambridge University Press.
Collier, V.P. (1989). How long? A synthesis of research on academic achievement in a second language. *TESOL Quarterly* 23 (3), 509–531.
Collier, V.P. (1992) A synthesis of studies examining long-term language minority data on academic achievement. *Bilingual Research Journal* 16 (1–2), 187–212.
Collier, V.P. (1995) *Promoting Academic Success for ESL Students: Understanding Second Language Acquisition for School*. Jersey City, NJ: Jersey City State College, New Jersey TESOL – Bilingual Education.
Cummins, J. (1979) Cognitive/academic language proficiency, linguistic interdependence, the optimal age question, and some other matters. *Working Papers on Bilingualism* 19, 197–205.
Cummins, J. (1981) The role of primary language development in promoting educational success for language minority students. In California State Department of Education (ed.) *Schooling and Language Minority Students: A Theoretical Framework* (pp. 3–51). Los Angeles, CA: CSU Evaluation, Dissemination and Assessment Centre.

Cummins, J. (1984) *Bilingualism and Special Education: Issues in Assessment and Pedagogy.* Clevedon, UK: Multilingual Matters.

Cummins, J. & Dolson, D.P. (1985) The effects of Spanish home language use on the scholastic performance of Hispanic pupils. *Journal of Multilingual and Multicultural Development 6,* 135–155.

Cummins, J. & Nakajima K. (1985) Age of arrival, length of residence, and interdependence of literacy skills among Japanese immigrant students. In B. Harley, P. Allen, J. Cummins, and M. Swain (eds) *The Development of Second Language Proficiency.* Cambridge, UK: Cambridge University Press.

Cummins, J. & Swain, M. (1986) *Bilingualism in Education.* London and New York: Longman.

Daily Yomiuri (1997) Article by Sato, G. Foreign students lack language skills. July 14.

Ezaki Y. & Moriguchi S. (ed.) (1988) *'Zainichi' gaikokujin* [Foreigners 'in Japan']. Tokyo: Shobunsha.

Freeman, D.E. & Freeman, Y.S. (1994) *Between Worlds: Access to Second Language Acquisition.* Portsmouth, NH: Heinemann.

Garcia, E. (1993) Language, culture and education. In L. Darling-Hammond (ed.) *Review of Research in Education,* Vol. 19 (pp. 51–98). Washington, DC: American Educational Research Association.

Genesee, F. (1987) *Learning Through Two Languages: Studies of Immersion and Bilingual Education.* Cambridge, MA: Newbury House.

Genesee, F. (1994). *Educating Second Language Children: The Whole Child, the Whole Curriculum, the Whole Community.* Cambridge, UK: Cambridge University Press.

Hakuta, K. (1986) *Mirror of Language: The Debate on Bilingualism.* New York: Basic Books.

Hamers, J.F. & Blanc, M.H.A. (1989) *Bilinguality and Bilingualism.* Cambridge, UK: Cambridge University Press.

Harada T. & Akabori T. (1992) *Kokusai rikai no kiiwaado* [Keywords for Internationalization]. Tokyo: Yuhikaku.

Itoh S. & Miyashita H. (1994) *Kanji wa mina, karuta de manaberu* [Kanji can all be learned with cards]. Tokyo: Tarojirosha.

Iwasaki Y. (1995) *Kokusaika ni taisuru kyōiku katei no unyō – Nihongo kyōshitsu wo chūshin to shita gaikokujin shijo kyōiku wo jissen wo tōshite* [Carrying Out the Process of Education For Internationalization: The Practice of Educating Foreign Children, Centreing on the JSL Classroom]. *Heisei 7 nendo gaikokujin shijo kyōiku kenkyū kyōryokukō renraku kyōgikai happyō shiryō* [Handout from a presentation made at the 1995 Conference for Consultation by Schools Cooperating in Research on the Education of Foreign Children].

Japan Times
(articles without by-lines)
Businesses asked to avoid hiring of illegal workers. *Japan Times* Kansai Edition, June 17, 1998.
Foreign residents total 1.48 million. *Japan Times* Kansai Edition, June 29, 1998.
(articles with by-lines)
Maeda T. (1997) Do traditional Bon and samba mix? Gunma town struggles to embrace Japanese-Brazilian returnees. *Japan Times* Kansai Edition, August 19, 1997.
Nagoya S. (1996) Government promoting policies to attract overseas students. *Japan Times* Kansai Edition, July 3, 1996.
Yamagiwa H. (1996) Recourse eludes illegal aliens: Employers' attitude, lack of rights main complaints. *Japan Times* Kansai Edition, June 13, 1996.

Lessow-Hurley, J. (1990) *The Foundations of Dual Language Instruction.* New York: Longman.

Lewis, C.C. (1995) *Educating Hearts and Minds: Reflections on Japanese Preschool and Elementary Education.* Cambridge, UK: Cambridge University Press.

McKay, S. & Freedman, S. (1990) Language minority education in Great Britain: A challenge to current United States Policy. *TESOL Quarterly* 24 (3), 385–405.

Ministry of Education (1991) *Kyōiku no kokusai kōryū ni kansuru jittai chōsa* [Study of Actual Conditions in International Exchange in Education]. Tokyo: Ministry of Education.

Ministry of Education (1992) *Heisei 3 nendo nihongo kyōiku ga hitsuyōna gaikokujin jidō seito no ukeire jōkyō ni kansuru chōsa no kekka* [Results of the 1991 Survey on the Acceptance and Instruction of Foreign Children and Students Needing Japanese Language Education]. Tokyo: Ministry of Education.

Ministry of Education (1994) *Heisei 5 nendo nihongo kyōiku ga hitsuyōna gaikokujin jidō seito no ukeire jōkyō ni kansuru chōsa no kekka* [Results of the 1993 Survey on the Acceptance and Instruction of Foreign Children and Students Needing Japanese Language Education]. Tokyo: Ministry of Education.

Ministry of Education (1996) *Heisei 7 nendo nihongo kyōiku ga hitsuyōna gaikokujin jidō seito no ukeire jōkyō ni kansuru chōsa no kekka* [Results of the 1995 Survey on the Acceptance and Instruction of Foreign Children and Students Needing Japanese Language Education]. Tokyo: Ministry of Education.

Ministry of Education (1998) *Heisei 9 nendo nihongo kyōiku ga hitsuyōna gaikokujin jidō seito no ukeire jōkyō ni kansuru chōsa no kekka* [Results of the 1997 Survey on the Acceptance and Instruction of Foreign Children and Students Needing Japanese Language Education]. Tokyo: Ministry of Education.

Ministry of Education Junior High School Section Student Guidance Study Group [*Mombushō chūgakkō kanai seito shidō kenkyūkai*] (ed.) (1994) *Heisei 5 nendoban dēta ni miru seito shidō.* [Student Guidance Needs Apparent in Data from 1993]. Tokyo: Daiichi hoki.

Ministry of Education Study Group (1996) *Newest Questions and Answers About School Administration.* Tokyo: Gyosei.

Murata Y. (1994) *Gaikokujin jidō kyōiku no jissen to sono kadai — Mōka, toyohashi chiku to tsukuba, kyōto chiku no hikaku chōsa wo tōshite* [Practice and Problems of Educating Foreign Children – A Comparison of Moka and Toyohashi to Kyoto and Tsukuba]. Final report on a 1993 Ministry of Education Science Research Grant Project.

Nakanishi A., Sugiyama M. & Hasegawa S. (1991) *Kyōshitsu karano kokusaika* [Internationalisation From the Classroom]. Tokyo: Gyosei.

Nihon daihyakka zensho [Encyclopedia Nipponica 2001]. Tokyo: Shogakukan.

Noyama H. (1992) *Zainichi gaikokujin jidō, seito e no nihongo kyōiku ni taisuru tabunka kyōikuteki ichikōsatsu* [Multicultural Aspects of Japanese Language Education of Foreign Children and Students in Japan]. Tokyo: *Kokuritsu kokugo kenkyūjo, nihongo kyōiku sentā* [National Language Research Institute, Japanese Language Education Centre], *Nihongo kyōiku ronshū [Japanese Language Education Bulletin]* No. 9.

Ruiz, R. (1984) Orientations in languge planning. *NABE Journal* 8 (2), 15–34.

Sakai H. (1992) *Kokusai rikai to kyōiku jissen* [International Understanding and Educational Practice]. Tokyo: Emuti shuppan.

Skutnabb-Kangas, T. & Toukomaa, P. (1976) *Teaching Migrant Children: Mother Tongue and Learning the Language of the Host Country in the Context of the Socio-Cultural Situation of the Migrant's Family.* Tampere, Finland: Tukimuksia Research Reports. (As summarised in *Encyclopedia of Bilingualism and Bilingual Education,* by Colin Baker and Syliva Prys Jones. (1998). Clevedon, UK: Multilingual Matters.)

Snow, C.E. (1990) Rationales for native language instruction: Evidence from research. In A.M. Padilla, H.H. Fairchild, and C.M. Valdez (eds) *Bilingual Education: Issues and Strategies.* Newbury Park, CA: Sage.

Swain, M., Lapkin, S., Rowen, N. & Hart, D. (1990) The role of native language literacy in third language learning. In S. P. Norris and L. M. Phillips (eds) *Foundations of Literacy Policy in Canada* (pp. 185–206). Calgary, AB, Canada: Detselig Enterprises Ltd.

Tada T. & Honda N. (1993) *Kokusai rikai kyōiku Q and A* [Education for International Understanding: Questions and Answers]. Tokyo: Kyoiku shuppan senta.

Takahashi M. & Vaipae, S. (1996a). Language minority students in Japanese elementary and junior high schools, Part 1. *Memoirs of the Faculty of Education, Niigata University* 38 (1), 21–40.

Takahashi M. & Vaipae, S. (1996b). *Gaijin seito ga yatte kita: ibunka toshite no gaikokujin jidō/seito wo dō mukaeru ka* ['Foreigner' Students Are Here: How Can We Welcome Foreign Children and Students as 'Cultural Others']. Tokyo: Taishukan shoten.

Takahashi M. & Vaipae, S. (1998) Language minority students in Japanese elementary and junior high schools, Part 2. *Memoirs of the Faculty of Education, Niigata University* 39 (2), 271–290.

Tinajero, J.V. & Ada, A.F. (eds) (1993) *The Power of Two Languages: Literacy and Biliteracy for Spanish-Speaking Students*. New York: Macmillan/McGraw-Hill.

Watanabe M. (1996) *Dekasegi nikkei burajirujin* [Nikkei Brazilian Migrant Workers]. Tokyo: Akashi shoten.

Wong Filmore, L. (1991). Second language learning in children: A model of language learning in social context. In E. Bialystok (ed.) *Language Processing in Bilingual Children* (pp. 49–69). Cambridge, UK: Cambridge University Press.

Chapter 9

Bilinguality and Bicultural Children in Japan: A Pilot Survey of Factors Linked to Active English-Japanese Bilingualism

MARY GOEBEL NOGUCHI

Introduction

As Japan emerged from its postwar obscurity and became renown for its thriving economy, it began attracting increasing numbers of long- and short-term immigrants despite its strict immigration policies. This trend, combined with increased foreign travel on the part of the Japanese themselves, has led to a vast increase in the number of marriages between Japanese and people of other nationalities (Yamamoto, 1995:64). Especially when the foreign marriage partner is a native English speaker, mixed couples often wish to raise their children bilingually because of the prestige English enjoys both within Japan and in the international arena. However in many cases, the children of mixed couples do not become active bilinguals, but instead, are passive bilinguals with substantial receptive capabilities but limited productive skills, or in some cases, display little ability to either understand or speak English (Yamamoto, 1987, 1992, 1995, 1996; Billings, 1990).

As part of a long-term project to investigate some of the variables related to whether children in bicultural families in Japan become active bilinguals or not, the author conducted an exploratory survey of members of the Japan Association for Language Teaching (hereinafter JALT) Bilingualism Special Interest Group (hereinafter SIG) in 1995. This was intended to be a pilot study to help refine a survey instrument that could be used on a wider scale to evaluate possible relationships between the bilinguality of children in bicultural families and factors such as the sex of the native English-speaking (NES) parent, the children's age and level in school, their parents' proficiencies in Japanese and English, family language strategies and communication patterns, and the children's ability to read both languages.

In designing the survey instrument and analysing the results, the difficulties in defining bilingualism (outlined in the book's introduction) were taken into account. Although, as Grosjean has pointed out, the lay person has a tendency to use the level of *fluency* in two languages as the 'main criterion of bilingualism' (Grosjean, 1982: 235), this study, like the others in the book, stressed the ability to *use* two languages as the deciding factor in categorising subjects as 'active bilinguals', 'passive bilinguals' or 'monolinguals'.

The results of this pilot study, including the discovery of another potentially influential variable, birth order, are reported here.

The foreign baby boom

A large-scale influx of foreigners into Japan began the late 1970s and continued on into the '90s, spurred by the nation's economic boom as well as the international image of Japan as one of the world's most powerful economies. (A graph of immigration trends based on figures from the government Statistics Bureau, Management and Coordination Agency is provided in Chapter 2 [Figure 1, p. 26].) As explained in Chapter 1, these immigrants came from a large number of countries and for a wide range of reasons.

Although the majority of these newcomers are from Asia and Latin America,[1] the number of native English speakers coming to Japan also rose dramatically during this period. As the nation moved into the international limelight, it attracted increasing numbers of young people from the West who came to explore the culture and the Japanese way of doing business. One programme that promoted this influx was the Working Holiday visa programme, which was established between Japan and Australia in 1980 and was extended to include New Zealand and Canada in 1985 and 1986, respectively. This programme alone now attracts approximately 4000 young student/workers from these British Commonwealth countries each year.[2]

Moreover, with the growth of Japan's export economy, there was increased demand for foreign copywriters and translators as well as foreign language teachers, especially those whose native language was English, the 'international language' of trade. To promote greater acquisition of communicative language skills by Japanese students, the Ministry of Education established the Japan Exchange and Teaching (JET) programme in 1978 and became the nation's largest recruiter of English teachers from outside Japan, bringing in 2874 in 1991 alone (O'Sullivan, 1994).

This influx of young people, complemented by a similar tide of young Japanese making long- and short-term trips overseas,[3] naturally led to a rise in the number of international marriages involving Japanese. It is estimated that in the 1990s, one in 30 Japanese marriages involved a non-Japanese partner (Lee, 1998: 33). The number of American women marrying Japanese men in Japan rose more than threefold, from 75 in 1970 to 243 in 1991, while the number of American men marrying Japanese women doubled between 1980, when it was 625, and 1991, when it reached 1292. (Statistics and Information Department, Ministry of Health and Welfare [1993], cited in Yamamoto, 1995).

The children resulting from these unions are not distinguished in government birth and citizenship statistics because 1985 revisions in the Japanese nationality law allow all children with one Japanese parent to acquire Japanese citizenship, and these children are therefore usually registered as Japanese. Until recently, accurate figures on the number of children born to international couples in Japan were therefore not available. However, Lee Setsuko, an associate professor at Tokyo Women's Medical University, has now extracted data from government surveys and used it to calculate the number of children born to mixed couples in Japan for her report *Zainichi gaikokujin no boshi hoken* [Insurance for Children of Foreign Mothers Residing in Japan] (1998).

According to Lee's study, there were 32,434 children born in Japan in 1996 who had at least one foreign parent. This is 1.8 times the 17,596 births to foreign residents in this country in 1987, when children born to foreign parents comprised 1.3% of all births in the country (Lee, 1998: 15). (See Figure 1.) Because the birth rate among couples in which both partners are Japanese steadily fell while the number of births to foreign residents continued to rise during that decade (1987–1996), children born to foreign parents accounted for 2.7% of all births in Japan in 1996 (Lee, 1998: 15). Moreover, in cities with large concentrations of foreign residents, the proportion of children born to foreign parents was even higher: over 7% in the city of Osaka, 6.7% in the 23 wards of Tokyo, 5.3% in the city of Kyoto and 4.6% in Kobe in 1997 (*Asahi shimbun*, Evening Edition, February 26, 1998).

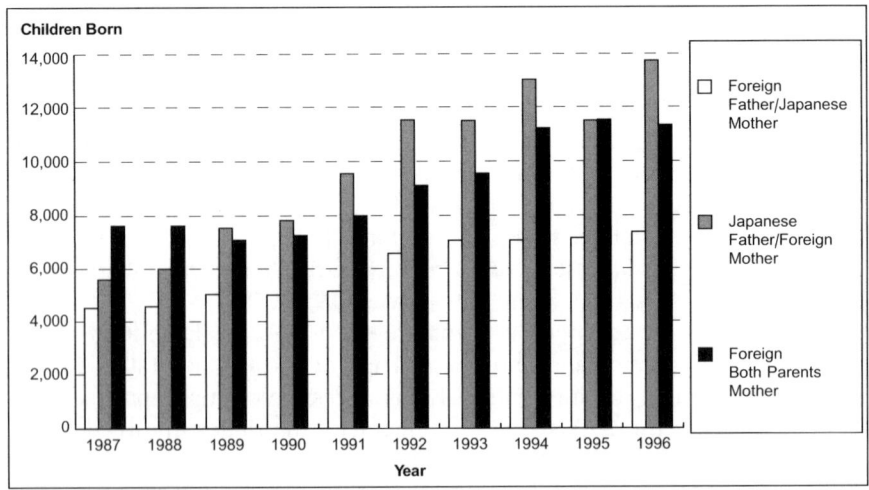

Figure 1 Increase in children born to foreign parents in Japan[4]

Mixed couples are the parents in a large percentage of these births, and the rate of increase for this group is also high. While births to couples in which both parents were non-Japanese rose 50.1% (from 7574 to 11,370) between 1987 and 1996, those to mixed couples increased 110.2% (from 10,022 to 21,064) during the same period (Lee, 1998: 15).

The total number of births to foreign mothers in Japan in 1996 was 25,122; of these, 22,856 were to mothers from countries whose main language is not English: Korea, the Philippines, China, Brazil, Thailand and Peru (Lee, 1998). This means that the number of children born to native English speaking mothers could have been no more than 2266 in 1996. Given the somewhat higher proclivity of Western men to marry Japanese women than of Western women to marry Japanese men (see Ma, 1995), the number of children born to native English-speaking fathers could be slightly higher, but obviously, cannot be higher than the total number of children born to foreign fathers in 1996, which was 7312 according to Lee.

Thus, one can safely say that the number of children born to native English speakers married to Japanese and living in Japan was well under 10,000 in 1996, but is also quite certainly on the rise. It is this increasing population of biracial, potentially bicultural children who are the subject of this study.

Bringing up Japanese-English bilinguals in Japan[4]

Many native English-speaking residents of Japan express a desire to have their children become bilingual. The general position of English as an 'international language', the valorisation of English in Japanese society, the inclusion of English reading skills on most high school and college entrance exams, and the fact that many native English-speaking parents in Japan earn their living by teaching English or using their English language skills, make them eager to have their children learn their native tongue.

In a survey of international families conducted in Japan in 1990, Yamamoto Masayo asked her subjects if they thought being bilingual was beneficial or detrimental,[5] and why they felt this way. She reported (Yamamoto, 1995) that 88% of her 49 subjects felt that being bilingual was beneficial. Many cited practical reasons for this belief, such as being able to communicate with foreign relatives or having a wider range of future career options or skills. The promotion of cognitive development was also mentioned. In addition, some of her respondents felt that bilingualism builds personality, enhancing open-mindedness and maturity. Bilingualism was also seen to promote intercultural understanding by helping bilinguals develop an ability to grasp various ways of thinking. Only five of the 49 families she surveyed (10%) noted possible negative aspects of bilingualism, such as the difficulty of dealing with two languages, cultures, and educational systems.

Bilingualism was also viewed positively by most of the respondents to a survey the present author made of 22 native English speakers living in Japan who had taught their children to read English in this country (reported in Noguchi, 1996a and Noguchi, 1999). In listing their objectives in teaching their children to read English, six respondents mentioned a desire to have their children master basic English communication and reading skills, three wanted their children's communication skills to be balanced by their English literacy skills, and one wanted them to become fully bilingual and bicultural. In addition, enjoyment or access to the minority parent's culture or religion was cited by four respondents, simple reading pleasure and expansion of the children's outlook or world by three respondents each, and the ability to communicate with English-speaking relatives by two. Answers that did not emphasise bilingualism included the possibility of a move to an English-speaking country (three respondents), and a possible transition to an international school if the child experienced trouble in the Japanese school system (one).

Despite such reasons for wanting their children to become bilingual and/or biliterate, many native English-speaking residents of Japan find that their children do not necessarily learn English. Indeed, research has shown that many children in international families in Japan do not become active bilinguals, but instead, are passive bilinguals with only limited productive ability in the minority language, or in some cases, display little or no receptive or productive ability in the minority language (Yamamoto, 1987; Yamamoto, 1992; Billings, 1990). There are a number of reasons for this.

First, the English-speaking young people who arrived during or after the seventies are widely scattered throughout the country, unlike the Western expatriates who settled in Japan before that time and tended to form enclaves near ports like Tokyo, Yokohama and Kobe, or near American military bases, where they established their own 'international' or mission schools, or relied on schools for dependents of members of the armed forces. The recent English-speaking immigrants live wherever their teaching or translating services may be needed or their Japanese spouse's family may reside. Thus, they do not generally belong to a foreign community that would provide an incentive for their children to learn English and offer schools to help develop English language skills.

Instead, many bicultural families send their children to local Japanese schools. In some cases this is because they cannot afford the high tuition fees of international schools; in others, it is because they live too far away from such schools. In many cases, however, this choice is due to their positive view of the Japanese education system. In the 1980s, American newspapers and magazines reported the results of a number of comparative tests that showed Japanese students outperforming their peers from other countries, especially the United States. Books such as *The Japanese Educational Challenge* by Merry White (1988) also provided a favourable picture of the Japanese education system. Thus a 1990 survey of members of the Association of Foreign Wives of Japanese (AFWJ) found that 88% of the respondents preferred to send their children to Japanese elementary schools, while only 12% chose international elementary schools or other types of educational institutions (*Japan Times*, Moon, 1991).

With their children attending Japanese schools and without a nearby community of fellow native speakers of English to provide linguistic, cultural and social support for bilingualism, many of the native English-speaking parents in mixed marriages in Japan have found that their children do not learn to speak much English, or even, in many cases, to understand it very well.

In addition to the lack of community support for and educational instruction in the language, another factor working against the development of English proficiency in these children is peer pressure to 'be like everyone else'. While such pressure is a salient feature of childhood in most societies, it is strengthened by the seemingly homogeneous nature of Japanese society and the emphasis on national identity explained in the introduction to this book. Yamamoto (1995) discussed the psychological effects of physical, linguistic or cultural conspicuousness in Japan, asserting that because Japanese society has a low degree of toleration for deviation from the norm, children from international families in Japan 'often face rejection from society ... [and] some may try to minimise their distinctiveness by behaving like the norm population' (p. 80). Thus for some biracial children, rejection of their foreign parent's language may be part of an attempt to reduce feelings of isolation.

Despite such barriers to bilingualism, many children from international families in Japan do learn the minority language with varying degrees of proficiency. A growing body of research has sought to determine what factors are conducive to the development of bilingualism in bicultural children. This paper seeks to further explore these variables.

Previous Research

Western research on childhood bilingualism has focused mainly on case studies of very young children raised in families where one parent speaks the minority language and the other, the majority language. Early studies by Ronjat and Volterra and Taeschner emphasised the importance of consistency in using the one person/one language system to help children keep the two languages separate (discussed in Arnberg, 1987: 33). In this strategy, each parent in a mixed marriage speaks his or her own language to their children. Saunders and Taeschner also found it helpful to use 'insistence strategies', in which the parent who speaks the minority language pretends not to understand utterances in the majority language or in some other way insists that children use the minority language (Dopke,

1992: 191). Metraux's research showed that children's personalities also have an effect, with extroverted children more likely to become bilingual (Arnberg, 1987: 33).

Dopke (1986, 1992) focused on the first-born children of six mixed German-English couples using the one person/one language strategy in Australia. She found that children are more likely to speak the minority language if the parent who speaks that language employs a more child-centred mode of interaction than the parent who speaks the majority language, or at least a mode of interaction that is similarly child-centred (Dopke, 1986). She also reported that child-centredness of discourse and language teaching techniques make a difference (Dopke, 1992). She did not find evidence of definite 'threshold levels' of input required to ensure active bilingualism, or that mothers were necessarily more child-centred than fathers (Dopke, 1992).

Lanza (1992, 1997) examined codeswitching and language mixing by two very young Norwegian-English bilinguals. She argued against the assumption promulgated by Volterra and Taeschner (1978) that bilingual competence is proven by language separation, which is defined as the ability to distinguish between the lexicon and syntax of two languages and use them without mixing. Lanza asserted, 'in many cases of bilingualism, language differentiation means both language separation and language mixing in appropriate contexts' (Lanza, 1997: 325). Parental discourse strategies may, in fact, either encourage or discourage language mixing by their children.

One larger-scale Western study that attempted to identify factors related to children's bilingual proficiency was made by Verhoeven (1991), who examined 72 six-year-old Turkish children living in the Netherlands and analysed variables related to the children themselves, their parents and their child-care experience to see if they could be used to predict the children's first and second language proficiencies prior to their entrance into elementary school. He found that the cultural orientation of the minority children and their parents, as well as the extent of caretaker interaction in the first language, were positively related to the children's bilingual proficiency.

In contrast to the prevalence of individual case studies of very young bicultural children in the West, much of the research in Japan to date has centred on surveys that strive to distinguish factors which may promote active bilingualism in children of mixed couples. Yamamoto Masayo has conducted several surveys which focused on the language environment in international families (reported in Yamamoto 1987, 1992, 1995, 1996, 1997). In her 1987 study, Yamamoto found that in all families where children were reported to be bilingual (i.e. they used English with the native English-speaking parent), the native English-speaking parent addressed the children exclusively in English. She also concluded that use of English among siblings was strongly suggestive: those who used English with their brothers and sisters also used it with their native English-speaking parent, while those who used Japanese with their siblings usually used Japanese with their native English-speaking parent as well.

In her 1992 study, Yamamoto noted that a discrepancy between the language used by foreign parents and children in international families did not 'necessarily mean that all these children are Japanese monolinguals' (p. 14). Children who sometimes or even always use the majority language with the minority language parent in international families may also be quite capable of speaking the minority language when necessary. Dodson (1985) argues that bilinguals have a preferred language, and will use it if the other person understands it. This means that even though a child may be able to speak English, s/he may not do so with a native English-speaking parent who understands Japanese. This theory is supported by Lanza's research, described above, which suggests that use of the majority language with the minority language parent may be appropriate under certain circumstances. This stance was adopted for the present study. While striving to build on Yamamoto's research, and like her, stressing language use rather than fluency, this paper assumes that children who use Japanese with their native English-speaking parent may be active bilinguals capable of speaking English with English monolinguals.

In addition to the surveys conducted by Yamamoto, a survey by Billings (1990) also explored factors that promote active bilingualism in children in international families living in Japan. Billings' questionnaire was completed by 38 members of the Association of Foreign Wives of Japanese who had decided at the time of their children's birth to raise their children bilingually. The survey covered a total of 43 children between the ages of seven and 12. Billings asked her respondents to assign one of three labels to each of their children: active bilingual, receptive bilingual or monolingual. She defined an active bilingual as a child who 'both speaks and understands Japanese and the mother's native language', a receptive bilingual as a child who 'understands but does not, or rarely speaks the mother's native language, while being fluent in Japanese', and a monolingual as a child who 'neither understands nor speaks the mother's native language, though his/her Japanese is fluent' (Billings, 1990: 94).

Billings concluded that the following 'intra-familial factors' had significant positive relationships to the probability that children were active bilinguals: (1) Being between seven and nine years old (as compared to children who were between ten and 12), (2) attending a combination of schools over the years, including Japanese schools, international schools, schools in the mother's home country, and/or home schools, (3) going to the mother's home country at least once a year, (4) living in a country outside Japan where the mother's home language is spoken as the majority language, and (5) experiencing being different from others as positive. She also suggested that parental effort plays a large part in whether or not children become bilingual, noting the importance of finding ways of encouraging children to speak the minority language, and stating that parental understanding of bilingualism may also help.

Billings admitted the limitations of her study. She asked mothers to fill in the questionnaire and rate their children as to their degree of bilingualism, but states,

> it cannot be assumed that the parents in the study ... accurately rated their children's bilingualism. Each mother who filled out the questionnaire may have used a separate set of criteria to answer this question; moreover, it would seem very difficult for parents to be unbiased when discussing their children's development. (p. 95)

She did cite a study by Kuo,[6] however, that found a positive relationship of significance between mother's ratings of their children's bilingualism and the results of a Peabody Picture Vocabulary Test given to the same children.

Billings' study suggests areas for further research. In particular, her finding that age plays a role, with older children less likely to be active bilinguals, was intriguing to this researcher, and is the reason that the age of the subjects was requested in the current study.

Another researcher who has looked at factors promoting bilingualism in Japan is Laurel Kamada (1995a, 1995b, 1996). Kamada interviewed a number of people who had experienced two cultures while growing up or who had children who had this experience, and told their stories in *Bilingual Japan*, the newsletter of the JALT Bilingualism SIG. She then formulated hypotheses on family factors that facilitate bilingual development (Kamada, 1995a, 1995b). A range of subjects were covered in her reports: some had mixed marriages, others were 'returnees' (young Japanese who had lived abroad for extended periods of time), and in some cases both parents were Japanese but had decided to raise their children bilingually. Her reports were not intended to be conclusive, but were used to uncover possible correlations, the significance of which could be explored more rigorously later.

Based on the stories of 22 children from twelve families, Kamada hypothesised that active bilingualism is more likely to result under the following circumstances: (1) when both parents use the minority language in the home, (2) when at least the mother uses the minority language with the child, (3) when siblings use the minority language to communicate with each other, (4) when subjects had resided overseas for at least one year or made frequent shorter trips, (5) when children were precocious in their first language ability, and (6) when parents or caretakers employed good language teaching techniques and used a lot of minority language material such as video and audio tapes and books. Factors hypothesized to work against the development of active bilingualism included mixing of the two languages, especially by the mother (Kamada, 1995a).

Thus, research in Japan to date suggests a number of possible factors that may affect the development of active bilinguality by children in international families in Japan: language use by parents and siblings, the child's age and schooling, overseas travel and residence, attitude toward bilingualism, natural linguistic ability, and parental language teaching techniques.

Research Focus

The current study was motivated by a desire to further investigate family and personal variables that might help or hinder bicultural children from becoming active bilinguals, capable not only of understanding both of their parents' languages, but also of speaking them. Some of these factors, such as language management strategies and family communication patterns, may be wholly or partly under the parents' control, while others, such as the sex of the minority language speaker and the child's age, are not. However, it was felt that identification of variables that have a positive relationship with active bilinguality might help parents make informed choices in child-rearing, while awareness of factors that might make it difficult for children to become active bilinguals might stimulate parents to try to offset them in some way.

The present author's survey on parents who had tried to teach their children to read English in Japan (Noguchi, 1996a; Noguchi, 1999) suggested that the sex of the native English-speaking (hereafter NES) parent might make a difference. Kamada's hypothesis on the importance of the mother speaking the minority language might also be interpreted to suggest that the sex of the NES parent is significant. Since mothers generally spend more time with their children and are thought to have a stronger influence over them, especially when they are young, it may be that bicultural children whose mothers are NESs are more likely to be active bilinguals than those whose fathers are the NES in the family. This trend might be particularly pronounced in Japan, since work patterns in this country do not generally take a father's family responsibilities into account, and mothers are held almost completely responsible for childraising, even when they work outside the home. This was therefore the first variable that was examined in relationship to the bilinguality of the children in the study.

A possible relationship between a child's age and active bilinguality was also probed. As was noted above, Billings' (1990) survey indicated that older children (those between the ages of ten and 12 in her survey) were less likely to be active bilinguals than younger children. Although Billings offered no explanation for this finding, the present author surmised that once children begin going to school, they spend less time with their NES parent and, if they attend a Japanese school, have less

English input as well as less motivation to use English. Their Japanese vocabulary would also expand at a higher rate than their English vocabulary, and they might find it harder to express their thoughts or explain what they've learned in school in English. Moreover, since peer pressure rises as children enter the teen years, the desire to be like their monolingual Japanese classmates might also lead children to stop using a language that would make them seem different. Checking this hypothesis became the second goal of this study.

English guidebooks for parents wishing to raise their children bilingually (e.g. Harding & Riley, 1986; Arnberg, 1987; Saunders, 1988) tend to emphasise language strategies as well as parental consistency in language use. The strategy most often suggested for mixed-marriage families is the one person/one language strategy, in which each parent speaks his or her own language to their children (Romaine, 1989: 166). Another strategy used to promote childhood bilingualism is the non-dominant home language strategy, also referred to as the home language/community language method, in which both parents speak a minority language in the home and the children learn the majority language in the outside community (Romaine, 1989: 167). This strategy is natural for immigrant families, but is also sometimes adopted by mixed couples who wish to increase the minority language input to ensure active bilinguality in their children.

Although a number of case studies made by linguists (including Fantini, 1985, and Saunders, 1988) suggest the efficacy of the one parent/one language strategy, little data is available to show that either of the above parental strategies is actually linked to active bilinguality in the children of ordinary bicultural families. In fact, Romaine (1989: 169) asserts that, 'A very common outcome of the "one person—one language" method was a child who could understand the languages of both parents, but spoke only the language of the community in which they lived.' It was therefore decided that the relationship between adoption of these strategies by parents and their children's degree of bilinguality should also be explored.

Since Yamamoto's studies (1987, 1992, 1995) suggested the importance of the language environment created by parents and siblings, it was decided to analyse this factor as well, using a wider definition of active bilinguality than Yamamoto used in her 1987 study in order to take into account theories advanced by Dodson (1985) and Lanza (1992, 1997), as explained above.

Finally, the author's survey on parents who had tried to teach their children to read English in Japan (Noguchi, 1996a; Noguchi, 1999) also suggested that both parents' proficiency in their non-native language might be relevant. The children of NES parents who spoke Japanese well tended to have lower English reading achievement levels, while the children's English reading achievement levels tended to be higher when their Japanese parent's occupation involved English. The survey also pointed to biliteracy as a support to bilinguality. It was therefore decided to include these variables in the current study as well.

Method

Questionnaire design

In designing the survey instrument (see Appendix), the author strove to refine the methodology used in Yamamoto's (1987, 1992 and 1995) and Billings' (1990) studies. To expand the definition of bilinguality beyond the range adopted by Yamamoto in her first study, the author incorporated Billings' 3-tiered assessment system of bilinguality, having respondents label each child an 'active bilingual', 'passive bilingual' or 'monolingual'. However, to promote accuracy in the assigning of these labels, the respondents were first primed to give a picture of their children's current language abilities and use by a paragraph that explained the unstable nature of language proficiency and the effects of external factors such as overseas trips, and requested 'A "snapshot" of each family member's skills *today*'.

Respondents were then asked to rate their own and their children's proficiency in both Japanese and English in each of the four language skills (speaking, listening, reading and writing) on a scale of 10 that the author had developed and pre-tested on friends and colleagues. Each even number on the scale was given a description of the proficiency it corresponded to, with different definitions for oral communication skills (speaking/listening) and literacy skills (reading/writing). For example, for speaking and listening, (0) was defined as 'Never says anything/ understands nothing', and (6) was defined as 'Can function on a practical level', while for literacy skills, these ratings were defined as 'No literacy skills' and 'Reads/writes simple materials at second-grade level or above but, if a non-native speaker, is not at the same level as a native speaker of the same age', respectively. Only the even numbers on the scale were defined in order to allow greater flexibility in rating language profiency. Respondents were told to use the odd numbers to indicate proficiencies that fell somewhere between the defined levels. This scale was intended primarily as a means of preparing the respondents to assign one of the three labels ('active bilingual', 'passive bilingual', or 'monolingual') to each member of their family, although it was also used in comparing the English proficiency of siblings and assessing the children's degree of biliteracy.

After this preparation, respondents were asked to choose the classification that most closely described the current oral language abilities and use of each member of the family: monolingual (defined as 'speaks and understands only one language'), passive bilingual ('speaks only one language, but understands normal conversation in the other language'), or active bilingual ('speaks and understands both languages well'). Respondents were also asked to specify the dominant language or note that the languages were balanced. This was done to allow them to make distinctions between family members with differing proficiencies and also to overcome the lay person's tendency (explained in the introduction to this paper) to use *fluency* in two languages rather than *use* of two languages as the 'main criterion of bilingualism' (Grosjean, 1982: 235). Since research has shown how difficult it is to accurately distinguish between 'balanced' and 'non-balanced' bilinguals (Grosjean, 1982: 232–5), these categories were not used in analysing the data of this study.

The questionnaire also investigated family language strategies and communication patterns. Respondents were asked if they were familiar with the one person/one language and home language/community language strategies, if they had used them, and if they had, how consistently they had applied them (rating their consistency on a scale of 0–10, with (2) defined as 'Rarely follow', (5) as 'Follow about half of the time', and (10) as 'Follow without fail'). Questions on the perceived advantages and disadvantages of these strategies were included for use in another paper (Noguchi, 1996b).

Finally, a chart similar to those employed by Yamamoto (1987, 1990, 1997) to report family language use was included, both as a means to check the respondent's assessments of bilinguality and to investigate the relationship between the family language environment and the development of bilinguality.

In analysing the data, the author relied mostly on the respondent's Billings-style assessments to determine the parents' and children's degree of bilinguality. The language proficiency ratings and family language use reports were used mainly to confirm these, and in some instances to make adjustments.

Subjects

To test the survey instrument, the author mailed it to members of the JALT Bilingualism SIG in the summer of 1995. JALT is an organisation composed mainly of foreign language teachers, and its Special Interest Group on Bilingualism is a sub-group of researchers in this field and parents interested in learning more about bilingualism so that they can foster it in their children. Since one of the goals of the group is the promotion of research on bilingualism, the SIG was seen as a ready source of subjects willing to participate in the pilot study. The availability of a mailing list and address labels also made this a convenient group on which to test a new questionnaire and get feedback on it. The cover letter asked only those SIG members who themselves were native speakers of English or whose spouse was a native speaker of English to fill in the questionnaire. The survey instrument was designed to allow subjects to remain anonymous: there was no space to write their names, and return envelopes with only the author's address were provided.

At the time of the survey the Bilingualism SIG had 203 members. The author and two close friends on whom an earlier version of the questionnaire had been tested were eliminated, and the group's mailing labels were used to send out 200 questionnaires. Of these, one was returned because the foreign addressee had moved back to her home country. Eighty-three questionnaires were completed, for a response rate of 41.7%. The low response rate can be partially attributed to the fact that not all SIG members have children or have a native English speaker in the family.

Sixty-nine of these responses were from people who were SIG members, had children who were old enough to talk, and had an NES in the family. Of those, nine families had two NES parents, three had native English speakers married to non-Japanese non-native English speakers, and one was headed by a single NES parent. For the purposes of this paper, these 13 families were excluded, and analysis was limited to the 56 respondents who had families in which a Japanese person was married to an NES.

In these 56 families, the NES parent was the mother in 16 and the father in 40 families. A breakdown of the parents' nationalities is shown in Table 1.

In the 56 families in this study there were 91 children who were old enough to speak. The breakdown of the children's ages is shown in Table 2.

The average age of the first child was 7.4 years, with the oldest first-born 18 years old and the youngest, two. The average age of the 30 second children, including one four-year-old who is the twin of one of the first-born children, was 5.3 years. There were five third-born children in the study; the age of two of these children was not reported. Two of the others were three years old and one was two years old. Thus in general, the children were quite young, with many not yet in elementary school.

Table 1 Parents' nationality

Nationality	Mother (N = 56)		Father (N = 56)	
	n	%	n	%
USA (American)	14	25.0%	27	48.2%
British	1	1.8%	10	17.9%
Australian	1	1.8%	1	1.8%
Japanese	40	71.4%	16	28.5%
Unknown	0	0.0%	2	3.6%

Table 2 Ages of children

Age	All Children (N = 91)		First Children (N = 56)		Second Children (N = 30)	
	n	*%*	*n*	*%*	*n*	*%*
2–4 years	28	30.8%	12	21.4%	13	43.3%
5–7 years	26	28.6%	16	28.6%	10	33.3%
8–10 years	16	17.6%	12	21.4%	4	13.3%
11–13 years	9	9.9%	7	12.5%	2	6.7%
14 or older	4	4.4%	4	7.1%	0	0.0%
Unknown	8	8.7%	5	8.9%	1	3.3%

Table 3 Language used in school

Language (s)	Children (N = 91)	
	n	*%*
Japanese	70	76.9%
English	6	6.6%
English & Japanese	3	3.3%
Not yet in school	12	13.2%

All but 12 of the children were enrolled in school or day care programmes. Seventy-one were attending a school or programme where Japanese was the medium of instruction, six went to an English-medium school, three were in institutions where both English and Japanese were used, and 12 were still being taken care of at home. Thus, as can be seen in Table 3, the majority of the children in this study (76.9%) were attending schools where the majority language was the medium of instruction. This is thought to reflect general trends in mixed families in Japan, as explained in the introduction.

Limitations

Several factors limit the reliability of this survey. First, the respondents were not a random sample of native English speakers married to Japanese and living in Japan. Members of the JALT Bilingualism SIG are more likely to be interested in bilingualism, to have more knowledge of the field, and to be actively encouraging it in their children than the average resident native English speaker.

Moreover, the response rate was not high. As mentioned above, only 83 of the 199 questionnaires that reached their destination were completed, making the response rate 41.7%, although this was partially attributable to the fact that not all SIG members have children or have a native English speaker in the family.

This survey is also subject to the limitations of all questionnaires, especially those relying on parental evaluations. Despite efforts to encourage the respondents to analyse their children's language proficiency and use carefully, it cannot be assumed that they did so. In some cases, inaccurancies were readily apparent. For example, the reading and writing skill rating system was designed to reflect the child's level in school but the speaking and listening skill rating system was not. Native speakers who were only in second grade in school were to be rated (6) in literacy skills, but (10) in speaking and listening. However several respondents obviously did not read the instructions carefully and gave their young children ratings of (10) for all four skills. Moreover, in some cases, respondents did not fill in all of the blanks on the questionnaire. The age was left out in several cases, presumably because the parent did not want to fill in his or her own age, and therefore left the whole age column blank. In addition, some of the parents' reports of language use at home contradicted the labels they chose for their children in assessing bilinguality. In two families (with a total of three children), the family language use data induced me to change the parents' assessment of their children from passive to active bilinguals, since the children were reported to speak English to their NES parent between 25% and 75% of the time. In this way, the 4-skills ratings and the family language use reports were used to check on the assessments of bilinguality and eliminate some inconsistencies in the parents' reports.

It must also be noted that although the questionnaire was meant to be anonymous, this was not specifically stated in the cover letter, and a number of the respondents signed the questionnaire and/or provided contact information to allow me to ask further questions. This limits the reliability of the results, as the approval motive may have induced respondents to be less than accurate in evaluating their children's and/or their own linguistic abilities. (See Oller & Perkins, 1978a and 1978b for a discussion of respondent bias when filling out attitude questionnaires.)

While these limitations must be acknowledged, the raw number of responses was as high as earlier surveys of bicultural families in Japan (56, as compared to 53 and 58 for the first two Yamamoto surveys, and 38 for the Billings survey).[7]

Analysis of data

The questionnaires of the 56 respondents were analysed to determine whether each member of the family was an active bilingual, a passive bilingual or a monolingual, as defined above. In tabulating these results, the respondent's choice of one of these three labels for each family member was checked against his or her evaluation of the same individual's proficiency in each of the four skills in both Japanese and English and the report of language use in the family. As mentioned above, several questionnaires had problems of internal consistency. However, careful consideration of all responses allowed determination of the individual's bilinguality.

Once the assessments of bilinguality were confirmed and/or adjusted, they were entered along with other data for each family member on a Microsoft Excel programme spreadsheet (Version 5.0), which was used to sort the data into the categories specified for analysis. The relationship between each child's bilinguality and the following variables were analysed: the sex of the NES parent, the child's age, level in school and position in the family (birth order), parents' bilinguality, parents' proficiency in their non-native language, language strategies used by the parents, consistency of language strategy application, language(s) used by the parents with the child, by the parents with each other and among the children in the family, and the child's literacy skills in both languages. In each case, the raw frequencies were determined and percentages calculated. Where large differences appeared in the percentage figures, significance of the differences between the frequency counts was tested using Chi-square procedures, with the alpha level set at $p < 0.05$. In some cases, categories were combined to ensure large enough cell sizes for the Chi-square analysis.

Results and Discussion

Subjects' bilinguality

The bilinguality assessments of the mothers, fathers and children in the survey families are presented in Table 4. The vast majority of the parents and children were labeled active bilinguals, with nearly 70% of the children assigned to this category. This is a high proportion, but it was not unexpected given the nature of the sample: members of a group

Table 4 Individual assessments of bilinguality

Assessment of Bilinguality	*Mothers* (N = 56)		*Fathers* (N = 56)		*Children* (N = 91)	
	n	*%*	*n*	*%*	*n*	*%*
Active Bilinguals	47	83.9%	39	69.6%	62	68.1%
Passive Bilinguals	8	14.3%	15	26.8%	26	28.6%
Monolinguals	1	1.8%	2	3.6%	3	3.3%

whose purpose is to foster bilinguality in their children. It is possible that the proportion of active bilingual children might be lower in a random sample of bicultural families in Japan. Only three of the 91 children (3.3%) were reported to be monolinguals. Two were Japanese monolinguals and one was a very young English monolingual who presumably would acquire the majority language as the amount of time s/he spent outside the home increased. Because the number of monolinguals was so small in this study, analysis concentrated on contrasting the active and passive bilingual subjects, and when Chi square procedures were used, the passive bilingual and monolingual categories were combined.

Sex of NES parent and children's bilinguality

The first variable that was checked to determine if it was related to the degree of bilinguality of the children in the survey was whether the NES in the family was the mother or the father. The results are presented in Table 5.

All three monolingual children were from families in which the NES parent was the father. As mentioned above, however, one of them was an English monolingual toddler who may become an active bilingual when s/he becomes old enough to go to school. The proportion of active bilinguals was slightly higher in families in which the NES parent was the mother (75.0% vs 65.1%). However, when Chi-square procedures were used to compare the degree of bilinguality of the children of NES mothers and NES fathers (active bilinguals vs. passive bilinguals and monolinguals), no significant difference was found (χ^2_{crit} (1 df) $= 3.841$; $\chi^2_{obs} = 0.85$).

These results suggest that it is not necessarily harder for children in international families to become active bilinguals when their father is the minority language speaker than it is when the NES is the mother. However, the fact that respondents were members of a group that promotes bilingualism may have made a difference. Further investigation of a possible relationship between these variables is therefore recommended.

Table 5 Sex of NES parent and children's bilinguality

Children's Bilinguality	Native English Speaking Parent			
	Mother (N = 28)		Father (N = 63)	
	n	%	n	%
Active Bilinguals (n = 62)	21	75.0%	41	65.1%
Passive Bilinguals (n = 26)	7	25.0%	19	30.1%
Monolinguals (n = 3)	0	0.0%	3	4.8%

Children's age and bilinguality

The second variable analysed in terms of its relationship to bilinguality was the children's age. It has been suggested that Billings' finding that older children are less likely to be active bilinguals might be the result of less English input and motivation to use English after the children began school (presuming they were going to a Japanese school, as almost 77% of the children in the current survey were).

However, when the data was examined, no relationship between the children's age and degree of bilinguality was apparent. As can be seen in Table 6, the monolinguals whose age was reported (one Japanese monolingual and one English monolingual) were found in the lowest age groups, while active bilinguals were found in all age groups. Thus, Billings' findings were not replicated in this study.

Since it was thought that Billings' finding regarding age might have been indicative of the effect of outside schooling upon the time the children

Table 6 Children's age and bilinguality

| | *Children's Bilinguality* ($N = 91$) | | | | | |
| *Age in Years* | *Active Bilinguals* ($n = 62$) | | *Passive Bilinguals* ($n = 26$) | | *Monolinguals* ($n = 3$) | |
	n	*%*	*n*	*%*	*n*	*%*
2 ($n = 8$)	4	50.0%	3	37.5%	1	12.5%
3 ($n = 12$)	6	50.0%	5	41.7%	1	8.3%
4 ($n = 9$)	8	88.9%	1	11.1%	0	0.0%
5 ($n = 8$)	6	75.0%	2	25.0%	0	0.0%
6 ($n = 10$)	7	70.0%	3	30.0%	0	0.0%
7 ($n = 7$)	6	85.7%	1	14.3%	0	0.0%
8 ($n = 6$)	5	83.3%	1	16.7%	0	0.0%
9 ($n = 7$)	4	57.1%	3	42.9%	0	0.0%
10 ($n = 3$)	3	100.0%	0	0.0%	0	0.0%
11 ($n = 3$)	1	33.3%	2	66.7%	0	0.0%
12 ($n = 4$)	4	100.0%	0	0.0%	0	0.0%
13 ($n = 2$)	1	50.0%	1	50.0%	0	0.0%
15 ($n = 2$)	2	100.0%	0	0.0%	0	0.0%
16 ($n = 1$)	1	100.0%	0	0.0%	0	0.0%
18 ($n = 1$)	1	100.0%	0	0.0%	0	0.0%
Unknown ($n = 8$)	3	37.5%	4	50.0%	1	12.5%

Table 7 Level in school and bilinguality

Children's Bilinguality (N = 91)	Level in School											
	Not Yet in School (n = 12)		Day Care or Kindergarten (n = 28)		Elementary School (n = 38)		Junior High (n = 2)		Senior High (n = 4)		Unknown (n = 7)	
	n	%	n	%	n	%	n	%	n	%	n	%
Active Bilinguals (n = 62)	9	75.0%	18	64.2%	28	73.7%	1	50.0%	4	100.0%	2	28.6%
NES Father	7	77.8%	13	65.0%	14	66.7%	1	50.0%	4	100.0%	2	28.6%
NES Mother	2	66.7%	5	62.5%	14	82.4%	0	0.0%	0	0.0%	0	0.0%
Passive Bilinguals (n = 26)	3	25.0%	8	28.5%	10	26.3%	1	50.0%	0	0.0%	4	57.1%
NES Father	2	28.6%	5	25.0%	7	33.3%	1	50.0%	0	0.0%	4	57.1%
NES Mother	1	33.3%	3	37.5%	3	17.6%	0	0.0%	0	0.0%	0	0.0%
Monolinguals (n = 3)	0	0.0%	2	7.1%	0	0.0%	0	0.0%	0	0.0%	1	14.3%
NES Father	0	0.0%	2	10.0%	0	0.0%	0	0.0%	0	0.0%	1	14.3%
NES Mother	0	0.0%	0	0.0%	0	0.0%	0	0.0%	0	0.0%	0	0.0%

spent with the minority language parent, the children's bilinguality was examined in relation to their level in school. The results are presented in Table 7.

One of the Japanese monolinguals and the English monolingual were in the lowest school levels (day care and kindergarten), while active bilinguals were found at all school levels. The fact that all four senior high school students were active bilinguals contradicts the hypothesis that as children advance in school and spend more time away from home and the minority language parent, they tend to use the minority language less.

However, two of these cases were rather unusual. One of the high school students lived in Hawaii until she was five and learned to read and write English there. After coming to Japan, she went to a combination of English-medium and Japanese-medium schools over the years, so her exposure to English was unusually high. Another high school student was attending an English-medium school, and thus enjoyed greater exposure to the minority language.

If we exclude these exceptional senior high school students, however, we are left with an extremely small sample of children in the higher levels of school (two each in junior and senior high school) and valid conclusions cannot be drawn. Since the sample group was unusual in that the parents were members of a group promoting research on bilingualism, further investigation of the relationship between children's level in school and their bilinguality is recommended.

Birth order and bilinguality

The survey instrument was not designed to examine the relationship between a child's place in the family and whether or not the child was bilingual; however, one of the respondents suggested that this be done. S/he asserted that in most bicultural families s/he had observed, the first child was an active bilingual while the second child was a passive bilingual. Billings (1990: 95) also reported that several of her respondents wrote that their first child was 'completely bilingual', their second, 'somewhat bilingual' and the third 'not at all' bilingual; however, a question about the position of the child in the family was not included in her questionnaire. Dopke (1992: 196–8) cites some general findings on later-born children's language ability as well as some reports on later-born bilingual children that suggest that this hypothesis might be true. However, Dopke's study was limited to first-born children, and no other researcher has investigated this area. The author's own experience as a parent as well as discussions with other parents indicated that the oldest child in a family tends to get more attention than later children, so this possibility was explored here.

Fortuitously, because the survey instrument had been designed to avoid the use of names, the spaces to record information about the children were numbered (Child 1, Child 2, etc.). It was therefore possible to check whether later-born children had lower degrees of bilinguality than first-born children.

Initial inspection of the questionnaires revealed several families who seemed to conform to this suggestion. In one family where the NES was the father, the first child was an active bilingual, the second, a passive bilingual, and the third, a monolingual Japanese speaker. In another family where the NES was the father, and in a third family where the NES was the mother, the first children were active bilinguals while the second and third children were passive bilinguals. On the other hand, there were two families – one where the NES was the father and the other where the NES was the mother – in which all three children were active bilinguals.

The data was therefore analysed to examine the relationship between birth order and bilinguality. The results are shown in Table 8.

While the proportions of only children and first-born children who were active bilinguals were fairly close (76.9% and 80%, respectively), the proportions of second and third children who were active bilinguals were lower (53.3% and 40%, respectively). It should be noted that the number of third-born children in this study was small (five), and one who was monolingual was a toddler who only spoke English – the minority language, so s/he may have developed into an active bilingual once s/he got out into Japanese society. Nonetheless, the decline in the proportion of active bilinguals among second children suggests that birth order is related to the likelihood of active bilinguality.

Table 8 Birth order and bilinguality

Children's Bilinguality (N = 91)	Children's Place in Family							
	Only Children (n = 26)		First Children (n = 30)		Second Children (n = 30)		Third Children (n = 5)	
	n	%	n	%	n	%	n	%
Active Bilinguals (n = 62)	20	76.9%	24	80.0%	16	53.3%	2	40.0%
NES Father	16	80.0%	15	75.0%	9	45.0%	1	33.3%
NES Mother	4	66.7%	9	90.0%	7	70.0%	1	50.0%
Passive Bilinguals (n = 26)	6	23.1%	5	16.6%	13	43.3%	2	40.0%
NES Father	4	20.0%	4	20.0%	10	50.0%	1	33.3%
NES Mother	2	33.3%	1	10.0%	3	30.0%	1	50.0%
Monolinguals (n = 3)	0	0.0%	1	3.3%	1	3.3%	1	20.0%
NES Father	0	0.0%	1	5.0%	1	5.0%	1	33.3%
NES Mother	0	0.0%	0	0.0%	0	0.0%	0	0.0%

Chi-square procedures were used to compare the differences in bilinguality according to birth order. To ensure a cell size of at least five, the passive bilingual and monolingual categories were collapsed, as were the second and third children categories. When this was done, the differences were found to be significant $(\chi^2_{crit} (2 \, df) = 5.991; \; \chi^2_{obs}$ (all children) $= 7.26, \; p < 0.05)$.

Differences were seen in both families where the NES parent was the mother and those in which the NES was the father; however, the decline in the proportion of active bilinguals among later children appeared to be steeper in those in which the NES was the father, falling to 45% for second children and 33.3% for third children, as opposed to 70% and 50%, respectively, in families where the NES was the mother. Because of the limited number of children with NES mothers $(N = 28)$, Chi-square procedures could not be carried out even when categories were combined. However, the sample of children with NES fathers was large enough $(N = 63)$ to carry out Chi-square procedures if the only children and first children categories were combined, the second and third children categories were combined, and the passive bilingual and monolingual categories were combined. When this was done, a significant difference was seen $(\chi^2_{crit} (1 \, df) = 3.841; \; \chi^2_{obs}$ (children of NES fathers) $= 7.45, \; p < 0.05)$.

The greater likelihood of the development of bilinguality in first-born children was also evident in the parents' ratings of their children's ability

Table 9 Birth order and English-speaking proficiency

	Higher		*Equal*		*Lower*	
	n	*%*	*n*	*%*	*n*	*%*
First Child's ESP* vs Second Child's	18	60.0%	11	36.7%	1	3.3%
First Child's ESP* vs Third Child's	4	80.0%	0	0.0%	1	20.0%
Second Child's ESP* vs Third Child's	1	20.0%	2	40.0%	2	40.0%

* ESP: English speaking proficiency as rated by parent.

to speak the minority language. Comparisons of the English speaking ability ratings of siblings are shown in Table 9. In 60% of the families who had more than one child, the first-born's English speaking ability was rated higher than the second child's, and in 80%, it was rated higher than the third-born's English speaking ability.

Although the survey data lends support to the hypothesis that birth order is related to bilinguality, it should be pointed out that in 11 families (36.7%), the second child's English speaking ability was seen to be equal to the first child's. Although the reasons for this are not evident from the survey data, it may be that if parents pay as much attention to the linguistic development of their later-born children as they do to that of their first-born, second and third children may well become active bilinguals.

Parent's language skills and children's bilinguality

The next variable analysed in relation to the children's bilinguality was the parents' linguistic skills, as indicated by their degree of bilinguality and their proficiency in their second language. The relationship between the mother's and children's bilinguality is shown in Table 10, and the relationship between the father's and children's bilinguality in Table 11.

Table 10 Mother's and children's bilinguality

	Children's Bilinguality (N = 91)					
Mother's *Bilinguality*	*Active Bilinguals* (*n* = 62)		*Passive Bilinguals* (*n* = 26)		*Monolinguals* (*n* = 3)	
	n	*%*	*n*	*%*	*n*	*%*
Mother is Active Bilingual (*n* = 77)	53	68.8%	21	27.3%	3	3.9%
Mother is Passive Bilingual (*n* = 12)	9	75.0%	3	25.0%	0	0.0%
Mother is Monolingual (*n* = 2)	0	0.0%	2	100.0%	0	0.0%

Table 11 Father's and children's bilinguality

Father's Bilinguality	Children's Bilinguality (N = 91)					
	Active Bilinguals (n = 62)		Passive Bilinguals (n = 26)		Monolinguals (n = 3)	
	n	%	n	%	n	%
Father is Active Bilingual (n = 65)	43	71.0%	21	32.3%	1	1.5%
Father is Passive Bilingual (n = 24)	18	75.0%	4	16.7%	2	8.3%
Father is Monolingual (n = 2)	1	50.0%	1	50.0%	0	0.0%

There did not appear to be a great difference in the children's bilinguality depending upon whether the parents (particularly the fathers) were active or passive bilinguals: Children were reported to be active bilinguals in roughly 70% of the cases where the parents were active bilinguals and in 75% of the cases where they were passive bilinguals.

When parents were monolingual, children were more often reported to be passive bilinguals (100% with monolingual mothers, 50% with monolingual fathers). However, there were no families with *both* a monolingual parent *and* a monolingual child. This suggests that for a child to be able to insist on using only one of the languages in the family, the parents have to speak or at least understand their non-native language.

Next, the parents' ability to speak their second language was compared with their children's bilinguality. It was thought that a greater ability on the part of the Japanese parent to speak English might facilitate their children's acquisition of the minority language and make it more likely for them to become active bilinguals. In contrast, a greater ability on the part of NES parents to speak Japanese might result in less pressure on children to learn English, and thus less likelihood of their becoming active bilinguals. However, the survey results did not support these suppositions. As can be seen in Tables 12 and 13, positive correlations were not evident in either case: proportions of active bilinguals appeared to rise and fall without pattern in both tables.

Thus, the data did not show a clear relationship between the parents' ability to speak their second language and the likelihood of their children to become active bilinguals. For NES parents, these results suggest that they do not have to limit themselves to their native language to ensure that their children become active bilinguals. In fact, minority language speakers can be highly proficient in the majority language without fearing that their children will refuse to actively learn the minority language.

Table 12 Japanese parent's English speaking proficiency and children's bilinguality

Respondent's Assessment of Japanese Parent's English Speaking Ability		Children's Bilinguality (N = 91)					
		Active Bilinguals (n = 62)		Passive Bilinguals (n = 26)		Monolinguals (n = 3)	
		n	%	n	%	n	%
3	(All Families)	2	50.0%	2	50.0%	0	0.0%
	(NES Mother)	2	100.0%	0	0.0%	0	0.0%
	(NES Father)	0	0.0%	2	100.0%	0	0.0%
4	(All Families)	3	75.0%	1	25.0%	0	0.0%
	(NES Mother)	2	66.7%	1	33.3%	0	0.0%
	(NES Father)	1	100.0%	0	0.0%	0	0.0%
5	(All Families)	2	100.0%	0	0.0%	0	0.0%
	(NES Mother)	0	0.0%	0	0.0%	0	0.0%
	(NES Father)	2	100.0%	0	0.0%	0	0.0%
6	(All Families)	6	85.7%	1	14.3%	0	0.0%
	(NES Mother)	3	100.0%	0	0.0%	0	0.0%
	(NES Father)	3	75.0%	1	25.0%	0	0.0%
7	(All Families)	6	66.7%	3	33.3%	0	0.0%
	(NES Mother)	1	100.0%	0	0.0%	0	0.0%
	(NES Father)	5	62.5%	3	37.5%	0	0.0%
8	(All Families)	32	69.6%	11	23.9%	3	6.5%
	(NES Mother)	10	66.7%	5	33.3%	0	0.0%
	(NES Father)	22	71.0%	6	19.3%	3	9.7%
9	(All Families)	10	66.7%	5	33.3%	0	0.0%
	(NES Mother)	2	100.0%	0	0.0%	0	0.0%
	(NES Father)	8	61.5%	5	38.5%	0	0.0%
10	(All Families)	1	50.0%	1	50.0%	0	0.0%
	(NES Mother)	1	50.0%	1	50.0%	0	0.0%
	(NES Father)	0	0.0%	0	0.0%	0	0.0%
Unknown	(All Families)	0	0.0%	2	100.0%	0	0.0%
	(NES Mother)	0	0.0%	0	0.0%	0	0.0%
	(NES Father)	0	0.0%	2	100.0%	0	0.0%

Table 13 NES parent's Japanese speaking ability and children's bilinguality

Respondent's Assessment of NES Parent's Japanese Speaking Ability		Children's Bilinguality ($N = 91$)					
		Active Bilinguals ($n = 62$)		Passive Bilinguals ($n = 26$)		Monolinguals ($n = 3$)	
		n	%	n	%	n	%
2	(All Families)	1	100.0%	0	0.0%	0	0.0%
	(NES Mother)	0	0.0%	0	0.0%	0	0.0%
	(NES Father)	1	100.0%	0	0.0%	0	0.0%
4	(All Families)	8	61.5%	5	38.5%	0	0.0%
	(NES Mother)	3	60.0%	2	40.0%	0	0.0%
	(NES Father)	5	62.5%	3	37.5%	0	0.0%
5	(All Families)	4	50.0%	2	25.0%	2	25.0%
	(NES Mother)	0	0.0%	1	100.0%	0	0.0%
	(NES Father)	4	57.1%	1	14.3%	2	28.6%
6	(All Families)	19	70.4%	7	25.9%	1	3.7%
	(NES Mother)	1	50.0%	1	50.0%	0	0.0%
	(NES Father)	18	72.0%	6	24.0%	1	4.0%
7	(All Families)	12	85.7%	2	14.3%	0	0.0%
	(NES Mother)	7	100.0%	0	0.0%	0	0.0%
	(NES Father)	5	71.4%	2	28.6%	0	0.0%
8	(All Families)	16	66.7%	8	33.3%	0	0.0%
	(NES Mother)	10	90.9%	1	9.1%	0	0.0%
	(NES Father)	6	46.2%	7	53.8%	0	0.0%
9	(All Families)	2	50.0%	2	50.0%	0	0.0%
	(NES Mother)	0	0.0%	2	100.0%	0	0.0%
	(NES Father)	2	100.0%	0	0.0%	0	0.0%

Language strategies

The next area explored was the relationship between parental language strategies and the children's bilinguality. As mentioned above, much of the literature on childhood bilingualism stresses strategies such as the one person/one language system and the home language/community language method, as well as parental consistency in language use. (See, for example, Saunders, 1988, Arnberg, 1987, and Gibbs, 1998.) Since such strategies are employed with the goal of promoting active bilingualism in children and this is one variable over which parents can exert control, the author decided to look at whether there was a relationship between their use and children's bilinguality.

The questionnaire asked respondents whether they were familiar with each of these strategies, whether or not they had tried them, and if they had, how consistent they had been in maintaining them. While reports of consistency cannot be considered accurate (as shown by Lanza in her 1997 study), they were used as a rough measure of parental determination in applying the strategies.

As was expected of members of a group which promotes research on bilingualism, most of the respondents were familiar with these two methods of family language management; 53 (94.6%) indicated that they knew of the one person/one language strategy and 49 (87.5%) were familiar with the home language/community language system. Many had also tried these strategies: 46 (82.1%) had adopted the former and 16 (28.6%) the latter strategy at some point. Some had used both.

The data on the children's bilinguality was sorted according to whether the respondents said they used the one person/one language approach or not, and also according to the degree of consistency they reported in their application of this strategy (on a scale of 1–10, where (2) indicates 'rarely follow', (5) indicates 'follow about half the time' and (10) indicates 'follow without fail'). Neither use of this approach nor level of consistency appeared to be related to the degree of the children's bilinguality. Thus, the present data does not suggest that the one person/one language strategy is particularly effective in raising active bilinguals, no matter how consistent the family may (intend to) be in applying it.

In contrast, respondents who said they used the home language/community language strategy had a higher proportion of active bilingual children than families who did not adopt this strategy or who had tried it but stopped, as seen in Table 14. This may be because this strategy ensures more minority language input than the one person/one language strategy.

Table 14 Home language/community language strategy and children's bilinguality

| Use of Strategy | Children's Bilinguality (N = 91) | | | | | |
| | Active Bilinguals (n = 62) | | Passive Bilinguals (n = 26) | | Monolinguals (n = 3) | |
	n	%	n	%	n	%
Used	12	85.7%	2	14.3%	0	0.0%
Used but stopped	3	50.0%	3	50.0%	0	0.0%
Didn't use	47	66.2%	21	29.6%	3	4.2%

Home linguistic environment

A family language use chart, adapted from the one developed for Yamamoto's surveys, was included to provide a clearer picture of the linguistic environment in the home. The language used by the NES parent was examined first, since this was a major focus of Yamamoto's early reports (1987, 1992). The relationship between the child's bilinguality and the language used by the NES parent with the child is shown in Table 15.

The parents of 71.4% of the children spoke to their children in English 90% to100% of the time. Another 13.1%, used English with their children most (60% to 89%) of the time. The proportion of active bilingual children in these families was high (roughly 75% in both cases), although it was somewhat lower for the NES fathers than it was for the NES mothers.

Table 15 NES parent's language use and children's bilinguality

Languages (s) Used by NES Parent	Children's Bilinguality ($N = 91$)					
	Active Bilinguals ($n = 62$)		Passive Bilinguals ($n = 26$)		Monolinguals ($n = 3$)	
	n	%	n	%	n	%
90–100% English (All)	48	73.8%	17	26.2%	0	0.0%
(NES Mother)	14	83.4%	3	17.6%	0	0.0%
(NES Father)	34	70.8%	14	29.2%	0	0.0%
60–89% English (All)	9	75.0%	2	16.7%	1	8.3%
(NES Mother)	6	100.0%	0	0.0%	0	0.0%
(NES Father)	3	50.0%	2	33.3%	1	16.7%
41–59% English (All)	3	60.0%	2	40.0%	0	0.0%
(NES Mother)	1	100.0%	0	0.0%	0	0.0%
(NES Father)	2	50.0%	2	50.0%	0	0.0%
60–89% Japanese (All)	0	0.0%	4	100.0%	0	0.0%
(NES Mother)	0	0.0%	4	100.0%	0	0.0%
(NES Father)	0	0.0%	0	0.0%	0	0.0%
90–100% Japanese (All)	0	0.0%	0	0.0%	0	0.0%
(NES Mother)	0	0.0%	0	0.0%	0	0.0%
(NES Father)	0	0.0%	0	0.0%	0	0.0%
Unknown (All)	2	40.0%	1	20.0%	2	40.0%
(NES Mother)	0	0.0%	0	0.0%	0	0.0%
(NES Father)	2	40.0%	1	20.0%	2	40.0%

None of the NES parents surveyed used Japanese 90% of the time or more, but when the NES parent's use of English dropped below 60%, the overall proportion of passive bilingual children increased. However, the one NES mother whose use of English fell in the 41–59% range had an active bilingual child. In families with native English speakers who used mostly Japanese with their children (60% or more), the children were all passive bilinguals. It is interesting to note that none of the NES fathers fell in this category; only NES mothers used this much Japanese with their children.

These results appear to lend some support to Yamamoto's (1987) assertion that exclusive use of English by the NES parent is an important support for bilinguality. However, we see that in some cases, the NES parent used Japanese about half of the time and still had active bilingual children. In fact, when the data for families in which the NES parent used English 90–100% of the time was compared to that for all families in

Table 16 Japanese parent's language use and children's bilinguality

Languages (s) Used by Japanese Parent	Children's Bilinguality (N = 91)					
	Active Bilinguals (n = 62)		Passive Bilinguals (n = 26)		Monolinguals (n = 3)	
	n	*%*	*n*	*%*	*n*	*%*
90–100% English (All)	4	50.0%	4	50.0%	0	0.0%
(Japanese Father)	1	33.3%	2	66.7%	0	0.0%
(Japanese Mother)	3	60.0%	2	40.0%	0	0.0%
60–89% English (All)	6	75.0%	2	25.0%	0	0.0%
(Japanese Father)	2	50.0%	2	50.0%	0	0.0%
(Japanese Mother)	4	100.0%	0	0.0%	0	0.0%
41–59% English (All)	9	90.0%	1	10.0%	0	0.0%
(Japanese Father)	7	87.5%	1	12.5%	0	0.0%
(Japanese Mother)	2	100.0%	0	0.0%	0	0.0%
60–89% Japanese (All)	18	90.0%	0	0.0%	2	10.0%
(Japanese Father)	7	100.0%	0	0.0%	0	0.0%
(Japanese Mother)	11	84.6%	0	0.0%	2	15.4%
90–100% Japanese (All)	24	54.5%	19	43.2%	1	2.3%
(Japanese Father)	4	66.7%	2	33.3%	0	0.0%
(Japanese Mother)	20	52.6%	17	44.7%	1	2.6%
Unknown (All)	1	100.0%	0	0.0%	0	0.0%
(Japanese Father)	0	0.0%	0	0.0%	0	0.0%
(Japanese Mother)	1	100.0%	0	0.0%	0	0.0%

which the NES parent reported to use English less than 90% of the time, Chi-square procedures did not reveal significant differences in the bilinguality of the children. Thus, rather than supporting the exclusive use of English by the NES parent, this data seems to suggest the importance of avoiding the predominance of Japanese when the NES parent talks to the children.

The data was also analysed to check if there was a relationship between the language the Japanese parent used with the child and the child's development of bilinguality. The results are presented in Table 16. For both Japanese mothers and fathers, the proportion of active bilingual children was higher when the Japanese parent used both Japanese *and* English than when s/he used either English or Japanese exclusively. This finding appears to contradict the conventional emphasis on consistent use of the one parent/one language strategy, while also suggesting that adherence to the home language/community language strategy may not be the best way to promote active bilingualism in children.

In addition to the language which the parents used with their children, the language which the parents used between themselves was examined to see if it was related to bilinguality in their children. The data included active and passive bilinguals in all types of families, from those in which the parents used English exclusively to those who relied on Japanese exclusively. Thus, the language used between parents did not appear to be related to the bilinguality of their children, although the proportion of active bilinguals was very low (33.3%) in the families with NES fathers who used almost exclusively Japanese (90–100%) to communicate with their wives.

The final aspect of the family communications chart that was analysed was the language used between the children, since Yamamoto (1987) suggested a link between bilinguality and use of the minority language by siblings. The results are presented in Table 17.

Table 17 Language used between children and children's bilinguality

Language (s) Used Between Children	Children's Bilinguality ($N = 91$)					
	Active Bilinguals ($n = 62$)		Passive Bilinguals ($n = 26$)		Monolinguals ($n = 3$)	
	n	%	n	%	n	%
90–100% English	1	50.0%	1	50.0%	0	0.0%
60–89% English	5	100.0%	0	0.0%	0	0.0%
41–59% English	3	75.0%	1	25.0%	0	0.0%
60–89% Japanese	15	100.0%	0	0.0%	0	0.0%
90–100% Japanese	17	47.2%	16	44.4%	3	8.3%
Unknown	2	100.0%	0	0.0%	0	0.0%

Table 18 Biliteracy vs bilinguality

Children's Reading Ability	*Children's Bilinguality* ($N = 91$)					
	Active Bilinguals ($n = 62$)		*Passive Bilinguals* ($n = 26$)		*Monolinguals* ($n = 3$)	
	n	*%*	*n*	*%*	*n*	*%*
3 or Less in Reading in One or Both Languages	31	57.4%	20	37.0%	3	5.6%
Minimum 4–5 in Reading in Both Languages	13	76.5%	4	23.5%	0	0.0%
Minimum 6–7 in Reading in Both Languages	11	84.6%	2	15.4%	0	0.0%
Minimum 8 or Higher in Reading in Both Languages	7	100.0%	0	0.0%	0	0.0%

There were both active and passive bilinguals in families with all types of sibling communication patterns, from exclusively English to exclusively Japanese. These results would appear to contradict Yamamoto's finding on the positive relationship between sibling use of English and active bilinguality, particularly since all of the children in families where the siblings used Japanese to communicate 60–89% of the time were active bilinguals. This difference in findings is probably at least partly due to the broader definition of bilinguality used in the current study.

Biliteracy and bilinguality

The final area explored in this study was a possible relationship between the children's ability to read both of their languages and their willingness to speak these languages. The questionnaire asked parents to rate their children's literacy skills on a scale of 10. (See Appendix for definitions of the even numbers on the scale). The highest level achieved in *both* languages (i.e. the reading level in the weaker language) was compared to the child's bilinguality. As shown in Table 18, the higher the children's ability to read both English and Japanese, the higher the proportion of active bilinguals.

Conclusion

While Japanese society generally expects children of mixed couples to be bilingual, especially when the foreign parent is a native speaker of

English, previous research has shown that in many cases these children do not speak the minority language proficiently. Even when parents in mixed marriages belong to a group aiming to promote bilingualism and their native language is highly valorised in the society at large, as English is in Japan, their children may not become active bilinguals. Lack of exposure to the minority language and social pressure to be like one's peers may lead children of mixed couples to reject the language of their foreign parent. This problem is demonstrated by the fact that in this survey of members of the JALT Bilingualism SIG, 30.8% of the children did not actively speak English and were rated by their parents as either passive bilinguals (28.6%) or Japanese monolinguals (2.2%).

All the same, many NES parents in Japan want their children to become bilingual, either because they feel English is an important language or because they see advantages inherent in bilinguality itself. This study aimed to build on previous research by determining individual and family characteristics that are related to the development of active bilinguality. It was hoped that the findings might help parents who want their children to become active bilinguals to choose childrearing patterns that will promote bilinguality and also to be aware of factors that they may need to correct or compensate for.

Interestingly, very few of the variables that were examined were shown to be related to children's bilinguality. There was no significant variation in the children's bilinguality depending on the sex of the NES parent, although when this factor was combined with birth order, a significant difference appeared: second children of NES fathers seemed to be less likely to be active bilinguals than first children of NES fathers and second children of NES mothers. Bilinguality was not shown to decrease significantly with age or with advancement in school. It was suggested, however, that the special nature of the respondents — members of a group of language educators interested in researching and promoting bilingualism — might have made a difference. Thus further investigation of all three of these variables — the sex of the NES parent, child's age and child's level in school — is recommended.

The one uncontrollable factor that had a significant relationship with the child's bilinguality was his or her position in the family. First-born and only children appeared to be more proficient at speaking English and were more likely to be active bilinguals, especially in families where the NES was the father. This may be due to the amount of time parents spend with individual children; as most parents will agree, it tends to decrease as the number of children in the family increases.

Parents hoping to promote bilinguality in all of their children are advised to devote ample time to later-born children. Moreover, given the lack of regard shown for fathers' parental duties in employment patterns in Japan, foreign fathers who want to encourage their bicultural children to become active bilinguals may need to take special measures to increase minority language input for their children, especially their later-born ones. Providing videos with English sounds tracks, organising a Saturday school or other outside English lessons, socialising with other native speakers of English and making frequent visits to the father's home country are recommended.

Another set of variables that was not shown to be related to children's bilinguality involved the parents' language abilities. Neither parents' bilinguality nor their ability to speak their second language was found to be related to their children's bilinguality. Moreover, their choice of language to use with each other was not shown to have a significant relationship to the likelihood of their children being active bilinguals.

Furthermore, parental language strategies — an area that parents can control and one that is often emphasised in advice to parents who wish to raise their children bilingually — were not necessarily related to active bilingualism. Use of the one person/one language approach was not shown to have a positive relationship to children's bilinguality. However the proportion of active bilinguals in families that employed the home language/community language strategy was higher than in families that did not.

Parental language choice was also considered. It was observed that the proportion of active bilingual children was high even when the NES parent used some Japanese to communicate with the children. However, the proportion of passive bilinguals was much higher when the amount of Japanese used by the NES parent exceeded 60%. As to language use by the Japanese parent, the proportion of active bilingual children was higher when *both* Japanese *and* English were used with the children than when either English or Japanese was used exclusively.

When considered together, the results concerning parental bilinguality, language strategies and family language use suggest that parents in mixed marriages do not need to restrict their communication with their children to their native language to ensure that their children become active bilinguals. It seems that minority language speakers can be highly proficient in the majority language and use that language with their children to a certain extent without fearing that their children will refuse to actively learn the minority language. These results lend some support to a theory argued elsewhere (Noguchi, 1996b) that parents in mixed marriages, rather than regarding themselves as models of a single language (and thus, serving as 'models of monolingualism'), might be better advised to see themselves as models of bilingualism for their children.

The data also suggested that a preponderance of Japanese language use in sibling communication does not rule out development of active bilingualism. There were no passive bilinguals in families in which the children used Japanese 60–89% of the time, although the proportion of active bilinguals was lower when Japanese was used 90% of the time or more.

Overall, these findings on family language strategies and communication patterns suggest that both languages can be used in bicultural families without fear of the children being monolinguals or passive bilinguals, as long as there is ample support for the minority language and the majority language is not allowed to dominate.

Because the respondents were members of a group that strives to promote bilingualism, this survey must be regarded as a preliminary investigation into variables that might influence the likelihood of children in international families becoming active bilinguals. Further research into the relationship between bilinguality and the sex of the minority language parent as well as the child's age is particularly recommended. The importance of birth order in promoting active bilinguality also needs to be confirmed. Likewise, the evaluation of family language patterns remains far from complete, although this study suggests that research to date may have over-emphasised the importance of strategies such as the one person/one language and home language/community language systems to the exclusion of language-use patterns involving bilinguality on the part of all family members.

Notes

1. Ministry of Justice figures showed that as of December 31, 1998, the number of foreigners registered to live in Japan totaled 1.51 million and accounted for 1.2% of the nation's population. Of these, Asians accounted for 1,123,409 (74.3%), while South Americans made up the second largest group (as reported in 'Foreign population totals 1.2%: Report', *Japan Times*, June 6, 1999.)
2. Figures from 'Working holidays elude some', *Japan Times*, August 16, 1995.
3. In 1997, 16,845 young Japanese went abroad on the Working Visa programme alone: 9444 to Australia, 3901 to New Zealand and 3500 to Canada (*Japan Times*, September 7, 1998). Tens of thousands more go overseas each year to take part in language and homestay programmes or to travel.
4. Adapted from table and statistics in *Zainichi gaikokujin no boshi hoken* [Insurance for Children of Foreign Mothers Residing in Japan] by Lee Setsuko (1998).
5. The term 'bilingual' was left undefined in order to test the subjects' general image of this word.
6. Kuo, Eddie Chen-Yu. (1974) The family and bilingual socialisation: A sociolinguistic study of a sample of Chinese children in the United States. *The Journal of Social Psychology* 92, 181–91.
7. Response rates were not indicated for the Yamamoto or Billings surveys, so these cannot be compared. Like the current survey, the Billings study used a convenience sample (Association of Foreign Wives of Japanese) rather than a random sample of bicultural families. Yamamoto does not explain how she selected her subjects.

Appendix

Questionnaire on Language Use in Families
With Native English Speaking Parents Living in Japan

1. **Wife's Nationality:**
2. **Husband's Nationality:**
3. **Number of Children:**

4. If children are in school, what language are they schooled in?

Child 1

Child 2

Child 3

Child 4

5. Age and language proficiency of each family member

On the chart below, please list the age and give a rough estimate of the *current* proficiency in each of the language skills shown below for each member of the family. I realise that language proficiency can change dramatically over time, rising to great heights at certain times (during trips to the States or England, for example), and dropping off at other times. For this survey, please try to give a 'snapshot' of each family member's skills *today*. Language proficiency should be given as a number according to the scales below. These are extremely rough, especially at the high end, but this is intentional. Odd numbers are not shown here, but can be used to indicate levels between those defined.

Speaking/Listening: 0: Never says anything/understands nothing
                                  2: Says/understands a few words and phrases
                                  4: Handles simple conversation
                                  6: Can function on a practical level
                                  8: Is highly proficient but not at native speaker level
                             10: Is a native speaker or on par with a native speaker of his/her age

Reading/Writing: 0: No literacy skills
                                  2: Reads/writes the alphabet/hiragana
                                  4: English – Reads simple sentences/writes simple sentences but may make many spelling mistakes
Japanese: Reads/writes words and sentences in hiragana and katakana
                                  6: Reads/writes simple materials at second-grade level or above but, if a non-native speaker, is not at the same level as a native speaker of the same age (Use this rating for second graders who are being schooled in the language.)
                                  8: Reads/writes adult-level materials but needs a dictionary and help from a native speaker for difficult passages
                             10: Reads/writes as a native speaker or on par with a native speaker of his/her age, or is doing all right in third grade or above in school in this language

	Age	Japanese Proficiency				English Proficiency			
		Speaking	Listening	Reading	Writing	Speaking	Listening	Reading	Writing
Mother									
Father									
Child 1									
Child 2									
Child 3									
Child 4									

6. Choose the classification below that most closely describes each family member's oral language abilities:

Monolingual: Speaks and understands only one language. Specify the language, i.e. Japanese monolingual.

Passive Bilingual: Speaks only one language, but understands normal conversation in the other language. Specify the dominant language, i.e.: English dominant passive bilingual.

Active Bilingual: Speaks and understands both languages well. Specify if one language is stronger than the other (i.e.: Japanese dominant active bilingual) or proficiency in the two languages is balanced (Balanced active bilingual).

Mother

Father

Child 1

Child 2

Child 3

Child 4

7. Are you familiar with the following language management strategies to help children become bilingual? (Circle yes or no.)
   One person/One language: Yes   No
   Home language/Community language   Yes   No

8. Have you employed either of these strategies or any other language management strategy to help your children become bilingual? (Check)
   One person/One language _____
   Home language/Community language _____
   Other _____ Specify:

9. If you have used one of these strategies, how consistent have you been in applying this strategy? Choose a number between 0 and 10, where 2 indicates 'Rarely follow', 5 indicates 'Follow about half of the time' and 10 indicates 'Follow without fail'. _____

10. If you have used one of these strategies, what advantages do you see in using the strategy you follow? Please write in as much detail as possible, adding an extra page if necessary.

11. If you have used one of these strategies, have you experienced any problems in using this strategy? If you have, please write about them in as much detail as possible, adding an extra page if necessary.

12. What language(s) is/are used between the members of the family? Specify the language(s) and a rough proportion of the time it is used (i.e.: English 60%, Japanese 40%) on the chart below.

From Mother to __	From __ to Mother	From Father to __	From __ to Father
Father		×	×
Child 1			
Child 2			
Child 3			
Child 4			

From Child 1 to __	From __ to Child 1	From Child 2 to __	From __ to Child 2
Child 1 ×	×		
Child 2		×	×
Child 3			
Child 4			

13. If you have any other comments on language use in your family, please write them here.

References

Arnberg, Lenore. (1987) *Raising Children Bilingually: The Pre-school Years.* Clevedon: Multilingual Matters.

Asahi shimbun (1998) *14 nin ni hitori oya ga gaikokujin* [1 child in 14 born to foreign parent(s)]. *Asahi shimbun* Evening Edition, February 26.

Billings, M.L. (1990) Some factors affecting the bilingual development of bicultural children in Japan. *AFJW Journal*, April 1990, 93–107.

Dodson, C.J. (1985) Second language acquisition and bilingual development: A theoretical framework. *Journal of Multilingual and Multicultural Development* 6 (5) 325–46.

Dopke, S. (1986) Discourse structures in bilingual families. *Journal of Multilingual and Multicultural Development* 7 (6) 493–507.

Dopke, S. (1992) *One Parent One Language: An Interactional Approach.* Amsterdam, Philadelphia: John Benjamins Publishing Company.

Fantini, A.E. (1985) *Language Acquisition of a Bilingual Child: A Sociolinguistic Perspective.* Clevedon: Multilingual Matters.

Gibbs, K. (1998) Sound advice to parents on bilingualism (translation of *Anna lapsellesi lahja/ Ge ditt barn en gava*). *The Bilingual Family Newsletter* 15 (3), 3.

Grosjean, F. (1982) *Life With Two Languages: An Introduction to Bilingualism.* Cambridge, MA and London, England: Harvard University Press.

Harding, E. and Riley, P. (1986) *The Bilingual Family: A Handbook for Parents.* Cambridge: Cambridge University Press.

Japan Times
    (Articles without bylines)
    Foreign population totals 1.2%: Report. *Japan Times*, Kansai Edition, June 6, 1999.
    Working holidays elude some. *Japan Times*, Kansai Edition, August 16, 1995.
    Working holiday visas offer growing challenges. *Japan Times*, Kansai Edition, September 17, 1998.
    (Article with byline)
    Moon, L. (1991) Foreign cross-cultural moms prefer Japanese schools for their children. *Japan Times*, Kansai Edition, March 31.

Kamada, L. (1995a) Report on bilingual family case studies in Japan: Significant factors affecting bilinguality. *Studies in the Humanities and Economics* 30 (3), 113–29. Hirosaki, Japan: Faculty of Humanities, Hirosaki University.

Kamada, L. (1995b) *Monographs on Bilingualism, No. 3: Bilingual Family Case Studies, Vol. 1.* Osaka, Japan: Japan Association for Language Teaching, Bilingualism National Special Interest Group.

Kamada, L. (1996) The nurture and nature of bilingual acquisition. In *On JALT '95: Curriculum and Evaluation* (pp. 146–50). Tokyo, Japan: Japan Association for Language Teaching.

Kuo, E.C. (1974) The family and bilingual socialisation: A sociolinguistic study of a sample of Chinese children in the United States. *The Journal of Social Psychology* 92, 181–91.

Lanza, E. (1992) Can bilingual two-year-olds code-switch? *Journal of Child Language* 19, 633–58.

Lanza, E. (1997) *Language Mixing in Infant Bilingualism: A Sociolinguistic Perspective.* Oxford: Clarendon Press.

Lee S. (1998) *Zainichi gaikokujin no boshi hoken* [Insurance for Children of Foreign Mothers Residing in Japan]. Tokyo: Igaku shoin.

Ma, K. (1996) *The Modern Madame Butterfly: Fantasy and Reality in Japanese Cross-Cultural Relationships.* Rutland, Vermont and Tokyo: Charles E. Tuttle Company.

Noguchi, M.L.G. (1996a) *Adding Biliteracy to Bilingualism: Teaching Your Child to Read English in Japan. Monographs on Bilingualism No. 4.* Osaka, Japan: Bilingualism National Special Interest Group of the Japan Association for Language Teaching.

Noguchi, M.L.G. (1996b) The bilingual parent as model for the bilingual child. *Seisaku kagaku,* Bessatsu, 245–61. Kyoto, Japan: Ritsumeikan University, Seisaku Kagakkai. (ERIC Document Reproduction Service No. ED 415 671)

Noguchi, M.L.G. (1999) *Katei de no dokuji shidō wa kano ka? 22 kazoku ni miru seikō no yōin* [Is it possible to teaching English-Japanese bilingual children to read English at home? Survey of 22 families on factors tied to success]. In M. Yamamoto (ed.) *Bairingaru no sekai* [The World of the Bilingual] (pp. 33–63). Tokyo: Taishukan shoten.

Oller, J. and Perkins, K. (1978a) Intelligence and language proficiency as sources of variance in self-reported affective variables. *Language Learning* 28, 85–98.

Oller, J. and Perkins, K. (1978b) A further comment on language proficiency as a source of variance in certain affective measures. *Language Learning* 28, 417–24.

O'Sullivan, J. (1994) *Teaching English in Japan.* Brighton, UK: In Print Publishing.

Romaine, S. (1989) *Bilingualism.* Oxford, England: Basil Blackwell.

Saunders, G. (1988) *Bilingual Children: From Birth to Teens.* Clevedon: Multilingual Matters.

Verhoeven, L.T. (1991) Predicting minority children's bilingual proficiency: Child, family, and institutional factors. *Language Learning* 41 (2), 205–33.

Volterra, V. and Taeschner, T. (1978) The acquisition and development of language by bilingual children. *Journal of Child Language* 5, 311–26.

White, M. (1988) *The Japanese Educational Challenge: A Commitment to Children.* New York: The Free Press (Macmillan Inc.).

Yamamoto M. (1987) Significant factors for raising children bilingually in Japan. *The Language Teacher* XI (10), 17–23.

Yamamoto M. (1992) Linguistic environments of bilingual families in Japan. *The Language Teacher* XVI (5), 13–15.

Yamamoto M. (1995) Bilingualism in international families. In J. Maher and K. Yashiro (ed.) *Multilingual Japan* (pp. 63–85). Clevedon: Multilingual Matters.

Yamamoto M. (1996) *Bairingaru wa dono yō ni shite gengo o shūtoku suru no ka* [How Do Bilinguals Acquire Language?]. Tokyo: Akashi shoten.

Yamamoto M. (1997) *Kokusai kekkon ni okeru gengo shiyō no jittai: Nigengo shiyō no jōkyō chōsa* [Research on Language Use in International Families: Survey on Bilingual Language Use]. The Ministry of Education, Science and Culture: Grant-in-Aid for Scientific Research (C), Project number: 07610517.

Chapter 10

Bilingual Education of Children in Japan: Year Four of a Partial Immersion Programme

R. MICHAEL BOSTWICK

Introduction

This chapter describes an evaluative study of the first English immersion programme in a Japanese elementary school. Although numerous studies have reported the effectiveness of immersion programmes in developing relatively high levels of second language proficiency without any tradeoff of first language development or subject matter mastery, little is known of immersion education in Japan. The implementation of the first immersion programme in a Japanese elementary school provides an opportunity to examine the appropriateness of such a programme in a non-Western socio-educational context. Moreover, because the immersion language is English and the students' native language Japanese, the programme provides a chance to examine the effectiveness of immersion in introducing a language which is very different from the students' first language. The study upon which this report is based is part of a comprehensive, longitudinal research project investigating the effects of partial immersion on Japanese childrens' academic achievement, first language development, and second language proficiency.

Immersion can be defined as a programme in which 50% or more of the school curriculum is done in the students' foreign language (Genesee, 1994a). It therefore represents the most intensive form of content-based foreign language instruction (Snow, 1986). In an immersion programme, the foreign language is not the subject of instruction, rather it is the medium through which a majority of the school's academic content is taught. Typically, in most immersion programmes this includes math, science, social studies and other 'serious' content classes. The intent of immersion programmes is to develop bilingualism and biliteracy in majority language students.

Research in North America has shown that this can be done at no cost to students' academic achievement or cognitive development in French immersion programmes (Genesee, 1983). Thomas, Collier & Abbott

(1993) have reported similar results in the early phases of Japanese immersion programmes in the United States. For an in-depth review of the research on immersion education in North America see Lambert & Tucker (1972), Swain & Lapkin (1982), Genesee (1983, 1987, 1995) and Baker (1996).

In recent years, immersion has spread to a number of other countries outside North America, but the effectiveness of programmes in these countries has been less well documented than their counterparts in North America (Baker, 1996). Overviews of research on immersion in other international contexts can be found in Artigal (1993), Artigal & Lauren (1992), Berthold (1992), Baker (1996), and Johnson & Swain (1997).

Most of the research on immersion to date has been with languages that share a common writing system with a relatively high number of cognates (e.g. the French *descendre, famille* and *ordinaire* and the English *descend, family*, and *ordinary*). Although there are a number of words from English that have been borrowed by the Japanese (e.g. *terebi, biiru* and *matchi* from the English *television, beer* and *match*), unlike English and French, English and Japanese do not belong to the same language family and therefore have fewer shared cognates. The two languages have very different grammar systems. The sentence order in Japanese is almost the reverse of equivalent sentences in English. Moreover, the Japanese writing system is not alphabet-based, so even the borrowed foreign words are written in different symbols.

In fact, Japanese has a very complex writing system that is fundamentally different from English. It is estimated that it takes 10 to 12 years for a Japanese student to learn the basics of reading and writing — a task which requires mastery of two different syllabaries (*hiragana* and *katakana*) with 46 symbols in each, plus approximately 2000 Chinese characters (*kanji*), most of which have multiple pronunciations that are differentiated by context. Shortly after the Second World War when there was a national debate in Japan about the need to simplify this writing system, a number of studies were conducted on the amount of time it takes to master written Japanese. Kuwabara (1953: 178) summarised many of these studies and noted that,

> In countries where the writing system is simple and there is nothing difficult like *kanji*, it does not require a lot of time to learn orthography — in Italy, it takes children approximately 900 hours of study, in Germany, 1300 hours, and in England, 2300 hours — that is, it takes only three to six years from the time children enter elementary school until they can sound out words. In Japan, it takes more than ten years. (Translation by Mary Goebel Noguchi.)

Japanese language classes therefore take up a large percentage of the elementary and secondary school curriculum in Japan and students spend a great deal of time in and outside of school learning the Chinese symbols used in the Japanese writing system (Benjamin, 1997).

Clearly, the distance between Japanese and English, linguistically speaking, is much greater than would be found in most immersion programmes in North America and Europe. As there are relatively few studies of immersion programmes in which two totally different language systems are paired, there is a great need to more fully investigate such programmes in order to understand the possibilities and limitations of immersion with very different languages. The implementation of an English immersion programme in a non-Western socio-educational context and in languages that are linguistically very different provides an chance to explore the extent to which immersion education can be applied to other socio-educational settings. Information regarding the generalisability of immersion research across settings and languages would be helpful as schools around the world consider the immersion option for teaching a foreign language.

Background

Although the study of English is not compulsory in Japan,[1] the overwhelming majority of students study English for at least six years before going on to college, where they often spend another two to four years studying the language. Even though Japan is clearly not as monolingual as it is reputed to be, and despite the significant amount of time and energy that is devoted to the learning of English, the outcomes of these efforts may be viewed as modest at best (Maher, 1984; Hansen, 1985).

Frustrated with the limited effect the Japanese English language education system had on students, Katoh Gakuen, a private Japanese school in central Japan, sought fundamental changes in its approach to English language instruction. This search ultimately led to the adoption of an early partial English immersion programme – the first of its kind in Japan (Katoh, 1993).

While immersion has generally enjoyed a strong track record in the North American context, and has demonstrated itself to be a very stable, viable educational model, there are any number of possible intervening variables that may affect the results of an immersion programme. Some of the most prominent factors mentioned by other researchers include parental interest and involvement, enthusiasm, commitment and training of teachers, material support and resources, and children's background and motivation (Ellis, 1994; Genesee, 1994b; Baker, 1996; Met & Lorenz, 1997).

In a study of Irish immersion students, MacNamara (1966) found that the children were approximately 11 months behind mainstream regular students in mathematical computation and problem solving by the end of fifth grade. In a study of English partial immersion students in Spain, Ballantine (1983) found that, among other problems, children had difficulty with subjects taught in the target language and did not achieve as well in these subjects as students not in the programme. Similar conclusions were reached by Ripple (1984) for English immersion students in Hong Kong. Immersion students in this study displayed limited flexibility and cognitive development in areas where the second language was used as the medium of instruction. There may be some risk, therefore, in generalising from the French immersion experience in Canada to other areas of the world because the conditions that foster the success of the programmes in North America may not necessarily be present in the same way in other parts of the world.

Moreover, there is ample evidence that immersion is not the panacea of language education it was once hoped to be: students in immersion programmes have been found to achieve less than native-like levels in their second language (Harley & Swain, 1984; Cummins, 1995; Johnson & Swain, 1997).

However, there is also a growing body of research that suggests that bilingualism can positively affect both intellectual and linguistic development. An important characteristic of the positive effects of bilingualism is that they tend to occur only in cases of what has been termed 'additive bilingualism' (Lambert, 1980), that is, when students were adding a second language at no cost to the development of their first language. The children in many (though not all) of the studies that suggest positive effects arising from bilingualism tended to come from majority language groups whose first language was strongly reinforced in the society they lived in. In contrast, minority children whose first language is not strongly reinforced by the schools tend to develop a subtractive form of bilingualism, in which the L1 is replaced by L2. Cummins (1998: 38) summarises the research on bilingualism by stating:

> The development of additive bilingual and biliteracy skills entails no negative consequences for children's academic, linguistic, or intellectual development. . . . Although not conclusive, there is evidence that points in the direction of subtle metalinguistic, academic and intellectual benefits for bilingual children.

Johnson and Swain (1997: 15) conclude that:

> under conditions favourable to immersion, claims based on research have gone beyond additive bilingualism to include cognitive, cultural and psychological advantages. . . . Under less favourable conditions, doubts have arisen concerning the potential of immersion programmes to achieve a full additive bilingualism.

This growing evidence of the successes of immersion in North America and of the possible positive benefits of additive bilingualism weighed heavily in the decision to try immersion in our school.

From the beginning, convincing our Japanese parents of the potential benefits of an immersion programme was not an easy task. Reporting on research that has taken place in other countries did not go far in allaying the concerns of parents about the immersion programme for their children. While this is probably true for parents all over the world, in international comparisons, Japanese parents appear to be more critical in their evaluation of their children's schools and place higher expectations on the schools and teachers than their counterparts in North America (Stevenson & Stigler, 1992; Lewis, 1995). Part of this may be explained by one aspect of Japanese culture: there is a tremendous emphasis on academic achievement as measured by the name of the college one enters. Entrance to a top university is seen as a sure 'ticket' to the best job opportunities after graduation. Therefore, there is growing pressure from the time the child enters the school system to acquire the necessary skills to pass the demanding college entrance tests. While not all parents fully support this type of exam-driven education, most do not want to penalise their children's chances for what is seen to be the key determiner of success in contemporary Japanese society.

Japanese parents are therefore constantly on the lookout for anything that might give their children an advantage in the fierce competition to get into the best colleges. Because Katoh Gakuen is a private school (with monthly tuition payments), parents must be convinced that their children will gain special advantages by receiving an education at our school. There are many factors involved in the parents' decision to enroll or not enroll their children in our programme. The most immediate advantage parents see is the potentially higher levels of English proficiency as a result of being in an English immersion programme. English is one of the three or four subjects most commonly tested on college entrance exams. Thus, greater English proficiency is seen as a possible plus in the exam 'war'. Many parents also believe that if their children are taught by a foreign teacher on a daily basis, they will become comfortable with foreigners and develop a more global perspective.

However, there are also several major reservations that many parents have when they consider our English immersion programme for their children. The first is academic achievement. Few parents completely believe that their children will not be penalised academically in some way by learning through a foreign language. Many are equally skeptical of claims that their children's Japanese language skills won't suffer as well. Still others fear that their children will lose their 'Japanese identity' by spending so much time learning in a foreign language with foreign teachers and will have difficulty adjusting to Japanese society as they grow older.

Therefore, although parents are frustrated with the level of English language proficiency achieved in most Japanese schools and see the immersion programme as a possible solution to this problem, few are actually willing to risk their children's academic and Japanese language development on an unproven programme. Our students are still a number of years from taking the college entrance tests, and until that time, the programme will be seen as 'experimental' by most parents and educators in Japan. Many of these concerns are likely to continue to surround the programme until our first graduates have completed their secondary schooling.

Currently, the parents that are most attracted to this programme have been either: (1) parents betting on immersion to provide an advantage for their children on the difficult university entrance tests, or (2) parents who desire a more internationally orientated education for their children and are hoping to escape what they perceive to be an over-emphasis on preparation for college entrance tests. This second group of parents generally places higher value on promoting international understanding, creative and critical thinking skills, and the possible benefits of being proficient in English in a global society.

The Founding of the First Immersion Programme in Japan

Many of the motives for starting the immersion programme at Katoh Gakuen were similar to the reasons North American parents and educators had for introducing immersion in their own schools. Dr Katoh Masahide, president of Katoh Gakuen, was frustrated with the foreign language proficiency of the Katoh high school graduates after six to twelve years of foreign language instruction and was eager to improve the level of English proficiency in his students. In the spring of 1991, he created a committee to explore alternative forms of English education and to consider the possibility of establishing a bilingual secondary programme for the school. At that time I was teaching at a local university and was invited to sit in on the committee as an outside consultant to help draw up a plan for the school.

The goal of the committee was to develop a programme that would enable students to conduct their academic studies in two languages. Planning quickly turned to the development of a preschool through grade 12 foreign language programme. The committee members were unanimous in their belief that more intense exposure to English at an earlier age would give the children time to develop better foreign language skills. This would better prepare them for the more difficult, abstract concepts introduced at the secondary level through the medium of the foreign language. It was also believed that if students were strong in two languages, we could offer immersion students classes in a third language in high school. It was at this stage in our discussions that our planning began to shift from a secondary bilingual programme to the creation of an early partial immersion programme.

Much time was spent reviewing research on immersion and other models of bilingual education at this stage. In the fall of 1991 several members of the committee had the opportunity to visit two Japanese immersion programmes in the state of Oregon: one in Portland and the other in Eugene. Both programmes were quite young at the time, but the visiting committee members were excited by the early successes of these programmes, and soon afterwards, the decision to proceed with the English immersion programme at our elementary school was made.

Once the decision to start the programme was reached, we had approximately six months to plan and design a programme before the start of the school year, since Dr Katoh was eager to start the new programme from the beginning of the following school year. Among the countless other things that needed to be completed before the start of the programme in April, 1992, we had to present and explain the plan to other Katoh Gakuen teachers and parents, hire immersion teachers, outline a curriculum and order instructional materials, most of which would come from North America and would take two or three months to arrive.

During this time I was appointed director of the immersion programme. One of my first jobs was to explain the proposed programme to the teachers in the elementary school. Understandably, they had questions and concerns about how the programme would affect the school as a whole, and how their roles and responsibilities might change. Although the teachers liked the idea of an immersion programme intellectually, many had serious concerns about implementing such an unknown and untested programme in Japan. Considerable time was spent with teachers (in and outside of school), discussing how the programme would operate. Although the teachers were initially very hesitant to introduce immersion in their school, by the time the programme began six months later, most had dropped their objection to the changes and were, in fact, cautiously excited about the prospects of the new programme at their school.

Interestingly enough, the decision to start an immersion programme came after the school had already enrolled 60 students for the 1992 school year. We therefore called the parents of these children for a meeting and explained the choice before them: keep their child in the traditional 'regular' programme, or select the new English immersion option. Between October and December 1991, we held several meetings with parents to explain the immersion programme to them. At the school's expense, we also sent a small group of parents and teachers to visit the Japanese immersion programmes in Portland and Eugene. Many of the parents were very impressed with what they saw and reported their impressions and observations to the other Katoh parents upon their return to Japan. It was at this time that enthusiasm for the immersion programme began to build (Bostwick, 1995).

It was also at this time that we started to design the curriculum to be taught in English. We began with an integrated, thematic approach to instruction – an approach that varied greatly from the traditional separation of subject areas found in most Japanese schools. It was felt that language could be more easily and more naturally developed using themes around which content and language outcomes could be organised. The study of water, for example, would include math, social studies, and science objectives, as well as provide for repeated opportunities to acquire high-frequency vocabulary and basic grammar in a natural, meaningful way.

We decided not to use a total immersion model, primarily because the writing systems in English and Japanese are so different. We felt that deferring first language literacy instruction (as is common in total immersion programmes) would put the students at too great a disadvantage later. Because the writing systems of the two languages are so different, we believed that fewer of the literacy skills would transfer over into Japanese, possibly making it difficult for students to catch up to their peers in Japanese language achievement in the upper grades. We were also legally required by the Japanese Ministry of Education to include Japanese language instruction from grade one.

A major objective in the planning of the programme was to ensure that students would have sufficient English skills to handle the difficult subject content in the upper grades that would be taught in English. Preparation for junior and senior high entrance tests is a big concern of parents and students, and we wanted to be sure the students would have sufficient language skills to continue their studies in English. Otherwise, instruction in these important content subjects in the foreign language might prove to be too difficult to do effectively in the later grades. It was therefore decided that a 'modified' partial programme model would be developed, in which the students would receive the same Japanese language instruction as non-immersion students, but all other classes would be taught in English. This meant that approximately two-thirds of the instructional day would be conducted in English. Our programme model would therefore be a hybrid between a total immersion programme, in which all instruction during the first several years of school is conducted in the foreign language, and partial immersion, in which half of the classes are usually conducted in the foreign language. (Bostwick, 1993).

In January, 1992, the parents of the incoming first graders were asked to make a commitment to either the regular programme or the new immersion programme. Of the 60 students who were accepted in October, the parents of 29 chose to enroll their children in the immersion programme, with the parents of the remaining 31 students choosing the regular programme. Results of an IQ test given to the students revealed that there was no significant difference in academic aptitude between the immersion and regular groups at the time of entrance into the programmes.

The school had expected to start with only one immersion class of about 20 students, and was surprised by the number of parents interested in immersion (especially given that there was an additional fee for this programme added to the regular school tuition). Because the class size is traditionally small at Katoh Gakuen, with 20 to 25 students in a class, the school was faced with a difficult decision. Either some of the immersion applicants had to be asked to enter the regular programme so that only one immersion class and two regular classes could be formed, or the school would have to create two small immersion classes and two small regular classes. The second of these two options was chosen, and the first two elementary immersion classes in Japan were formed. Since that first year, we have easily filled two immersion classes at each grade level in the elementary school.

Immersion Programme Description

The elementary school at Katoh Gakuen is a private Japanese elementary school in the city of Numazu, Shizuoka Prefecture, which is accredited by the Japanese Ministry of Education and the Shizuoka Prefectural Board of Education. The city has a population of approximately 210,000 and is situated on the Pacific coast about 120 kilometres south of Tokyo.

Dual tracks

The immersion programme is housed within Gyoshu Elementary School along with the 'regular' (non-immersion) elementary school programme. Applicants for the school must take an entrance test and be accepted by the teachers before they are admitted to the school. At the time that the students in the study applied for entrance to the school, the entrance test involved having the children come to the school for an entire morning. During that time the children were closely observed. They received scores on how well they could do the following things: change out of their preschool uniform and into their gym clothes, put away their belongings, interact with other children during free play, listen to the first part of a book read by the teacher, and draw a picture of how they thought the story would end. The teachers also gave the students a colouring, cutting and pasting task, and students were evaluated on the quality of their completed product. The students received a grade for each of these areas during the class observation. The Wechsler Preschool and Primary Scale of Intelligence (WIPPSI) − Japanese Version (Nippon Bunka Kagakusha, 1967) was also individually administered to all the students. Finally, the parents were interviewed to determine their understanding of the school's programme and their motivations for enrolling their child. There were no formal criteria for passing this 'test', but each student was discussed by the teachers and all three areas − class observation, academic aptitude, and parent interview − were considered in their decision concerning whether to accept the child in the school. Generally speaking, a very high percentage of the applicants pass the school's entrance test and only children with exceptionally low 'scores' in all three areas are turned away by the school.

In the years that followed the introduction of immersion to the school, the entrance test has been somewhat modified. Upon application to the school, parents indicate their choice of programme (immersion or regular). The school no longer routinely administers an individual intelligence test

Table 1 1996–1997 Student enrollment

Grade	Program	
	Regular	Immersion
1	41	40
2	31	40
3	28	44
4	38	33

to all students. In its place is a locally designed, group academic aptitude test for which no validity or reliability figures are available. The WIPPSI is now given only to 'borderline' students to supplement the information gained from the class observation and the group test. There is no English test for the children applying for the immersion programme, but children are given the opportunity to listen to a story and learn a short song in English during their time at school. The children are observed during this time to see how attentive they are and how well they participate in the English activities. These observations supplement the earlier classroom observations. The total numbers of students accepted into the school at each grade level at the time of the evaluation is noted in Table 1.

Preschool/kindergarten programme

Two years after the start of the elementary immersion programme, an immersion programme for the preschool/kindergarten was implemented. The children in the preschool/kindergarten range in age from three to five years of age. Most children arrive shortly after 10.00 a.m. and return home around 2.00 p.m., with approximately 50% of the immersion students' time in the programme conducted in English. Like the elementary school, the preschool/kindergarten is 'dual track', and parents may choose to enroll in either the regular or immersion programme. Because the programme wasn't begun until several years after the start of the elementary programme, none of the grade three or grade four elementary students, who are the subjects of this study, had any prior immersion experience.

Immersion programme students

Ninety-eight percent of the students in the immersion programme are Japanese, and nearly all of these students started the programme with little or no English speaking ability. While students come from a fairly wide range of socioeconomic backgrounds, the majority of students come from middle or upper-middle class families. Not all of the students live in the immediate area: a number commute as much as an hour or more one-way. Few parents actually understand or speak English, and most of the students come from homes where English skills are limited. The first cohort began in grade one of elementary school, and this pilot class had completed grade four at the time of the study.

Class size and student-to-teacher ratio

Ministry of Education regulations dictate a maximum class size of 40 for public and certified private elementary schools. Local schools are able to create smaller classes if they want, but budget constraints usually mean that the typical class size in a Japanese public school runs between 35 to 40 students. Traditionally, Katoh Gakuen has offered smaller class sizes. In the elementary school, most classes range between 20 to 25 students. Compared to Japanese public school standards, this allows for a relatively high teacher/student ratio.

Goals and purpose

The immersion programme at Katoh Gakuen places a high priority on becoming bilingual and biliterate while maintaining high academic standards. The programme attempts to achieve a form of 'additive bilingualism' (Lambert, 1980) in that it is designed to maintain and develop students' first language skills while adding a second language. The intent of the programme is not to replace Japanese with English. Japanese language and culture are valued and supported by the teachers and school, and many of the traditional events and festivals of the Japanese culture are part of the school programme. The immersion students also follow the same Japanese language arts programme as the non-immersion students. Students are expected to maintain normal academic and first language development despite the fact that the instruction is through a second language medium. Assessment of students' academic achievement is done in both English and Japanese.

Teachers

At the time of the study, the immersion programme's faculty included four Americans, three Canadians, two Australians, and one British national. All of the teachers in the programme are trained and certified elementary school teachers in their home countries, and all have had prior elementary school classroom teaching experience before coming to the immersion programme. The average length of classroom experience for the teachers in the immersion programme is approximately eight years. All are also native speakers of English. Many of the teachers have had experience living in Japan before joining the programme, with the average length of prior residence in Japan being approximately four years in total. Approximately half of the teachers had conversational Japanese speaking ability, although only three of the teachers could actually conduct parent conferences without the aid of a translator.

Four Japanese teachers (one for each grade) were teamed with the immersion staff. Three of the four could effectively communicate in English with their immersion teaching partner and assisted in the immersion teachers' communications with the parents.

Proportions of English and Japanese instruction

The Katoh Gakuen English Immersion Programme could be considered a modified early partial-immersion programme. The students in the pilot group spent approximately two-thirds of their instructional day in English in Grades 1, 2, and 3. This means that during the six-period school day, four class periods were conducted in English. Each period is 45 minutes long.

During these first three grades all of the elementary school subjects, with the exception of Japanese language arts and a few music classes, are conducted in English in the Immersion Programme. From Grade 4, the students take half their classes in English and half in Japanese. Math, Science, Physical Education and Computer Skills are taught in English, and Japanese Language Arts, Social Studies, Music and Art are taught in Japanese. Technical math and science terminology in Japanese is reviewed during Japanese language arts class. Although no content is re-taught in Japanese at this time, the students are given practice with math story problems in Japanese and are taught the Japanese equivalents for the technical terminology learned in English.

The Japanese teachers are also asked to assess the students' math, science, and social studies knowledge in Japanese after the students have passed the end-of-unit tests on the English side of the programme. This assessment is done to confirm that the students understand the technical terminology in Japanese for the subjects taught in English. Underlying this practice is the need to confirm for parents that the children remain competitive in academic achievement compared to the non-immersion students. Table 2 shows a breakdown of the subjects by language medium for the students in the present study.

Mirroring regular programme

The Ministry of Education requires that schools adhere to the Course of Study curriculum guidelines in order to maintain accreditation. Students who do not graduate from accredited elementary, junior and senior high schools are not eligible to directly apply for entrance to a Japanese university. Because most Japanese parents hope to sent their children to a Japanese university, few are willing to send their children to an

Table 2 Distribution of classes by language medium

Grade	Average Number of Classes in English (Per 30-Period Week)	Classes Conducted in English (Number of Classes Per Week)*	Classes Conducted in Japanese (Number of Classes Per Week)*
1	20	Math (6) Life Studies (6) PE (3) Music (2) Art (2) Computer Skills (1)	Japanese (9) Homeroom (1)
2	20	Math (6) Life Studies (6) PE (3) Music (2) Art (2) Computer Skills (1)	Japanese (9) Homeroom (1)
3	20	Math (5) Social Studies (3) Science (3) PE (3) Art (2) Music (1) English (2) Computer Skills (1)	Japanese (8) Music (1) Homeroom (1)
4	15	Math (5) Science (3) PE (3) English (2) Computer Skills (1) Homeroom (1)	Japanese (8) Social Studies (3) Music (2) Art (2)

*Each class is approximately 45 minutes long.

unaccredited school. [See Chapter 5, 'Affiliation, Not Assimilation: Resident Koreans and Ethnic Education' for more on the matter of school accreditation and problems faced by students attending non-accredited schools.]

The content and goals of the curriculum in the immersion programme are therefore designed to mirror those of the regular programme. The textbooks used in the regular programme are translated into English and given to the immersion students to use in the immersion classroom. Immersion students also take the same end-of-unit and end-of-year tests as students in the regular programme. The number of hours in each subject per week is also the same as that in the regular course. In addition, the immersion students receive the same number of Japanese language arts classes as the regular students — approximately nine classes per week in Grades 1 and 2, and approximately eight classes a week in Grades 3 and 4. The major difference between the two programmes is that the immersion students receive instruction in most of these subjects in English.

Aside from the differences in the language of instruction, two other differences between the two programme's curriculum can be noted. One is the greater emphasis on integrated study in the early grades in the immersion programme, as discussed earlier. The second difference can be found in the content and goals of the English classes, which are taught three periods a week starting in the first grade in both programmes. The English classes in the regular programme are EFL instruction and tend to focus on aural/oral conversational skills. In the immersion programme, however, the focus of instruction in the classes where English is the subject tends to be on literacy skills.

Language separation

In the immersion programme, foreign teachers are paired with Japanese partners in each grade and the two teachers work together to plan weekly schedules and develop activities for the children. However, instruction in English and Japanese are clearly separated in the programme by time, location and teacher. During the English portion of the day, the immersion teacher takes responsibility for the class. Except in extraordinary cases, Japanese is not used by the immersion teacher during the English portion of the day. In addition, the students' day is blocked off into periods of English or Japanese, and every effort is made to avoid switching students back and forth between languages. Students move to one room to receive instruction in Japanese during the Japanese portion of the day and another room for classes conducted in English. Subject areas are also divided by language. Rarely is the same subject taught in both languages, and when follow-up or remedial instruction is needed in one of the English-based classes, the content is never re-taught in Japanese. If a student experiences a problem in math or some other subject taught in English, the immersion teacher takes responsibility and provides remedial instruction in English.

Purpose of Study

The overall purpose of this study was to assess the effect that four years of immersion has had on our students in three key areas. It was believed that four years in the programme was sufficient time to see if there were systematic programme effects that could be identified.

The first three research questions focused on students' academic and language progress:

(1) What is the level of academic achievement in mathematics[2] for students in the partial-immersion programme at the end of four years in comparison to other Katoh Gakuen students?

(2) What is the level of academic achievement in Japanese reading and writing (*kokugo*) for students in the partial-immersion programme at the end of four years in comparison to other Katoh Gakuen students?

(3) What is the level of English proficiency for students in the partial-immersion programme at the end of fourth grade?

The fourth research question was intended to determine parents' and students' perspectives of the programme:

(4) How do parents and students view the partial-immersion programme after four years in the programme?

Method

Participants

The focus of the present study was the progress of the pilot class at the end of Grade 4. In the four years since the start of the programme in first grade, one student moved out of the area and five students have been added to this initial group, making a total of 33 students in the pilot class at the time of the study. Of the five new students, two were Japanese children returning from America, and two were from bicultural families which were living in the area and had one parent whose native language was English. Several of these late enrollees had limited Japanese literacy skills. Although it would have been instructive to include the following immersion classes in the comparison, this was not done because there was no comparable IQ data available for the subsequent immersion classes. Therefore the study was limited to the first immersion class.

Two major problems arose in establishing a control group for this study. First, parents selected the programme – the children were not randomly assigned to the immersion or regular groups. This introduces many unknown variables to the study that are nearly impossible to control. Any number of unforeseen factors may cause parents to choose one programme over the other, possibly causing systematic differences between the two groups that can not be totally controlled experimentally. This is a problem for nearly all quasi-experimental immersion studies.

The second major problem was that direct comparisons between the immersion and regular classes are limited by school policy. Because the school is private, it has a vested interest in not doing anything that might damage one programme in its discussion of the other. Early experiences with parents demonstrated how politically sensitive direct comparisons could be for the school. At the end of the first year of the programme, comparisons of test scores in math and Japanese between the regular and immersion classes were made public. No statistically significant difference was found, but the immersion class outscored the regular class in math by a few tenths of a point. This was misinterpreted by parents and created the impression that the regular teachers were lax in the instruction of their children, despite the fact that both groups were one standard deviation above the prefectural and national averages and that the difference between the scores was likely due to measurement error. Because of the extremely competitive nature of Japanese schools, parents are very sensitive to test scores. The prevalent logic for parents at that time was, 'If the immersion students, studying through a foreign language are doing that well, then the non-immersion students, studying in their mother tongue, should be able to do even better.' This is a point I will return to later in the paper. Although we continue to monitor the students' progress and report individual student progress to the parents, as a result of this experience, all direct group comparisons between the immersion and regular classes have essentially been banned by the school.

The preferred design would be to compare immersion and non-immersion groups moving through their treatment/non-treatment at the same time. However, because direct comparisons of the immersion students in the current Grade 4 class with the students on the regular side of the programme was not possible, an alternative strategy was employed. Test scores from the previous two fourth grade classes at Katoh Gakuen (before the immersion programme was introduced) were used in this study. The comparison classes were the 1994–95 fourth grade class and the 1993–94 fourth grade class. The 1994–95 school year had 48 fourth grade students and the 1993–94 school year had 46 fourth grade students. All three groups at the time of this evaluation were enrolled in Katoh Gakuen, comprising Grades 4, 5 and 6.

This type of design is less rigorous than a more direct comparison of immersion and non-immersion groups or a random assignment of students to the two classes. However, by using the previous fourth grade classes at Katoh Gakuen, it was possible to maintain positive parent and teacher relations within the school while providing the study with a comparable control group. In order to establish comparability of the three groups, an attempt was also made to account for three variables that were believed to have a potentially significant impact on student achievement: socio-economic status, IQ and private after-school lessons.

Socioeconomic status

Data taken from school application forms indicated that the family background variables (parents' occupation and education) for the immersion and control groups were comparable, with a majority of children in both groups coming from middle to upper-middle class Japanese families. In most families, at least one parent was a university graduate. The range of occupations was also equally diverse within groups, with many holding highly technical/professional, or middle to upper management company positions.

IQ

All three groups were given the Wechsler Preschool and Primary Scale of Intelligence (WIPPSI) – Japanese Version (Nippon Bunka Kagakusha, 1967) before entering the school in first grade. No significant differences between the three groups in IQ scores were found.

Private after-school class attendance

There is a variety of after-school, extracurricular activities available to Japanese students. Classes range from swimming and piano to accelerated classes in math, Japanese, and English. After-school programmes have become a multi-million dollar industry in Japan and are an essential supplement to the regular school system in the minds of many Japanese parents (White, 1987). As was noted earlier, Japanese parents are often preoccupied with providing every possible advantage to their children in passing the difficult university entrance tests. Accordingly, there is widespread use of after-school programmes that specialise in preparing students for the highly competitive high school and college entrance exams, and the percentage of students attending these programmes dramatically increases in the years preceding these school entrance tests.

During parent-teacher conferences, teachers often check with parents about the type and amount of time spent in activities outside of school. Data collected on students' after-school study habits reveal that while the overall amount of time spent on after-school lessons did not differ significantly between the immersion and regular groups, the subjects of study did differ. English was the most common subject studied after school for the students in the regular class, followed by piano, math, Japanese, and swimming. The order of frequency for the immersion students, however, was piano, swimming, math and Japanese classes, and English was not a subject they commonly studied after school. Parents in both groups reported that their children, on average, attended after-school classes for approximately two hours a week. Overall, no significant differences in the total number of hours of after-school study were found between the groups.

Based on the information gathered, all three groups were considered to be comparable on the variables of academic aptitude, socioeconomic status and study habits outside of school.

Test materials and other programme evaluation procedures

The students in the study took the *Zenkoku hyōjun shindanteki gakuryoku kensa* (National Norm-Referenced Diagnostic Academic Achievement

Exam) published by Tosho Bunka-sha (1992). The Math (*sansū*) and Japanese Language Arts (*kokugo*) test components were administered to the students at the end of their academic year (February). The tests measure the progress of students' academic achievement in relation to all students in Japan and to the curriculum guidelines set forth by the Japanese Ministry of Education. The Japanese test assesses students' knowledge of Chinese characters (*kanji*) and general reading and writing ability in Japanese, while the math test assesses concepts and skills associated with the Japanese elementary math curriculum. The tests were administered in Japanese, and therefore also assess the immersion students' ability to transfer knowledge of mathematical concepts and skills into Japanese, as all instruction in mathematics in the immersion classes was provided primarily in English.

Three instruments were used to assess students' English proficiency. The first was a mock version of the STEP Level 3 Test taken from the *Eiken san-kyū zen mondaishū* [Collection of Questions Included in Previous STEP Level 3 Tests] (Ohbunsha, 1995). The STEP tests, known in Japanese as the *Eigo kentei shiken* [Official English Examination], or *Eiken* for short, are authorised by the Japanese Ministry of Education and are the most commonly used English proficiency tests for secondary and college students in Japan. Well over 40,000,000 students have taken the tests since the founding of the *Eigo kentei kyōkai* [Society for Testing English Proficiency, or STEP] in 1963 (*Eiken Guide*, 1995).

Eigo Kentei Kyokai, the test makers of the *Eiken* (STEP) tests, routinely publish past exams. The test administered by Eigo Kentei Kyokai in October, 1994 and published in *Eiken san-kyū zen mondaishū* (1995) was used to assess the immersion students' English proficiency in comparison to other students in Japan. Although no specific age levels are assigned to the test, generally speaking, the lowest level test, Level 5, is designed to test students on the English covered by the curriculum for the first year in junior high school, the Level 4 test covers the material they've learned up until the end of the second year in junior high school, and the Level 3 (*san-kyū*) test is intended for junior high school graduates. Written at a 2100-word level, the Level 3 (*san-kyū*) test that was administered to the immersion students consists of sections on sentence completion, conversation completion, passage completion, reading comprehension, and listening comprehension.

On the *Eiken* Level 3 passage completion task, the students read a passage of approximately 200 words in length with five sentences missing from various parts of the passage. The students' task is to find the most appropriate sentences from the choices given to complete the passage. On the reading comprehension task, the students are given two 200–220 word passages with five comprehension questions for each passage. The average Flesch-Kincaid readability of the two passages was at the 5.6 grade level. The listening comprehension section of the test was comprised of 20 multiple-choice questions on short dialogs and listening passages on topics related to daily life. The test publishers do not provide data on the test's reliability or validity.

The actual *Eiken* Level 3 Test involves an oral interview in addition to the written test. However, this was not administered to the students because a separate instrument (LAS) was used to assess students' oral proficiency. The *Eiken* Level 3 was administered to immersion students in September, 1995 — half way through their fourth year in the programme.

In order to get a fuller perspective of the immersion students' English language ability, the English subtests of the Iowa Tests of Basic Skills (1993) Level 8 were administered in December, 1995. The English subtests of the Core Battery include the following sections: Reading Vocabulary, Word Attack Skills, Reading Comprehension, Spelling, Capitalisation, Punctuation, Usage and Expression, and Listening. The tests use a multiple-choice format and all of the directions are in English. The Iowa Tests of Basic Skills are designed for English-speaking students in schools with an American-based curriculum and are standardised and norm-referenced. They are popular academic achievement tests used throughout the US and in many international schools around the world with an American-based curriculum. The tests provide grade-equivalent scores as well as a wide range of other standardised scores. They furnish teachers with an estimate of students' English language and literacy development and identify areas of strength and weakness relative to the US school population.

The third instrument used to assess the immersion students' English proficiency was the oral component of the Language Assessment Scale (CTB/McGraw Hill, 1990). This test is comprised of several listening comprehension and short answer subtests as well as a story retelling task using a series of picture cues. The LAS test is typically used in the US to assess the oral language skills of English as a Second Language (ESL) students and to recommend placement in or exit from bilingual/ESL programs. Scores are compared to native speaker norms and classify students into five levels of proficiency, from 'non-English speaker' (Level 1), to 'Limited English Speaker' (Levels 2 and 3) and 'Fluent English Speaker' (Levels 4 and 5). The test is administered entirely in English.

In order to determine the attitudes and perspectives of the fourth grade students and their parents, a Parent Survey and a Student Questionnaire were developed. The instruments were based on similar instruments previously developed by other programme evaluators in North America (Day & Shapson, 1983; Genesee, 1978; Lambert & Tucker, 1972). The questions were designed to elicit responses to issues which developed during the implementation of the immersion programme and to provide parent input regarding how the programme could be improved. The parent survey was pilot tested and the revised form was distributed to all the parents in the programme in February, 1995. The survey was anonymous and parents returned the questionnaire in unmarked envelopes. Space was provided on the form for parents to write additional comments or questions.

The student survey was completed in May, 1996 (two months into their fifth grade year). The questionnaires were administered in English and the class went through each question together with the researcher. Students were instructed to work alone and not to share their answers with other students during the administration of the questionnaire.

Results and Analysis

Math achievement

The results of the math assessment are presented in Table 3. The scores are reported as T-scores.[3] A score of 50 represents the national average with a standard deviation of ten. The results of the math assessment demonstrate that all three groups are approximately one standard deviation above the national average in math. Not only are the immersion students performing as well as past Katoh Gakuen students, but they are performing significantly above most of their peers in Japan. The scores indicate that as a group, the immersion students are at approximately the 85th percentile of all students nationwide in mathematics.

A one-way ANOVA was carried out on the math scores of the three classes. The results indicate that the immersion class is performing at approximately the same level in math as past Katoh Gakuen students. Of the three classes in the test comparison, the immersion class slightly outperformed the past two classes in mathematics achievement, but the differences were not statistically significant ($p > 0.05$).[4] In other words, statistically speaking, the scores were comparable scores, and there is very little confidence that any differences seen are actual and not due to sampling error.

These results are remarkable in that even though nearly all math instruction for the previous four years had been given in English to the immersion students, they were achieving at the same level as comparable students whose instruction was entirely in Japanese.

Table 4 summarises the results of the statistical comparison between the three classes. No significant differences were found, so no post hoc tests were performed.

Table 3 Comparative Math and Japanese achievement, end of Grade 4

	Math Mean Score	*Math Standard Deviation*	*Japanese Mean Score*	*Japanese Standard Deviation*	*n*
Immersion Pilot Class	61.15	5.38	59.15	4.60	33
Regular Class (1995–96)	59.34	6.84	59.92	6.55	48
Regular Class (1994–95)	61.00	7.19	55.76	8.09	46

Table 4 Math achievement – results of one-way ANOVA

Source	df	Sum of Squares	Mean Squares	F Ratio	F Probability
Between Groups	2	87.9107	43.9554	0.9996	0.3710
Within Groups	123	5408.7956	43.9739		
Total	125	5496.7063			

Japanese language achievement

On the Japanese language test, immersion students again performed as well as students on the regular side of the programme and at nearly one standard deviation above the national mean (50). The results of this test verify that the immersion students' reading and writing skills in Japanese are well above the national average. As shown in Table 3 above, the immersion class as a whole scored 0.77 points below the 1995–96 regular class but 3.39 points above the 1994–95 regular class.

A second ANOVA analysed the Japanese language test scores. The results summarised in Table 5 indicate that there was a significant difference between the group means ($p < 0.05$). In the subsequent post hoc test (Table 6), it was determined that the scores between the two regular classes were significantly different. No other group means were found to be significantly different from each other. In other words, there was no significant difference between the immersion class and the two regular classes. The only significant difference found was between the 1995–96 regular cohort and the 1994–95 regular cohort. The Japanese

Table 5 Japanese achievement – results of one-way ANOVA

Source	df	Sum of Squares	Mean Squares	F Ratio	F Probability
Between Groups	2	444.9812	222.4906	4.8931	0.0090
Within Groups	124	5638.2787	45.4700		
Total	126	6083.2598			

Table 6 Japanese achievement – Scheffé Test

Group Means	Immersion	Regular (95–96)	Regular (94–95)
59.15 Immersion			
59.91 Regular (95–96)			* significant at 0.05
55.76 Regular (94–95)			

achievement score for the 1994–95 regular class was several points below the immersion class and the 1995–96 regular class, but statistical significance was only reached in its difference with the 1995–96 regular class. The scores indicate that the English immersion programme did not have a negative effect on first language literacy skills and that the immersion students were developing first language literacy on par with students who were not in the immersion programme.

These results reveal a notable accomplishment for the immersion students, as they spent less than half of their instructional day in Japanese. They support other research that shows that knowledge gained in the process of developing a second language can assist children in promoting their first language (Cummins, 1984; Harley, 1987). Thus, the immersion students demonstrated normal literacy development even though they received less formal instruction through the medium of Japanese. The additive bilingual nature of the immersion programme appears to more than compensate for the reduction of time spent studying in their first language. The fact that the immersion students were able to maintain normal first language development despite the large portion of their school day that they spent in a language system that is completely different from their own is an especially noteworthy accomplishment.

Table 7 Summary of English proficiency measures

Test	Mean Score	Mean Grade Equivalent	Standard Deviation	Minimum Score	Maximum Score
Eiken (STEP) Level 3 Test	67.00	—	15.08	41	93
ITBS Reading Vocabulary	—	2.1	0.56	0.9*	3.3*
ITBS Reading Comprehension	—	2.5	0.62	1.5*	4.1*
ITBS TOTAL Reading	—	2.2	0.47	1.4*	3.7*
ITBS Listening	—	2.9	0.85	1.0*	5.4*
ITBS Language	—	2.4	0.79	1.0*	4.4*
ITBS TOTAL Language	—	2.6	0.68	1.1*	4.2*
ITBS Word Analysis	—	2.4	1.10	1.0*	6.6*
LAS (oral proficiency)	70.51	—	3.83	64	77.5

* Grade Equivalent Scores

English proficiency

English proficiency testing was only done with the immersion students because no comparable test data was available for the two non-immersion classes. Therefore no direct comparisons were made between the groups. Table 7 summarises the results of the *Eiken* (STEP) Level 3 test, the ITBS and the LAS.

Eiken *(STEP) test*

The written test (*1-ji shiken*) of the Level 3 *Eiken* (STEP) Test was administered to the fourth grade immersion class to determine how the students performed in comparison to junior and senior high school students in Japan who typically take this test. The level of English required to pass the test is that of a 'junior high graduate' (*Eiken Guide*: 2) in Japan. The Eigo Kentei Kyokai indicates that each year, approximately 45% of the students sitting for the written and oral sections pass this test (*Eiken Guide*: 16).

The *Eiken* test publishers state that a score of approximately 65% correct on the test is considered a passing score. The immersion class average on this test was 67.00% correct. Of the 33 students who took the *Eiken* Level 3 Test, 19 passed the 65% criterion. Of the 19 who passed the test administered by the school, three students passed the *Eiken* Pre-Level 2 (*Jun ni-kyū*) Test administered at an *Eiken* testing centre in October of that year. The Pre-Level 2 Test is a much more difficult test and is intended for high school students in Japan.

Passing Level 3 (or better) of the *Eiken* is a significant accomplishment for elementary school students in Japan. As noted above, the percentage of students who pass is not high, and many schools know that even junior high school graduates find it difficult to pass this test. The fact that over half of the immersion students are passing Level 3 or better by fourth grade is a significant accomplishment.

By way of an indirect comparison between the immersion and non-immersion groups, it can be noted that the *Eiken* test is an option for fifth and sixth grade non-immersion students. Each year a few fifth grade regular students take the lowest level of the *Eiken* (Level 5) and a somewhat larger number of sixth grade regular students try either the Level 5 or the next highest level (Level 4) test. While over half of our fourth grade immersion students passed the more difficult Level 3 test, very few of the sixth grade non-immersion students even sit for the Level 3 test.

The Iowa Tests of Basic Skills (ITBS)

The unique properties of the ITBS allow schools to make detailed interpretations of the results. The mean Reading Comprehension grade equivalent score of 2.5 for the immersion class indicates that the average student in the fourth grade immersion programme scored as well as a typical second grader in the fifth month of school in America. Listening was the strongest area for the immersion students, with the average student in the class scoring at the end of second grade (2.9). The listening test was very challenging and was designed to evaluate the listening comprehension ability of native English speaking students.

In general, the immersion students' English skills appear to approximate those of second grade students in the United States. Comparisons of the immersion students' literacy development to both Japanese and American native speaker norms show that not only have they mastered the skills expected of them in their first language, but they have also made significant progress in acquiring a second language. Several of the students appear to be working at or near grade level in several English language areas. High grade equivalent scores were recorded in English Reading Comprehension (4.1), Listening (5.4), Language (4.4) and Word Analysis (6.6). Several of these high-scoring students had never been abroad and had attained all of their English proficiency through the immersion programme.

The results of the ITBS indicate that the immersion students' English literacy skills lag behind students in the US but also reveal significant language development in a foreign language learning environment where only part of their day is in English.

Language Assessment Scale (LAS)

The LAS was used to assess the immersion students' oral language proficiency. While the *Eiken* and ITBS have listening comprehension components, both tests are primarily written tests that assess students' reading skills and knowledge of language usage. In contrast, the LAS provides an assessment of students' speaking proficiency relative to native English speakers. Results of the LAS indicate that while the students' oral proficiency is not native-like, most students have little difficulty communicating their intended message. In the story retelling section of the test, students listened to a story (with picture cues) in English about an alien that lands in a little girl's yard to ask for directions as she is raking the leaves. The following are typical retellings of the story by the immersion students (verbatim).

> 'Pam raking leaves then spaceship came with, with a flashing blue and red light. Pam go near, uh, spaceship and the blue creature with large green eye came from of Pam. And then blue creature touch green belt and ask to Pam, "What planet is here?" Pam said "Its Earth." Blue creature said "Thank you" and ... and ... get, go into spaceship. Then Pam said to her friend all about it. But nobody think that is truth. But Pam know because rake leaves one ... one more time.'

'One day, see ... uh ... the yard leaf ... and the UFO come slowly down and with red and blue light. And the door open and huge head and green eyes, and, and, went out. She said, "Hello" and that creature pushed green button and that speaker said, "Hello, what planet is this?" She said, "Earth" and that speaker said, "Oh, wrong planet." "We should go to Neptune." and they go. Then tell every friend but no one, no one that true, no one believe but she knows because leaf are ... have been, go, everywhere.'

The retellings indicate a number of grammatical errors in tense (*think* for *thought, go* for *went*), number agreement (*eye* for *eyes*), determiners and preposition usage (*a, the, to, with*). The retellings point to a simplified verb system, and an incomplete mastery of a number of basic structures. An absence of idiomatic expressions can also be noted in the retellings. In general, the students' English grammar still appears to be influenced to some extent by their first language system (Japanese).

A native English speaking child of the same age would also likely retell this story with a number of grammatical errors and unfinished sentences. However, the types of mistakes made by the immersion students indicate that they have not yet established the level of control over the language that a typical native English speaking child their same age would exhibit. Nevertheless, the students are able to communicate their thoughts, albeit with a number of grammatical inconsistencies.

The LAS rates students' oral proficiency on a scale from one (Non-English Speaker) to five (Fluent), relative to native English speaking children of the same age. Table 8 indicates how students are categorised and shows the number of immersion students who achieved each level of oral proficiency on the LAS. Most of the immersion students are at level three (Limited English Speaker) in relation to other native English speaking students their age. The class average was 70.51 points.

These results should help prevent parents and educators from setting unrealistic expectations concerning students' oral English proficiency. While the full benefits of being in an immersion programme accumulate

Table 8 LAS oral proficiency levels

Category	Level	Test Score Range	Number of Students in the Grade 4 Class at Each Level
Fluent English Speaker	5	85–100	0
Fluent English Speaker	4	75–84	5
Limited English Speaker	3	65–74	27
Limited English Speaker	2	55–64	1
Non-English Speaker	1	0–54	0

over time and may not be seen in the initial stages of the programme, clearly, students' use of English has not reached native-like levels. Experience in North America also indicates that while students in total immersion programmes may approach native-like ability in receptive skills (listening and reading) they rarely reach that same level in the productive areas of speaking and writing (Genesee, 1995; Cummins & Swain, 1986). Research findings in North America suggest that there may be an upper limit to second-language proficiency that can be achieved in a school context that does not include substantial opportunities for peer inter-action in the second language (Genesee, Holobow, Lambert, Cleghom & Walling, 1985). Parents and educators should not expect native-like skills in speaking unless there is extensive interaction outside of school with native English speaking peers.

Parent and student perceptions

An English translation of the parent survey instrument and the ques-tions in the student survey are presented in full in the Appendices, along with the compiled responses for each survey instrument.

Eighty-five percent of the parents returned the anonymous survey to the school. The parent survey results indicated that a great majority of parents were generally satisfied with the overall programme at Katoh School, although a number of specific recommendations were offered by the parents. The average rating given to the question concerning overall satisfaction with the programme was 2.48 on a scale of (1) to (5) (with (1) being the highest rating). The statement, 'My child is comfortable in the English immersion programme' was given a very high rating of 1.78, indicating that the vast majority of parents felt their children were not experiencing any stress by spending so much of their school day in a second language.

Clearly, however, the fourth grade parents felt some concerns. They indicated in their comments that they were uncomfortable being the lead group. Because their children are the first group to go through the immersion programme, many parents hoped for more advance planning and curriculum development. Some frustration with homework in English and anxiety regarding matriculation to the junior high immersion programme was also expressed. Some parents also wanted even greater emphasis on English.

One somewhat surprising finding was the parents' rating of satisfaction regarding academic progress in the core subjects – Math, Science, Social Studies and Japanese. The parents' mildly positive score – 2.92 on a scale from (1) (very satisfied) to (5) (very dissatisfied) – did not seem to match the high academic achievements of the students in the programme and indicated some concern by the parents in an area in which the students were clearly doing very well. One possible reason for this discrepancy is that although the parents are informed of their individual child's' test scores, the parents have not been given group data comparing the immersion and non-immersion classes.

Many of the parents' concerns could be directly attributed to the fact that this was the first group in Japan learning through an immersion approach and to insufficient information regarding the programme. Parents wished there was a 'path already cleared away for them to follow' and were somewhat envious of the classes following them. It seems that the role of 'pioneer' is not always a comfortable one when it concerns the education of your child. However, most parents indicated in their comments that, overall, they felt the benefits of the programme far outweighed the difficulties and drawbacks encountered in establishing the programme. Moreover, since the beginning of the immersion programme, no child has moved from the immersion programme to the regular programme.

Most parents indicated that they chose the programme because of its bilingual nature and because they felt that being in the programme would broaden the perspectives of their children. Many parents indicated that they hope to prepare their children not only for a role in Japan but also for a role in a larger global society. The statement (in Question 5), 'The ability to communicate in English is very important. I would like my child to be bilingual' was the highest ranked reason given by the parents for enrolling their children in the immersion programme.

The student questionnaire (see Appendix B) revealed a number of interesting points. Use of English outside of class was, as expected, quite limited. While there have been occasional opportunities to use English with native English speaking peers, these opportunities were extremely rare. The use of English with friends or family was also very limited.

The questionnaire also revealed that the students appeared to have a great deal of confidence in their English ability. Seventy-five percent of the students stated that they could understand 'very well' or 'most' of a movie or television programme in English. Nearly the same percentage indicated that they 'definitely' or 'probably' could communicate their most important ideas in English to a native speaker their age. In general they ranked their English abilities in all four skill areas (reading, writing, listening, and speaking) as 'good.' Listening ('your ability to understand others') was ranked the highest and grammatical accuracy ('your ability to speak correctly'), the lowest.

The students generally had a very positive attitude towards their experience in the immersion programme. Ninety percent said they enjoyed studying English in school and all of the students stated that given the choice, they would like to study in a school that used both English and Japanese. None of the students indicated that they wanted to leave the programme. The responses indicate a strong positive attitude towards learning English, and a belief that learning English is valuable and important for their future.

Discussion

There is no evidence that the students' academic and cognitive development has been slowed in any way by their immersion experience, even though the language used as a medium of instruction in most of their core academic classes was very different from their native language and has a completely different writing system. Overall, the students participating in the immersion programme have scored at least as well as other comparable Katoh School students. Test results also reveal that the immersion students are able to maintain academic achievement in math and Japanese at approximately one standard deviation above the national average. This is remarkable, given that nearly all of their math instruction was presented in the foreign language and that the students spent less than 50% of their instructional day in Japanese, a language with a complex writing system that takes a great deal of time to master. It is instructive to note that these results mirror results typically achieved in North American immersion programmes. The results of this study indicate that the immersion students have not experienced any delay in academic achievement or first language development as a result of being in a partial English immersion programme.

In English language proficiency, the immersion students have made steady progress in all skill areas since their start in grade one of the programme. LAS scores indicate that, as a class, the immersion students are at Level 3 in oral proficiency (with (1) representing non-English speaker and (5) representing fluent English speaker). Results from the ITBS suggest that linguistically speaking, students are operating in English at approximately the same level as second grade students in the US. This is remarkable considering that most of the students have never lived abroad. When we compare the immersion students to students here in Japan in terms of English language skills as measured by the *Eiken* test, we find that a majority of students are operating at or beyond the junior high level. The results suggest that listening comprehension is the student's strongest skill, and it is believed that competency in this area is essential in laying the groundwork for future progress in the language. Classroom teachers have also observed that the productive skills of speaking and writing tend to lag behind the receptive skills of listening and reading in their work with the children.

Although the primary design of the study was to appraise the progress of the immersion students after four years in the programme, tentative inferences may be made regarding the effect the distance between two languages may have on children's first and second language development in an immersion programme. There is substantial evidence from second language research with adult learners that suggests that the distance between two languages can affect the rate of acquisition as well as the degree of positive and negative language transfer (Ellis, 1994). The importance of this factor may be seen in the number of weeks that the United States Foreign Service Institute calculates are needed to achieve intermediate level proficiency in various languages. For English speaking students, the Foreign Service Institute allocates more than twice as many weeks of Japanese instruction as it does for French instruction to achieve the same level of proficiency. Further indication of the importance of this factor comes from a study by Ringbom (1986). In this study Swedish speaking adults in Finland were able to acquire English much faster than Finnish speaking adults. Ringbom concluded that this was largely because, linguistically speaking, Swedish is much closer to English than Finnish is. In a somewhat related finding, Sundquist (1986) found that Swedish speaking Finnish children could reach nearly the same level of English reading ability in half the time required by Finnish speaking children.

Although a substantial amount of second language learning occurred, the partial immersion students in the study were far from achieving native-like ability in speaking and literacy skills. Whether this could be attributed to the less than total immersion experience provided these students or was due to the distance between the two languages (or any number of other possible intervening variables) cannot be fully addressed in a study of this design. Further research is needed to determine if, and in what ways, the linguistic distance between languages may influence the acquisition of a second language within an immersion context.

More obvious inferences may be drawn in regard to first language development. Research in North American immersion programmes has clearly shown that there is no negative effect on first language development when the language pairs are similar (e.g. French and English, or Spanish and English). Less was known about the possible affects on the first language when the language pairs in an immersion programme are very different. This is a major concern for parents and educators because children entering such programmes have not yet developed literacy skills in their first language. The data from this study would suggest that even in immersion programmes where the paired languages are very different, students' first language literacy skills are not impaired. The results tend to mirror the results from studies of French and Spanish partial immersion programmes in North America in regard to first language development. However, it is believed that introduction of first language literacy instruction from the beginning of the programme was a major factor in achieving normal first language development. It is far from clear that similar results could be achieved in a total immersion programme where first language literacy instruction may be delayed until second, third or even fourth grade. It is possible that the linguistic distance may become a more important factor in a total immersion programme.

The strong positive attitudes of the students towards learning English also parallels the generally positive responses of children toward learning a second language in North American immersion programmes. This is in sharp contrast to the attitudes of many students towards learning a second language through traditional language classes. The results of the study would suggest that the intensive immersion experience develops much higher levels of second language ability in students with less emotional stress and more personal enjoyment than a typical 'drip feed' foreign language class that meets only once or twice a week.

Conclusion

Some educators in Japan have warned of the possible negative effects on first language development or academic achievement as a result of too much emphasis on foreign language education for children. One can still hear statements by researchers and educators that English language education should wait until students have mastered their first language. For example, in an article discussing a proposal to begin English language training in elementary schools in Japan, a university professor was quoted as stating:

> English language education should wait until children become ten years old or older. Before that age children have not generally developed their fundamental language ability and therefore, learning of a foreign language can confuse them. (*Asahi Evening News*, May 13, 1996)

There is also the belief by some that children exposed to two languages too early in life will lose their ability to function effectively in either language, becoming, in effect, 'semilingual', as asserted by another university professor in a recent newspaper article.

> If the parents place emphasis on learning English ahead of the mother tongue, the child's ability in both languages will probably be limited considerably. In that case, the child will become what we call 'semilingual'. (*Daily Yomiuri*, January 21, 1997)

Fundamentally, there is the fear that learning a foreign language at an early age will place constraints on the child's first language development.

Informal inquiries made to parents in the regular programme revealed that some parents chose not to enroll their child in the immersion programme because they were worried that too much time in English would interfere with the development of their children's first language. These concerns are reminiscent of the naive 'balance theory' of bilingualism, or what Cummins (1980) called the Separate Underlying Proficiency model. Conceptually this is seen as two language balloons inside the head. As the second language balloon expands, the first language balloon is reduced in size because the brain can only hold a limited amount of language. The assumption is that spending large amounts of time acquiring a second or foreign language will mean that you cannot fully acquire your first language because you will have 'filled your second language balloon' with too much language. The two languages are seen as operating separately without transfer and with a very restricted amount of 'room' for either language. Baker (1996: 145) notes that these theories

> ... appear to be held intuitively by many people. Many parents and teachers, politicians and large sections of the public appear to latently, subconsciously take the balloon picture as the one that best represents bilingual functioning.

This would seem to be true for us in Japan as well. It is difficult for parents and educators to accept data that contradict these deeply held, 'common sense' beliefs regarding language learning and bilingual education. These conceptions about language have enormous sway over people's thinking about language learning and bilingualism.

The results of the parent survey also pointed to a potential gap in the parents' perception of their children's academic progress and the children's actual progress. Without evidence to the contrary, parents are more likely to accept the 'common sense' logic that first language learning and academic achievement may be delayed. Comments by parents on the survey indicate that some of these misconceptions about bilingualism may still colour their thinking.

The results of this study and the long history of success with immersion in North America directly contradict the 'common sense' logic outlined above. Evidence from this study suggests that even when the distance between the languages is great, students do not experience a delay of first language development as a result of being in an immersion programme. Cummins (1984) and Genesee (1987) have pointed out a number of possible reasons why students' first language development may not suffer in an immersion setting. Among the most important is the principle that 'additive bilingualism' can develop under certain conditions — that is, in a setting in which a second language is being learned by choice and where the second language is not likely to displace or replace the individual's first language or home culture. Additive bilingual contexts have been consistently associated with positive cognitive and linguistic effects (Diaz & Klingler, 1987; Cummins & Swain, 1986). The results of this study would seem to indicate that language learning in an immersion programme has effects that are much more complex than the simple 'logic' offered in the above 'common sense' conceptions about bilingualism. The truth may be that the interaction between bilingualism, cognitive functioning and language development is much more complicated than what 'common sense' would dictate.

The results of the study provide support for the claim that an early partial immersion education can be a viable option for schools wishing to promote English language proficiency while maintaining first language development and academic achievement within a Japanese elementary school setting. The results suggest that when first language literacy instruction is provided from the beginning of the programme within the context of a partial immersion programme, no delay in academic achievement need be expected. The immersion students' strong performance on Japanese language assessments provide further support to the claim that the distance between English and Japanese does not hinder the students' first language development within a partial immersion programme.

The study offers fewer clues as to the possible affect linguistic distance may have on immersion students' foreign language development. A future study designed to compare the foreign language proficiency levels of students from very different language backgrounds in an immersion programme would more directly address this issue.

Notes

1. The standard curriculum set out by the Ministry of Education for compulsory education includes foreign language instruction at the junior high school level, but does not stipulate which language must be studied. However, most junior and senior high schools offer English, either as the only foreign language or as one of the foreign languages from which students must choose.
2. Math was chosen as the main indicator of academic achievement for two reasons. First, students are not tested in science or social studies in grades one through four and therefore data was only available for math and Japanese. Second, absence of testing in the other subject areas reflects the school's and parents' heavy emphasis on math. Math is seen as one of the most important subject areas in the elementary school curriculum. Therefore it seemed reasonable to assign math as the key indicator of academic success in this study.
3. The T-score, known as *hensachi* in Japanese, is commonly used in Japan to report student achievement.
4. Two one-way ANOVA tests were performed in this study. Doing multiple F tests in one study compromises the confidence of the probability that differences truly exist between groups. (See Brown, 1992). Doing multiple F tests in a study is rarely recommended because it increases the possibility that a Type 1 error (saying one group is different from the other, while in fact, they weren't) may occur. However, in this study, a Type 2 error (saying there was no difference between the groups when in fact there was) was deemed to be a much more serious error. Therefore, no adjustments to the *p* value of the tests were made to compensate for the possibility of a Type 1 error – and thereby increase the chances that a Type 2 error may occur.

Appendix A

Parent Survey

All responses have been re-ordered to reflect the rank order given to the items by the parents. Note: The lower the number on the scale the more positive (higher) the ranking is for the item.

1. **How satisfied are you with your child's progress in the English immersion programme in the following areas? Please rate your satisfaction with your child's development in each of the following areas by circling one of the numbers according to the scale below. Please add any comments that you feel would help us to further understand your responses.**

Very Satisfied	Satisfied	Neutral	Dissatisfied	Very Dissatisfied
1	2	3	4	5

Average Ratings

Progress in learning English	1.96
Progress in Japanese (*kokugo*)	2.23
Academic progress in Social Studies	2.24
Personal and social development	2.59
Progress in special skills (Art, Music, PE, Computer Skills)	2.60
Academic progress in Math	2.65
Academic progress in Science	2.72

2. **How satisfied are you with the English immersion programme in the following areas? Please rate your satisfaction for each item by circling one of the numbers according to the scale below. Please add comments to help us to further understand your responses.**

Very Satisfied	Satisfied	Neutral	Dissatisfied	Very Dissatisfied
1	2	3	4	5

Average Rating

Overall level of satisfaction with the programme	2.65
Communication between immersion teachers and child	2.72
Special subjects (Art, Music, PE, Computer, etc.)	2.81
Core subjects (Math, Science, Social Studies, etc.)	2.92
Communication between child's teachers and parent	2.93

3. **How strongly you would agree with the following statements. Rate your level of agreement for each item by circling one of the numbers according to the following scale. Add comments at the end to help us understand your responses.**

Strongly Agree	Agree	Neutral	Disagree	Strongly Disagree
1	2	3	4	5

Average Rating

My child feels good about school	1.48
My child is comfortable in the English immersion programme	1.78
In general, I feel that the immersion programme has been a valuable experience for my child	1.79
As a result of the immersion programme my child has become more aware of and open to people of other cultures	2.04
Overall, the immersion programme has made a positive contribution to the Katoh Elementary School programme	2.48

4. **Where do you hope your child will go for college?**

Average Rating

I'll leave it completely up to my child	58%
Japanese college	32%
College abroad	12%
Other:	4%

5. **Rank order of reasons why parents enrolled their children in the immersion programme:** (The options given to parents have been listed in the rank order of responses by parents.)
   1. The ability to communicate in English is very important. I would like my child to be bilingual.
   2. To prepare my child for future academic opportunities.
   3. To help my child become more comfortable with and open to other people and ways of thinking.
   4. To prepare my child for future personal opportunities.
   5. To prepare my child for future professional opportunities.
   6. I want to provide my child with a more challenging and stimulating school experience.

   Other reasons volunteered for enrolling child: (number of parents with similar comments)
   Disappointed with public school education (3)
   Disappointed with traditional English education (2)
   One parent is an English speaker (1)

6. **What do you think are some of the GOOD things about the immersion programme?**
   (Free response item with the number of similar responses indicated in parentheses)
   Children can naturally master English as a tool of communication. (7)
   Children naturally exposed to English (North American) culture and environment. (5)
   Programme enhances interest, creativity, and divergent thinking. (4)
   Children maintain Japanese and academic achievement while mastering English. (3)
   Positive student and teacher relationships. (2)
   Teachers use various instructional strategies. (2)
   There are many opportunities to meet English speaking students the same age. (1)

7. **What do you think could be done to IMPROVE the immersion programme?**
   (Free response item with the number of similar responses indicated in parentheses)
   English speaking skills need to be improved. (4)
   Immersion teachers should stay longer; teacher turnover is too high. (3)
   Students must be encouraged more to use English with each other outside of class. (2)
   More detailed curriculum development should be completed before instruction begins. (2)
   Difficult to monitor homework that is in English. (2)
   More thorough follow-up of academic achievement needed. (2)
   More opportunities to exchange with English speaking students the same age needed. (1)
   Better parent-teacher communication needed. (1)

8. **What do you think have been some of the BENEFITS for your child or your family of being in the immersion programme?**
   (Free response item with the number of similar responses in parentheses)
   English has become a part of my child's life. (8)
   The 'fear' of foreigners is gone. (3)
   Our conversation topics and personal perspectives have widened. (3)
   My child shows a positive interest in cultures and languages other than Japanese. (2)
   My child loves English and school. (2)
   My child's interest in Japanese language and culture has increased. (2)
   It is convenient for family trips abroad. (2)
   My child is becoming more independent and expresses himself clearly. (2)
   It helps to prevent my child from forgetting the English learned while abroad. (1)
   We do not have to rent videos dubbed in Japanese. (1)

Appendix B

Student Survey

I. **Use of English**
    1. **How often do your parents speak English with you at home?**
At least once a day	7
At least once a week	8
At least once a month	8
Almost never	10

    2. **During the past year, how often have you used English outside of class (during recess, lunch, after school, etc.) with your friends?**
At least once a day	4
At least once a week	4
At least once a month	11
Almost never	14

    3. **During the past year, how often did you have a chance to use English with native speakers outside of school?**
10 or more times	10
3–9 times	10
1–2 times	12
Never	1

    4. **Have you ever been asked to translate?**
Yes	31
No	2

    5. **How much time do you spend reading English books?**
Less than 15 minutes a week	7
Between 15–30 minutes a week	6
Between 30–60 minutes a week	7
More than 1 hour a week	13

    6. **How much time do you spend reading Japanese books?**
Less than 15 minutes a week	0
Between 15–30 minutes a week	1
Between 30–60 minutes a week	3
More than 1 hour a week	29

II. **Language Ability**
    7. **How well do you understand TV or movies in English?**
I understand very well	7
I understand most of it	18
I understand some of it	8
I don't understand any of it	0

    8. **Is studying in English more difficult than studying in Japanese?**
Yes, learning in English is more difficult than in Japanese	10
They're about the same	17
No, learning in Japanese is more difficult than in English	6

9. **Do you think you could communicate your most important ideas in English to a native English speaker that is your age?**

Definitely. I'm sure I could communicate my most important ideas   8
Probably. Yes, most likely I could communicate my most important ideas   14
Maybe. I'm not sure. Perhaps I could communicate my most important ideas   11
Probably not. I don't think I could communicate my most important ideas   0

10. **How good do you think you are in English in the following areas. Using the scale below, write your level for each area listed.**

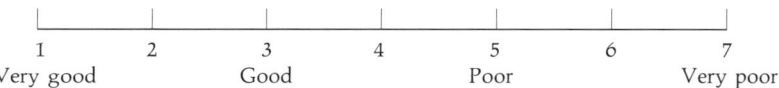

1	2	3	4	5	6	7
Very good		Good		Poor		Very poor

Average Rating (Listed in order from highest to lowest ranking by students)

2.88	Your ability to understand others
2.97	Writing
3.09	Your ability to be understood when you speak
3.12	Reading
3.33	Your pronunciation when you speak
3.36	Your ability to say what you want to say
3.36	Your ability to speak correctly

III. **Motivations and Attitudes Towards Learning English**

For questions 11–16, circle the response that shows how strongly you agree or disagree with each statement.

11. **My parents feel that it is important to learn English.**

Strongly agree	Agree	Disagree	Strongly disagree
17	13	2	1

12. **I think it is important to be able to understand and speak English.**

Strongly agree	Agree	Disagree	Strongly disagree
20	12	1	0

13. **My friends think that it is important to understand and speak English.**

Strongly agree	Agree	Disagree	Strongly disagree
7	12	12	2

14. **I enjoy school.**

Strongly agree	Agree	Disagree	Strongly disagree
15	13	5	0

15. I enjoy studying English at school.

Strongly agree	Agree	Disagree	Strongly disagree
10	20	3	0

16. I would like to speak a third language someday.

Strongly agree	Agree	Disagree	Strongly disagree
11	17	4	1

17. What kind of school would you like to be in?

An only English speaking school   0
An only Japanese speaking school   0
An English & Japanese speaking school like Katoh School   33

18. After studying English for several years, some children seem to change their personalities while others seem to stay the same. How about you? Do you think you have become less Japanese in your thoughts and feelings; or do you see yourself now as being both foreign and Japanese, or more Japanese?

I think I am more Japanese than I would have been without the immersion
    programme   4
I think I am both Japanese and foreign in the way I think and feel   15
I think I am more foreign than Japanese   10

19. If you had a younger brother or sister who was going to start school next year, would you advise him or her to take the immersion programme?

Yes   27
Not sure   4
No   2

Reasons for stating 'Yes'
Because its fun (7)
Because we learn to speak English (6)
Because it wouldn't be fair if I get to be in the programme and s/he can't be in the
    programme (2)
Because we need both English and Japanese (3)
Because we will be able to talk to foreigners (3)
Because we can travel/live abroad someday (3)
Because learning a second language is good (1)

Reasons for stating 'Not Sure'
I don't want to be responsible for that decision. (2)
English is difficult. (1)

Reasons for stating 'No'
My brother doesn't like English. (1)
My brother is already in the regular programme. (1)

20. **Finish the sentence below. Circle any and all responses that are true. You may circle more than one answer.**

I think it is important to learn English because ...
Number of students that selected the item (listed in descending order selected by students)

26 then I might be able to make more friends from other countries.
26 in the future it will be important to speak English in Japan.
24 it will help me to get a better job when I graduate from school.
24 then I can travel more freely in foreign countries.
24 then I can watch movies and TV in English.
23 it is nice to know another language.
23 English is an international language.
17 then I might be able to live in a foreign country someday.
12 most of my class work and homework is in English.
 9 many of my friends are also studying English.

References

Artigal, J.M. (1993) Catalan and Basque immersion programmemes. In H.B. Beardsmore (ed.) *European Models of Bilingual Education* (pp. 30–53). Clevedon: Multilingual Matters.

Artigal, J.M. and Lauren, C. (1992) Immersion programmemes in Catolonia and Finland: A comparative analysis of the motives for the establishment. *Rassegna Italiana di Linguistica Applicata* 3, 165–9.

Baker, C. (1996) *Foundations of Bilingual Education and Bilingualism* (2nd edn). Clevedon: Multilingual Matters.

Ballantine, S. (1983) *A Study of the Effects of English-Medium Education on Initially Monoglot Spanish-Speaking Gibraltarian Children.* University of Wales.

Benjamin, G. (1997) *Japanese Lessons: A Year in a Japanese School Through the Eyes of an American Anthropologist and Her Children.* New York and London: New York University Press.

Berthold, M. (1992) An Australian experiment in French immersion. *The Canadian Modern Language Review* 49 (l), 112–25.

Bostwick, R.M. (1993) Immersion education: Introducing a new era in English education. *Fuji-Phoenix Review* l (l), 173–84.

Bostwick, R.M. (1995) After 30 years: The immersion experiment arrives in Japan. *The Language Teacher* 19 (5), 3–6.

Brown, J.D. (1992) Statistics as a foreign language – Part 2: More things to consider in reading statistical studies. *TESOL Quarterly* 26 (4), 629–64.

Cummins, J. (1980) The construct of language proficiency in bilingual education. In J.E. Alatis (ed.) *Georgetown University Round Table on Languages and Linguistics 1980* (pp. 25–59). Washington, DC: Georgetown University Press.

Cummins, J. (1984) Wanted: A theoretical framework for relating language proficiency to academic achievement among bilingual students. In C. Rivera (ed.) *Language Proficiency and Academic Achievement* (pp. 2–19). Clevedon: Multilingual Matters.

Cummins, J. (1995) Canadian French immersion programs: A comparison with Swedish immersion programmes in Finland. In M. Buss and C. Lauren (eds) *Language Immersion: Teaching and Second Language Acquisition. University of Vaasa: Research Papers.* 192 (pp. 17–26). Vaasa: University of Vaasa.

Cummins, J. (1998) Immersion education for the millennium: What we have learned from thirty years of research on second language immersion. In M. Childs and R.M. Bostwick (eds) *Learning Through Two Languages: Research and Practice* (pp. 34–58). Numazu, Japan: Katoh Gakuen.

Cummins, J. and Swain, M. (1986) *Bilingualism in Education.* London and New York: Longman.

Ellis, R. (1994) *The Study of Second Language Acquisition.* Oxford: Oxford University Press.

Day, E. and Shapson, S. (1983) *Elementary French Immersion Programs in British Columbia: A Survey of Administrators, Teachers, and Parents:* Burnaby: Simon Fraser University.

De Avila, E.A. and Duncan, S.E. (1990) *Language Assessment Scale.* Monterey: CTB/McGraw Hill.

Diaz, R. and Klingler, C. (1991) Towards an exploratory model of the interaction between bilingualism and cognitive development. In E. Bialystok (ed.) *Language Processing in Bilingual Children* (pp. 167–192). Cambridge: Cambridge University Press.

Eigo kentei kyōkai [Society for Testing English Proficiency] (1995) *Eiken san-kyū zen mondaishū – 3.* Tokyo: Ohbunsha.

Eigo kentei kyōkai [Society for Testing English Proficiency] (ed.) (1995) *Eiken Guide.* Tokyo: Nihon eigo kentei kyokai.

Genesee, F. (1978) Second language learning and language attitudes. *Working Papers on Bilingualism* 16, 19–42.

Genesee, F. (1983) Bilingual education of majority-language children: The immersion experiments in review. *Applied Psycholinguistics* 4, 1–45.

Genesee, F. (1987) *Learning Through Two Languages.* (First Edition). Cambridge, MA: Newbury House Publishers (Harper and Row).

Genesee, F. (1994a) Second language immersion programmes. In R.M. Bostwick (ed.) *Immersion Education International Symposium Report on Second Language Acquisition Through Content Based Study: An Introduction to Immersion Education* (pp. 14–25). Numazu, Japan: Katoh Gakuen.

Genesee, F. (1994b) *Integrating Language and Content: Lessons From Immersion* (Educational Practice Report 1). Santa Cruz: National Center for Research on Cultural Diversity and Second Language Learning.

Genesee, F. (1995) The Canadian second language immersion programme. In O. García and C. Baker (eds) *Policy and Practice in Bilingual Education* (pp. 118–133). Clevedon: Multilingual Matters.

Genesee, F., Holobow, N., Lambert, W.E., Cleghom, A. and Walling, R. (1985) The linguistic and academic development of English-speaking children in French schools: Grade 4 outcomes. *Canadian Modern Language Review* 41 (4), 669–685.

Hansen, H.E. (1985) English education in Japanese universities and its social context. In C.B. Wordell (ed.) *A Guide to Teaching in Japan* (pp. 145–70). Tokyo: Japan Times.

Harley, B. (1987) *The Development of Bilingual Proficiency* (Final Report) Toronto: Ontario Institute of Studies in Education.

Harley, B. and Swain, M. (1984) The interlanguage of immersion and its implications for second language teaching. In A. Davies, C. Criper and A.P.R. Howatt (eds) *Interlanguage* (pp. 291–311). Edinburgh: Edinburgh University Press.

Hoover, H.D., Hieronymus, D.A.F. and Dunbar, S.B. (1993) *Iowa Tests of Basic Skills.* Iowa City, Iowa: The Riverside Publishing Company.

Johnson, R.K. and Swain, M. (1997) *Immersion Education: International Perspectives.* Cambridge: Cambridge University Press.

Katoh, M. (1993) The start of the English immersion programme: Toward educational innovation. *Fuji-Phoenix Review* 1 (l), 151–62.

Kuwabara Takeo. (1953) *Minna no nihongo* [Everyone's Japanese]. *Bungei shunju,* April, 1953. Reprinted in *Shinsen nihon gendai bungaku zenshū* [New Anthology of Modern Japanese Literature], 38 Vols., Chikuma shobo, 1958–60, Vol. 34, 257–8; excerpted in Hibbett, H. and Itasaka G. (1968) *Modern Japanese, A Basic Reader* 2nd edn, Vol. II, 178. Cambridge, MA: Harvard University Press.

Lambert W. (1980) The social psychology of language: A perspective for the 1980s. In H. Giles, W.P. Robinson and P.M. Smith (eds) *Language: Social Psychological Perspectives* (pp. 415–24). Oxford: Pergamon Press.

Lambert W. and Tucker, R. (1972) *Bilingual Education of Children: The St. Lambert Experiment.* Rowley, MA: Newbury House.

Lewis, C. (1995) *Educating Hearts and Minds.* Cambridge: Cambridge University Press.

MacNamara, J. (1966) *Bilingualism and Primary Education, A Study of Irish Experience.* Edinburgh: Edinburgh University Press.

Maher, J.C. (1984) English language education in Japan: Historical and macro issues in the teaching of English in schools. *Language Learning and Communication* 3 (1), 71–92.

Met, M. and Lorenz, E. (1997) Lessons from US immersion programs: Two decades of experience. In R.K. Johnson and M. Swain (eds) *Immersion Education: International Perspectives* (pp. 243–64). Cambridge: Cambridge University Press.

Nippon Bunka Kagakusha (ed.) (1967). *Wechsler Preschool and Primary Scale of Intelligence (WIPPSI) – Japanese Version.* Tokyo: Nippon bunka kagakusha.

Ringbom, H. (1986) *The Role of the First Language in Foreign Language Learning.* Clevedon: Multilingual Matters.

Ripple, R. (1984) Cognitive and affective costs of bilingual education: A look at the Hong Kong experience. Paper presented at AERA, New Orleans.

Snow, M.A. (1986) *Innovative Second Language Education: Bilingual Immersion Programs* (Report-Evaluative/Feasibility 142). Los Angeles, CA: UCLA Center for Language Education and Research.

Stevenson, H. and Stigler, J. (1992) *The Learning Gap.* New York: Simon and Schuster.

Sundquist, L. (1986) Lexical inferencing among Swedish- and Finnish-speaking primary-school pupils. Unpublished Masters thesis. Abo Akademi University: Ado (Turku), Finland.

Swain, M. and Lapkin, S. (1982) *Evaluating Bilingual Education: A Canadian Case Study.* Clevedon: Multilingual Matters.

Thomas, W., Collier, V. and Abbott, M. (1993) Academic achievement through Japanese, Spanish, or French: The first two years of partial immersion. *The Modern Language Journal* 77 (2), 171–9.

Tosho bunka-sha (ed.) (1992) *Zenkoku hyōjun shindanteki gakuryoku kensa* [National Norm-Referenced Diagnostic Academic Achievement Exam]. Tokyo: Tosho bunka-sha.

White, M. (1987) *The Japanese Educational Challenge.* Tokyo: Kodansha International.

Chapter 11

English/Japanese Codeswitching Among Students in an International High School

YURIKO KITE

Introduction

In so-called 'monolingual Japan' there is a growing number of bilingual/ multilingual communities (Maher & Yashiro, 1995). One such group consists of school children between kindergarten and high school age who are attending English-medium international schools in Japan. In 1994 it was estimated that there were about 8500 students in 27 such schools (Japan Council of International Schools, 1994) throughout the country. These K-12 schools were founded to provide an English language education for expatriates' dependents, such as children of businessmen, diplomats, missionaries and scholars, and some of these institutions have been in existence since as early as 1859 (Fujisawa, 1994). Originally the schools educated only a select group of expatriates, and Japanese nationals were not enrolled. Therefore, they were isolated in many respects until fairly recently.

However, in the past few decades the composition of the student body has changed (Willis, 1992). Due to the growing Japanese economy, the international schools expanded in size and began to open their doors to non-native English speaking students. School-age children of immigrants and long-term resident Koreans, Chinese, and Indians began to enroll in these schools, and although they are foreigners, most of these children were born and raised in Japan and are bi/multilingual in their home language, English and Japanese.

Furthermore, since the 1970s Japanese nationals have also begun to show interest in this type of school. Not only Japanese who had expatriate experience, but also parents with no exposure to Western education started to select international schools for their children. They were willing to do so even if they were taking a risk, since the international schools are not accredited as official schools by the Japanese Ministry of Education, and it is a violation of Japan's compulsory education laws for Japanese nationals to attend non-accredited schools. Nonetheless, according to a recent survey on the proportion of Japanese native speaking learners in these schools

(Japan Council of International Schools, 1994), roughly 30% of the total enrollment at the 27 international schools were Japanese nationals. Linguistically, it was estimated that approximately 38% of the students spoke Japanese as their first (L1) or dominant language.

This chapter will examine Japanese-English language alternation, or codeswitching, in a sample of bi/multilingual students attending an international school in Japan. Different types of codeswitching will be identified, and the situational factors which motivate the switch will be explored.

Codeswitching

Definitions

Codeswitching (CS) is defined as 'alternations of linguistic varieties within the same conversation' (Myers-Scotton, 1993b: 1). CS can be any alternation between language varieties, including a switch between a standard variety and non-standard variety within the same language, as well as switches between two distinct languages. CS has also been explained as:

> The process whereby bilingual or bidialectal speakers switch back and forth between one language or dialect and another within the same conversation. (Trudgill,1992: 16)

Two types of CS

CS can occur either inter- or intra-sententially. Inter-sentential CS refers to switches which occur between sentences, as in Example 1 below, where two students (represented by their initials, IER and LIM) enrolled in an English medium international school discussed cross-cultural issues as an assignment. In response to a specific question on how language barriers affect groups, one student's response was:

Example 1
(In this and all examples that follow, Japanese words are shown in italics and actual English words spoken are shown in boldface type. English equivalents of each Japanese word and explanations of Japanese auxiliary verbs and case markers are shown in the line below the Japanese words. For example, TOP indicates topic marker, ACC indicates accusative case marker, NOM indicates nominative case marker, COMP signifies verb compliment, STA stands for a verb showing a state, and POL indicates the polite form of a verb. In all cases, a complete translation into English is shown in brackets below the example, as it is here.)

IER: *kotoba no*   *chiga-tteru*   *hito*   *wa*   *gurūpu mo*
        language of   different-STA   person TOP   group also

        chigatte i-masu
        different STA-POL

**Because people will speak Japanese most of the time in
talking to people who speak English most of the time
because the words they use and even the way they talk is
different. And it doesn't go. You know.**

[People with different languages are in different groups.
Because people will speak Japanese most of the time in talking
to people who speak English most of the time because the
words they use and even the way they talk is different. And it
doesn't go. You know.]

On the other hand, CS can also occur within a sentence, in which case it is
referred to as intra-sentential CS. In Example 2 below, a continuation of
the above conversation, the same student begins to express to a second
student (LIM) how she copes with the variety of linguistic and cultural
backgrounds she encounters.

Example 2
IER: **Well,** *watashi*   *wa*   **variety**   *no* **culture** *to-ka*   *wo*
                I   TOP   of   such as   ACC

I like to learn.
[Well, as for me I like to learn a variety of culture and so on.]

LIM: Yeah

IER: **About variety** *no* **culture** *to-ka* **variety**   *no*   **language**
                              of   or   of

        you know. *Sore ga*   *ii*   *to*   *omoi-masu.*
                        This NOM   good   COMP   think-POL

**Like I like to know a bit of Spanish and then I like to know
stuff about um Arabic people or I like to learn about this
other religion other than my own ...**

[About variety of culture or variety of language, you know.
I think that this is good. Like I like to know a bit of Spanish and
then I like to know stuff about, um, Arabic people or I like to
learn about this other religion other than my own. ...]

In this example the speaker IER switches both inter-sententially and intra-
sententially. In the first line, *watashi wa* [as for me] functions as a topic
marking, which initiates her utterance in Japanese. She then switches and
inserts several English nouns as objects of the English verb phrase I *like to*

learn. In addition to these intra-sentential switches in the first turn, she continues in Japanese for a full sentence (*Sore ga ii to omoimasu* [I think this is good]) and then switches to full English sentences starting with *Like I like.*

Research Focus

This paper focuses on the alternation of two languages, Japanese and English, in the discourse of high school students ages 14 to 17 who are enrolled in one of the international schools in Japan. It explores the use of Japanese-English CS as part of the bi/multilingual international school students' language repertoire – a style of speech used for peer interactions. The first research focus is on the patterns of language use reported by these students on a questionnaire and in discussions. The second focus uses a survey interview to examine how CS is viewed both by the students and the faculty in the same speech community.

The following brief review presents the theoretical framework for this study, particularly two models which will be used to explain the determinants of the switch.

Theoretical Background

Codeswitching is reported to be a persistent phenomenon in numerous bilingual/multilingual communities around the world, although not all bilinguals codeswitch (McClure & McClure, 1988). The perspective taken in this paper is that CS is one code choice in a bilingual's linguistic repertoire (Gumperz, 1964), and it is assumed to occur within the norms and conventions of individual speech communities. However, it is necessary to understand who chooses to CS with whom, and in what settings in a bi/multilingual speech community. Also, it is necessary to determine where the choice of CS lies among the patterns of language usage. Two theoretical frameworks for discussing these issues will be presented and used in this preliminary investigation: the construct of Domain and the Markedness Model.

Domain

In accounting for a bilingual speaker's language choice, the framework of Domain (Fishman, 1965, 1972) is considered first. Fishman defines Domain as 'the major cluster of interaction situations that occur in particular multilingual settings' (1972: 19). In other words, it is the configuration of interlocutors, topic and setting that structures language choice; e.g. when a teacher and a student (interlocutors) discuss how to solve an algebra problem (topic) at school (setting). These three factors comprise the domain of education, which is different from the domains of home, friendship or employment. Therefore, the key element in Fishman's notion of Domain is the congruence among the three components of interlocutor, topic and setting.

The notion of Domain also involves the following assumptions. First, Fisherman suggests the allocation of a specific language variety to one domain. He (1972: 15) states:

> Proper usage dictates that only one of the theoretically co-available languages or varieties *will* be chosen by particular classes of *interlocutors* on particular kinds of occasions to discuss particular kinds of *topics*. (original emphasis)

Second, it is assumed that language choice is selected at the societal level. Fishman considers language choice to be:

> much more clear-cut, polarised in 'usual' situations governed entirely by sociolinguistic norms of communicative appropriateness than they are in 'unusual' situations which must be resolved by individual interpretation. (1972: 25)

Examples of domains presented by Fishman (1972), along with empirical examples from his questionnaire survey of Spanish/English bilingual high school students, are presented in Table 1.

Using the Domain framework, McGregor & Wei (1991) investigated language usage among Chinese students at the University of Newcastle upon Tyne. A survey of 117 students showed, among other things, the context of their CS usage. Here the researchers found that the use of CS was observed frequently in in-group interactions for both same- and mixed-gender interlocutors. However, CS was used regardless of whether the topics were personal, social or academic, or whether the setting was a student's apartment, a shop, or an academic gathering. No CS was reported for situations where the students talked with strangers, or with people of higher social status or in the presence of a third party. Less CS was reported when they talked with either older or younger Chinese people in town. Thus, this study suggested that Domain-based CS may

Table 1 Example of domains for Puerto Rican students

Domain	*Interlocutor*	*Place*	*Topic*
Family	Parent	Home	How to be a good son or daughter
Friendship	Friend	Beach	How to play a certain game
Religion	Priest	Church	How to be a good Christian
Education	Teacher	School	How to solve an algebra problem
Employment	Employer	Workplace	How to do your job more efficiently

(Adapted from Fishman 1972: 22.)

not always involve the interplay of the three components of interlocutor, setting and topic, but could be based on only one component – in this case, friends. Here 'friends' made up a domain for switching. This report will note a similar finding.

The Markedness Model

The more recent Markedness Model (Scotton, 1983; 1988, Myers-Scotton, 1993a, 1993c) is the second framework considered. The Markedness Model (MM) is based on two assumptions. First, this model suggests that it is the speaker who makes the language choice and not the norms of the society which determine which language will be used, as Fishman's analysis of Domain implies. According to this model, a speaker uses a code as a tool of negotiation in each interaction.

Second, a speaker is equipped with what is called a markedness metric and a sense of indexicality. The latter involves the idea that a code (speech variety) indexes or points out a social identity. A speaker, as a member of a speech community, knows the norms and can assess which code is marked (unusual) or unmarked (normal) for a particular kind of interaction, in order to index a rights and obligations set. Thus, the speaker assesses societal factors such as setting or topic as contributing to the relative markedness of a code choice. In other words, through exposure to language in use, a speaker understands what is the expected (unmarked) and unexpected (marked) language choice for a particular interaction. This knowledge of norms is developed from the speakers' experiences indicating how interaction with certain interlocutors or in a given setting will be interpreted. Taking these factors into account, the speaker then makes a choice of language usage, since s/he wishes to index the rights and obligations set which s/he prefers or thinks feasible to establish.

Why does a speaker select one language over the other? The MM explains that any language choice is a tool used to achieve a communicative goal in an interaction. CS is one of the choices a bilingual can make from his/her language repertoire. Writing on why people use CS, Myers-Scotton states (1993c: 478):

> Speakers use the possibility of making code choice to negotiate interpersonal relationships, and by extension to signal their perceptions or desires about group memberships.

When CS is a common code choice in a speech community, it often is characterised as including rapid switching without pauses. The MM identifies this type of CS as the Unmarked Choice (Unmarked CS) for a particular discourse context. Unmarked CS often occurs to signal dual identity in the two cultures indexed by use of the two languages (this is called 'cohort co-identity' in Myers-Scotton, Jake & Okasha, 1995). For example, Myers-Scotton (1993a, 1993c) reports that educated Kenyans codeswitch to negotiate two group identities: one, with the international language of English indicating education and authority, and the other with Swahili indexing solidarity with East Africans.

With regard to the speaker's psychological domain, the MM sets forth the following conditions in which unmarked CS occurs: (1) the two languages are positively evaluated for the speakers' in-group identities, and (2) the speakers are proficient in two languages. Further, the MM predicts that CS as an unmarked choice occurs in informal in-group interactions and that the interlocutors are likely to be peers.

Thus, the current study is an exploratory investigation to determine if unmarked CS exists among Japanese-English bilingual students in the educational community of their international school and, if so, what is its relationship to the various domains of interaction: school, home and the Japanese community at large.

Method

The first step in this study was to determine the patterns of language usage among high school students in an English-medium international school in Japan. To investigate this, a questionnaire was developed based on the Domain framework discussed above. To determine whether language use varied with the interlocutor, the students were asked, 'When you talk about life in school, in which language do you usually speak to the following people?' The students were asked to indicate the language used with their father, mother, brothers and sisters, close friends, friends, neighbours, and strangers. To determine whether language use varied with the setting, the students were asked, 'When you talk about life in school and you are in the following place, in which language do you usually speak?' The settings included were school, classroom, with friends, at home, and on the bus. The survey instrument also asked for information on CS according to topic: 'When you talk about the following topics with your friends at lunch or recess time, which language do you usually speak?' Five topics were presented: friends, family, personal matters, school work and current events.

The questionnaire was administered to a convenience sample of 99 high school students attending the same international school. In addition, audio-taped discussions by the students on their language use were arranged on two occasions and were analysed by the researcher.

The students were also asked to evaluate CS by writing a passage presenting their views about it. These passages were read and coded by three Japanese/English bilinguals. A five-point scale was used, 5 being most positive and 1 the most negative toward CS. The rating assigned by the coders, or the average if there was a lack of agreement, was assigned to each passage.

An additional questionnaire was administered to a convenience sample of 16 faculty members at the international school. These teachers were asked to answer questions after listening to a four and a half minute discussion of cross-cultural issues by two students in which substantial CS occurred. The teachers' L1 in all cases was English. This questionnaire and the teachers' responses are given in Appendix I and II.

Analysis of the Data

Logistic regression analysis was used to investigate if there was a significant correlation between occurrence of CS and the kind of interlocutors: friends (the categories of friends and close friends), home (the categories of father, mother and siblings), and community (the categories of neighbours and strangers). Calculation of the Z statistic was used to measure the effect of the variable of interlocutor type on the likelihood of CS taking place. Since each question represented repeated measurements for each subject (17 questions for 99 subjects) Generalised Estimating Equations (GEE) were used. This procedure was necessary because individuals appeared multiple times in the analysis, violating the assumption of independence necessary for standard Logistic Regression procedures. If the Z score was larger than (2) for any effect, the effect was significant at the 0.05 level, $p < 0.05$.

Results

Part of the students' discussion offers a good example of the patterns of language use investigated here. In the following example, two female students responded to the question, 'How is speaking Japanese evaluated by other students?' In the course of their discussion, they clearly mention the different domains and interlocutors with whom different languages are used.

Example 3

01　IKA:　Or it's something like this. For me, I have to speak Japanese at home. I have two brothers. They are in a Japanese school and can't speak English. Besides, with my grandmother, I have to speak Japanese, right? This kind of switch, I can't do it with a snap of the fingers. In the morning when I get up, I speak Japanese, then go to school and speak English there, then switch to Japanese again. I can't change it with a snap of the fingers. Then [unexpected language] 'pops in' and I can't do anything about it.

02　LAK:　For me, I have been in the same pattern for a long time. Japanese at home, with my mother a little (use English?), speak English with my big sister,* Japanese with my

Mom and Dad, with my mother and my father. When I go to school, I speak English, then little by little Japanese is creeping in. When I go home, I switch to Japanese.

03   IKA: Uhn.

04   LAK: Well, then if you have been familiar with, you get used to it.

05   IKA: That's right. It comes down to this. For those who speak both Japanese and English, that Japanese and English becomes one language.

06   LAK: Uhn.

07   IKA: What I mean is that it is not English and Japanese, English and Japanese becomes one.

08   LAK: Yeah, Japlish?

09   IKA: Yeah (laugh). Something like that.
          * The student's sister is also a student at the same international school.

According to the two students, language choice depends on the setting (home or school) and the interlocutors (brother, grandmother, sister, parent). This result is also apparent in the responses to the questionnaire, given in Table 2.

The general pattern is for English to be used with most interlocutors, in most settings and for most school-related topics. This is expected since English is the language of instruction at school, and English is the L1 for 38% of the students. Fourty-five percent of the students report using English with their siblings, 48% report using English with their fathers and 37% report using English with their mothers. However, Japanese is commonly used when the respondents are talking with neighbours (56%) or strangers (54%). This is not surprising, as the students live in Japan and speak Japanese in the larger community. It is also interesting that 56% of the students report the use of Japanese while riding the school bus. Perhaps the bus is seen as an extension of the Japanese community rather than as part of the school domain, where students report use of English only (29%) or a mixture of Japanese and English (35%), but zero use of Japanese only.

Regarding CS, the questionnaire results suggest that its use is positively related to the domain of friends. Forty-one percent of the students report that they use CS with close friends, and when indicating CS according to setting, 30% report that they codeswitch with friends in school — far higher proportions than for any other type of interlocutor. For topics, the highest proportion of CS (36%) is reported for discussing matters concerning their friends. In contrast, only a few students indicate that they used CS with neighbours, strangers, or on a bus — an anticipated finding given the fact the these settings are characterised by the use of the Japanese language exclusively. Therefore, it appears that the domain of friends motivates the choice of CS as the major communication strategy.

Table 2 Patterns of language use according to domain (interlocutor, setting and topic)

Interlocutor	E (%)	E/J (%)	E & J (%)	CS (%)	J/E (%)	J (%)	Total No. of Responses
Father	48	13	6	6	5	22	83
Mother	37	8	1	13	8	31	83
Siblings	45	18	7	13	4	8	74
Close Friends	25	21	4	41	6	3	96
Friends	21	22	17	30	7	3	96
Neighbours	19	6	5	5	7	56	95
Strangers	11	10	4	8	10	54	97
Setting	E	E/J	E & J	CS	J/E	J	
School	29	35	9	25	1	0	95
Classroom	49	37	5	8	1	0	98
Friends	19	29	11	32	6	2	96
Home	35	17	10	13	6	20	84
Bus	11	6	1	6	8	56	71
Topic	E	E/J	E & J	CS	J/E	J	
Friends	28	19	7	36	6	3	95
Family	33	22	6	25	9	5	93
Personal	36	17	8	27	8	3	95
School Work	46	22	10	19	3	0	96
Current Events	43	21	9	19	7	0	97

Key E = English only
E/J = English more often than Japanese
E, J = English and Japanese about equally
CS = Mixing of J and E
J/E = Japanese more often than English
J = Japanese only

Logistic regression analysis was used to determine whether there was a significant correlation between the effect of different variables on frequency of CS. The results of the test for the choice of CS and three kinds of interlocutors are shown in Table 3. These results suggest that CS is more likely to occur when the students are at their friends' house than at home, at school or on a bus, each with lesser chance of occurrence, respectively. Thus the choice of CS is more related to the domain of friends than to other domains.

The topic variable is not correlated with the occurrence of CS. As long as the students are with their friends, the topic of their conversation did not matter, although topics such as current events or schoolwork are less likely to be discussed using CS than personal matters or family affairs.

Table 3 Interlocutor and choice of CS

Interlocutors Compared	Z Score
Z (Friends vs. Community)	13.50*
Z (Friends vs. Home)	5.80*
Z (Community vs. Home)	−1.17
Source	**Beta**
Friends	1.50
Community	−0.52*

* Significant at 0.05, $p < 0.05$

As mentioned, this questionnaire is based on Fishman's notion of Domain. Fishman claims that Domain is a clustering of three components (interlocutors, setting and topic) which require one variety of language. Another assumption of Domain theory is that there is a one-to-one relationship between the domain and the language choice.

It is true that the domain of friends in this study indicates informal setting and in-group conversations. However, in contrast to choices such as only English, or only Japanese, CS centres around friends: talking with friends, talking about friends, and at friend's houses. This finding suggests that the notion of Domain proposed by Fishman (1972) may be too rigid in its prediction that language choice is determined by a cluster of factors. The results presented here suggest that CS during interactions with friends is not always related to a specific topic or setting. When the addressee is a friend, bilingual students tended to select CS as a code choice, regardless of topic or setting. Thus, similar to the findings of McGregor & Wei (1991), one factor − interlocutor (friends) − not a congruent set of factors, is the strongest predictor for the occurrence of CS among the subjects here.

The MM, a micro-level model, is better at accounting for why the bilingual students in this report choose to codeswitch. MM analysis suggests that for the high school students investigated:

(1) English is the unmarked choice for many of the students.
(2) CS is one of the unmarked choices for much of the students' interactions with friends.
(3) Under the MM, CS is used to signal dual identity in the two cultures indexed by the two languages, English and Japanese.

Evaluations of Codeswitching

Student evaluations

Codeswitching in general is evaluated negatively as a grammar-less mixture of two languages (Grosjean, 1982; Olshtain & Blum-Kulka, 1989) which is met with a lack of societal acceptance (Lüdi, 1986). It is suggested that CS indicates low status in education and personality (Bentahila, 1983), and that CS is disapproved of in teaching/learning contexts (Legenhausen, 1991).

Researchers also note that in many, if not all, bilingual/multilingual communities, the terms used to refer to CS are pejorative. The idea is that when language use is not pure, it is not good. For example, Jacobson (1982) talks about such terms as *Tex-Mex* or *Spanglish* used among Spanish and English bilinguals (also mentioned in Chana & Romaine, 1984, and Gumperz, 1982). Chana & Romaine report that in a Panjabi speaking community, CS is labeled as *tuti futi* (broken up), and they add that 'Panjabi do not consider it to be real or pure Panjabi' (1984). Willis (1992), who conducted an anthropological study in the same community as the current study, called CS *chanpon-go* (a hodgepodge language). In the interviews from this study, the students often referred to CS as *Japlish*, as is seen in Turn 8, Example 3 above.

However, the speakers' negative evaluation of CS seems to coexist with its robust use in almost all bilingual/multilingual communities around the world. This discrepancy between reported speaker attitudes towards CS and actual usage has been referred to as 'covert prestige' (Trudgill, 1974).

However, the notion of covert prestige in CS has not received much attention in the CS literature. There are only a few studies which are specifically concerned with the attitudes towards CS by members of the speech community. Two studies (Bentahila, 1983 and Gibbons, 1983, 1987) used matched-guise experiments (Lambert, Hodgson, Gardner & Fillenbaum, 1960) and one study (Hidalgo, 1986) was based on interviews. The Gibbons studies were conducted in Hong Kong with Chinese students who used Cantonese and English and the findings note the subjects' hostility towards CS since it was perceived to be arrogant. Bentahila's study on Moroccan Arabic/French CS also suggested that CS is negatively evaluated. For example, the informants indicate that codeswitchers were victims of colonisation (31.90%), were incompetent in both Arabic and French (29.78%), were showing off (23.40%) and so on. Hidalgo (1986) studied Spanish/English CS in Juarez, a Mexican town on the United States border. One interesting finding was that half of the informants claim that they do not understand Mexican Americans when they switch continuously, an unlikely event and one which signals negative perceptions of CS.

Can one then predict that CS will be negatively evaluated in a speech community where it is actively observed? In the speech community under consideration here, when students were asked if they used CS, 82% said that they did. The presence of a positive attitude towards CS by these bilingual students is shown by the results of the student essays (Table 4). Here, CS was generally evaluated favourably by the students, with 48% giving a positive response, 32% a neutral response and only 19% a negative response. Thus, the majority of students who used CS evaluated it positively.

Table 4 Evaluation of CS

5-Point Scale	*No. of Students*	*(%)*	*Meaning*
1	5	(5%)	most negative
2	14	(14%)	
3	32	(33%)	
4	39	(40%)	
5	8	(8%)	most positive
Total	98	(100%)	

Teacher evaluations of CS

The overall evaluations by the 16 teachers of CS are much more positive than anticipated (see Appendix I and II). All of the teachers noticed the use of CS on campus. When asked, 'Why do you think people mix the two languages?' the majority of them gave one or more of four reasons. One is Creative Repertoire, meaning that the students use CS to enhance their discourse in order to be more expressive. Two teachers who speak German or Russian as well as some Japanese suggested that CS was used as a communication-enhancing strategy (e.g. see Færch & Kasper, 1983) for purposes such as clarity, humour, and secrecy. In addition, most of the informant teachers seemed to recognise that some things are best described in one language rather than the other language, suggesting the relationship of CS to specific topics. Teachers also perceived that CS was used as a Compensatory Strategy (Færch & Kasper, 1983); that is, CS is used when students lack vocabulary in one language.

Only two teachers mentioned that CS is used to mark speakers' membership, to include members of a group or exclude outsiders, a usage called Membership Marking. They stated that, 'speakers seek identification with another member of a similar linguistic or ethic group.' These two teachers were the only ones who spoke three or more languages, and in their answers, they demonstrated their insights into language choice in a multilingual community. One of them even said that, 'CS is a useful skill for classroom management.'

The teachers were also asked to express their views on CS. (See Appendix II for some of their comments.) Unexpectedly, the teachers appeared to be quite open to the use of CS, contrasting with reports in the CS literature, where evaluation of CS is normally negative. [See the review in Chapter 12 for positive evaluations of classroom CS.] An interesting observation is that three teachers who viewed CS as a negative phenomenon actually codeswitched themselves with their French-speaking relatives. This mismatch of attitudes and behaviour suggests the concept of 'covert prestige' mentioned earlier. The teachers who evaluated

CS negatively listed many reasons why they felt CS was detrimental. One wonders how these negative views of a commonly used code are manifested in their classroom in response to the discourse of their bilingual students.

The findings of the teacher evaluations can be summarised as follows:

(1) The teachers' overall evaluation of CS seemed positive.
(2) The teachers identified four general purposes for the use CS by the students: as creative repertoire for enhancing communication, as a topic indicator, as a compensatory strategy, and for membership marking.
(3) There did not seem to be any relationship between the evaluation the teachers made and their own language capability (monolingual or bi/multilingual) or their personal use of CS.

Conclusions

The results of this limited exploratory study suggest that CS is the unmarked language choice for peer interactions in a variety of settings for these bilingual high school students in an international school in Japan. CS is an element of their linguistic repertoire and seems to be used to index their membership in their unique speech community. Heller (1995: 160) views CS as 'a means of drawing on symbolic resources and deploying them in order to gain or deny access to [bilinguals'] resources, symbolic or material'. Thus, it can be argued that bilinguals have the right to access CS as part of their resources in spite of notions that CS is a sign of a lack of linguistic competence. In the case of the students in this study, English is the language of instruction, but CS also has its place in the students' linguistic resources, and they have a right to use it. In considering those rights, future research needs to address the following question: Do students who codeswitch lack academic proficiency?

Two issues are involved here. One is the suggestion in both the literature and in some teachers' comments that CS is used primarily as a compensatory strategy and, thus, is bad. However, the limited results presented here seem to indicate a range of behaviour among the 99 students who participated in the discussion sessions. Some students codeswitched and some did not.

Furthermore, although there was no correlational analysis of the relationship between achievement and reports of CS — something which must be done in future research — anecdotal evidence suggests that there was no negative correlation between CS and academic performance. A number of students who participated in this study indicated that CS was their unmarked language choice in interaction with friends, yet these students were later enrolled in top-ranking universities in the US such as Harvard, Yale and Princeton.

The second issue concerns the students who truly use CS as a compensatory strategy, even when talking to a monolingual classroom teacher. Teachers have observed that some students are not able to sustain discourse in a single language, regardless of whether it is their L1 (Japanese) or L2 (English). The number of these students is not large, but their linguistic performance implies different motivation for language choice than discussed here. It is a challenge to identify the types of CS they produce, and a framework to test the syntax of CS is available (e.g. Myers-Scotton, 1993b) for future investigation.

A second question is whether teachers respond differently to code-switchers than to monolinguals in a classroom. Investigating how students actually use CS in a classroom and how teachers respond to it must be the focus of future research. CS in educational settings has received only limited attention. [See Chapter 12.] Classroom discourse studies with teachers who have negative views of CS and the use of Japanese in an English-language environment would be revealing.

Finally, although this paper is not intended as an argument in support of the use of CS in the classroom, it must be recalled there are more bi/multilinguals than monolinguals in the world. Japan has a reputation as a monolingual country, but it is actually not, and it must develop general tolerance for other language usage as a step towards the goal of globalisation. Thus, it is vital that further empirical studies of language alternation in Japanese contexts be undertaken.

APPENDIX I

Teacher Views on Why Students Codeswitch

Compensatory Strategy ($n = 11$)

- They feel insecure in a non-native language
- A lack of an adequate way to express themselves in one of their codes
- Easier way out

Creative Repertoire ($n = 14$)

- They sense the addressee is more fluent in another language
- To be more expressive (to express ideas which are not easily stated in one language)
- Topic becomes more personal
- To endear the speaker to others by using 'cute' Japanese or 'cool' English words
- For clarity, humour and secrecy

Membership Marking ($n = 2$)

- Speakers seek identification with another member of a similar linguistic or ethnic group
- There may be a social stigma (coolness) in mixing
- To include/exclude members of a group
- When they know that the teacher does not understand, they CS

APPENDIX II

Teachers' Views on CS
'What are your views on the mixing of English and Japanese?'

Detrimental/Disadvantageous

- From an academic standpoint, I believe that it hinders their English development.
- Academically it is not acceptable (if growth and accuracy are going to happen). It is not the way to properly develop a language.
- If a whole idea is given in one language, it is not good but perhaps acceptable in an informal setting. When a word or two are thrown in, they should be corrected. This form will eventually destroy both languages. There are times when using two languages is fine. If the person is going to learn from someone else by doing so.
- Obviously if you are trying to improve your English skills, it is best to use English as much as possible. If one cannot express oneself sufficiently, the mixing becomes a problem.
- Educationally, I should think that stressing one language is best. Speak English during my English class.
- Mixing may have disadvantages because it is a habit; when communicating to only English speaking people or only Japanese speakers it could be a problem.

No Problems, But ...

- I don't see any problems with mixing.
- It depends on one's expectations and priorities in using a language (i.e. total fluency).

Neutral

- They seem to communicate more effectively and comfortably with each other when they use two or three languages.
- I think it is natural for people to mix English and Japanese.

Useful Skill

- I think CS is a really useful skill for classroom management. My biggest difficulty is deciding when my students have stopped CS and have crossed into the realm of translation – possibly to the detriment of their language learning.

References

Bentahila, A. (1983) *Language Attitudes Among Arabic-French Bilinguals in Morocco*. Clevedon, UK: Multilingual Matters.

Chana, U. and Romaine, S. (1984) Evaluative reactions to Panjabi/English Code-switching. *Journal of Multilingual and Multicultural Development* 5 (6), 447–473.

Færch, C. and Kasper, G. (1983) Plans and strategies in foreign language communication. In C. Faerch and G. Kasper (eds) *Strategies in Interlanguage Communicator* (pp. 20–60). London: Longman.

Fishman, J. (1965) Who speaks what language to whom and when? *LA Linguistique* 2, 67–88.

Fishman, J. (1972) The relationship between micro- and macro-sociolinguistics in the study of who speaks what language to whom and when. In J.B. Pride and J. Holmes (eds) *Sociolinguistics* (pp. 15–32). Harmondsworth: Penguin Books.

Fujisawa K. (1994) *Kokusai gakkō no genjō to kadai* [International Schools and Their Issues]. In Nakanishi A. (ed.), *Kokusai rikai kyōiku ni okeru kokusai gakkō no kyōiku* [Education in International Schools for Global Understanding] (pp. 27–30). Tokyo: MT Publishers.

Gibbons, J. (1983) Attitudes towards languages and code-mixing in Hong Kong. *Journal of Multilingual and Multicultural Development* 4 (2), 129–47.

Gibbons, J. (1987) *Code-Mixing and Code Choice: A Hong Kong Case Study*. Clevedon: Multilingual Matters.

Grosjean, F. (1982) *Life With Two Languages*. Cambridge, MA: Harvard University Press.

Gumperz, J.J. (1964) Linguistic and social interaction in two communities: The ethnography of communication. *American Anthropologist* 66 (6), 137–154.

Gumperz, J.J. (1982) Conversational code-switching. In J.J. Gumperz (ed.) *Discourse Strategies* (pp. 59–99). Cambridge: Cambridge University Press.

Heller, M. (1995) Code-switching and the politics of language. In L. Milroy and P. Musken (eds) *One Speaker, Two Languages: Cross-Disciplinary Perspectives on Code-Switching* (pp. 158–74). Cambridge: Cambridge University Press.

Hidalgo, M. (1986) Language contact, language loyalty, and language prejudice on the Mexican border. *Language in Society* 15, 193–220.

Jacobson, R. (1982) The social implications of intra-sentential code-switching. In J. Amastae and L. Elias-Olivares (eds) *Spanish in the United States: Sociolinguistic Aspects* (pp. 182–208). Cambridge: Cambridge University Press.

Japan Council of International Schools. (1994) *Outline of International Schools in Japan*. Tokyo: Ministry of Education, Science and Culture, Japan.

Lambert, W.E., Hodgson, R.R., Gardner, R.C. and Fillenbaum, S. (1960) Evaluational reactions to spoken language. *Journal of Abnormal and Social Psychology* 60, 44–51.

Legenhausen, L. (1991) Code-switching in learners' discourse. *International Review of Applied Linguistics in Language Teaching* 29, 61–73.

Lüdi, G. (1986) Forms and functions of bilingual speech in pluricultural migrant communities in Switzerland. In J.A. Fishman (ed.) *The Fergusonian Impact* (pp. 217–236). Berlin: Mouton de Gruyter.

Maher, J. and Yashiro K. (1995) Multilingual Japan: An introduction. *Journal of Multilingual and Multicultural Development* 16 (1 and 2), 1–17.

McClure, E. and McClure, M. (1988) Macro- and micro-sociolinguistic dimensions of code-switching in Vingard (Romania). In M. Heller (ed.) *Code-Switching: Anthropological and Sociolinguistic Perspectives* (pp. 77–96). Berlin: Mouton de Gruyter.

McGregor, G. and Li W. (1991) Chinese or English? Language choice amongst Chinese students in Newcastle-upon-Tyne. *Journal of Multilingual and Multicultural Development* 12 (6), 493–510.

Myers-Scotton, C. (1983) The negotiation of identities in conversation: A theory of Marked-ness and code choice. *International Journal of the Sociology of Language* 44, 115–136.

Myers-Scotton, C. (1988) Codeswitching as indexical of social negotiation. In M. Heller (ed.) *Code-Switching: Anthropological and Sociolinguistic Perspectives* (pp. 151–186). Berlin: Mouton de Grunter.

Myers-Scotton, C. (1993a) Common and uncommon ground: Social and structural factors in codeswitching. *Language in Society* 22, 475–503.

Myers-Scotton, C. (1993b) *Duelling Languages: Grammatical Structure in Codeswitching*. Oxford: Oxford University Press.

Myers-Scotton, C. (1993c) *Social Motivations for Codeswitching: Evidence From Africa*. Oxford: Oxford University Press.

Myers-Scotton, C., Jake, J. and Okasha, M. (1995) Arabic constraints of codeswitching. Paper presented at the Arabic Linguistics Association Annual Convention.

Olshtain, E. and Blum-Kulka, S. (1989) Happy Hebrish: Mixing and switching in American-Israeli family interactions. In S. Gass, C. Madden, D. Preston and L. Selinker (eds) *Variation in Second Language Acquisition: Discourse and Pragmatics* (pp. 59–83). Clevedon: Multilingual Matters.

Trudgill, P. (1974) *The Social Differentiation of English in Norwich*. Cambridge: Cambridge University Press.

Trudgill, P. (1992) *Introducing Language and Society*. Middlesex, England: Penguin English.

Willis, D. (1992) Transnational culture and the role of language: An international school and its community. *The Journal of General Education* 41, 73–95.

Chapter 12

Codeswitching by Japan's Unrecognised Bilinguals: Japanese University Students' Use of Their Native Language as a Learning Strategy

SANDRA FOTOS

Introduction

The widely-held view of Japan as a monocultural, monolingual nation has been challenged recently by several books and theme issues of journals[1] which suggest that the country is actually neither. These works document and discuss ethnic pluralism and multilingualism ranging from the Ainu in Hokkaido to the Ryukyuan people in Okinawa. Aimed at destroying a similar myth, a recent article (Susser, 1998) challenged stereotypic assumptions held by many Western teachers of English as a Foreign Language (EFL) about the nature of English education in Japan and criticised their tendency to 'other' their students — a term used by Edward Said in expounding his concept of Orientalism[2] (1978/1994). Susser argues that a polarisation similar to that described by Said in his treatment of the Middle East can be seen in many Western teachers' reductive view of Japanese students, stereotyping them as inscrutable group members, hierarchically oriented, and quiet and shy in the classroom. Susser considers such generalisations to be unjustified and suggests that they obscure the fundamental nature of the language acquisition process.

Following the tradition of challenging received views, this report examines Japanese-English language alternation in a large but unacknowledged group of bilinguals, Japanese students of EFL, and asserts the benefits of native language (L1) use within the EFL classroom. Since it has been suggested that many teachers of English use considerably more Japanese than the target language during instruction (Kaneko, 1991; LoCastro, 1996), it might appear that use of the L1 is exactly what is *not* needed to promote second language acquisition (SLA) and an increased sense of membership in a multicultural society. Nonetheless, this report will suggest that foreign language classrooms can become linguistic microclimates which function as distinct speech communities within the native culture. Use of the students' L1 during study of their second language (L2) within this microclimate can enhance community membership, creating favourable affective conditions for learning, and can also serve as a strategy for increasing the salience of input from the target language. In particular, language alternation within the same utterance, or code-switching, can serve a dual function: promoting SLA through negotiation of meaning and focus on form, and fostering the students' sense of their bilingual identity.

Japanese EFL students as limited proficiency bilinguals

The great number of EFL students at the secondary and tertiary levels makes this pool of bilinguals the largest in Japan. However, due to often-expressed feelings of communicative inadequacy in English on the part of these students (Koike, 1985) and because of the erroneous concept that bilinguals must have equal proficiency in each language,[3] the essentially bilingual nature of Japanese students of English has been almost completely ignored – if not actively denied, as seen in the commonly-held view that 'Japanese cannot learn foreign languages easily.'

This paper argues for the recognition of the essentially bilingual nature of Japanese EFL students and recommends a movement away from Orientalist arguments about possible innate limitations of the English language learner in Japan. In support of this position, the inevitability of language alternation in bilingual classrooms will be shown through a review of research, and the positive results noted from reserving specific language codes for distinct functions will be introduced and discussed.

L1 use in the L2 classroom

Changing views in the ESL situation

In English as a Second Language (ESL) education in the US there has been a traditional distinction between bilingual education, where students study core subjects in their L1 and learn the L2 as a separate subject, and immersion programmes, where students are placed in an English-only environment, albeit 'sheltered' or simplified English. The theory behind the English-only programmes is that maximum exposure to the target language in communicative contexts will result in its successful acquisition. Consequently, use of the students' first language must be actively discouraged, as it does not contribute to the L2 acquisition process. However, in 1993 an influential paper (Auerbach, 1993) argued strongly for the use of the students' first language in ESL classrooms, thus creating a third instructional option. Auerbach suggested that permitting use of the students' first language during predominately English-based instruction would send a message that the first language was valuable and held a status equivalent to English. It would promote a humanistic classroom environment with affective and cognitive conditions which enhance the acquisition process, and it would assist in maintenance of the students' L1 in an English-speaking society.

Although language rights and bilingual instruction have long been issues in multilingual nations such as Canada (Heller, 1996) and other areas, particularly those with a colonial past (e.g. Akinnaso, 1994; Gfellar & Robinson, 1998; Phillipson & Skutnabb-Kangas, 1995), and articles in periodicals such as the *Journal of Multilingual and Multicultural Development* and *World Englishes* have addressed problems of mother tongue main-tenance and the status differentials inherent in language choice (e.g. see Garrett *et al.*, 1994), the emergence of this argument in the ESL situation was highly significant. Follow-up studies[4] have continued to emphasise the benefits of use of the primary language to mediate target language learning processes in regular ESL classes. At this point, it is necessary to examine research specifying the positive nature of such mediation.

The language classroom as a linguistic microclimate and a community of practice

Essential to a positive view of L1 use in the L2 classroom is the concept of the second/foreign language classroom as a cultural community. The applicability of cultural adaptation models to second/foreign language classrooms has been suggested for the past several decades (Damen, 1993), and such classrooms, particularly when staffed by native speakers of the target language who may not have the capability to 'native-ise' their discourse, have been compared to the ecological concept of a micro-environment (Conden, 1976; Gay, 1978). A microenvironment is a phys-ical entity within the larger environment, differing from it by a number of variables (Gay, 1978). When Japanese students enter the microenviron-ment of an EFL classroom staffed by a native-speaker teacher, the class-room has the potential to become a distinct subunit within the native culture (Fotos, 1984). This situation has been termed 'microcosm' and 'linguistic micro-climate' by researchers who have investigated issues of cross-cultural communication and cultural adaptation (Condon, 1976; Damen, 1993; Gay, 1978).

More recent investigations of the collabourative construction of meaning in the language classroom by researchers working within the sociocultural tradition of Vygotsky[5] conclude that such classrooms often become 'communities of practice' (Donato & McCormick, 1994: 454). This has been defined as 'a social area in which learning is constructed as gradually increasing participation in the values, beliefs and behaviours' (p. 454) [of the classroom] takes place. One study (Donato & McCormick,

1994) found that learners who became skilled in participating in inter-active classroom tasks were able to use this skill to develop a classroom community for practice of the target language. The community was created through collabourative activities such as group work, peer evaluation, and reviewing and discussing performed language tasks, and the authors suggested that the 'culture of the classroom' played an important role in fostering learning.

The key role of the teacher in creating motivation to learn and facili-tating the development of a 'community of practice' has been investigated widely (see Ellis, 1994 and Note 5); however discussion of this research is beyond the scope of the present report. One aspect is relevant, however, and that is the extent to which L1 use by L2 teachers has been found to contribute to a positive learning environment. The following section will examine research on teacher use of the students' native language during instruction in English, and determine its impact upon the learning situation.

Teacher codeswitching in L2 classrooms: Modality-splitting for motivation and learning enhancement

Defined as 'alternation of two languages within a single discourse, sen-tence or constituent' (Poplack, 1980: 158), codeswitching (CS) has been the subject of extensive sociolinguistic and syntactic research (see Nishimura, 1998, and Myers-Scotton, 1993a and b for overviews). The categories and functions of CS will be examined in a subsequent section.

Research on L1 use in the L2 classroom often appears in the form of studies of 'situational' or setting-specific codeswitching (Adendorff, 1993; Canagarajah, 1995; Martin, 1996; Merritt *et al.*, 1992; Mustafa & Al-Khatib, 1994; Pennington, 1995; Polio & Duff, 1994; Rose, 1997). Many studies of classroom CS report that teachers use the students' L1 during L2 instruc-tion as a means of facilitating understanding of difficult L2 material and as a way of motivating students. Research on Zulu-speaking teachers and students in English class (Adendorff, 1993) noted that frequent switches into Zulu assisted the students to comprehend English literary passages. The switches were L1 repetitions of the L2 material, paraphrases, reiterations of important L2 information or statements of encouragement. It was suggested that such L1 switches facilitated the lesson through clarification of L2 information and encouragement of the students, and served as a valuable resource for classroom management and the promo-tion of a community identity (p. 155). Similar findings were reported in a study of Arab-speaking professors teaching science in English (Mustafa & Al-Khatib, 1994). This study concluded that CS was a prominent feature of all lectures.

Research on teacher CS in India (Caragarajah, 1995) again found that the L1 was especially used for clarification of difficult L2 content and for classroom management. English, the L2, served as the formal code for instruction, whereas teacher use of the L1 expressed informality, group membership and a sense of classroom community. Such consistent division of language use according to purpose has been called 'modality splitting CS' (Merritt *et al.*, 1992: 109), and means that specific codes are reserved for distinct functions. Garrett *et al.* (1994) found that modality splitting CS characterised teacher talk in ESL classrooms in the UK and a similar form of modality splitting was found in American classrooms (Polio & Duff, 1994). However, although Polio & Duff (1994) found that classroom communities were promoted by CS, they suggested that teacher use of the L1 may have operated against learner development of negotiation of meaning skills in the target language.

A study of classroom CS in Kenya (Merritt *et al.*, 1992) found modality splitting CS among teachers and analysed the determinants of the switch. It was suggested that four main factors motivated CS: '(1) official school policy; (2) cognitive concerns; (3) classroom management concerns; and (4) values and attitudes about appropriate use of the languages in society at large' (p. 118).[6]

Similar findings were reported in a study of CS in Hong Kong high school English classes (Pennington, 1995). Here, CS served both compensatory and strategic purposes. Teacher use of the students' L1 compensated for lexical gaps, low motivation and discipline problems, and even for the lack of time to cover content. Strategically, English was used to emphasise the teacher's authority, to control classroom communication, to establish discipline, and to instruct. In contrast, the L1 was used in informal exchanges, to explain or discuss content presented in English, to de-emphasise the teacher's authority and to allow the students to control classroom communication. These findings reflect the results of earlier research on high school teachers' CS in Hong Kong (Lin, 1990) which also regarded modality splitting CS to be a significant classroom resource for management and instruction.

Although many studies indicate that teachers feel uneasy about using the L1, particularly when school policy stresses exclusive use of the target language (Adendorff, 1993; Auerbach, 1993; Caragarajah, 1995; Martin, 1996; Merritt *et al.*, 1992; Pennington, 1995), these same studies acknowledge the positive role of teacher CS in facilitating classroom management, assisting learner comprehension of target language material and promoting the sense of classroom community. These studies further suggest that L1 use by bilingual teachers and students in L2 classrooms is not only the norm, but is inevitable.

Learner codeswitching in L2 classroom: A community-building learning strategy

The research presented so far indicates generally positive results from L1 use in L2 classrooms by teachers. However, reports on CS among learners are not as numerous. Although Caragarajah's study (1995) suggested that learners used the L1 in a positive way for community building, there was no actual data showing this. On the other hand, an American study (Polio & Duff, 1994) suggested that teacher CS did not promote learner negotiation skills in the L2, but again, there was no analysis of learner data to determine whether this was, in fact, the case. The following section will therefore briefly review studies of learner CS to determine whether it functions positively in the classroom.

One study of L1 and L2 classroom language use (Tarone & Swain, 1995) examined language choice over time by students in L2 immersion programmes. Surprisingly, the researchers found that use of the L2 did not increase as the students gained L2 proficiency. Instead a type of modality splitting existed, where the students used the L1 as a peer register when chatting with each other and chose the L2 when engaged in academic discourse. The researchers presented a review of sociolinguistic features which indicated that such classes were true speech communities in the sociolinguistic sense, since a variety of speech styles and registers existed and were used for different purposes. The authors concluded, as did Pennington for Hong Kong classrooms (1995), that bilingual classrooms inevitably become diglossic. Similar to what was found for modality splitting CS by teachers in L2 classrooms in Africa and India, here English was the formal language, associated with power and prestige, and the L1 was reserved for affective or informal interaction, paraphrasing, supplying lexical items, explaining difficult L2 material, and classroom management. Thus, student CS was similar to teacher CS.

Research on Chinese university EFL learners in Hong Kong (Hird, 1996) examined CS during group performance of language tasks. Switching because of a lexical gap was not as frequent as might be expected. Instead, the author presented five more common reasons for CS: (1) to signal direct quotations, (2) to address someone particular in the group, (3) to emphasise by repetition, (4) to manage task performance, and (5) to distinguish 'between objectivity and subjectivity' (p. 167). Thus, CS during task performance was not motivated by low proficiency in the target language, but was rather used for management of conversation and as a strategy to deal with task material.

A study of Spanish-speaking English learner CS (Hancock, 1997) used Goffman's frame theory (1974) to interpret student CS during performance of an English role play. Again students used the L1 to frame their task utterances, manage task business, make requests for lexical items and to negotiate meaning. The L1 was also the unmarked code for peer discussion. The author concluded that when the L1 was selected for a particular communicative purpose, it did not impact negatively on L2 learning.

Thus, although studies of learner CS are not as common as research on teacher CS, the results indicate that learner CS is also characterised by modality splitting and has a positive impact on language learning and classroom community building. The next section will review studies of CS among Japanese EFL learners to determine whether similar findings have been reported.

Japanese EFL learner codeswitching

Japanese-English CS by Japanese university EFL students has been investigated by the present author (1995, 1996). The first study (Fotos, 1995) examined CS by Japanese university EFL students performing interactive tasks in the English classroom, and suggested that this group could be regarded as bilinguals, but with limited proficiency in their second language. This data was compared with Japanese-English balanced bilingual children's CS (Fotos, 1990) to see whether the switching by the limited-proficiency bilingual EFL students was less skillful than that by bilinguals who were equally fluent in both languages (Fotos, 1995). It was found that Japanese-English switching by the EFL students was grammatical and served the same type of discourse management functions in the conversation as the switching of the balanced bilinguals. A subsequent study (1996) of Japanese university EFL learners' CS indicated that it was important for making aspects of the target language salient and in creating a supportive classroom community. Part of these results will be presented in the next section.

A recent investigation of Japanese-English CS in adult EFL conversation classes (Ogane, 1997) noted extensive switches to the L1 for discourse items such as tags, fillers, and repair signals during L2 conversation. It was suggested that these switches were used to focus attention on important L2 utterances and to express personal feelings, thereby creating classroom solidarity. Quoting Nishimura (1995), who noted the 'reach out' function of such L1 switches to connect with particular linguistic audiences, Ogane (1997: 119) suggested that the students, 'may want or need to involve both the teacher and each other in communication or they may be appealing to their dual identities of L1 speaker and L2 learner.'

There have been several studies of Japanese-English CS by university EFL learners during the composition process. These report favourable results from L1 use while writing in the L2. Research examining essays which were written first in Japanese, then translated into English (Kobayashi & Rinnert, 1992) concluded that allowing initial composition in the L1 was beneficial to the final writing quality. A study of Japanese university ESL students' private-speech CS which was audio-recorded during the composing process (Hara, 1996) concluded that the learners actively used CS as a meta-strategy for organising and reflecting on their production of the L2, and as a prompt to elaborate or correct ideas. Switching from English into Japanese was positively related to writing quality and seemed to facilitate the flow of thought. These findings receive support by what is known about the nature of bilingual writing – that learners retrieve schemata and background knowledge in the language in which it was originally prcessed − and confirm suggestions in the literature that L1 use during the L2 writing process improves ideas, organisation and details, produces a greater variety of sentence structures and, allows the exploration of ideas more fully at the writer's intellectual and cognitive level (Hara, 1996: 3).

Summary of findings from classroom CS studies

Several trends are clear from this review of L1 CS during L2 instruction:

(1) CS is inevitable when students and their teachers share an L1.
(2) Teachers use the L1 for classroom management, for clarification of L2 material and for establishing an informal rapport with the students; the L2 is used for instruction, to emphasise teacher authority and to set a formal classroom tone.
(3) L1 CS is the unmarked choice for peer interaction among students who share an L1, and its use promotes a positive atmosphere and a sense of classroom community.
(4) Students also use the L1 to request lexical or content assistance with difficult aspects of the L2, and as a strategy for organising and managing L2 activities.
(5) When working on L2 activities such as composition, students use the L1 to facilitate the flow of ideas and maintain their focus on the L2 content and language.

Two general uses for classroom CS by learners emerge from this overview. First, CS is the language of peer discourse; its use promotes a classroom discourse community of the same type as noted in monolingual studies. Second, many learners seem to use aspects of CS as a learning strategy to control and manage their cognitive processes in dealing with the L2, and to enhance their focus on the L2 activity they are performing.

Research Focus

There has been extensive research on strategy use by second language learners (see Oxford, 1990), and the conclusion is that active use of learning strategies promotes language acquisition. However, this area has been approached only from the monolingual perspective. The use of CS as a possible learning strategy by bilinguals is an important topic for research and will be investigated here. This report examines CS during interactive L2 task performance by Japanese university EFL students. CS is analysed quantitatively in terms of the number and syntactic type of switches, and qualitatively in terms of the functions the switches performed in the discourse. The research focus of this report is whether Japanese EFL learners used classroom CS as a learning strategy to focus on L2 content.

Before introducing the study it is necessary to consider the roles of negotiated interaction, comprehensible input and comprehensible output in SLA to understand how CS might function as a learning strategy during task performance. There is a substantial body of research on the role of interaction in promoting SLA (see Ellis, 1994 and Robinson, 1996 for discussions), so only the most general points will be mentioned here as they apply to the current study.

The requirement for both comprehensible L2 input (target language use which is understandable) and comprehensible L2 output (opportunities for students to produce the target language themselves, notice their own language use, and receive feedback from others) in promoting SLA is now widely accepted. (See reviews in Braidi, 1995; Ellis, 1994; Fotos, 1998; Swain & Lapkin, 1995.) Grammar instruction by itself has been shown to be inadequate, since it mainly develops formal knowledge of L2 rules, not the ability to use the L2 successfully in meaning-focused communication. This is usually based on implicit knowledge, which is not directly developed through instruction.

Therefore, an interactional approach has been recommended by a number of researchers (see Swain and Lapkin, 1995) to provide the learners with opportunities for meaning-focused input and output in the target language. Often task-based, this approach requires the students to 'negotiate meaning' by asking and answering questions when L2 utterances are not understood or L2 instructional material is not clear. The many studies of negotiated interaction by L2 learners during task performance (reviewed in Braidi, 1995; Fotos, 1994; Ellis, 1994; Kowal & Swain, 1994; Swain & Lapkin, 1995) suggest that during the negotiation process:

> Learners focus on the meaning of individual words, phrases, or unanalysed chunks. Semantic transparency is also evident, because more self-repetitions and object identifications, which serve to make the input more transparent, are found ... Meaning is also monitored ... (Braidi, 1995: 153)

Codeswitching as a learning strategy

Although the exact nature of the relationships among input, output, and negotiation of meaning to ultimate levels of SLA has not been determined (see Note 7), it is generally thought that when L2 structures become salient to the learner, such awareness triggers a restructuring of the learner's internal linguistic system (Braidi, 1995; Ellis, 1994; Fotos, 1993; Robinson, 1996). Thus, learner attention to and awareness of specific L2 forms is a preliminary step to acquisition. Negotiating meaning by asking and answering questions assists the development of awareness of L2 forms, as does recognition of one's own linguistic inadequacies. 'Noticing the gap' (Kowal & Swain, 1994: 74) between what learners want to say in the L2 and what they are able to say has been suggested to be one requirement for successful SLA, and activities which promote such awareness are considered to be beneficial (Robinson, 1996; Swain & Lapkin, 1995).

From this interactionist perspective, CS which calls attention to L2 forms, emphasises their usage in meaning-focused interaction, and clarifies aspects of their structure through negotiation of meaning can be suggested to facilitate SLA. Use of CS to focus on the L2 and to call attention to usage patterns can therefore be regarded as a learning strategy which assists in triggering L2 acquisition.

The Study

Subjects and method

The subjects were 53 first-year Japanese university EFL students enrolled in the author's weekly 90-minute Oral English class. The data consisted of six and a half hours of audio-taped recordings of the students as they performed three interactive, problem-solving L2 tasks dealing with specific grammar points. (See Fotos, 1994 for details regarding task design and administration.) The three audio-recorded task performances took place during three-week intervals and the students worked in groups of three or four in separate rooms. The first task was on adverb placement and took nearly eight minutes to perform on average. The second task was on indirect object placement and took an average of 23 minutes, and the final task was on relative clause usage and took an average of nine minutes.

The second and third task were information-gap tasks where each student received information written on a task card which had to be shared with the rest of the group. Each card was different, and the students had to read their cards to the group and listen carefully to the sentences read by the other members. These sentences contained correct and incorrect usages of the grammar point they were studying and the students had to decide which were correct. The first and third tasks required the students to develop grammar rules based on the correct use of the grammar point. These activities promoted discussion on correct and incorrect usage of the grammar forms, discussion of grammar rule formation and also questions as to how to perform the tasks.

The audio-tapes were transcribed by a bilingual Japanese graduate student and analysed by the writer. As in the previous study (Fotos, 1995), codeswitching was defined as a change of language within the same utterance, and cases where students were asked a question in one language and replied in another were not counted in the present report. This largely eliminated requests in the L1 for lexical assistance with L2 terms.

Analysis of the data

There are two general approaches to the study of CS (see Nishimura, 1998 for an overview). The first is linguistic research on the syntactic nature of the switch, meaning the part of speech which is switched, and the type of constraints on switching which maintain grammaticality. In this study, switches were first analysed according to their syntactic nature, and adjusted one-way Chi-square procedures were used to test the significance of differences in frequency counts between Japanese and English utterances and among the different syntactic categories. The alpha level was $p < 0.05$. Preliminary results were reported in Fotos, 1995.

The sociolinguistic function of CS is also studied. Switching for the establishment and maintenance of social relationships in particular settings has been identified and is termed 'situational' CS (see Myers-Scotton, 1993a and Nishimura, 1998). A second type of CS investigates the function of the switch at the individual level as a personal communication strategy. Such 'conversational' codeswitching can perform a number of discourse functions.[8] A switch can be used to indicate a particular topic – for example, bilinguals have been found to discuss certain topics only in one language. Or the switch may signal that the topic is going to change (Nishimura, 1998). Switching can focus attention on key words (Auer, 1988) and can emphasise an idea by restatement in the second language. A confusing utterance can be clarified by switching it into the L1 and perhaps elabourating it with further explanation. Switches can be used to set off reported speech and codeswitched discourse markers can be used to attract and hold attention during speech in the other language (Koike, 1987). The use of CS discourse markers to 'frame' a situation was noted by Hancock (1997), and the present author found many examples of switches used to set off events in Japanese-English CS (1990, 1995). CS can also be used to distinguish between personal feelings and objective issues. Both the Hancock study (1997) of Spanish native speakers and the Hird study of Hong Kong Chinese (1996) noted this function, and Fotos (1990, 1995) and Ogane (1997) found this type of switching in Japanese-English CS as well.

Functional categories for conversational codeswitching

In this report, seven functional categories were used to analyse the conversational CS of the Japanese university EFL learners during interactive task performance. (Categories are from Auer, 1988; Goffman, 1974; Koike, 1987; McClure, 1977; Nishimura, 1995; and Poplack, 1980 and 1988.) The examples of each category given below for illustration are from the present study.

Two types of switching to emphasise the topic
Use of Japanese topic markers wa *and* ga *in English sentences.*
In the example below, the Japanese topic marker *wa* is used to emphasise that the topic is Task Sentence One.

Example 1
Sentence one *wa*, I think correct.

Nishimura (1998) found that this type of topic-nominating function was common in her data on Japanese-Canadian CS.

Switching to indicate task terms.
Other switches involve the insertion of English task terms into otherwise Japanese utterances, as in the following example.

> Example 2
> Task recording *haitteru* ?
> > [is (it) being recorded?]

Previously this author (Fotos, 1990) found that such topic-related switches were common among balanced bilingual children, who used English for school-related concepts and Japanese for reference to money.

Switching for emphasis

The emphatic function of switching is usually achieved by repetition of the same message in the other language, as in Example 3.

> Example 3
> *Tsugi wa*, next one ... is incorrect.
> [next + subject-bound topic marker *wa*]

Here, 'next' is repeated in the L2 for emphasis. The use of the Japanese topic marker *wa* also adds emphasis, suggesting that this item (the next one) is different from the previous one.

Switching for clarification

This type of switch may or may not involve repetition, but always includes an elabouration of previous information, as in Example 4.

> Example 4
> We will read the directions.   *Minna de yomu no? Hitori de yomu no?*
> > [Should we all read (them together) or just one of us read (them)?]

The English statement is elaborated by a switched clarification request as to how the reading should be done.

Switching to frame discourse and attract attention

This type of switching consists of short switches at the boundaries of discourse and is used to attract attention and to move the discourse forward (Koike, 1987; Nishimura, 1995). Nishimura (1998: 141–142) also refers to these switches as 'involvement intensifiers' which show the speaker's commitment to the conversation.

> Example 5
> *Ano*, between subject and verb?
> [uh, well]

Here, the L1 utterance focuses the listeners on the correct placement of an important grammatical form.

Switching to separate personal feelings from factual or objective material

In this type of switch, the L1 serves as the personal voice or 'private speech' in the Vygotskian sense (see Donato & McCormick, 1994 and Note 5), whereas the L2 is used for making objective statements. In Example 6, the student says in English (his L2) that he does not know whether the Task Sentence is correct or not, but comments very frankly in his L1 that he thinks it is a bad sentence.

Example 6
I don't know.   *Zettai kore mazui to omou yo!*
                 [I definitely think this is bad!]

Switching to indicate that a repair of the preceding utterance will be made

This type of switch occurs when the speaker notices a problem in the previous utterance and wishes to signal that s/he will correct it. In the author's data, the repaired portion was always a task-related utterance in the L2, whereas the repair signal was an emphatic negation in the L1.

Example 7
The verb 'report' is ... is *jeneiya!*   The verb 'report' does not have
                            [isn't!]
two object.

The student repairs his use of the incorrect English verb 'is' by signaling in the L1 that he has made a mistake. This switch is followed by a repeat using the correct L2 verb form.

Fillers

Fillers in the other language may be used to allow the speaker to gain time to think about what s/he will say next. Most of the fillers in the author's data occurred within English utterences, as in the example below.

Example 8
Name ... name ... ah ... *eto* ... I'm Sato.
                         [uhmmm]

Here use of an L1 filler gives the student time to think of the correct L2 form.

Inter-rater reliability

Reliability estimates for coding the switches into the seven conversational categories were obtained by having a second researcher independently code 100 switches into the categories presented above, then comparing this with the coding done by the author. The switches were randomly selected by reading the transcripts and writing down every third switch until a total of 100 was reached. The percent of agreement between the two coders was 75%. Researchers usually hope for inter-rater agreement percentages in the mid to high 80s, but for this type of qualitative analysis, it is difficult to determine what the motivation for a particular switch might be, so the figure of 75% was deemed acceptable. In cases where there was disagreement, the author examined the switch and its linguistic environment carefully to determine which coding was most representative of the probable reason. Although some switches could be coded into more than one category, only the first coding is reported here.

Results and Discussion

Syntactic analysis

A total of 359 switches was made, which is a rate of about one switch per minute (Fotos, 1995). As shown in Table 1, significantly more switches were made from English into Japanese (207 switches) than from Japanese into English (152 switches) (X^2_{crit} (1 df) = 3.85; χ^2_{obs} = 9.1008, $p < 0.05$). For single-item switches, the difference between Japanese and English switches was close to significant (X^2_{crit} (1 df) = 3.85; X^2_{obs} = 3.0806, $p > 0.05$) and for multi-item switches, significantly more switches were made into Japanese (X^2_{crit} (1 df) = 3.85; X^2_{obs} = , $p < 0.05$). These results suggest that the learners were speaking mainly English during their task performance, although no morpheme counts were made to determine whether English was the base or matrix language (Myers-Scotton, 1993b).

Single-item switches comprised 74% of the total number of switches. This high percent is in line with Nishimura's results for Japanese-English CS among Canadian Nisei and her survey of other codeswitching studies (Nishimura, 1995, 1998). However, only 40% of the single-item Japanese switches consisted of nouns and verbs, compared with 91% of the single-item English switches. The latter result is similar to what Nishimura found in her survey of other studies (1998): English nouns were always the most common switch, regardless of the data or the nature of the L1. This was somewhat surprising here because, given the difficult nature of the tasks, one would have expected more switches into the L1 due to lexical gaps in the students' L2 knowledge.

Whereas non-noun or verb switches in the category 'Other' made up only 9% of the English switches, they constituted nearly 60% of the single-item switches into Japanese. As in reports by Nishimura (1998) and Ogane (1997), these switches consisted of *wa/ga* topic markers, the possessive *no*, conjunctions such as *dakara* (so, then), attention-getters preceding English task sentences, such as *de, ano* or *ne* (well, uh), *ja* (well), or *ikuyo* (here I go), various exclamations and interjections such as *nanda!* (what!), *yoshi!* (good), and pronouns such as *kore* (this) and *dotchi* (which), as well as adjectives,

Table 1 Type and frequency of switched items

	Switches into Japanese	*Switches into English*	*Total*
Total	207*	152	359
Single Item **(76% of total)**	**153 (74%)**	**123 (81%)**	**276**
Nouns, etc. (36% of total)	21 (14%)	109 (88%)	130
Verbs (12% of total)	41 (27%)	3 (2%)	44
Other (28% of total)	91 (59%)	11** (9%)	102
Multi-Word **(23% of total)**	**54* (26%)**	**29 (19%)**	**83**
Dependent Clauses (3% of total)	9	3	12
Independent Clauses (1% of total)	3	2	5
Sentences (13% of total)	31	17	48
Phrases as Asides (3% of total)	11	0	11
Paraphrases (2% of total)	0	7	7

Table adapted from Fotos, 1995.
 * Differences between Japanese and English switches were significant at $p < 0.05$, using one-way Chi-square tests corrected for continuity.
** For English switches, this category refers to all single task words.

adverbs, fillers and tags. A special class of negation item such as *janakute* and *janai* (that's not it) said within or immediately following an English utterance served as a signal that repair of the previous utterance was about to take place. Since the students were nearly all male, their L1 language was masculine, as shown by the form of the short negation items.

Grammaticality

There is a pejorative designation in Japanese for mixing languages: *champon*, which means a noodle dish made with a crude mixture of ingredients. Similar to the findings of early studies on CS in Europe and the US which showed that CS was viewed very negatively, many people in Japan assume that CS must be random and meaningless. However, as was found in other studies of CS (Myers-Scotton, 1993b), the switches in this study were found to be nearly always grammatical. Nishimura's research (1998) on the syntax of intrasentential Japanese-English CS concluded that government-binding considerations based on the direction of the sentence head are responsible for switching constraints. English is a head-initial language whereas Japanese is head-final; when these directions are maintained within phrases, CS is grammatical, as in the example below.

Example 9
After verb and front *ni mo aruka?*
[in (the front of verbs) too?]

In the data of this study, there were only three utterances where English was in the final position and grammaticality was compromised because of the lack of a verb. These results suggest that although they had only limited proficiency in the target language, the bilingual Japanese EFL students were nonetheless grammatical codeswitchers (Fotos, 1995).

Switching as a learning strategy

The hundred randomly chosen switches used for the inter-rater reliability estimate will now be examined to determine the frequency of switches within the seven conversational CS categories and to identify their possible role in promoting language learning.

Two types of topic-related switches
Use of Japanese topic markers wa *and* ga *in otherwise English sentences.*
This type of switch signalled that the previous word was important and that the utterance which followed should be noted carefully. Ten percent of the 100 functional switches examined were in this category. These switches focused attention on both the preceding utterance and that which followed, as in the examples below.

Example 10
Correct *wa*, correct is 'indirect.'

Example 11
Rule One *ga*, not understand.

Switching to indicate task terms.
This was the second most frequent type of switch, with 22% of the switches falling in this category. These switches were always into English and reinforced the importance of the task content, as in Example 12.

Example 12
Direct *mo* indirect *mo dotchimo dekiru.*
[It can be both a direct (object) and an indirect (object)]

It can be suggested that such consistent use of the L2 may have contributed to the development of two types of target language knowledge schemata, explicit knowledge about grammatical rules and correct usage, and implicit knowledge about meaning-focused language use (see Note 7). The current view is that learners benefit from formal instruction on grammatical rules if the rules are simple, but need repeated exposure to meaning-focused input to trigger processing if the rules are complex (Robinson, 1996). When they performed the grammar tasks, the EFL learners in this study received both types of input: direct instruction on grammar rules and communicative exposure to the target form. Development of both types of knowledge was also promoted by consistent switching into the L2 for task information and terms.

Emphasis

Important L2 task information was often repeated in the L1 for emphasis, as in Example 13, so this type of switch appeared most frequently in the data, comprising 25% of the 100 switches.

Example 13
Place adverbs between noun and noun. *Meishi to meishi no aida.*
[Between noun and noun.]

As suggested by previous studies of teacher and learner CS, repeating key L2 information in the L1 is a common function of classroom codeswitching and has been widely suggested to facilitate the learning process. Hara (1996) especially notes this type of switch in her analysis of Japanese writers' private speech during English composition, and suggests that translation into the L1 confirms the meaning of the L2 and clarifies the students' thoughts. In this study such switches attracted the learner's attention to both the grammar rules and to communicative use of the target form.

Clarification

In this type of switch, more information is always provided after the switch than in the original utterance. Thus it functions to promote awareness of the L2 form and perhaps assists in the triggering process. Hara (1998) suggests that such switches from the L2 into the L1 permit Japanese writers to develop and elaborate their thoughts in the L1, thereby facilitating the addition of further information to the English text. She also notes that the process happens in reverse, with the initial utterance in Japanese serving as a rehearsal for the production of English. Both types of clarification were observed in this data, and examples are provided below. Clarification switches comprised eight percent of the 100 switches examined.

Example 14
How write? How? *Koko ni nante kaku? Nante hyōgen suru?*
                              [What should I write here? How do I express it?]

Example 15
Dō omou? What do you think second?
[What do you think?]

Switching to frame discourse and attract attention

The body of the students' task-related discourse tended to be in English, framed by short Japanese switches. These were usually the coordinating conjunction *dakara* (so, then) or *ja* or *ne* (well, then), as in the examples below.

Example 16
Ja! I read Number Three Sentence.
[Well then!]

Example 17
Dakara! 'asked' and 'suggested' is OK!
[So!]

A study by Flowerdew and Tuaroza, (1995) found that positive learning outcomes resulted from use of L2 discourse markers during L2 lectures. The discourse markers promoted learner attention to and retention of the lecture material. Although only eight percent of the 100 randomly selected switches were of this type, a full 59% of the single-item switches into Japanese were in this category, so the random sample may have under-represented the frequency of the switches in the data.

Switching to separate feelings from facts

This type of switch has been described in other studies of Asian bilinguals' task performance (Hara, 1996; Hird, 1996; Ogane, 1997). In the present study, it occurred when learners talked about their feelings in the L1 and used English for task-related utterances, as in Example 18. Fourteen percent of the 100 switches were of this type.

Example 18
We need three rules but *ikko mo wakarimasen.*
                              [I don't even know one (rule)]

In the present data, these switches often expressed the learners' frustration at not being able to say what they wanted in English or at their lack of knowledge of the L2 grammar rule. Such switches are very important because they indicate that the learners recognised the limitations of their own linguistic knowledge and output ability and were aware that they were unable to use the L2 as they desired. Such awareness is thought to facilitate the 'pushing' of learner output towards increasingly target-like use of the L2 (Braidi, 1995; Fotos, 1993; Kowal & Swain, 1994; Swain & Lapkin, 1995).[9]

Switching to signal repair

The students used this type of switch to take advantage of the impact value of a strong Japanese negation placed in the middle of an English utterance, as in Example 19.

> Example 19
> Direct object ... *chigau!* Indirect object
> > [Wrong!]

This highly marked usage attracted attention to the error and emphasised the repair which was to follow. By strongly focusing attention on the correct usage of the form, such switches would appear to promote learner awareness. Seven percent of the 100 switches were in this category.

Fillers

It has also been suggested that, in addition to social functions of identity promotion, switched fillers keep the flow of thoughts going and create time for the speaker's cognitive processing to take place (Myers-Scotton, 1993a; Hara, 1997). In this data, only 6% of the 100 switches were of this type, which may be an under-representation of their frequency. The following example illustrates the use of a lexically motivated switch followed by fillers used as a learning strategy to facilitate retrieval of the correct form from the student's memory.

> Example 20
> Adverbs may also occur ... verb *mae. Doshi no mae* ... Verb *no* front
> > [in front of.] [In front of the verb] [of]
> ... ah, ... before ... before *eh* ... *eh* ... before ... before verb.

After considerable self-negotiation, assisted by switching into the L1, the student produces the correct phrase. In this switch, the scaffolding effects of the L1 allow the learner to finally fill the lexical gap with the correct L2 form.

Summary

Studies of good language learners (see the review in Ellis, 1994: 546–550) have identified four characteristics of successful learning:

(1) Attention to language form.
(2) Use of meaning-focused communication.
(3) An active, involved approach where students manage their own learning process and set their own goals.
(4) A conscious awareness of the learning process which takes the form of making decisions about study habits and strategy use.

The Japanese EFL learners' CS appears to have been valuable in promoting all of these features. Use of CS discourse markers, *wa/ga* topic markers, topic-specific switches to indicate task terms, switched repetitions and clarifications of important grammatical information, and switches indicating that previously stated task material was incorrect and would be repaired, all contributed to a focus on the target form. In addition, switched fillers and self-corrections during meaning-focused speech in the L2 indicated that the learners were aware of their limits in the L2 and were managing its use. As mentioned above, such awareness has been suggested to 'push' the learners' subsequent output to higher levels of accuracy. As Swain and Lapkin conclude:

> It might be that producing language forces the learners to recognize what they do not know or know only partly. This may trigger an analysis of incoming data, that is, a syntactic analysis of input, or it may trigger an analysis of existing internal linguistic recourses, in order to fill the knowledge gap. (1995: 375)

In this study, CS appeared to function as a learning strategy to increase learner awareness of target L2 grammar forms and attract attention to their correct use.

Conclusion

In this report, the bilingual Japanese university EFL students have been seen to use the various emphatic, repair, and clarification functions of CS as a learning strategy to enhance important L2 input and to focus on and correct their own L2 output during group performance of interactive tasks. They also used switching to indicate that they recognised their own linguistic limitations. Such active strategy use has been found to facilitate processing of L2 input and to ultimately promote language acquisition (Oxford, 1990). It is interesting that this group of students made significant proficiency gains in use of the grammar structures which were the task contents (Fotos, 1994a), and perhaps CS was one means of producing the favourable learning outcome.

The results of this study have suggested that Japanese EFL learners are indeed bilingual and can use CS skillfully to dramatise their conversation, create a feeling of community with their fellow-students, and also to focus on aspects of the target language during group work in such a way as to encourage successful learning.

Acknowledgements

A version of this paper was presented in 1996 at the Annual Convention of the American Association of Applied Linguistics. Chicago, IL, March 24.

Notes

1. *Special issues of journals*: See the 1995 special issue of the *Journal of Multilingual and Multicultural Development* 16 (1 and 2) edited by John Maher and Yashiro Kyoko, the 1995 special issue of *Language, Culture and Curriculum* 8 (1) on Multilingualism and Language Learning, and the 1998 special issue of *Language, Culture and Curriculum* 11(1) edited by Michael Lessard-Clouston.
   Books: See D. Denoon, M. Hudson, G. McCormack and T. Morris-Suzuki (eds) (1996) *Multicultural Japan: Paleolithic to Postmodern*. Cambridge: Cambridge University Press; and M. Weiner (ed.) (1997) *Japan's Minorities: The Illusion of Homogeneity*. London: Routledge.
2. Said's concept of Orientalism (1978/1994) suggests that European analysis of the Arab world exaggerates differences and creates distinctions between the West and the East, rendering the latter unknowable and obscure in a pejorative fashion. 'Othering' is a philosophical term (Susser, 1998: 52) indexing the separate identity of the Other. It often leads to stereotyping and casts the Other in opposition to oneself. Susser suggests that Japanese learners must be viewed as individuals, not as monolithic representatives of 'The Japanese.'
3. For a discussion of what constitutes bilingualism and how it can be measured, see G. Valdes and R. Figueroa (1994). *Bilingualism and Testing: A Special Case of Bias*. Norwood, New Jersey: Ablex.
4. For more work in this direction, see Lucas and Katz (1994) and papers in the 1996 special issue of *TESOL Quarterly* 30 (3), on language planning and policy.
5. See the 1994 theme issue of *The Modern Language Journal*, 87, for additional classroom research in the Vygotskian tradition. Also see Schinke-Llano (1993).
6. For a discussion of language choice as a political strategy, see Myers-Scotton (1993a).
7. Explicit knowledge refers to conscious knowledge, or knowledge about something, whereas implicit knowledge refers to knowledge of how to do something and is often unconscious. The present report cannot take up the debate concerning these types of knowledge and the nature of the interface between them. The reader is referred to Anderson's thorough discussion (1995) of explicit and implicit knowledge and the closely related constructs of declarative and procedural knowledge. However, most SLA researchers agree that there are mechanisms to transform one form to the other and that formal instruction, exposure to meaning-focused language, and conscious awareness or attention to material which must be learned all have a part in the conversion process (Ellis, 1994; Robinson, 1996).
8. See Poplack, 1988 and Auer, 1988 for studies of the discourse-enhancing functions codeswitching can serve in a conversation.
9. Ellis (1994: 282) notes that although direct evidence for student output leading to SLA is lacking, research indicates that situations which force students to generate accurate target language are beneficial.

References

Adendorff, A. (1993) Code-switching amongst Zulu-speaking teachers and their pupils. *Language and Education* 7 (3), 141–162.

Akinnaso, F. N. (1994) Linguistic unification and language rights. *Applied Linguistics* 15 (2), 139–168.

Anderson, J. (1995) *Learning and Memory: An Integrated Approach*. New York: Wiley.

Auer, J. (1988) A conversational analytic approach to codeswitching and transfer. In M. Heller (ed.) *Codeswitching: Anthropological and Sociolinguistic Perspectives* (pp. 187–214). The Hague: Mouton de Gruyter.

Auerbach, E. (1993) Reexamining English only in the ESL classroom. *TESOL Quarterly* 27, 9–32.

Braidi, S. (1995) Reconsidering the role of interaction and input in second language acquisition. *Studies in Second Language Acquisition* 17, 141–175.

Canagarajah, A. (1995) Functions of codeswitching in ESL classrooms: Socializing bilingualism in Jaffna. *Journal of Multilingual and Multicultural Development* 6 (3), 173–195.

Damen, L. (1983) Reading, writing and culture shock. *Cross Currents* 10, 51–70.

Donato, R. and McCormick, D. (1994) A sociocultural perspective on language learning strategies: The role of mediation. *Modern Language Journal* 78, 453–464.

Flowerdew, J. and Tauroza, S. (1995) The effect of discourse markers on second language lecture comprehension. *Studies in Second Language Acquisition* 17, 435–458.

Fotos, S. (1984) The need for a cultural adaptation model in creating a humanistic EFL classroom. *Bulletin of the Foreign Language Center*, Tsukuba University, 147–163.

Fotos, S. (1990) Japanese-English codeswitching in bilingual children. *JALT Journal* 12, 75–98.

Fotos, S. (1993) Consciousness raising and noticing through focus on form: Grammar task performance versus formal instruction. *Applied Linguistics* 14, 385–407.

Fotos, S. (1994) Integrating grammar instruction and communicative language use through grammar consciousness-raising tasks. *TESOL Quarterly* 28, 323–351.

Fotos, S. (1995) Japanese-English conversational codeswitching in balanced and limited proficiency bilinguals. *Japan Journal of Multilingualism and Multiculturalism* 1 (1), 2–15.

Fotos, S. (1996, March) Language choice as strategy in an EFL classroom discourse community. Paper given at the Annual Convention of the American Association of Applied Linguistics. Chicago, IL.

Fotos, S. (1998) Shifting the focus from forms to form in the EFL classroom. *ELT Journal* 52 (4), 301–307.

Garrett, P., Griffiths, Y., James, C. and Scholfield, P. (1994) Use of the mother-tongue in second language classrooms: An experimental investigation of effects on the attitudes and writing performance of bilingual UK children. *Journal of Multilingual and Multicultural Development* 15 (5), 371–383.

Gay, G. (1978) Viewing the pluralistic classroom as a cultural microcosm. *Special Education, E.R.Q.* 2, 46–73.

Gfeller, E. and Robinson, C. (1998) Which language for teaching? The cultural message transmitted by the languages used in education. *Language and Education* 12 (1), 18–32.

Goffman, I. (1974) *Frame Analysis*. New York: Harper and Row.

Hancock, M. (1997) Behind classroom code switching: Layering and language choice in L2 learner interaction. *TESOL Quarterly* 31 (2), 217–235.

Hara Y. (1996) Codeswitching as a strategy in the process of second language writing: A preliminary report. *Japan Journal of Multilingualism and Multiculturalism* 2 (1), 1–19.

Heller, M. (1996) Legitimate language in a multilingual school. *Linguistics and Education* 8, 139–157.

Hird, B. (1996) The incomparable objectives of group work in FL learning: A study of Chinese-English codeswitching. *Language, Culture and Curriculum* 9 (2), 163–175.

Kaneko T. (1991) The role of the first language in the foreign language classroom. Unpublished doctoral dissertation, Temple University Japan, Tokyo.

Kobayashi H. and Rinnert, C. (1992) Effects of first language on second language writing: Translation versus direct composition. *Language Learning* 42, 183–215.

Koike, D. (1987) Code switching in the bilingual Chicano narrative. *Hispania* 70, 148–154.

Koike I. (1985) *General Survey of English Language Teaching at Colleges and Universities in Japan — Students' View*. Tokyo: JACET.

Kowal, M. and Swain, M. (1994) Using collabourative language production tasks to promote students' language awareness. *Language Awareness* 3 (2), 73–94.

Lin A. (1990) *Teaching in Two Tongues: Language Alternation in Foreign Language Classrooms*. City Polytechnic of Hong Kong, Department of English, Research Report 3. Hong Kong: City Polytechnic of Hong Kong.

LoCastro, V. (1996) English language education in Japan. In. H. Coleman (ed.) *Society and the Language Classroom* (pp. 40–58). Cambridge: Cambridge University Press.

Lucas, T. and Katz, A. (1994) Reframing the debate: The role of native languages in English-only programmes for language minority students. *TESOL Quarterly* 28 (3), 537–561.

Martin, P. (1996) Codeswitching in the primary classroom: One response to the planned and unplanned language environment in Brunei. *Journal of Multilingual and Multicultural Development* 17 (2–4), 128–144.

McClure, E. (1977) Aspects of code-switching in the discourse of bilingual Mexican-Americans. In R. Duran (ed.) *Latino Language and Community Behavior* (pp. 69–94). Norwood, NJ: Ablex.

Merritt, M., Cleghorn, A., Abagi, J. and Bunyi, G. (1992) Socializing multilingualism: Determinants of codeswitching in Kenyan primary classrooms. *Journal of Multilingual and Multicultural Development* 13 (1 and 2), 103–121.

Mustafa, Z. and Al-Khatib, M. (1994) Code-mixing of Arabic and English in teaching science. *World Englishes* 13 (2), 215–224.

Myers-Scotton, C. (1993a) *Social Motivations for Codeswitching: Evidence from Africa*. Oxford: Oxford University Press.

Myers-Scotton, C. (1993b) *Duelling Languages: Grammatical Structure in Codeswitching*. Oxford: Clarendon Press.

Nishimura M. (1995) A functional analysis of Japanese/English code-switching. *Journal of Pragmatics* 23, 157–181.

Nishimura, M. (1998) *Japanese/English Codeswitching: Syntax and Pragmatics*. New York: Peter Lang.

Ogane, E. (1997) Codeswitching in EFL learner discourse. *JALT Journal* 19 (1), 106–122.

Oxford, R. (1990) *Language Learning Strategies: What Every Teacher Should Know*. Boston, MA: Heinle and Heinle.

Pennington, M. (1995) Pattern and variation in use of two languages in the Hong Kong secondary English class. *RELC Journal* 26 (2), 80–105.

Phillipson, R. and Skutnabb-Kangas, T. (1995) Linguistic rights and wrongs. *Applied Linguistics* 16 (4), 483–504.

Polio, C. and Duff, P. (1994) Teachers' language use in university foreign language classrooms: A qualitative analysis of English and target language alternation. *Modern Language Journal* 78, 313–326.

Poplack, S. (1980) Sometimes I'll start a sentence in English *y termino en Espanol*: Toward a typology of code-switching. *Linguistics* 18, 581–618.

Poplack, S. (1988) Contrasting patterns of codeswitching in two communities. In M. Heller (ed.) *Codeswitching: Anthropological and Sociolinguistic Perspectives* (pp. 215–244). Amsterdam: Mouton de Gruyter.

Robinson, P. (1996) Learning simple and complex second language rules under implicit, incidental, rule-search and instructed conditions. *Studies in Second Language Acquisition* 18, 27–68.

Rose, K. (1997) Pragmatics in teacher education for nonnative-speaking teachers: A consciousness-raising approach. *Language, Culture and Curriculum* 10 (2), 125–138.

Said, E. (1978/1994) *Orientalism*. New York: Vintage Books.

Schinke-Llano, L. (1996) On the value of a Vygotskian framework for SLA theory and research. *Language Learning* 43 (1), 121–129.

Susser, B. (1998) EFL's othering of Japan: Orientalism in English language teaching. *JALT Journal* 20 (1), 49–82.

Swain, M. and Lapkin, S. (1995) Problems in output and the cognitive processes they generate: A step towards second language learning. *Applied Linguistics* 16, 371–391.

Tarone, E. and Swain, M. (1995) A sociolinguistic perspective on second language use in immersion classrooms. *Modern Language Journal* 79 (2), 166–178.

Chapter 13

Language Attrition in Contexts of Japanese Bilingualism

LYNNE HANSEN

Introduction

Language attrition is part and parcel of bilingualism. Defined as 'the loss of any language or any portion of language by an individual or a speech community' (Lambert and Freed, 1982: 1), it occurs in every corner of the world. Not only do all of us as individuals lose parts of the languages we know, but we live at a time when a large proportion of the languages spoken on earth appear to be destined for imminent extinction (Harmon, 1995; Hale, 1991). The ubiquitous scenario we see played out in settings from pole to pole is that as a language is forgotten by an individual or a society, it is replaced by another. That is, the disappearing language does not simply vanish, leaving a linguistic vacuum, but rather, the functions it previously filled are taken over by a different language. Thus, bilingualism is inextricably associated with natural language loss (as opposed to pathological loss which is not treated in this paper) and, in a sense, when we describe language attrition we are describing bilingualism.

Only recently, however, has this aspect of bilingualism received much scholarly attention. During the past three decades the efforts of researchers in several disciplines have converged in a new area of language study. The facts dealt with are relevant to the perspectives of these various fields because they relate not only to what in a language is lost (the focus of linguists) but, in addition, to how it is lost (the focus of psycholinguists and neurolinguists) and to why the loss occurs (the focus of sociolinguists, sociologists and anthropologists).

A succession of edited volumes has marked the development of language attrition as a field of study. The first of these included papers from a convention on language loss convened at the University of Pennsylvania in 1980 which laid the groundwork for the field (Lambert & Freed, 1982). The second presented reports from a conference in 1986 in the Netherlands, including investigations done in Dutch, Swedish, British and Israeli contexts (Weltens *et al.*, 1986). In the late 80s three journals devoted entire issues to the theme of language attrition: *Applied Psycholinguistics* in 1986, *ITL Review of Applied Linguistics* in 1988, and *Studies in Second*

Language Acquisition in 1989. The earliest volume to focus on first language attrition appeared in 1991 (Seliger & Vago, 1991), while a collection of papers on second language attrition in Japanese contexts appeared in 1999 (Hansen, 1999).

The aim of the present chapter is to put the study of language loss in Japanese bilingualism into its historical and international contexts, and then to highlight the rich potential of Japanese settings as research sites for the future investigation of language attrition. In so doing we first review the literature in the area of mother tongue attrition, and secondly the work that examines second language attrition. We then narrow the focus to Japanese bilingualism. Within a typology of attrition categories, we highlight previous work on language maintenance and loss, and suggest applications of this research in Japanese contexts.

First Language Attrition

Two separate strands of research have contributed to progress in our understanding of mother tongue loss. The dominant one, a sociolinguistic perspective, emphasises shifting patterns of general language choice; the second, a linguistic perspective, focuses on the language of individual speakers of varying degrees of competence in an attriting language.

In the sociolinguistic approach researchers have looked at language maintenance and shift across generations. As one might expect, language shift is generally in the direction of the language of the most powerful group. The typical pattern is for an initial switch to occur, during which the dominant language begins to be used in settings that had been previously reserved for the language of lesser power. As the dominant language gradually takes over, the attriting language suffers structural loss. Transmission to the next generation, to the extent that it occurs, is in a reduced form. The nontransmission of the mother tongue, an increasingly frequent outcome around the world, is referred to as language death. Because of the ongoing spread of a few dominant languages, smaller languages are dying out at a speed that has no historical precedent. In fact, if the present trend continues, as many as 90% of the world's 6000 languages will die out during the next century (Diamond, 1993; Krauss, 1991; Wheeler, 1994).

The pattern of language shift outlined above is seen currently among indigenous minorities in virtually every part of the world: in North America (Hill, 1993), Australia (Fesi, 1987; Schmidt, 1985; McConvell, 1988), Papua New Guinea (Hooley, 1987; Kulick, 1992), and many other areas. A similar phenomenon also occurs with nonindigenous minorities − immigrant groups − whose original L1 diminishes in function and is often replaced by the language of their new homeland within two or three generations. Examples of this phenomenon are also widespread: in North America (Fenyesi, 1995; Levine, 1995), Australia (Clyne, 1991;

Pauwels, 1986, 1994; Waas, 1996), Europe (Py, 1986; Schaufeli, 1995), Israel (Olshtain & Barzilay, 1991, 1994), and elsewhere.

Much of the research on L1 loss in L2 settings involves a search for the set of conditions that cause language shift. Macrosociological characteristics of ethnic groups in contact situations are compared in order to find the cluster of factors that determine either language maintenance or loss (e.g. Hernandez Chavez *et al.*, 1995; Kloss, 1966). Numerous features have thus been considered: social class, economic status, educational level, number of speakers in relation to other language groups, religion, extent of exogamous marriage, government policy toward language, and education of minorities. In the scores of studies examining such factors to date, there has been a confounding lack of success in locating some unique set of social conditions which can reliably be identified as causal in language shift.

Although almost none of the external factors that have been investigated is, on its own, a reliable predictor of the outcome of any particular situation of language contact, there are a few common elements in all of them. One of these, of course, is bilingualism; another, codeswitching, is seen in the language use of individual speakers. Defined as 'the juxtaposition within the same speech exchange of passages of speech belonging to two different grammatical systems or subsystems' (Gumperz, 1982: 59), codeswitching has been identified in some bilingual situations as a symptom of the progressive advance of language shift, e.g. Gal's (1979) report on a shift to German in a village on the Austrian/Hungarian border.

The lack of predictive or explanatory power in macrosociological variables has led to a greater ethnographic orientation in recent research. From the census data or surveys of large populations in earlier work, research on language shift has increasingly moved to the intensive analysis of a single limited community, and the language use of its members (Kulick, 1992; Rhydwen, 1995; Schmidt, 1985). Such a dichotomy of approaches is seen in Neustupny's (1994) two-way classification: (1) the community language approach, which places emphasis on what happens to the language at the macrolevel, and (2) the contact situation approach, which concerns itself primarily with interaction between community members.

In recent L1 investigations (Seliger & Vago, 1991) with a shift in primary focus to linguistic aspects of attrition, two main forces are seen influencing the linguistic forms of attriting grammars: (1) internally induced changes, in which the modification of linguistic forms is either related to features in the particular grammar of the L1 itself, or is motivated by universal principles of language, and (2) externally induced changes – influences on the L1 from structures in the attriters' L2. Second language influence would include, for example, rule generalisation in syntax, meaning extension and loan translation in semantics, and intermingling of L2 lexical items, phrases, and grammatical categories within L1 utterances. Such language mixing – described in the literature on bilingualism under such headings as code-mixing and codeswitching – is found in both native language and second language attrition.

Second Language Attrition

In this section we will review variables and processes that have come to the fore in the study of second language attrition over the past two decades.

Attrition thresholds: 'The more you know, the less you lose'

'The higher the degree of attainment, the lower the degree of attrition,' was the conclusion reached by Vechter, Lapkin & Argue (1990) in a review of the L2 attrition literature. Similarly Bahrick (1984) and Hansen (1996) state that high levels of proficiency predict better survival of skills over time. Especially receptive skills such as vocabulary recognition and reading comprehension show high correlation between advanced learners and second/foreign language maintenance (Bahrick, 1984; Cohen, 1989; Olshtain, 1989).

The idea of thresholds in attrition, where learners would 'become immune to interference or decay' (Neisser, 1984: 33), finds support in the research. Bahrick (1984) presents evidence that there is an initial decline followed by a plateau of retention. Ishiguro (1994) posits two plateaus in language attrition: an initial one for passive/listening skills and a second for productive/speaking skills. The claim is that when these points have been reached, ability levels can be maintained even when input to the attriting language is drastically reduced.

For advanced second language speakers as well as mature native speakers, an initial period has been observed during which little attrition is observed despite language disuse. Residual learning or improvement of second language skills has even been reported in some cases (Scherer, 1957; Cohen, 1975; Weltens and Cohen, 1989; Hansen-Strain, 1992).

We think we lose more than we actually do

Self assessments of language loss have been widely used in language attrition research. Can-do scales, patterned after Clark (1981) and Gardner, Lalonde and MacPherson (1985), have contributed to the instrumentation for data elicitation in studies of language loss conducted by Weltens (1989), de Bot & Lintsen (1989), Waas (1996), Hansen & Newbold (1997), Hansen & Chantrill (1999) and Hansen & Shewell (1999). However, self assessments of language loss generally exceed test-measured results, although they do correlate highly with non-use (Clark & Jorden, 1984; Bahrick, 1984; Hansen-Strain, 1993; Weltens, 1988).

Lack of language use appears to generate a lack of confidence that possibly magnifies self assessments of loss. For example, after a summer vacation, high school learners of Japanese in Hawaii reported significant loss of their L2, while no loss was found in a comparison of their L2 morphology before and after the break in instruction (Hansen-Strain, 1993). Weltens' (1989) young adult subjects believed that their proficiency in French had deteriorated dramatically, while their test data showed hardly any signs of attrition. DeBot & Weltens (1995: 157) suggest that the discrepancy between (high) test results and (low) self assessments may be due to attriters' awareness 'that their retrieval is slowed down when they are forced to come up with the right word in time, and so they (rightly) say that they have experienced language attrition.'

Lack of use as a key variable in attrition

Considerations of language use and exposure after the learner has been effectively separated from the language environment have emerged as important factors. Actual use relates to maintenance more than exposure. Through self-report data, Clark & Jorden's (1984) study showed that attriters' speaking and listening proficiencies were directly related to their degree of current use of Japanese (their L2). Bahrick (1984) demonstrated that lack of target language exposure and use affected recall vocabulary more than recognition vocabulary. In a longitudinal study comparing groups that varied in L2 use, Weltens (1989) found that lack of use of the L2 led to lexical loss. That vocabulary use is related to recall was demonstrated by Cohen (1986, 1989), Weltens (1989) and Weltens & Grendel (1993).

However, Gardner & Lysynchuk (1990) stand virtually alone in maintaining that L2 use during the period from the end of L2 training to the time of L2 retention testing is essential for retention. In fact, a number of studies have shown that high frequency words and phrases, including idiomatic expressions and phrases that carry a high pragmatic load, are resistant to attrition (Cohen, 1986, 1989; Olshtain, 1986, 1989; Olshtain & Barzilay, 1991; Hayashi, 1999; Reetz-Kurashige, 1999).

Attitudes and motivation in language retention

In Canadian bilingualism research, social factors, particularly attitudinal and motivational variables have been integral parts of language acquisition and retention research. From the beginnings of the field in 1980, Gardner argued that attitudinal/motivational factors are related to retention since they influence the degree to which individuals seek out opportunities to use a language, as shown in Edwards' (1976, 1977) work on second language retention among Canadian government workers in Ottawa (Gardner, 1982).

The effects of attitudes, motivation and language use on L2 attrition were subsequently studied in Canadian students who had taken intensive French courses in Quebec (Gardner *et al.*, 1985). Less favourable attitudes and lower language use among the subjects correlated with the attrition of speaking and understanding, but not with reading. Gardner, Lalonde, Moorcroft and Evers (1987) examined the role in L2 attrition of motivation and use of the language by high school students of French over the summer vacation. They claim that language attitudes cause motivation and motivation has an effect on L2 exposure after the acquisition period which, in turn, has an effect on language retention.

The age advantage in childhood

The importance of age as a variable in child language attrition has been substantiated in recent empirical work. In case studies of siblings who experienced similar linguistic environments, Cohen (1989), Hansen (1980), Hansen-Strain (1990) and Yukawa (1997b), found that the older siblings retained their language skills better than the younger (losing L2 Portuguese, L2 Hindi-Urdu, L2 Japanese, and L1 Japanese respectively). A single exception, Kuhberg's (1992) report of the more rapid L2 German attrition of a Turkish nine year old than a seven year old, is explained by the researcher as being due to the 'stronger pressure for the older child to give absolute priority to Turkish' (Kuhberg 1992: 145). Group studies of child language attrition have also shown that, in general, 'older is better' for language retention (Olshtain, 1986, 1989; Yoshida & Arai, 1990).

Age eight to nine emerges as a decisive time when, if youngsters have reached a certain level of language stability in a second language, retention is more likely than attrition (Berman & Olshtain, 1983; Olshtain, 1986, 1989; Cohen, 1989; Yoshida, 1989; Yoshida and Arai, 1990; Yukawa, 1997a, 1997b; Reetz-Kurashige, 1999). A combination of maturity and literacy has been shown to correlate with the retention of language skills (Cohen, 1989; Dutkova, 1997; Hansen-Strain, 1990; Olshtain, 1986, 1989). Both lexical retrieval and compensatory strategies vary between younger (under eight years old) and older (8 to 12 year-old) children according to Olshtain (1986), Yoshida (1989), Tomiyama (1999) and Yoshitomi (1999).

Yoshitomi (1992: 300) concluded from a review of studies in psycholinguistics and neuroscience that there appears to be 'a common critical period for language development (especially productive syntactic skills) generally occurring by the end of the first decade of life'. Since children's neural networks and their cognitive abilities are continually developing, lack of maturity of both L1 and L2 language skills can probably account for the contrast between attrition rates of younger and older children.

In the language acquisition literature, Long (1990) argues convincingly for the idea of multiple sensitive periods which may have applications to attrition as well. Up to age five is posited as the sensitive period for native-like phonology acquisition; age fifteen for native-like acquisition of syntax. Less is known of age constraints on the acquisition or attrition of vocabulary and pragmatic knowledge, but it may well be that sensitive periods for them extend into adulthood.

The regression hypothesis: First learned, last forgotten

Dating back to Jakobson (1941), the regression hypothesis describes the path of language attrition as the mirror opposite of acquisition. The fact that so few studies have tested this idea over the subsequent six decades has surely been influenced by the inherent difficulties involved. Documenting that the stages of development are reversed in attrition is time consuming, and a universal or predictable development ladder has been established for only a limited number of linguistic structures. However, Berman & Olshtain (1983), Cohen (1975), Hansen (1980, 1999a), Hayashi (1999), and Olshtain (1986) have demonstrated through testing that the reverse order hypothesis holds. In a longitudinal study of the acquisition and attrition of negation in Hindi-Urdu by American children, Hansen (1980: 169) concludes that 'the forgetting data from both children could be interpreted as a recapitulation in reverse of the acquisitional sequence.' Similarly, Kuhberg (1992: 138) in his study of Turkish children's attrition of L2 German concluded that 'attrition was largely a mirror image of acquisition.'

Nonetheless, a universal or predictable development ladder has been established for only a limited number of linguistic structures. Yoshitomi (1992: 295) concluded that 'the generalisability of reverse order at the intra-skills level is limited, ... because the hypothesis has been tested only on a limited number of specific syntactic structures.' (For a fuller discussion, see de Bot & Weltens, 1991).

Processes in attrition: L1 influence and retrieval failure

The interference theory of second language loss holds that forgetting is actually interference between the attriting language and the language replacing it. The transfer that occurs across linguistic systems in the process, however, has just begun to engage the attention of researchers. In a pioneering study of features of first language (Hebrew) transfer in second language (English) attrition, Berman & Olshtain (1983) found that structural properties where the attriting language differs quite markedly from the dominant language showed the greatest attrition. Additional work on the attrition of English as a second language by Hebrew speakers led Olshtain (1989) to suggest that typological universals affect interference from the dominant language in the use of the more restricted one.

Similarly Reetz-Kurashige (1999), in her study of the L2 English of Japanese returnee children drew upon typological universals as an explanation for the widespread use of uninflected English verb stems, rather than analysed forms, by her subjects. This difference between the L2 English data of the Japanese returnees and that of the L2 English of the Israeli returnee children reported by Olshtain (1989) is seen as a possible consequence of the frequent use of the base form, *shūshikei*, in Japanese. A further example of Japanese influence in returnee English is reported by Tomiyama (1997), who concludes that her subject's switching of the noun modification pattern in English, from post-modification to pre-modification, is likely a transfer from head-final Japanese. Kaufman's (1997) analysis of the attriting Hebrew verbs of Israeli children in the United States found forms unprecedented in acquisition, providing another apparent example of influence from the structure of the replacing language, in this case English.

The retrieval failure theory follows current thinking in memory research with the view that knowledge is not lost once it has been acquired. A consequence of non-use of a language, however, is a reduction in the availability of the knowledge of that language. Thus, forgotten information is not gone, but has become inaccessible (Cohen, 1989; Yukawa, 1997a). A decrease in accessibility to one's knowledge of a language is evidenced by strategies such as circumlocution (Olshtain & Barzilay, 1991; Turian & Altenberg, 1991), progressive retrieval (Sharwood-Smith, 1983a; Cohan, 1986, 1989; Olshtain, 1989) and other hesitation and repair behaviour (Russell, 1996; Hansen *et al.*, 1998). In the retrieval failure view, processing time is a critical element in the measurement of language attrition. An early sign of attrition is an increase in the amount of time needed to retrieve linguistic items (Olshtain, 1994). Thus, well-controlled timed experiments which force subjects to apply rules they are uncertain about is essential in gaining a complete picture of language attrition (de Bot & Weltens, 1995).

The Savings Paradigm and Language Relearning

The savings paradigm from memory research in psychology, brought to the attention of language attrition researchers by de Bot & Stoessel (forthcoming), offers a new approach to the study of language loss and to the reactivation of lost language. Based on the assumption that once language is learned it remains indefinitely in the brain, the approach suggests that, even when linguistic items can no longer be recognised using traditional test procedures, there are residues of knowledge that might be used in reactivating them. Thus, it is necessary to distinguish between different memory levels. For recall, the ability to produce a linguistic item, the highest level of activation is needed; for recognition, a lower level is sufficient. As the activation drops still lower, the item can no longer be retrieved. The memory studies have shown that, through relearning, the forgotten item will become reactivated while, at the same time, newly learned items not previously known cannot reach that level in the same learning period.

In their first study, de Bot & Stoessel (forthcoming) used the savings approach to assess long-term retention of words learned in a second language during childhood. The subjects were two German adults who no longer remembered the Dutch they had learned thirty years previously in the Netherlands. Their residual lexical knowledge was demonstrated to still be considerable. In the second study (de Bot & Stoessel, 1999), data from foreign languages learned by adults (French in the Netherlands, German in the United States) indicated that, for short-term learners as well, part of the L2 lexical knowledge that appears to have been forgotten is still available and helpful in a relearning task. These findings are interesting not only to language attrition researchers but also to practitioners of language teaching and testing, and have already stimulated several studies which are now in progress in Japanese contexts.

Language Attrition in Contexts of Japanese Bilingualism

Contributions of studies in Japanese contexts

In this section we will focus on the promising potential of Japanese bilingual contexts as sites for the study of language loss. The peculiar history of Japanese as it has developed in its insular setting has resulted in spoken and written languages of singular structure; the genetic affiliation of Japanese to other languages has not been proven to this day (Shibatani, 1990). By providing sharp structural contrasts with other languages studied, the examination of attrition in Japanese contexts promises fruitful insights by presenting new evidence from a non-Indo-European language spoken in a non-Western culture. The Japanese attrition data can make an important contribution to cross-linguistic comparisons for testing hypotheses about putative language universals and markedness conditions.

Not only the linguistic structures of Japanese, but also the patterns of language use – developed over centuries of relative isolation – contribute to the potential value of attrition studies in Japan. The Japanese language features levels of speech that are chosen according to the relationship between the people involved in a conversation, as well as the context in which they find themselves. The language evolved in such a way as to include the most finely differentiated styles of speech between men and women, and between other 'superior' and 'inferior' persons, by means of intricate levels of distinctions between humble and honorific words and patterns of speech. Japanese contexts provide valuable opportunities for examination of the acquisition and use, as well as the attrition, of such sociolinguistic subtleties. Furthermore, information on language use in Japanese speech communities, in comparison with groups already studied, can contribute to our understanding of such societal causes of loss-related phenomena as code switching, language shift, and language death.

A typology of Japanese bilingual contexts

Virtually the entire population of the Japanese archipelago – some 124,000,000 people, speak one or another dialect of the Japanese language. Although Japan has traditionally been characterised as monolingual, the papers in the present volume suggest a different picture, one of a multilingual area rich in examples of language loss. Among the strongest candidates for attrition of their mother tongues are Japan's linguistic minorities, including Okinawans, Koreans, Chinese, and Ainu.

Increasing numbers of permanent or temporary residents who speak various European languages contribute to Japan's linguistic mosaic. For example, at any one time, about 1500 Mormon missionaries are scattered throughout the country, mostly young Americans who stay for two years. Representatives of other religious denominations are present, often staying in the country for even longer periods. Foreign representatives of various business interests are numerous as well, particularly in major cities. From the 1980s onward an influx of refugees and foreign workers from Asia and South America has brought additional languages to Japan. [See Chapters 1, 6 and 7 for more on these immigrants.] Since all of these linguistic minorities have a need to communicate in Japanese, most become bilingual to some extent.

In addition to linguistic minorities and foreigners in Japan, increasing numbers of Japanese native speakers are becoming bilingual. English, for example, is now studied by virtually everyone for six years in secondary schools as a compulsory subject. Furthermore, in harmony with the nation's emergence as a major world power, Japanese nationals in increasing numbers are taking up residence outside of Japan. For those who live away from their language group for very long, some form of language attrition is inevitable; upon their return to their homeland, the languages they learned abroad may also be at risk. Since 1985 over 10,000 Japanese school-age returnees annually have experienced this on their return to Japan.

A further increase in bilingualism involving the Japanese language is also occurring as the language spreads far beyond the nation's borders. Japanese is fast becoming the foreign language of choice in a growing number of school systems and universities in such far-flung places as Australia, New Zealand and the United States. In the latter, for example, between 1983 and 1990, a 135% increase occurred in the number of college students studying Japanese, the highest rate of growth for any foreign language over this period (Modern Language Association, 1991). Such student populations can also be expected to experience L2 attrition after leaving their Japanese classrooms.

The Japanese contexts of natural language attrition discussed above can be fitted into a categorisation of attrition types based on (1) what is lost, whether mother tongue (L1) or a later learned language (L2); (2) the

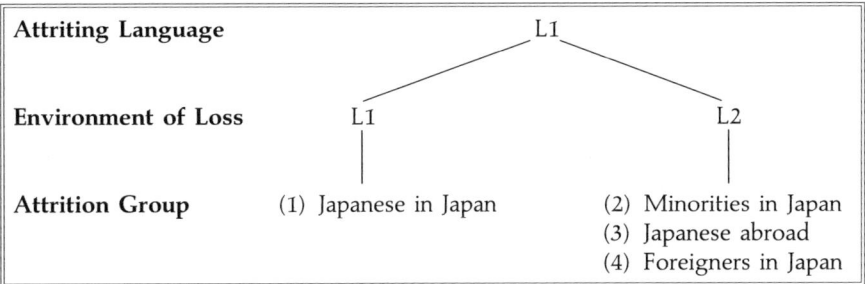

Figure 1 First language loss in Japanese contexts

environment in which it is lost, whether L1 or L2; and, in the case of second language attrition, (3) the environment in which it was learned, whether in a natural milieu, as a second language (L2), or in the classroom, as a foreign language (FL). This categorisation of language attrition types is based partially on de Bot & Weltens (1985).

In Figure 1, the typology shows four groups of L1 attriters in Japanese contexts: first, those in an L1 environment, e.g. elderly Japanese who experience deterioration of language skills in their mother tongue; and second, those in an L2 environment, including minority groups of Japan such as the Ainu and the Koreans, as well as Japanese who take up residence abroad, and foreigners in Japan such as businessmen, missionaries and guest workers.

The study of first language attrition in Japanese bilingual contexts to date has consisted of sociolinguistic investigations of the use of minority languages, including Ainu and Korean, spoken by Attrition Group 2 on the above table (DeChicchis, 1995; Maher, 1993, 1995; Maher & Kawanishi, 1995; Kim, 1991), and studies of mother tongue loss of Japanese nationals or emigrants living abroad, Attrition Group 3 (Minoura, 1981; Noro, 1990; Yukawa, 1997b). Although anecdotal accounts of first language loss by foreigners in Japan, Attrition Group 4, are plentiful, the only study we are aware of that touches on this phenomenon is Smout (1988).

Turning now to second language loss, Figure 2 displays a similar typology with one additional parameter, the setting in which acquisition occurred: in a classroom alone (FL), or in a second language milieu (L2). This distinction in learning environment has practical significance because of the enormous expenditures made for foreign language education. Looking separately at the attrition of languages learned at school, and examining the effects of various instructional variables on retention, can help us be more efficient, not only in teaching our students to learn a language but also to better keep that language after leaving the classroom. Thus, the study of foreign language retention surely deserves greater attention in research than it has thus far received.

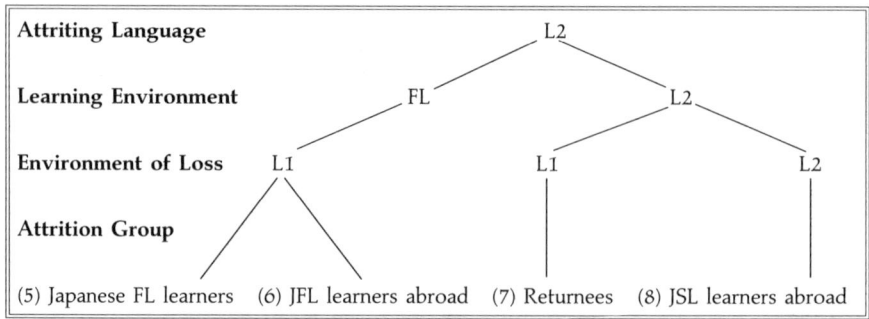

Figure 2   Second language loss in Japanese contexts

We are aware of no studies of the retention of English or other foreign languages learned by Japanese students in Japan, Attrition Group 5. Learners of Japanese as a foreign language outside of Japan, Attrition Group 6, however, are the focus of Nagasawa's (1999) study of American university students, and Hayashi's (1999) study of elderly Micronesians who had learned Japanese as children in school.

With regard to Attrition Group 7, the Japanese returnee children have attracted the most language attrition research, with dozens of studies extending over more than two decades, including Ishiguro (1994), Koike (1990), Kamijo, Ishiguro & Ito (1992), Nakazawa (1989a, 1989b), Nakazawa & Yoshitomi (1990), Reetz-Kurashige (1999), Seya (1990); Tomiyama (1995, 1996, 1999), Yashiro (1987, 1991), Yoshida, Arai, Fujita, Hattori, Nagano, Okamura, Tanaka, Yanaura & Yoshitomi, (1989), Yoshida & Arai (1990), and Yoshitomi (1992, 1994, 1999). The language loss of foreigners returned home after learning Japanese in Japan has also recently attracted the attention of a few researchers (Hansen, 1996, 1999; Hansen, *et al.*, 1997; Hansen & Newbold, 1997; Hansen-Strain, 1990, 1992, 1993; Hansen-Strain & Iwata, 1992; Russell, 1996, 1999). Attrition Group 8, JSL attriters in a second language environment, remains unstudied.

Applications of Attrition Studies in Japanese Contexts

A good deal more is known about the learning of languages in Japan than is known about their loss. Yet language attrition is as common as is acquisition, and its study is just as important for positive applications in contexts of Japanese bilingualism. For example, an understanding of what, when and under what conditions language regression occurs can lead us to teaching methods which engender more durable language skills for learners after instruction has ended. Relevant questions in this connection are whether particular teaching methods are superior to others in terms of the long-term retention of the language, the effects on retention of intensive vs. non-intensive programmes, the effects of emphasis on particular language skills, and the extent to which literacy anchors knowledge of a language (Hansen & Newbold, 1997; Hansen & Chantrill, 1999; Hansen & Shewell, 1999).

Likewise in language maintenance programmes such as the ones in place in Japan among linguistic minorities (Maher, 1993, 1995) and in the form of Saturday classes for returnees, the insights coming out of research on language attrition are requisite to the development of effective teaching. Yoshitomi (1999), in important pioneering work in this area, found that the ability of Japanese returnees to use sub-skills erodes more slowly than global language ability, prompting her to suggest that communicative activities involving real-time spontaneous interaction may be vital for the childrens' second language maintenance.

A further application of language attrition research is to provide attriters with instruction on personal strategies for keeping their hard-won linguistic skills. In the same way that language acquisition research on characteristics of the 'good language learner' (Dickenson 1992; McDonough 1995; O'Malley & Chamot 1990; Oxford 1990) has led to materials for teaching strategies for successful language learning (Brown 1989, 1991; Ellis & Sinclair 1989; Rubin & Thompson 1994), so too will our investigation of individual differences in language attrition allow us to develop materials for teaching strategies for successful language retention. Thus, with the progress of language attrition research in Japan, the Japanese bilingual will have a better chance in the new millenium of being a 'good language keeper'.

APPENDIX

Symposia on Language Attrition, 1996–99
(with current e-mail addresses of the presenters)

AILA'96, 11th World Congress of Applied Linguistics; Jyväskylä, Finland; August 5, 1996. Papers presented at the Symposium on Language Attrition from Cross-Disciplinary Perspectives organised by Lynne Hansen:

Hansen, L. (Brigham Young University, Hawaii). Fitting the pieces together: Attrition curves in the longterm loss of a second language. hansenl@byuh.edu

Russell, R. (Brigham Young University). Hesitation and repair behaviour in L2 Japanese attrition. robert_russell@byu.edu

Tomiyama M. (Toyo Gakuen University). L2 attrition processes: A four-year case study of a Japanese returnee. tomiyama@icu.edu.jp

Yoshitomi A. (Tokyo University of Foreign Studies). A case study of Japanese returnee children's loss of ESL: Methodological and theoretical suggestions for future research. yasako@fs.tufs.ac.jp

Yukawa E. (Center for Research on Bilingualism, Stockholm University). L1 Japanese attrition: Three case studies of two early bilingual children. VED04614@niftyserve.or.jp

Waas, M. (National Chung Cheng University, Taiwan). Absence of sounds in language attrition. waasm@nie.edu.sg

AAAL'97 Annual Meeting of the American Association for Applied Linguistics. Orlando Florida. March 11, 1997. Papers presented at the Symposium on First and Second Language Attrition: Insights from Production Data organised by Dorit Kaufman and Lynne Hansen:

Dutkova, L. (The University of Arizona, Tucson). Assessing child L1 and L2 narrative competence: Evidence for L1 attrition. 1dutkova@olemiss.edu

Hansen, L. and Newbold, J. (Brigham Young University, Hawaii). Literacy as an anchor for the spoken language: Evidence from adult attriters of L2 Japanese. hansenl@byuh.edu and newbold@byuh.edu

Kaufman, D. (State University of New York at Stony Brook). Children's tales and the story of first language attrition. dkaufman@cs.sunysb.edu

Tomiyama M. (Toyo Gakuen University). L2 attrition and L1 influence. tomiyama@icu.edu.jp

Reetz, A. (UCLA Extension, American Language Center) Tracking Japanese returnees' English verb usage ... back home. reetz@usc.edu

Waas, M. (Universidad Europea de Madrid). Attrition of immediate responses in adult immigrants. waasm@nie.edu.sg

PacSLRF'98 Second Language Research Forum of the Pacific. Tokyo, Japan. March 26, 1998. Papers presented at the Explaining Language Attrition: Predictors from Language Acquisition Symposium organised by Lynne Hansen and Tomiyama Machiko.

Hansen, L. (Brigham Young University, Hawaii). The effects of instruction and other pre-attrition variables on second language maintenance. hansenl@byuh.ed

Nagasawa S. (Kurume University). The effects of initial achievement, learning experiences, and classroom instruction on adult attrition/retention of L2 Japanese. nagasawa@cec.mii.kurume-u.ac.jp

Russell, R. (Brigham Young University). Measuring attrition in L2 Japanese syntactic competence. robert_russell@byu.edu

Tomiyama M. (International Christian University). The later stages of natural L2 attrition. tomiyama@icu.edu.jp

Yukawa, E. (Stockholm University, Center for Research on Bilingualism). L1 Japanese attrition and regaining: The age and pre-attrition variables. VED04614@niftyserve.or.jp

AILA 12th World Congress of Applied Linguistics. Tokyo, Japan. August 2, 1999. Papers presented at the Language Attrition: Retrospection and Directions for the New Millennium symposium, organised by Lynne Hansen and Dorit Kaufman.

Hansen, L. (Brigham Young University, Hawaii) What we think we know about second language attrition: A twenty year retrospect. hansenl@byuh.edu

Kaufman, D. (State University of New York at Stony Brook) The L1 verbal system in an L2 environment: The case of Hebrew. dkaufman@cs.sunysb.edu

Olshtain, E. (Hebrew University of Jerusalem) Discussant. mseliteo@mscc.huji.ac.il

Tomiyama M. (International Christian University) The longitudinal study of the L2 English attrition of a Japanese returnee. tomiyama@icu.edu.jp

Yukawa, E. (Notre Dame Women's College) L1 Japanese attrition as a result of retrieval failure of intact linguistic knowledge: Evidence from bilingual children. VED04614 @niftyserve.or.jp

References

Bahrick, H. (1984) Fifty years of second language attrition: Implications for programmematic research. *Modern Language Journal* 68, 105–111.

Berman, R.A. and Olshtain, E. (1983) Features of first language transfer in second language attrition. *Applied Linguistics* 4 (3), 222–234.

Brown, H.D. (1989) *A Practical Guide to Language Learning: Fifteen-Week Program of Strategies for Success.* New York: McGraw-Hill.

Brown, H.D. (1991) *Breaking the Language Barrier: Creating Your Own Pathway to Success.* Yarmouth, ME: Intercultural Press.

Clark, J.L.D. (1981) Language. In T.S. Barrows (ed.) College students' knowledge and beliefs: A survey of global understanding. New Rochelle, NY: *Change Magazine Press*, 25–35 and 87–100.

Clark, J. and Jorden, E. (1984) *A Study of Language Attrition in Former U.S. Students of Japanese.* Final Project Report. Washington, DC: Center for Applied Linguistics (ED243 317).

Clyne, M. (1991) *Community Languages: The Australian Experience.* Cambridge: Cambridge University Press.

Cohen, A.D. (1975) Forgetting a foreign language. *Language Learning* 25, 127–138.

Cohen, A.D. (1986). Forgetting foreign language vocabulary. In B. Weltens, K. deBot and T. van Els (eds) *Language Attrition in Progress* (pp. 143–158). Dordrecht, Holland: Foris.

Cohen, A.D. (1989) Attrition in the productive lexicon of two Portuguese third language speakers. *Studies in Second Language Acquisition* 11, 135–149.

de Bot, K. and Lintsen, T. (1989) Perception of own language proficiency by elderly adults. *I.T.L. Review of Applied Linguistics* 83, 51–61.

de Bot, K. and Stoessel, S. (1999) Finding residual lexical knowledge: The 'savings' approach to testing vocabulary. Paper presented at the AAAL Conference. Stamford, Connecticut.

de Bot, K. and Stoessel, S. (forthcoming) In search of yesterday's words: Reactivating a long forgotten language. *Applied Linguistics.*

de Bot, K. and Weltens, B. (1991) Recapitulation, regression, and language loss. In H.W. Seliger and R.M. Vago (eds) *First Language Attrition* (pp. 31–52). Cambridge: Cambridge University Press.

de Bot, K. and Weltens, B. (1995) Foreign language attrition. *Annual Review of Applied Linguistics* 15, 151–164. Cambridge: Cambridge University Press.

DeChicchis, J. (1995) Ainu, Formosan, and Mayan: Is there a road to oblivion? Paper presented at the Symposium on Language Loss and Public Policy. Albuquerque: University of New Mexico.

Diamond, J. (1993) Speaking with a single tongue. *Discover* 14 (2), 78–85.

Dickinson, L. (1992) *Learner Training for Language Learning.* Dublin: Authentic Language Learning Resources Ltd.

Dutkova, L. (1997) Assessing child L1 and L2 narrative competence: Evidence for L1 attrition. Paper presented at AAAL'97. Orlando, Florida.

Edwards, G. (1976) Second language retention in the Canadian Public Service. *Canadian Modern Language Review* 32, 305–308.

Edwards, G. (1977) *Second Language Retention in the Public Service of Canada.* Ottawa: Public Service Commission of Canada.

Ellis, G. and Sinclair, B. (1989) *Learning to Learn English: A Course in Learner Training.* Glasgow: Cambridge University Press.

Fenyvesi, A. (1995) How assimilation affects assimilations: The loss of some phonological processes in American Hungarian. Paper presented at the Conference on Language Loss and Public Policy. Albuquerque: University of New Mexico.

Fesi, E. (1987) Language death among Aboriginal languages. *Australian Review of Applied Linguistics* 10, 12–22.

Fishman, J.A., Nahirny, V., Hofman, J. and Hayden, R. (eds) (1966) *Language Loyalty in the United States.* The Hague: Mouton.

Gal, S. (1979) *Language Shift: Social Determinants of Linguistic Change in Bilingual Australia.* New York: Academic Press.

Gardner, R.C. (1982) Social factors in language retention. In R.D. Lambert and B. Freed (ed.) *The Loss of Language Skills* (pp. 24–39). Rowley, MA: Newbury House.

Gardner, R.C., Lalonde, R.N. and MacPherson, J. (1985) Social factors in second language attrition. *Language Learning* 35, 519–540.

Gardner, R.C., Lalonde, R.N., Moorcroft, R. and Evers, F.T. (1987) Second language attrition: The role of motivation and use. *Journal of Language and Social Psychology* 6, 29–47.

Gardner, R.C. and Lysynchuk, L.M. (1990) The role of aptitude, attitudes, motivation and language use in second language acquisition and retention. *Canadian Journal of Behavioral Science* 3, 254–270.

Godsall-Myers, J. (1981) The attrition of language skills in German classroom bilinguals: A case study. Dissertation Abstracts International, 43, 57A.

Gumperz, J.J. (1982) *Discourse Structures*. Cambridge: Cambridge University Press.

Hale, K. (1991) On endangered languages and the safeguarding of diversity. Paper delivered at the Annual Meeting of the Linguistics Society of America, Chicago.

Hansen, L. (1980) Learning and forgetting a second language: The acquisition, loss and reacquisition of Hindi-Urdu negative structures by English-speaking children. PhD dissertation, University of California, Berkely. Dissertation Abstracts International, 42, 193A.

Hansen, L. (1983) The acquisition and forgetting of Hindi-Urdu negation by English-speaking children. In K.M. Bailey, M.H. Long and S. Peck (eds) *Second Language Acquisition Studies* (pp. 93–103). Rowley, MA: Newbury House.

Hansen, L. (1996) Fitting the pieces together: Attrition curves in the longterm attrition of a second language. Paper presented at the AILA Eleventh World Congress of Applied Linguistics, Jyvaskyla, Finland (*Conference Abstracts*, 48).

Hansen, L. (1999a) Not a total loss: The attrition of Japanese negation over three decades. In L. Hansen (ed.) *Second Language Attrition in Japanese Contexts* (pp. 142–153). Oxford: Oxford University Press.

Hansen, L. (1999b) Language regression in bilingualism: A retrospect of language attrition research over two decades. Plenary address presented at the Applied Linguistics Association of Korea Conference on Bilingualism: Language acquisition and language attrition. Seoul.

Hansen, L., Gardner, J. and Pollard, J. (1998) The measurement of fluency in a second language: Evidence from the acquisition and attrition of Japanese. In B. Visgatis (ed.) *Trends and Transitions: Proceedings of the 23rd International JALT Convention (JALT'97)*. Tokyo: Japan Association for Language Teaching.

Hansen, L. and Newbold, J. (1997) Literacy as an anchor of the spoken language: Evidence from adult attriters of L2 Japanese. Paper presented at the AAAL annual conference, Orlando, Florida.

Hansen, L. and Chantrill, C. (1999) The effects of literacy on the attrition of L2 Chinese by English-speaking adults. Paper presented at the AAAL Convention. Seattle.

Hansen, L. and Shewell, J. (1999) The role of alphabetic literacy in second language retention: The case of Korean. Paper presented at the Applied Linguistics Association of Korea Conference on Bilingualism: Language Acquisition and Language Attrition. Seoul.

Hansen-Strain, L. (1990) The attrition of Japanese by English-speaking children: An interim report. *Language Sciences* 12 (4), 367–77.

Hansen-Strain, L. (1992) Language loss over a break in instruction: Negation in the L2 Japanese of American high school students. In Yoshioka K., B. Murdoch, J. Smith and Kato Y. (eds) *Proceedings of the 4th Conference on Second Language Research in Japan* (pp. 123–134). Niigata: The International University of Japan.

Hansen-Strain, L. (1993) The attrition of Japanese negation by English-speaking adults. Paper presented at AILA 10th World Congress of Applied Linguistics, Amsterdam (*Conference Abstracts*, 114).

Hansen-Strain, L. and Iwata Y. (1992) The loss of Japanese negation by English-speaking children. Paper presented at the 26th Annual TESOL Convention. Vancouver.

Harmon, D. (1995). The status of the world's languages as reported in *Ethnologue*. Paper presented at the Symposium on Language Loss and Public Policy. Albuquerque: University of New Mexico.

Hayashi, B. (1999) Testing the regression hypothesis: The remains of the Japanese negation system in Micronesia. In L. Hansen (ed.) *Second Language Attrition in Japanese Contexts* (pp. 154–168). Oxford: Oxford University Press.

Heller, M. (ed.) (1988) *Codeswitching*. Berlin: Mouton de Gruyter.

Hernandez Chavez, E., Hudson, A. and Bills, G.D. (1995) Socioeconomic and demographic factors in language shift. Paper presented at the Symposium on Language Loss and Public Policy. Albuquerque: University of New Mexico.

Hill, J.H. (1993) Structure and practice in language shift. In K. Hyltenstam and A. Viberg (eds) *Progression and Regression in Language: Sociocultural, Neuropsychological and Linguistic Perspectives* (pp. 68–93). Cambridge: Cambridge University Press.

Hooley, B.A. (1987) Death or life: The prognosis for Central Buang. In D.C. Laycock and W. Winter (eds) *A World of Languages: Papers Presented to Professor S.A. Wurm on His 65th Birthday* (pp. 275–285). Pacific Linguistics, Series C-100. Canberra: Australian National University Press.

Ishiguro T. (1994) Two suggested threshold levels in L1 and L2 attrition processes. *Studies in Humanities*, 121. Kanagawa, Japan: Kanagawa University.

Jakobson, R. (1941) *Kindersprache, Aphasie und Allgemeine Lautgesetze*. Uppsala: Almquist and Wiksell. [English translation (1972): *Child Language, Aphasia, and Phonological Universals*]. The Hague: Mouton.

Kamijo M., Ishiguro T. and Ito K. (1992) The returnees' processes of language acquisition and attrition. *Language Studies* 14, 101–140.

Kaufman, D. (1997) Where have all the verbs gone? Autonomy and interaction in attrition. *Southwest Journal of Linguistics* Special Issue on Language Loss and Public Policy, I. Hernandez-Chavez, E. and G. Bills (eds) 14, 1–2, 43–66. Albuquerque, NM: Linguistics Association of the Southwest.

Kim D.R. (1991) *Zainichi chōsenjin shijo no bairingarizumu* [The bilingualism of resident Korean children]. In J. Maher and Yashiro K. (eds) *Nihon no bairingarizumu* [Bilingualism in Japan] (pp. 125–148). Tokyo: Kenkyusha.

Kloss, H. (1966) German-American language maintenance efforts. In J.A. Fishman, V. Nahirny, J. Hofman, and R. Hayden (eds) *Language Loyalty in the United States* (pp. 206–252). The Hague: Mouton.

Koike I. (1990) How the Japanese children lose English as a second language. Paper presented at the AILA 9th World Congress of Applied Linguistics. Thessaloniki (*Conference Abstracts*, Vol. 1, 8).

Krauss, M. (1991) The world's languages in crisis. Paper delivered at the Annual Meeting of the Linguistics Society of America, Chicago.

Kuhberg, H. (l992) Longitudinal L2-attrition versus L2-acqusition in three Turkish children: Empirical findings. *Second Language Research* 8 (2) 138–154.

Kulick, D. (1992) *Language Shift and Cultural Reproduction*. Cambridge: Cambridge University Press.

Lambert, R.D. and Freed, B.F. (eds) (1982) *The Loss of Language Skills*. Rowley, MA: Newbury House Publishers.

Levine, G.S. (1995) Elderly second-generation speakers of Yiddish: A model of L1 loss, incomplete L1 acquisition, competence and control. Paper presented at the Symposium on Language Loss and Public Policy. Albuquerque: New Mexico.

Long, M. (1990) Maturational constraints on language development. *Studies in Second Language Acquisition* 12 (3), 251–285.

Maher, J. (1993) Ainu: Undeniably alive. *Japan Times Weekly*, August 12, 7–8.

Maher, J. (1995). Ainu in Japan: language loss, language recovery. Paper presented at the Symposium on Language Loss and Public Policy. Albuquerque: New Mexico.

Maher, J. and Kawanishi Y. (1995) On being there: Korean in Japan. In J. Maher and K. Yashiro (eds) *Multilingual Japan* (pp. 87–103). Clevedon: Multilingual Matters.

McConvell, P. (1988) MIX-IM-UP: Aboriginal codeswitching, old and new. In M. Heller (ed.) *Codeswitching* (pp. 97–150). Berlin: Mouton de Gruyter.

McDonough, S.H. (1995) *Strategy and Skill in Learning a Foreign Language*. London: Edward Arnold.

Minoura Y. (1981) *Amerika bunka to no sesshoku ga nihonjin no katei sekatsu to kodomo no shakaika katei ni oyobosu eikyō* [The Effect of Contact with American Culture on Japanese Families and the Socialization Process of Their Children]. *Kaigai no nihonjin to sono kodomotachi* [Japanese People and Their Children Abroad]. *Toyota zaidan dai-12-kai jōsei kenkyū hōkokukai shiryō* [Report based on a research grant from Toyota Corporation].

Modern Language Association. (1991) *Fall 1990 Survey of Foreign Language Enrollments in U.S. Colleges and Universities*. New York: MLA.

Nagasawa S. (1999) Learning and losing L2 Japanese: A multiple case study of American university students. In L. Hansen (ed.) *Second Language Attrition in Japanese Contexts* (pp. 169–200). Oxford: Oxford University Press.

Nakazawa Y. (1989a) *Kikoku shijo no gaikokugo shori katei to sono sokute hōhō nitsuite* [On the foreign language processing of returnees and its measurement]. In *Kikoku shijo no gaikokugo hoji ni kansuru chōsa kenkyū hōkokusho* [A survey on the foreign language retention of returnees] Vol 1 (pp. 820–822). Tokyo: Kaigai shijo kyoiku shinko zaidan [Japan Overseas Student Education Foundation].

Nakazawa Y. (1989b) *Kikoku shijo no nihon kikokugo no gaigokugo iji teido wo ketteisuru yōin nitsuite no chōsa* [A report on the factors that determine foreign language retention of returnees after returning to Japan.] In *Kikoku shijo no gaikokugo hoji ni kansuru chōsa kenkyū hōkokusho* [A survey on the foreign language retention of returnees] Vol. 1 (pp. 29–59). Tokyo: Kaigai shijo kyoiku shinko zaidan [Japan Overseas Student Education Foundation].

Nakazawa Y. and Yoshitomi A. (1990) *Kikoku shijo no gaikokugo shori katei to sono sokute hōhō nitsuite 2* [On the foreign language processing of returnees and its measurement 2]. In *Kikoku shijo no gaikokugo hoji ni kansuru chōsa kenkyū hōkokusho* [A survey on the foreign language retention of returnees] Vol. 2 (pp. 42–52). Tokyo: Kaigai shijo kyoiku shinko zaidan [Japan Overseas Student Education Foundation].

Neisser, U. (1984) Interpreting Harry Bahrick's discovery: What confers immunity against forgetting? *Journal of Experimental Psychology, General*, 113, 32–35.

Neustupny, J.V. (1994) Language management and problems of community languages. Paper read at the Second National Language Research Institute (of Japan) International Symposium. Tokyo.

Noro H. (1990) Family and language maintenance: An exploratory study of Japanese language maintenance among children of postwar Japanese immigrants in Toronto. *International Journal of the Sociology of Language* 86, 57–68.

Olshtain, E. (1986) The attrition of English as a second language with speakers of Hebrew. In B. Weltens, K. de Bot and T. van Els (eds) *Language Attrition in Progress* (pp. 187–204). Dordrecht, Holland: Foris.

Olshtain, E. (1989) Is second language attrition the reversal of second language acquisition? *Studies in Second Language Acquisition* 11, 151–165.

Olshtain, E. and Barzilay, M. (1991) Lexical retrieval difficulties in adult language attrition. In H. Seliger and R. Vago (eds) *First Language Attrition* (pp. 139–150). Cambridge: Cambridge University Press.

Olshtain, E. and Barzilay, M. (1994) Metalinguistic accessibility as an indication of adult primary language attrition. Paper presented at the AAAL Annual Conference. Baltimore, Maryland.

O'Malley, J.M. and Chamot, A.U. (1990) *Learning Strategies in Second Language Acquisition*. New York: Cambridge University Press.

Oxford, R. (1990) *Language Learning Strategies: What Every Teacher Should Know*. New York: Newbury House.

Pauwels, A. (1986) *Immigrant Dialects and Language Maintenance in Australia*. Dordrecht, Holland: Foris.

Pauwels, A. (1994) Managing multilingualism in Australia: Issues in language maintenance and intercultural communication affecting ethnolinguistic minorities. Paper read at the Second National Language Research Institute (of Japan) International Symposium. Tokyo.

Py, B. (1986) Native language attrition amongst migrant workers: Towards an extension of the concept of interlanguage. In E. Kellerman and M. Sharwood-Smith (eds) *Cross Linguistic Influences in Second Language Acquisition* (pp. 163–171). Oxford: Pergamon.

Reetz-Kurashige, A. (1999) Japanese returnees' maintenance and loss of English speaking skills: Changes in verb usage over time. In L. Hansen (ed.) *Second Language Attrition in Japanese Contexts* (pp. 21–58). Oxford: Oxford University Press.

Rubin, J. and Thompson, I. (1994) *How to be a More Successful Language Learner* (2nd edn). Boston: Heinle and Heinle.

Russell, R. (1996) Pause and repair behaviour in L2 Japanese attrition. Paper presented at the AILA Eleventh World Congress of Applied Linguistics, Jyväskylä, Finland.

Russell, R. (1999) Lexical maintenance and attrition in Japanese as a second language. In L. Hansen (ed.) *Second Language Attrition in Japanese Contexts* (pp. 114–141). Oxford: Oxford University Press.

Rhydwen, M. (1995) Why did we give up our language? Paper presented at the Symposium on Language Loss and Public Policy. Albuquerque: University of New Mexico.

Schaufeli, A. (1995) Word order in a language contact situation. Paper presented at the Symposium on Language Loss and Public Policy. Albuquerque: University of New Mexico.

Scherer, G. (1957) The forgetting rate in learning German. *German Quarterly 30*, 275–277.

Seliger, H.W. and Vago, R.M. (eds) (1991) *First Language Attrition*. Cambridge: Cambridge University Press.

Seya H. (1990) *Kikoku shijo no eigo shiin no onchikaku to goi sutorateji no shiyō* [The perception of English consonants and use of lexical strategies by returnees]. In *Kikoku shijo no gaikokugo hoji ni kansuru chōsa kenkyū hōkokusho* [A survey on the foreign language retention of returnees] Vol. 2 (pp. 29–41). Tokyo: Kaigai shijo kyoiku shinko zaidan [Japan Overseas Student Education Foundation].

Sharwood-Smith, M. (1983a) On first language loss in the second language acquirer: Problems of transfer. In S. Gass and L. Selinker (eds) *Language Transfer in Language Learning* (pp. 22–31). Rowley, MA: Newbury House.

Sharwood-Smith, M. (1983b) On explaining language loss. In S.W. Felix and H. Wode (eds) *Language Development at the Crossroads* (pp. 49–62). Tubingen: Gunter Narr Verlag.

Shibatani M. (1990) *The Languages of Japan*. Cambridge: Cambridge University Press.

Smout, K.D. (1988) *Senkyoshigo*: A missionary English of Japan. *American Speech 63*, 137–149.

Tomiyama M. (1995) A longitudinal study of natural second language attrition. Paper presented at the 29th Annual TESOL Convention, Long Beach, CA.

Tomiyama M. (1996) A process of L2 attrition: A four-year case study of a Japanese returnee. Paper presented at the 11th World Congress of Applied Linguistics, Jyvaskyla, Finland.

Tomiyama M. (1997) L2 attrition and L1 influence. Paper presented at the AAAL '97 Convention. Orlando, Florida.

Tomiyama M. (1999) A longitudianal study of natural second language attrition – Stage I: A case study of a Japanese returnee. In L. Hansen (ed.) *Second Language Attrition in Japanese Contexts* (pp. 59–79). Oxford: Oxford University Press.

Turian D. and Altenberg, E.P. (1991) Compensatory strategies of child first language attrition. In H.W. Seliger and R.M. Vago (eds) *First Language Attrition* (pp. 207–226). Cambridge: Cambridge University Press.

van Els, T. (1986) An overview of European research on language attrition. In B. Weltens, K. de Bot and T. van Els (eds) *Language Attrition in Progress* (pp. 3–18). Dordrecht, Holland: Foris.

Vechter A., Lapkin, S. and Argue, V. (1990) Second language retention: A summary of the issues. *The Canadian Modern Language Review 46* (2), 189–203.

Waas, M. (1996) *Language Attrition Downunder*. Frankfurt: Peter Lang.

Waas, M. (1998) Language Attrition: A Comprehensive Bibliography.
http://www.nie.ac.sg:8000/~wwwlib/biblio/lattrition/intro.htm

Weltens, B. (1987) The attrition of foreign language skills: A literature review. *Applied Linguistics 8* (1), 22–36.

Weltens, B. (1989) *The Attrition of French as a Foreign Language*. Dordrecht, Holland: Foris.

Weltens, B. and Cohen, A.D. (1989) Language attrition research. *Studies in Second Language Acquisition* 11, 127–133.

Weltens, B. and Grendel, M. (1993) *Attrition of Vocabulary Knowledge*. Studies in Bilingualism, 6. Nijmegen, Holland: Katholieke Universiteit.

Weltens, B., de Bot, K. and van Els, T. (eds) (1986) *Language Attrition in Progress*. Dordrecht, Holland: Foris.

Wheeler, D.L. (1994) The death of languages. *The Chronicle of Higher Education* April 20, A8, A9, A16.

Yashiro K. (1987) Second language maintenance for returnee students in Japan. Paper presented at AILA'87. Sydney, Australia.

Yashiro K. (1991) Bilingualism of Japanese returnees. Presentation at JALT National Conference. Kobe, Japan.

Yoshida K., Arai K., Fujita T., Hattori M., Nagano K., Okamura A., Tanaka M., Yanaura K. and Yoshhitomi, A. (1989) *Kikoku shijo no gaikokugo hoji ni kansuru ichi chōsa* [A Consideration of the Retention of a Foreign Language by Returnees]. In *Kikoku shijo no gaikokugo hoji ni kansuru chōsa kenkyū hōkokusho* [A Survey on the Foreign Language Retention of Returnees] Vol. 1 (pp. 12–28). Tokyo: Kaigai shijo kyoiku shinko zaidan (Japan Overseas Educational Services).

Yoshida K. and Arai K. (1990) *Kikoku shijo no gaikokugo risuningu nōroyoku no hoji ni kansuru kōsatsu* [On the Retention of Listening Skills of Returnees]. In *Kikoku shijo no gaikokugo hoji ni kansuru chōsa kenkyū hōkokusho* [A Survey on the Foreign Language Retention of Returnees] Vol. 2 (pp. 9–28). Tokyo: Kaigai shijo kyoiku shinko zaidan [Japan Overseas Educational Services].

Yoshitomi A. (1992) Towards a model of language attrition: Neurobiological and psychological contributions. *Issues in Applied Linguistics* 3 (2), 293–318.

Yoshitomi A. (1994) The attrition of English as a second language of Japanese returnee children. Unpublished Ph.D. dissertation. University of California, Los Angeles.

Yoshitomi A. (1999) On the loss of ESL of Japanese returnee children. In L. Hansen (ed.) *Second Language Attrition in Japanese Contexts* (pp. 80–112). Oxford: Oxford University Press.

Yukawa E. (1997a) L1 Japanese attrition of a 5 year-old bilingual child. *Japan Journal of Multilingualism and Multiculturalism* 3 (1), 1–22.

Yukawa E. (1997b). *L1 Japanese Attrition: Three Case Studies of Two Early Bilingual Children.* Stockholm: Centre for Research on Bilingualism, Stockholm University.

Contributors

Editors

Mary Goebel Noguchi is a Professor of English in the College of Law at Ritsumeikan University in Kyoto, Japan. She holds a master's degree in East Asian Studies from the University of Wisconsin — Madison, with Japanese literature as her area of concentration. In addition to research and translation in the field of Japanese studies, particularly in reference to modern Japanese society and Japanese women, she has taken an interest in the development of bilingualism by bicultural children in Japan and Japanese returnees. In 1995 she helped found the *Japan Journal of Multilingualism and Multiculturalism* and has since served as its editor.

Sandra Fotos is Professor of English in the School of Economics at Senshu University, Tokyo, Japan. She holds an EdD in Applied Linguistics from Temple University and her research interests include bilingualism and the effects of formal instruction on second language acquisition. She has published in journals such as *Applied Linguistics, Language Learning, ELT-Journal* and *TESOL Quarterly* and is a contributor to *New Ways in Teaching Grammar*, which was published by TESOL. She has edited a book on multimedia language teaching and is first author of *Grammar in Mind*, a task-based approach to grammar instruction. Dr Fotos is editor of the *JALT Journal*, published by the Japan Association for Language Teaching, and is a member of the editorial board of the *Japan Journal of Multilingualism and Multiculturalism*.

Authors

John C. Maher is an Associate Professor of Linguistics in the Department of Communications and Linguistics at International Christian University in Tokyo, Japan. His research and editing work on various minority groups in Japan has played a major role in helping the English-speaking world see the linguistic and cultural diversity that exists in the country. Among the research collections he has coedited are *Nihon no bairingarizumu* [The Bilingualism of Japan] (Kenkyusha, 1991), *Multilingual Japan* (Multilingual

Matters, 1995) and *Diversity in Japanese Culture and Language* (Kegan Paul International, 1995).

Yamamoto Masayo is a Professor in the Language Center of Kwansei Gakuin University in Hyogo Prefecture, Japan. She holds a PhD in linguistics from International Christian University. Her research focuses on the language acquisition of simultaneous bilinguals and language use in interlingual families. She is the author of two books and numerous articles on bilingualism and currently the co-Convenor of the AILA Scientific Commission on Child Language.

Fred E. Anderson is a Foreign Lecturer (*Gaikokujin koshi*) of English and Intercultural Communication Studies in the Program in English Education at Fukuoka University of Education. He holds a PhD in Linguistics from the University of Hawaii, with areas of concentration in ethnolinguistics, language learning/teaching, and Japanese linguistics. His research interests focus on the sociocultural context of language learning, including classroom discourse studies and bilingualism. His publications include 'Language development in social context: Ethnographic, sociohistorical, and biological perspectives' (*Reviews in Anthropology*, forthcoming) and 'First-language socialisation and second-language learning' (*Proceedings: The 8th International University of Japan Conference on Second Language Research in Japan*, 1997).

Masami Iwasaki-Goodman is an Associate Professor of Anthropology in the Department of Humanities at Hokkai Gakuen University. She holds a master's degree in linguistics from the University of Minnesota and a PhD in anthropology from the University of Alberta, Canada. Her research interests include the cultural and social importance of whaling in Japan and Norway, issues regarding aboriginal rights, and the management of marine resources by aboriginal peoples. Her published papers include 'Social-cultural significance of whaling in contemporary Japan' (in T. Burch and L. Ellanna [eds] *Key Issues in Hunter-Gatherer Research*, 1994, Oxford: Burge) and '*Sake shigen no gensho to "Nagmis no hitobito"*' [Decline of salmon resources and the people of the 'Nagmis'] (in Akamichi T. [ed.] *Shizen wa dare no mono ka* [Who Owns Nature?], Kyoto: Showado, 1999).

Osumi Midori is a Professor of Linguistics in the Department of Languages, College of Culture and Communication, Tokyo Woman's Christian University. In addition to postgraduate studies at the University of Tokyo and the University of Paris, she completed a doctorate in linguistics at the Australian National University. She has published extensively on sociolinguistics and the languages of Oceania, with a special focus on Tinrin, a previously undescribed language of Melanesia, in addition to the changing language situation of Okinawa.

Ann B. Cary is an Associate Professor in the English Department at Kobe Women's University, where she currently teaches English language and composition, translation and interpreting. Ann was raised in Japan but graduated from Oberlin College in Ohio. She worked as an interpreter in both the United States and Japan before earning her master's degree in bilingual education at the School of Education, Boston University. After returning to Japan she began teaching, first in Otaru, Hokkaido, then from 1992 to 1999 at Matsuyama Shinonome College in Shikoku, where she taught English language classes as well as courses on bilingualism.

Tomozawa Akie is an Associate Professor in the Faculty of Letters, Momoyama Gakuin University (St.Andrew's University). After graduating from Osaka University of Foreign Studies, she earned a master's degree in American history at the University of Wisconsin–Madison. She has published extensively on teaching Japanese language to foreign students as well as on bilingualism and bilingual education in the United States.

Hirataka Fumiya is an Associate Professor in the Faculty of Policy Management, Keio University at Shonan Fujisawa, Japan. After post-graduate studies at Tokyo University of Foreign Studies, he earned a doctor's degree in philosophy at the Free University of Berlin, Germany. His research focuses on the second language acquisition, language policy and the history of teaching Japanese as a second language.

Koishi Atsuko is an Associate Professor in the Faculty of Policy Management at Keio University–Shonan Fujisawa Campus. In addition to a master's degree in applied linguistics from the University of Paris III and another MA in linguistics from the French Department of Tokyo University, she earned a PhD in linguistics at University of Paris VIII. Her recent research focuses on language policy in education. Together with Professor Hirataka, she organised the JUMP Project (1993–97), a student volunteer project to aid Japanese Language Classes for foreign students at Shonandai Elementary School, and the LAPO Project (1994–98) to survey the language environment of immigrant workers and their families in Fujisawa City. Her other publications in this field include *Gengo kyōiku kara mita imin jidō/seito no ukeire: 'Fransu-shiki tōgō moderu' no kenshō* [Languages in schooling for immigrant children: Examination of the French model of integration] in *Gengo to funsō* [Language and Conflict]. Fujisawa, Japan: Keio University Graduate School, 1997.

Kato Yosuke earned a master's degree in media and governance at Keio University at Shonan Fujisawa, Japan. He is now working in the General Planning and Policy Division, Minister's Secretariat in the Ministry of Posts and Telecommunications.

Sharon Siebert Vaipae has a BA in Special Education from Drake University, an MEd in TESL from the University of California, and California state teaching credentials in Political Science, History and Sociology with CLAD certification. She has 28 years experience teaching native and second-language learners in the United States, Samoa and Japan. As a Foreign Lecturer at Niigata University, she began a long-term research project on language minority students in Japan that led to her coauthorship, with fellow Niigata University faculty member Takahashi Masao, of *Gaijin seito ga yatte kita: ibunka toshite no gaikokujin jidō/seito wo dō mukaeru ka* ['Foreigner' Students Are Here: How Can We Welcome Foreign Children and Students as 'Cultural Others'] (Taishukan, 1996). Now back in the United States, Sharon maintains a continuing commitment to advocacy of language minority students' equal access to quality education.

R. Michael Bostwick earned an EdD at Temple University, Japan and currently serves as Director of the English Immersion Programme at Katoh Gakuen. Since his pivotal role in founding the first immersion programme in an elementary school in Japan, he has actively promoted the dissemination of research on immersion education by organising symposiums at Katoh Gakuen featuring leading researchers in the field and by publishing the results of research on the progress of the Katoh Gakuen immersion programme pupils.

Yuriko Kite earned a PhD in linguistics from the University of South Carolina with areas of concentration in sociolinguistics and second language acquisition, and is currently a Professor of Linguistics in the Faculty of Letters at Kansai University. She has done extensive research on codeswitching and language choice by children at international schools in Japan, and is now working on a study comparing these students to children in Japan's first English immersion programme in an elementary school in terms of their development of English pragmatics.

Lynne Hansen is Professor of Applied Linguistics at Brigham Young University–Hawaii. Her research focuses on bilinguals' language learning and loss. Her most recent publication is *Language Attrition in Japanese Contexts*. Oxford: Oxford University Press, 1999.

Index

377